PT405 G05

OXFORD MODERN LANGUAGES AND LITERATURE MONOGRAPHS

Editorial Committee

Exotic Spaces in German Modernism

JENNIFER ANNA GOSETTI-FERENCEI

OXFORD
UNIVERSITY PRESS

OXFORD
UNIVERSITY PRESS

Great Clarendon Street, Oxford OX2 6DP

Oxford University Press is a department of the University of Oxford.
It furthers the University's objective of excellence in research, scholarship,
and education by publishing worldwide in

Oxford New York

Auckland Cape Town Dar es Salaam Hong Kong Karachi
Kuala Lumpur Madrid Melbourne Mexico City Nairobi
New Delhi Shanghai Taipei Toronto

With offices in

Argentina Austria Brazil Chile Czech Republic France Greece
Guatemala Hungary Italy Japan Poland Portugal Singapore
South Korea Switzerland Thailand Turkey Ukraine Vietnam

Oxford is a registered trade mark of Oxford University Press
in the UK and in certain other countries

Published in the United States
by Oxford University Press Inc., New York

British Library Cataloguing in Publication Data
Data available

Library of Congress Cataloging in Publication Data
Data available

Typeset by SPI Publisher Services, Pondicherry, India
Printed in Great Britain
on acid-free paper by
MPG Books Group, Bodmin and King's Lynn

ISBN 978–0–19–960412–8

1 3 5 7 9 10 8 6 4 2

For Milan and Arthur

Acknowledgements

Thanks are due for support that enabled the research for and writing of this book. Professor Ritchie Roberston of The Queen's College, Oxford, gave generous advice throughout its development. St John's College, Oxford and the Clarendon Fund of Oxford University provided support, and Fordham University gave me leave to pursue the project. Many colleagues and friends, including Professor T. J. Reed and Dr. Guy Kahane, offered helpful discussion. I am indebted as well to my family, especially Arthur Ferencei and Dr. Milan Ferencei.

Contents

Abbreviations

A	Stefan Zweig, *Der Amokläufer. Erzählungen*
Adorno, GS	Theodor Adorno, 'Aufzeichnungen zu Kafka', *Gesammelte Schriften*, 10.1
AL	Alfred Kubin, *Aus meinem Leben. Gesammelte Prosa mit 73 Zeichnungen*
AS	Alfred Kubin, *Die andere Seite. Ein phantastischer Roman*
AW	Alfred Kubin, *Aus meiner Werkstatt. Gesammelte Prosa mit 71 Abbildunggen*
B	Robert Musil, *Briefe 1901–1942*
Benjamin, GS	Walter Benjamin, *Gesammelte Schriften*
Benn, SW	Gottfried Benn, *Sämtliche Werke. Stuttgarter Ausgabe*
B/I	Rainer Maria Rilke, *Briefe. Erster Band 1897 bis 1914*
BMBS	Stefan Zweig, *Begegnungen mit Menschen Büchern Städten*
Brecht, GW	Bertolt Brecht, *Gesammelte Werke. Werkausgabe Edition Suhrkamp*
Dauthenday, GW	Max Dauthendey, *Gesammelte Werke*
FA	Thomas Mann, *Große kommentierte Frankfurter Ausgabe*
GA	Max Weber, *Gesammelte Aufsätze zur Religionssoziologie*
GA7	Georg Simmel, *Gesamtausgabe Band 7. Aufsätzte und Abhandlungen 1901–1908, I*
GA8	Georg Simmel, *Gesamtausgabe Band 8. Aufsätze und Abhandlungen 1901–1908, II*
GA16	Georg Simmel, *Gesamtausgabe Band 16. Der Krieg und die geistigen Entscheidungen. Grundfragen der Soziologie. Vom Wesen des historischen Verstehens. Der Konflikt der modernen Kultur. Lebensanschauung*
GVW	Max Dauthendey, *Geschichten aus den vier Winden*
GWE/A	Hugo von Hofmannsthal, *Gesammelte Werke in Einzelausgaben. Aufzeichnungen*
Hesse, SW	Hermann Hesse, *Sämtliche Werke*
Hofmannsthal, GW	Hugo von Hofmannsthal, *Gesammelte Werke in zehn Einzelbänden*
Hofmannsthal, SW	Hugo von Hofmannsthal, *Sämtliche Werke. Kritische Ausgabe*
KA	Rainer Maria Rilke, *Kommentierte Ausgabe in Vier Bänden*
KA/DL	Franz Kafka, *Kritische Ausgabe, Drucke zu Lebzeiten*
Kafka, GW	Franz Kafka, *Gesammelte Werke*
Kafka, GW/A	Franz Kafka, *Gesammelte Werke, Amerika*
Kafka, GW/B	Franz Kafka, *Gesammelte Werke, Beobachtungen*
Kafka, GW/E	Franz Kafka, *Gesammelte Werke, Erzählungen*

KA/T	Franz Kafka, *Kritische Ausgabe, Tagebücher*
KG	Friedrich Nietzsche, *Werke. Kritische Gesamtausgabe*
L	Max Dauthendey, *Lingam. Zwölf asiatische Novellen*
Mann, GW	Thomas Mann, *Gesammelte Werke in zwölf Bänden*
Musil, GW	Robert Musil, *Gesammelte Werke in neuen Bänden*
NS/I	Franz Kafka, *Kritische Ausgabe, Nachgelassene Schriften und Fragmente I*
NS/II	Franz Kafka, *Kritische Ausgabe, Nachgelassene Schriften und Fragmente II*
Schopenhauer, SW	Arthur Schopenhauer, *Sämtliche Werke*
SM	Max Dauthendey, *Sieben Meere nahmen mich auf*
T	Robert Musil, *Tagebücher*
W	Bertolt Brecht, *Werke. Berliner und Frankfurter Ausgabe*
WA	Sigmund Freud, *Werkausgabe in zwei Bänden*
WB	Hölderlin, Friedrich, *Werke und Briefe*
WG	Stefan Zweig, *Die Welt von Gestern. Erinnerungen eines Europäers*

Introduction

The 'Exotic' and the Geographical Imagination in Modern German Literature

The subject of this study is the evocation of exotic spaces in modern German prose. This evocation may be principally descriptive (as in travel writings), symbolic (as in metaphorical renderings of familiar spaces as exotic), imaginative (where the spaces are wholly imagined and may not bear much likeness to the regions they evoke), or aesthetic or philosophical (where the exotic space is only fragmentarily evoked as a cipher for an idea of freedom, wholeness, or mystical fulfilment). Differing from both post-colonial and utopian readings of modern literature, this study demonstrates that exotic spaces in some essential modernist texts are not principally sites of domination, but rather of contest and recoding of the relationship between the familiar and the exotic, the self and the foreign other. Exotic spaces may serve not only to affirm the subject in a symbolic conquering of territory, or project the fantasy of escapism to a lost paradise, but condition the moral, aesthetic, or imaginative transformation of the subject, promoting new possibilities of perceiving or being, and yet not without risking disaster or dissolution of the self and compromising the boundaries of a familiar world.

While not giving an exhaustive survey of the evocations of exotic spaces in German modernism,[1] this study examines a selection of texts (1892–1927) from both major canonical and lesser studied German authors, and from these establishes five possibilities of transformation in the exposure to exotic spaces. These transformative possibilities include: re-enchantment through epiphany (as illustrated through Hugo von Hofmannsthal, Max Dauthendey, and Hermann Hesse in Chapter 1);

---

[1] While giving little in-depth analysis of individual texts, Wolfgang Reif (1975) offers a broad survey of works from the first quarter of the twentieth century. More recent accounts covering a wider historical span include Fuchs and Harden (ed.) (1995); Honold and Simons (ed.) (2002); Kontje (2004); Dunker (ed.) (2005); Görner and Mina (eds.) (2006).

the collapse of self when confronted with an exotic space conceived as
erotically and pathologically infectious (in works by Thomas Mann and
Stefan Zweig analysed in Chapter 2); liberation of the imagination from
the confines of the familiar and the actual (in Franz Kafka's fictional spaces
examined in Chapter 3); aesthetic transformation, whether or not that
involves collapse of the subject's integrity or being (in Robert Musil,
Gottfried Benn, and Alfred Kubin, considered in Chapter 4); and revelation of the 'primitive' nature of modern experience (in Bertolt Brecht
in Chapter 5). Not mutually exclusive, these categories of the exotic
experience testify to the fragility of the boundaries of the European or
Germanic subject as depicted in modern literature and to the complexity
of its responses to the spaces of the exotic. Significantly, evocation of
exotic spaces also reveals—by a process akin to what Shklovsky called
'defamiliarization'—the usually unconsidered boundaries of the subject's
own familiar world.[2]

THE RELATIONAL AND MOBILE CONCEPT OF THE EXOTIC

The notion of 'exotic' space must be defined from the outset. Just as a far-
off foreign place must be far from somewhere proximal and familiar, the
'exotic' must be understood as a relational or relative, not an absolute,
concept.[3] Post-colonial criticism of literature, propelled by Edward Said's
Orientalism (first published in 1978) has established the constructed
nature of the exotic qualities of places, in particular that of the 'Orient'.[4]
Said's theory has been expanded to describe, beyond colonial spaces, the
politics of cultural imagination with respect to any contested or dominated topography, and to texts of national literatures less directly, or only
briefly, involved with historical colonialism (discussed in the next section
of this Introduction). Said is not, however, the first to examine the
imaginatively constructed nature of space; Said himself acknowledges
Gaston Bachelard, who showed how space is endowed with 'an imaginative or figurative value' through literary description.[5] And German modernist writers had already theoretical means to consider the constructed

[2] Shklovsky (1965: 18).
[3] While quotation marks throughout this study will be reserved for particular emphasis,
the term 'exotic' is meant as a relative concept throughout, as are terms such as 'primitive'
and the 'Orient'.
[4] Said (1979/2003).
[5] Bachelard (1957); Said (1979/2003: 55).

nature of space. For instance, Georg Simmel, in *Soziologie des Raumes* (*Sociology of Space*) and other works, examined the cultural and subjective conditions of spatial experience, including the boundaries between familiar and foreign spaces.[6] Simmel argued that space, with respect to a given familiar place, neighbourhood, or foreign region, must be understood not as absolute or positively measurable, but as lived; such space, Simmel claims, is 'überhaupt nur eine Tätigkeit der Seele' ('only at all an activity of the soul') (GA7, 133).

In light of this understanding of space, it will be shown that the exotic is not an attribute of any specific place or a given set of regions of the world,[7] although historical conditions promote the characterization of particular spaces as exotic. In this study the exotic can be attributed to a place or space experienced as: (1) foreign, where such foreignness is also felt as (2) alluring (even if also frightening) and (3) mysterious, that is, inherently unknowable or epistemologically resistant to a transparent understanding. These qualities are also often accompanied by a fourth feature, (4) a temporal-historical anachronism in contrast with the modern, as is the case with the topography of so-called 'primitive' cultures, or the locale of a lost golden age, such as classical Greece. Recognition of the constitution of the 'exotic' allows the use of the term, in this study, of 'exoticization', which highlights the active rendering (through description, metaphor, symbolism, and so forth) of a place or culture in terms that evoke the exotic as defined here.

The notion of 'exoticization' can be further elaborated in noting that the concept of the 'exotic' is not only relative but also mobile. The same geographical space can be regarded from varying points of view, and can be differently 'coded', to use Said's notion.[8] Italy may signify primarily the connection to a classical culture and vital sensuality (as in Goethe's *Römische Elegien* (*Roman Elegies*)) or a scene of perversion and deception (in Mann's *Der Tod in Venedig* (*Death in Venice*) and 'Mario und der Zauberer' (*Mario and the Magician*) for example). America can signify a space of uncorrupted vitality (as it does for Hofmannsthal's narrator of the *Briefe des Zurückgekehrten* (*Letters of One Returned*)) or a force of hypermodern, corrupting capitalism (as when the American visitor threatens the nostalgic *Traumreich* or dream-world in Kubin's *Die andere Seite*

---

[6] Among the modern writers acquainted with Simmel were Rilke, Hofmannsthal, George, and Musil. See Frisby (1978); Dahme and Rammstedt (1984); Frisby (1991); Faath (2000) and Schings (2002).

[7] For Said (1979/2003: 31), for example, the 'Orient' to which Western writers refer is not an empirical place but a primarily moral and cultural designation, usually applied to various lands and cultures East or South of Europe.

[8] See Said's discussion of Orientalist 'codes' (1979/2003: 39).

(*The Other Side*)). In Kafka's *Der Verschollene* (*The One Who Disappeared*), the same national topography serves as an ambiguous space of both hyper-modernity and uncivilized vastness: Karl makes his way through New York as through the machinery of the modern city and its commerce, and travels to the lawless frontier region of 'Oklahama'.[9] The mobility of the concept of the exotic is no more evident than in the rendering of the modern city (for instance, Chicago and, implicitly, Berlin by Brecht) as a jungle or other 'primitively' driven realm. Like some German Expressionist painters, Brecht illustrates the paradox of representing the modern metropolis as both hyper-modern and precariously primitive. The mobility of the exotic also pertains to its ephemerality. Given radical progression of communication and transportation technology, places that were perceived as foreign or exotic at the outset of the twentieth century are not necessarily perceived as foreign today. Thus, to examine the exotic spaces and places in literature written in German a century or more ago is also to engage the historical imagination.

The exotic is, further, often associated with *Fernweh*, the European or German subject's longing for radically distant and different places, as discussed in Chapter 1, which deals with writings based on authors' travels. The alluring mystery of places perceived as foreign promises a liberation from the usual course and understanding of things or a development of the self not possible within the familiar confines of home. In this vein Bachelard, examining imagery of exploration and wandering, argues for the psychic effects of spatial change: 'en quittant l'espace des sensibilités usuelles, on entre en communication avec un espace psychiquement novateur' ('in leaving the space of usual sensibility, one enters into communication with a psychological innovative space').[10] While Wolfgang Reif's survey of exotic settings characterizes such liberation in terms of the escapist projection of *Wunschräume*, this study shows in what ways the experience of the exotic may be more significantly integrated into the aesthetic, moral, and imaginative possibilities and transformations of the self. These transformations may be positively realized—Hofmannsthal's *Andreas* fragment points to this outcome, and it is actualized in Musil's story 'Die Portugiesin'—or result in destruction of the self, as in Mann's *Der Tod in Venedig*, Benn's *Gehirne* (*Brains*) narratives, Zweig's *Der Amokläufer* (*The Runner Amok*), and Musil's 'Grigia'.

---

[9] Sokel (1975: 247–248) characterized the ambiguity of place in Kafka's novel in terms of 'Drohung' and 'Errettung'. For an account of varying *Amerikabilder* throughout the German literary tradition, see Bauschinger, Denkler, and Malsch (eds.) (1975: 9–16), and in particular the introduction by Malsch. 'Oklahama' is Kafka's misspelling.

[10] Bachelard (1957: 187).

Approaches like that of Reif emphasize flight and wish-fulfilment, as well as compensation for modern alienation;[11] others describe the cultural history of travel as a 'curative dream', a solution for the 'collective sense of the unsatisfactoriness of European life'.[12] Or they point out that the aestheticization of the colonial landscape is correlative to a sense of freedom from the social restrictions of life at home.[13] In light of these characterizations, these texts may be labelled exoticist or anti-exoticist, according to the outcomes for the protagonist, leaving the precise nature of these transformations, and their implications, unexamined. More recent studies associate the projection of magical exotic worlds outside Europe with the 'identification of another consciousness that recognized but did not challenge European superiority',[14] and this more politically charged criticism is extended in other accounts to symbolic territorialism within Europe. In either case the treatment of foreign places as mysterious and irreducibly 'other' invites post-colonialist critique. Colonialist domination or xenophobia is a theme in critical responses to Hofmannsthal's travel writings, as well as those of Hesse and the stories, based on travel to Asia, of Dauthendey (all discussed in Chapter 1); it appears in criticism of symbolic or descriptive presentations of the Eastern and Asian in Mann and Zweig (the subject of Chapter 2), and of China and the penal colony in Kafka (Chapter 3). The African and Oriental motifs in Benn, Musil, and Kubin call for such criticism (Chapter 4). And racial categories are both problematic and problematized in Brecht's depiction of Asian immigrants in Chicago (Chapter 5). In post-colonial terms, the depiction of places (or people or cultures) foreign to the Northern or Western European writer as inherently mysterious, sensual, mystical, or in some other way radically 'other' is thought to contribute to justifications for exploitation or appropriation by imperial powers and to invite symbolic domination. In Said's view, the mysteriousness attributed to exotic places—the element of mystery rendered in what will be called throughout this study 'exoticization' of place—is precisely what is problematic. For this mysteriousness allows dominated geographies and cultures to serve as symbolic receptors for projections of otherness in contrast to which dominant cultures can define themselves; or they are seen as blank spaces ripe for appropriation.[15] Exoticized spaces within Europe (in particular Southern or Eastern Europe) have also been described in 'Orientalist' terms and have been

---

[11] Reif (1975: 10, 12). In this vein see, more recently, Kundrus (ed.) (2003).
[12] Porter (1993: 53).
[13] Kundrus (2003: 145–161).
[14] Murti (2001: 4).
[15] Said (1979/2003: 3).

shown to be implicated in an imperialist or racialist geopolitics, as will be seen in the case of the texts by Mann discussed in Chapter 2.[16] It will be argued here that, despite these problems associated with the 'exotic', its evocation also introduces other, non-appropriating ways to view the mysteriousness and allure of foreign places. For the mysteriousness attributed to the exotic may also serve symbolically to protect the differences of foreign places (and peoples) from being absorbed into a dominant aesthetic or world-view. Mysteriousness may be invoked implicitly in justifications for exploitation, but it can also serve to suspend or limit epistemological and even moral arrogance, as well as implementation of would-be practical aims. While Said claims that the European subject of discourse is complicit in 'dramatizing the distance and difference between what is close to it and what is far away' in order to affirm itself (in coming to terms with and symbolically conquering the foreign),[17] this need not necessarily characterize every depiction of the exotic by the modern European writer. The representation of differences may register and preserve, rather than obliterate, real differences between the writers' familiar expectations and the places they encounter or imagine.[18]

Moreover, as will be described in Chapters 2 and 4, the exposure to the exotic can also be a disempowering experience for the subject or self. Mann's *Der Tod in Venedig* demonstrates the disastrous consequences of attempting to appropriate the exotic 'other' in terms of a fabricated aesthetics of self-affirmation. Mann's protagonist submits to *Fernweh*— initially dismissed as 'Reiselust' ('urge to travel')—provoked by the appearance of an exotic stranger, and eventually collapses in the seductive and infectious atmosphere of Venice. Musil's 'Grigia' also depicts the seduction by an other-worldly, sensuous Italy—a mountain region with its earthy, physical peasant culture—from which the bourgeois German protagonist, drawn away from his domestic life, will never return, as he dies abandoned by his peasant lover in a cave. Zweig's novella *Der Amokläufer* seems to present a critique of the projections of the exotic, as a disastrous fate results from erotic-infectious aggression in the East Indies. These texts suggest that the operations of a self-affirming or escapist subject do not exhaust the possibilities of exotic experience, that

---

[16] Boa's (2006) study of cultural geography in Mann not only offers an account of geographical politics within Europe but also of the anxiety attending globalization and the erasure of cultural boundaries in general.

[17] Said (1979/2003: 55).

[18] The tensions of post-colonial discourse within German studies are discussed in R. Berman (1998) and Uerlings (2005). Zantop (1997), while condemning colonialism and xenophobia, finds resistance to these in nineteenth-century canonical texts.

there are other driving motives and meanings to be found in modernist texts in their reflections on self, other, and modernity.

While post-colonialist criticism looks for evidence of authors' mapping, surveying, and symbolically appropriating the exotic, this study shifts the focus to consider in detail the transformations of self and the implicit criticism of a disenchanted world occasioned by experiences of foreign places. For the exotic challenges a view of reality as wholly comprehensible through the rational calculation dominant in Western thought, and so it necessarily limits what Weber identified as the most characteristic features of modern Occidental culture, rationalization and intellectualization (GA, i. 94). This is evident in Benn's explicit critique of Western rationality in the Rönne narratives and in Kubin's fantastical novel *Die andere Seite*, in which aesthetic rather than political alternatives to the crisis of modernity are imagined. In Musil's stories, the evocation of the exotic can offer both radical critique of disenchantment and the possibility of mystical and aesthetic renewal. All of these texts are discussed in Chapter 4.

Post-colonialist criticism is to be credited with uncovering insidious or harmful representation of dominated places and cultures, and so with subverting the effects of domination. Yet the critic may also take pains to avoid, as Russell Berman puts it, reducing any presentation of the foreign to 'the power of overriding paradigms or epistemes, which structure the possibilities of consciousness in advance'—the exclusive emphasis on which 'loses the sense of . . . the concrete subjectivity of human experience in particular contexts'.[19] The dominant scholarship of cultural studies and post-colonial criticism, for all its merits, has overlooked the service of unknown and exotic spaces to the politically unaccountable needs of the human imagination. The affirmation of imaginative possibility beyond the confines of one's given cultural actuality is, as will be demonstrated in Chapter 3, the most significant function of exotic spaces in Kafka's writings. The imaginative power of the exotic in many of these texts affirms Bachelard's suggestion that literary images of very different places, even as they engage risk, seem to rescue the self from sedimentation or stasis. In respect to this rescue, he proposes: 'Il faut toujours laisser ouverte une rêverie de l'ailleurs' ('One must always leave open a reverie of elsewhere').[20] But such images of elsewhere, while rarely wholly unproblematic, may also be necessary for different relations with and responses to others, for imagining the world otherwise than strictly within the framework of familiar expectations.

---

[19] R. Berman (1998: 4, 14).   [20] Bachelard (1957: 69).

ORIENTALISM, GERMAN LITERATURE, AND THE
GEOGRAPHICAL IMAGINATION

Before turning to specific interpretations of modern literary works, the relevance and influence of post-colonial criticism and Orientalist theory on the interpretation of modern German literature must be addressed more directly. Leaving critical accounts of individual authors for the following chapters, three aspects of symbolic geography as interpreted by Said and other post-colonialist critics may be identified at the outset and will be discussed in this section: (1) the relevance of German colonialism for interpreting modern German literature; (2) the affirmation of the European or German subject in its opposition to an 'other' represented as exotic; and (3) the politics of representation in terms of the productive and discursive theory of power. Where these aspects are analyzed at length in recent scholarship, they will be treated here only briefly, with reference to relevant sources.

Said's *Orientalism* focuses on British and French colonialism and the relationships between its policies and politics and compliant or collaborative representations of colonized 'others' by British and French writers. Said leaves German literature mainly out of the account because Germany was not, in comparison with France and Britain, a considerable colonial power, and because he regards German 'Orientalism' as a principally scholarly matter that can be separated from any national or imperialist interest. He writes, 'The German Orient was almost exclusively a scholarly, or at least a classical, Orient: it was made the subject of lyrics, fantasies, and even novels, but it was never actual.'[21] That this considerably underestimates the case has been the subject of much subsequent scholarship.[22] The application of Said's theory to the colonial context of German literature and culture has yielded considerable historical evidence of national if not imperial interest in Africa, Asia, and South America where, it has been pointed out, even Nietzsche and Kafka had colonial relatives.[23]

Extending beyond actual colonial activity is, further, a 'kulterelle[r] Resonanzraum kolonialer Bestrebungen' ('cultural sphere of resonance

---

[21] Said (1979/2003: 19).

[22] See for instance Fuchs-Sumiyoshi (1984); Pratt (1992); Zantop (1997); Zantop (eds.) (1998); Gründer (ed.) (1999), (2004); Murti (2001); Honold and Simons (ed.) (2002); Friedrichsmeyer, Lennox, Kontje (2004); Dunker (ed.) (2005); Irwin (2006).

[23] On Nietzsche, colonialism, and his sister and brother-in-law's investments in Paraguay, see Holub (1998). On Kafka's familial relation to colonialism, see Zilcosky (2003).

of colonial ambitions') as Honold and Simons put it in their introduction to a recent anthology. 'Neben seiner ideologischen und politischen Geschichte... ist der Kolonialismus ein strukturelles Phänomen, das auch an Wissenschaften und Texten mitschrieb' ('Alongside its ideological and political history... colonialism is a structural phenomenon, which also inscribes on sciences and texts').[24] Suzanne Zantop has shown that the relatively brief period of German colonialism—initiated by Bismarck in 1884 in South-West Africa and expanded in Tongo, Cameroon, East Africa, and the Pacific in the 1880s, and engaged until the First World War—is preceded by centuries of colonialist discourse and fantasies. According to Zantop's argument, these fantasies established a sense of 'colonial mastery' that became 'so firmly entrenched in Germany's collective imagination that they formed a cultural residue of myths about the self and other(s) that could be stirred up for particular political purposes'. This 'collective mentality' in Germany is identified by Zantop as a kind of counter-response to Germany's 'lack of actual colonialism', which spurred the desire for and 'sense of entitlement to such possessions in the minds of many Germans' during the colonial period.[25] Said's notion that Germany prevailed over an 'intellectual authority' in the matter of colonialist Orientalism may be read, in sharp contrast to Zantop's emphasis on fantasy, as an 'active collusion to further colonial ambition in all its brutality'. German philosophers and writers including Hegel and some Romantics are complicit, in Kamakshi Murti's account, in reinforcing 'the image of the Orient congruent to nineteenth-century European colonialism's agenda'.[26] Todd Kontje, following Mary Louise Pratt, points out the connection between acts of writing and colonialist subordination of 'natives'; racist anthropology, for example, is not equivalent to a physical act of violence but may serve as implicit or explicit justification or promotion of such acts.[27] Yet even the seemingly more neutral activity of describing landscape in travel writing can work as a symbolic form of colonial imperialism. In Pratt's account, to 'survey' descriptively entails a symbolic command of territory achieved through literary form.

Those scholarly accounts that have applied Said's thesis more widely to German literature may offer a differentiated view. Zantop includes accounts of the counter-discourse to the prevailing fantasy she outlines (in Kleist, Heine, and Keller). In favour of such differentiation, Kontje also

[24] Honold and Simons (eds.) (2002: 9–10, 13).
[25] Zantop (1997: 3, 4, 7).
[26] Murti (2001: 7, 22). See also the introduction by Görner and Mina (eds.) (2006: 7–10) and Loop in the same volume, 11–25.
[27] Pratt (1992: 7); Kontje (2004: 5).

refers to 'German *Orientalisms* rather than a single German Orientalism'.[28] Russell Berman defends the possibility of contact and responses
between German or European writers and exotic 'others' that cannot be
foreseen or explained on ideological or political grounds alone. His view is
that 'real travel through space and the encounter with foreign cultures and
society certainly has the potential to elicit qualitatively new experiences'
that are not reducible to the background of inherited assumptions against
which they are projected. 'The travel through space permits new experiences, even if those experiences and the reactions to them are repressed
because of colonial ideology.' Thus Berman, in *Enlightenment or Empire*,
examines 'how German travellers in the non-European world—especially
to regions that would come under the sway of European colonization—
encountered alterity and came to grips with it (or not)'. This also applies to
the imagination of such travels. Kafka's *In der Strafkolonie* (*In the Penal
Colony*), for instance, has been read as an exposure of colonial brutalities
and as a discursive perpetuation of them. But the work in either case
breaks down the oppositions between primitive and civilized, as Berman
argues, by showing that the 'real "primitives"... are not the "natives" or
"noble savages" but the colonizing riffraff and the colonial policies that
horrify the European explorer.[29]

   The substance of Said's indictment of European literary representations
of non-Western places or peoples is not merely the negative characterization of such, but concerns the use of projected differences to reflect, and
eventually affirm, the familiar self as superior. 'For there is no doubt', Said
argues, 'that imaginative geography and history help the mind to intensify
its own sense of self.' In regarding exotic others, Orientalism works as a
conceptual and metaphoric 'grid' of interpretation that guarantees a
'*positional* superiority' for the European. Even if this position is flexible,
as Said argues, the encounter with an exotic other cannot but affirm the
'sovereign Western consciousness' and its 'unchallenged centrality'.[30] The
principal thesis of the present book, in contrast, suggests that such
affirmation is not the only outcome or motivation of the encounter with
or imagination of alterity, in particular in the evocation of exotic spaces.
Others include forms of challenge and contest to the self that dismantle
the oppositional hierarchy of self and other, of 'us' and 'them'. This
challenge may, but need not, entail a rejection of all things familiar,
European, German, or Western, in order to undermine any presumptive
authority over an 'other' based on epistemological, moral, racial, aesthetic,
or cultural prejudice. Most of the depictions of such encounters in the

[28] Kontje (2004: 12).   [29] R. Berman (1998: 5, 232).
[30] Said (1979/2003: 55, 6–7, 8).

works studied in this book, even if they evidence such prejudice, challenge the stability, the self-understanding, and the self-assurance of their European or German protagonists (and often their authors), and almost always express their loss of control or authority over their surroundings. In addition, the exotic or 'primitive' other may, in fact, be revealed to be in some way (aesthetically, morally, or spiritually) superior when assumptions about the self break down. When it is deemed dangerous or corrupting, the exotic may be located precisely not in some foreign realm, but the heart or psyche of the 'rational' European self. To represent the modern European or American metropolis, for instance, as the truly 'primitive' realm, must be distinguished from representing the 'Orient' or exotic places as Europe's 'surrogate and even underground self'.[31]

Such differentiations and distinctions, however, do not register within certain conceptual frames of Said's theory, which combines a discursive and productive model of power with a particular view of language. Said, on his own account, borrows heavily from Foucault's account of power, articulated in *La Volunté du savoir* (*The Will to Knowledge*) and *Surveiller et punir* (*Discipline and Punish*).[32] In Foucault's view, power is not essentially repressive but productive, not primarily exercised by juridical prohibitions but by discourse (the production of knowledge, for instance in writing a history or anthropology of the 'Orient') and the techniques of domination with which they are intertwined. For Said the 'Orient'—and this could apply to the related concepts of the 'exotic' and the 'primitive'—is a production of the Western imagination that is always operative within a network of tactics of empirical or ideological domination. While this view importantly accounts, for instance, for the complicity of insidious misunderstandings of the 'other' in colonial, racial, and cultural hierarchies, or the racism and ethnocentrism inherent in, for instance, Flaubert's description of an Egyptian courtesan, it paints nearly every written account of the 'other' by any 'non-other' with the same brush, and aligns it with acts of domination. Even Foucault's view that power is ubiquitous insistently registers resistance within its operations. Said has adopted Foucault's thesis of the discursive and productive nature of power and knowledge without acknowledging how radically Foucault has dismantled the representation of polarized relations of power between oppressor and oppressed.

---

[31] Said (1979/2003: 3).
[32] These were published in 1975 and 1976, respectively.

As some critics have pointed out, Said overlooks aspects of resistance to domination, such as irony, calls to reform, ambiguity, and complexity in representing the other, in many of the texts he analyses.[33] His view of the construction of the 'Orient' as a single geographical imaginary correlates to his identification of a fixed network of 'Occidental' responses to whatever can be represented accordingly.[34] Said argues of scientific, literary, and spiritually minded writer alike, and of those who travelled or merely imagined the 'Orient': 'To be a European in the Orient *always* involves being a consciousness set apart from, and unequal with, its surroundings. . . . In all cases the Orient is *for* the European observer. . . .'[35]

While Said is to be credited with establishing the consistency of representations of places that chronically disadvantage 'Orientals' at the hands and pens of Europeans, and of the ubiquity of power relations within them, the necessity and universality in his account demands scrutiny. For in Said's account, any representation of the non-European or 'Oriental' space by the European writer involves a 'strategic location' of power over, of 'containing the Orient, and finally, representing it or speaking in its behalf'.[36] Representation as such is always exterior, as the author always takes up a position vis-à-vis the 'other', and so immune to dialogical influence. This exteriority, Said argues, usurps any possibility of self-representation of those others.[37] And this usurpation is grounded not only in the particular nature of power but also of language. Said writes, 'The exteriority of the representation is always governed by some version of the truism that if the Orient could represent itself, it would.' This usurpation is not only due to the power inherent in Western discourse of 'dominating, restructuring, and having authority' over the object of its representation. Rather, it is also grounded in regarding a linguistic fact as a fact of power: that language or 'discourse', in particular the act of writing, operates on the basis of the absence of its referent. Said writes, 'The written statement is a presence to the reader by virtue of its having excluded, displaced, made supererogatory any such any real thing as "the Orient".'[38] The absence of the referent from the written utterance, and the corresponding relative autonomy of the sign, so celebrated in postmodern theories of language, indicate for Said, in the context of geopolitics, the inevitable political, social, or geographical marginalization

[33] Varisco (2007: 103, 127). Warraq (2007: 399).
[34] See Varisco (2007: 10).
[35] Said (1979/2003: 157–158).
[36] Said (1979/2003: 20).
[37] Irwin (2006: 292–293) addresses Said's view of Arab self-representations in his critique.
[38] Said (1979/2003: 21, 3, 21).

or erasure of that to which such language refers. The fact that postmodern theory (in Barthes, Blanchot, and Foucault, for instance) has also decentralized the author as the arbiter of meaning, and thus neutralized the authority Said assumes belongs to the act of writing, does not register in Said's account.

Moreover, a basic ontological confusion occurs here between signified and referent. If the 'Orient' is in fact a construction of Western imagination, the referent is already in question, and it is not possible to misrepresent it simply by speaking of or writing about it.[39] To put it another way, one cannot obliterate the autonomy and autochthonous reality of that which one has invented. What Said means, of course, is that a certain invention, a cohesive set of ideas and images on the part of the European imagination, has been projected onto real places and peoples in collaboration with other acts of imperial domination. While this is a compelling and important argument, it does not follow that the very fact of writing or speaking, any invoking or evoking the 'other', is itself *always and in every case* an act of domination on the part of the speaker or author, even if he or she is speaking or writing about, rather than to or with, that other. Moreover, while other post-structuralists such as Barthes, Foucault, and Blanchot affirmed the 'death' of the author, that is to say demoted to relative insignificance his or her intentions, individual motivations, and generating consciousness as the 'original' source of the work and its meaning, Said argues for the author's fixed sovereignty, and for the effective authority of his or her cultural grid of interpretation. The linguistic fact of the absence of referent from the utterance, along with the maintenance of authorial presence, is interpreted in moral terms: 'The Orientalist, poet or scholar . . . is never concerned with the Orient except as the first cause of what he says.'[40]

But the coupling of these linguistic assumptions and a theory of power as productive is problematic in the case of post-colonial critique, in that it obscures the many ways in which language also connects self and other, and the ways in which representation, even by another, can empower or ennoble. It overlooks the multiplicity of possible responses by framing the 'Occidental' or Western subjectivity of the writer in fixed, essentialized, and inalienable terms. Foucault's view of power as ubiquitous and channelled by discursive tactics of domination includes the not inessential caveat that it is nearly coextensive with resistance to power. This ought to lend currency to potential transformations within the ideologically well-guarded dichotomies of self and other, familiar and exotic. Even

---

[39] Said's inconsistency here is noted by Irwin (2006: 291).
[40] Said (1979/2003: 20).

problematic representations of the 'Oriental' may contain ambiguities, ironies, contradictions, and other elements that destabilize a dominant interpretive code. As a much broader and mobile concept, the 'exotic' does not demand any absolutely fixed framework of reference, does not depend upon a single cohesive 'imaginary', but rather invokes patterns of attribution that include, as defined above, relative foreignness, mysteriousness, and (potentially threatening) allure.

The sovereignty and authority of the Western subject or self as represented in literature are not inalienable in the works to be studied here. This does not presume that any 'authentic' contact with any 'real referent' of the exotic can be established or guaranteed, nor does it preclude evidence of ethnocentrism, colonial tropes, and racial stereotypes. While these need to be critically examined, and have been subject to much scholarly attention, so too the varying possibilities of response, and the ambiguities of representation which respect the potential transformation of self in its encounters in a foreign exotic place, deserve elaboration. Yet these possibilities have received relatively scant scholarly attention. Most significantly for this study, the experiences of the 'exotic' as represented in the texts to be examined here offer means for critical self-reflection on European modernity and its forms of thought and life. Even while the 'exotic' here still usually services the European perspective on its own self and culture, this is often critical rather than affirmative, contemplative rather than assertive, and sometimes evidences the humility of genuine inspiration by 'exotic' others.

The following five chapters in this study outline several different modes of transformation made possible through the evocation of exotic spaces: epiphany, breakdown, imaginative liberation, aesthetic-mystical transformation, and the recognition of the primitive within modern experience itself. An analysis of these literary phenomena establishes that exotic spaces enable modern German authors to imagine various modes of transformation of self and, in so doing, formulate literary responses to perceived problems of the modern self and its culture, as theorized by Nietzsche, Simmel, Weber, Freud, and others, including some of the literary authors cited here. The analysis progresses through a varied textual topography. The first chapter's account of exotic spaces described on the basis of the author's *travel through real places* is followed by an account, in the second chapter, of *spaces imaginatively exoticized* through projections of metaphor and imagery. In the texts of the third chapter, the *spaces are imagined or invented realms*, with but slight correspondence to real spaces, in some cases symbolizing the vastness of an elsewhere as such. In the fourth chapter, exotic voyages are turned inward, so that exotic spaces serve in charting contours and transformations of *inner topographies* experienced through dream, artistic discovery, and mystical fulfilment. In the fifth chapter, the imaginative *'inner' rendering of the exotic and the depiction of external spaces converge*. The modern city becomes a scene for the primitive conflicts of modern experience. These travelled, metaphorically exoticized, imaginatively invented, inner literary, and symbolically converging spaces present the exotic as a varied site of contest for and challenge to the modern European self and its familiar culture.

Before proceeding to the following chapters, the notion of 'self' requires at least a brief initial elaboration. Like the concept of the exotic, the 'self' that is here claimed to be at stake in these presentations is relational, but not, as is the case of the 'exotic', mobile. At least since Descartes's epistemological reflection and Shakespeare's characterization, with Hamlet, of existential reflection—or, to point to earlier sources, Socrates' performances of the ethical mantra of self-knowledge and Augustine's confessional examinations—the 'self' signifies at minimum that which can be accessed in immediate referral, as well as the source of such reference. The self is the subjective proximal pole of what is not 'other'; it is precisely the core of what is not exotic, but rather familiar. 'Selfhood' would then suggest some state of continuity of the reflective being in this immediacy and access, and involves as well—for instance through memory, sedimented expectations, and embodied habit—the history of such a subject as centre, if not anchor and originating principle, of wilful engagements with the world. The self therefore can be said to be a more or less coherent, but in any case dynamic, structure of subjective reflection, exertion, and receptivity that generally maintains a familiar individuation throughout its various experiences. That in modernity the 'self' is also gradually attenuated with a sense of depth and mystery, and therefore is seen (with Nietzsche and Freud, for instance) to harbour an unknowable otherness within, is discussed in Chapter 4. But first it must be considered, as in the next three chapters, how the very familiarity, immediacy of access, and transparency of the self, as well as the specific connotations of the Western self with respect to the dominance of rationality, individuation, and autonomous will, are put into question in literary examinations of the exotic.

1

Fernweh, Travel, and the Re-enchantment of the World in Hofmannsthal, Dauthendey, and Hesse

Post-colonialist critics have regarded evocations of foreign places in European literature in terms of imperialism, mystification, and symbolic appropriation of the foreign. Literary description of foreign places has been interpreted as a form of descriptive mapping and surveying of territory, and the evocation of the 'exotic' has been aligned with justifications for dominating foreign cultures. *Fernweh*, the longing for distant and different places, might contribute to the problematic exoticization of places by projecting an ever-inaccessible mystery that breaks radically with the familiar order of things, a mystery that could exaggerate differences and justify the self-assertion of a dominant culture even as it represents otherness. Modern prose based on a European author's travels is particularly vulnerable to this form of critique, as *Fernweh* inevitably motivates not only authors' travel but also a seeking out of the 'exotic' in particular. The issue of colonialist domination or symbolic imperialism arises in scholarship on Hugo von Hofmannsthal's descriptions of Africa, as it does on Max Dauthendey's and Hesse's Asia, with critics suggesting, often in Said's terms, that the modern European self is reaffirmed in these writings as a colonialist subject.[1]

---

[1] For example, Nina Berman (1998: 8), aiming to expand Said's critique to German authors, claims that, in the context of Austro-German economic and political (rather than national) interests, 'Hofmannsthal's writings take part in the creation of a non-occupational imperialist ideology'. Gabriella Rovagnati (1994: 311) regards Hofmannsthal as a typical 'Repräsentant der Wiener Kultur' ('representative of Vienna culture') and its turn-of-the-century consumption of Oriental culture. See also Görner (2006: 165–175) on 'Hofmannsthals Orientalismus'. While more generous to Dauthendey's later writings, Klaus Börner (1997: 186) dismisses *Lingam* as 'Exotismus pur' ('pure exoticism') and its author as 'Flaneur und Voyeur'. See also Vidhagiri Ganeshan's (1975) critique of Dauthendey. Reif (1975: 44–45) critically compares the superficially exoticizing descriptions of native perspectives in Dauthendey and Hesse. Mileck (2003: 124) views Hesse's 'Eastern quest' as intent 'primarily upon comforting affirmation of his own evolving view of . . . life'.

Yet while exoticization of foreign places may symbolically affirm the colonialist subject, it can also liberate the self from a sedimented identity, from cultural constraints and habits, from the perception of an already determined future, and force a re-examination of one's own familiar world. *Fernweh* in Hofmannsthal, Dauthendey, and Hesse involves complexities that cannot be accounted for solely in post-colonialist terms.

Places radically different from a narrator's or protagonist's familiar world need not be projected, either, as a mere *Wunschraum* or paradisal escape from the burdens of self and self-consciousness. These writings need not be regarded as expressing a wholesale rejection, grounded in 'Zivilisations-müdigkeit' ('civilization fatigue') of Northern European culture, as Wolfgang Reif has argued, for they also offer critical reflection on and reinvigoration of the familiar world.[2] For these writers, the appearance of reality itself and the very structure of perception seem to be altered by the experience of distant and exotic places. Ever pointing towards distant places, *Fernweh* signifies a longing for a vaguely imagined freedom, either through an apparent dissolution of self, or through cultivation of its untested possibilities; but it also leads to critical self-reflection. A critical account of *Fernweh* in modern German literature may open up a critique of the modern perception of the world, while highlighting the significance of place, distance, and the spatial imagination in constituting this perception.

Just as the exotic always remains mysterious, *Fernweh* also suggests a desire for something ever out of reach, pointing at once to the finitude of human experience and to the contrary imagination of endlessness. But *Fernweh* is a paradoxical longing: if a culturally or geographically distant place is reached, and so the mere imagination of it is replaced by concrete perceptions, it no longer promises endless discovery. This is what Dauthendey called 'der Fluch und zugleich die Wollust des Reisens' ('the curse and at the same time the excitement of travel'): an unbounded imagination becomes limited by real perceptions, and so the world might seem smaller, rather than vaster, for the traveller (GVW, 43). The seeking of the exotic can lead to disillusionment, as Hesse's narrator repeatedly expresses in the travel essays of *Aus Indien* (*From India*), writings which will be discussed here in contrast to Dauthendey's descriptions of the same locale. Yet in the experience of enchantment as Dauthendey presents it, or in moments of epiphany as Hofmannsthal describes, exotic places can offer liberation from the constraints of the familiar world, precisely by calling that familiarity into question. It will be shown in this chapter how the description of distant and exotic spaces raises questions about the self

---

[2] Reif (1975: 42).

and its relation to reality, while promoting critical alternatives to what Weber calls the 'Entzauberung der Welt' in the rationalized culture of modern Europe (GA, i. 94).[3]

Modernity's disenchantment, according to Weber, results from its instrumentality and abstraction, its elimination of the role of myth, magic, and religion in reconciling the self with the world. Disenchantment could be described as the loss of what Freud (albeit in a critical vein) called, in *Das Unbehagen in der Kultur* (*Civilization and its Discontents*), 'das "ozeanische" Gefühl' ('the oceanic feeling'), the sense of being enveloped in a whole, infinite, and sacred nature: 'ein Gefühl von etwas Unbegrenztem, Schrankenlosem, gleichsam "Ozeanischem"' ('a feeling of something unbounded, limitless, that is, "oceanic"') (WA, ii. 370, 368).[4] In the exotic settings presented in Dauthendey's *Lingam* and longingly recounted by the narrator of Hofmannsthal's *Briefe des Zurückgekehrten*, among their other works, and in travel writings by Hesse, the rational calculation and intellectualization[5] with which Weber (GA, i. 94) characterizes modern Western disenchantment seem to lose their power to define reality. Experiences within exotic settings tend to resist the simplicity and economy of rational explanation—as William James describes the 'sentiment of rationality'—but rely upon vivacity and intensity for their validity and truth.[6] Not merely symbolic colonialism or escapism, but disenchantment with modernity and the hope for re-enchantment, become major motives for the modern European writer's interest in exotic spaces. These writers seek nothing less than a new sense of reality, as Hofmannsthal expresses in a text in which Asia and its spiritual vision are evoked as an ideal for a disenchanted Europe, affirming that 'Die Wirklichkeit besteht nicht nur aus konkreten Dingen, aus exakt Greifbarem: genau ebenso leben wir in einer Welt von Mysterien und ganz ungreifbaren allerwirksamsten Lebendigkeiten' ('Reality consists not only of concrete things, of that which can be precisely grasped: we live

---

[3] See Stephen Kalberg's (1980: 1146) critique of the translation of 'Entzauberung' as 'disenchantment' and of the use of Weber's term to refer to the romantic yearning for an earlier, simpler world. 'Disenchantment' is used here for Weber's term, but it is meant to include the sense, which Kalberg sees as missing from the English term, that the 'magical' no longer has a place in the modern understanding of reality.

[4] Freud's notion was influenced by Romain Rolland's studies of Indian culture. For a discussion of Weber's notion of disenchantment in Freud's terms, see Scaff's (2000: 105) summary of Weber's theses on modernity.

[5] Weber refers to *Zweckrationalität* or means-end rationality and the role of abstraction (such as the notion of efficiency or bureaucracy in general), which dominates in modernity to the diminishment of other forms of rationality.

[6] William James (1948: 4). Hofmannsthal read James's *Varieties of Religious Experience* while at work on *Andreas*. See Alewyn (1960: 142); Hamburger (1961). See Hofmannsthal's (SW, xxi. 138) citation from James in the notes for *Andreas*.

equally in a world of mysteries and entirely ungraspable, most effective vivacities') (Hofmannsthal, GW, ix. 52).

ATMOSPHERE AND EXOTIC SPACES IN HOFMANNSTHAL'S TRAVEL WRITINGS

Hofmannsthal, among other writers, renders culturally or geographically distant places as rich alternatives to the realities of modern European experience. His fiction and travel narratives provide a suitable starting point for examining exotic places in modern German prose and their reflections of cultural and individual identity; relevant works by Hofmannsthal span the chronological parameters for this study (1892–1925). It is important that non-Germanic places within Europe, especially those relatively untouched by modernization, such as parts of Italy and Greece, can be as exotic for Hofmannsthal as Africa; all of these places are exoticized by Hofmannsthal's descriptions of them, for instance, as 'Oriental'. By contrast with Vienna, the countryside of Carinthia through which the protagonist of the *Andreas* novel fragment first travels is also exotic, in one way, while Venice is exotic in quite another. Venice, with its long literary history as an exotic space,[7] situates labyrinthine adventures in which disorientation might be the condition for becoming conscious of one's relation to reality. Exoticizations of place in Hofmannsthal's less frequently discussed travel essays 'Reise im nördlichen Afrika' ('Travels in Northern Africa'), 'Sizilien und wir' ('Sicily and Us'), and 'Augenblicke in Griechenland' ('Moments in Greece'), provide occasions for rich awakenings of mind, invigoration of sensuous perception, and the sense of a newfound access to the deeper essence of things, including the past, from which the superficiality of everyday life in modern Europe is thought to be alienated. The experience of defamiliarization by and fascination with a place regarded as exotic can then provoke a feeling of the strangeness of one's own home and the penury of its familiar way of life; and in the writings discussed in this chapter, this reflection is grounded in the author's direct observation of a foreign world. These writings bring to light, and often explicitly reflect upon, the process of constituting a unified experience of place through what may be a whirlwind of fragmentary and disorienting impressions of the foreign. But the driving motive for the exploration of exotic spaces is critical and

---

[7] The literary history of Venice as exotic space is presented in, for instance, Pabst (1955), Nienhaus (1992), Tanner (1992), and will be discussed in Chapter 2 in the context of Mann's *Der Tod in Venedig*. See also Simmel's 1907 essay on Venice (GA8, 258–263).

reflexive: it offers, by radical contrast, a means to reflect upon the experience and problems of modern European life.

The texts of Hofmannsthal to be discussed in this chapter, from the unfinished novel to the travel writings and epistolary essays, are connected in three ways: (1) all of them describe experiences of travel, and all to places that are unfamiliar, traditionally exotic, or exoticized through metaphoric or other narrative means; (2) they all present experiences of disorientation or disconnection, and then a striving to establish orientation within or connection to an unfamiliar place; (3) in all of them epiphanies are central, suggesting a transcendence through which the self or experience is reoriented or unified. A general development (though not strictly chronological, for central themes reappear) can also be established in Hofmannsthal's treatment of *Fernweh* and the exotic in these writings. It begins with a fascinated exploration of foreign environments within Europe and their exoticization, such as in the earliest text here considered, 'Südfranzösische Eindrücke' ('Impressions of Southern France') (1892). Not only exotic comparisons by the narrator (in which a European landscape, for instance, is likened to Egypt or the Orient) but also a relation to the remote but longed-for past may be involved in exoticization. A critical turn occurs with the harsh and explicit critique of modern (Northern) European life presented, through juxtaposition with exotic spaces, in *Die Briefe des Zurückgekehrten* (1907). This critique can be understood as providing momentum for Hofmannsthal's depiction of a fragmented self and his progress towards unification in *Andreas*, in which the experience of travel is central (1907–1927). Despite the eighteenth-century setting of that novel fragment, the problems of self that emerge are particularly modern, an anachronism that also characterizes 'Ein Brief' ('A Letter') (1902). In the later travel essays 'Augenblicke in Griechenland' and 'Sizilien und wir', the distances to be crossed by the modern traveller invoke a temporal, as well as spatial, *Fernweh*, but they also offer the possibility of a re-enchantment through epiphany. In the last of the travel writings, the most foreign setting of North Africa occasions not merely a reaffirmation of the European subject, but rather reflection upon European culture in respect to a foreign environment.

Hofmannsthal's travel writings are also of particular interest because the task of evoking exotic space through description is an explicit subject of reflection; the writer must assemble the foreign impressions into a meaningful whole and may thereby make apparent the cognitive and imaginative means through which a space or place is constituted. In a discussion of recollections of travel in 'Südfranzösische Eindrücke', Hofmannsthal suggests that 'die Bilder des Lebens folgen ohne inneren Zusammenhang aufeinander und ermangeln gänzlich der effektvollen Komposition' ('the images of life succeed one another with no internal connection and entirely lack effective composition') (GW, vii. 589). Yet he argues that the writer must re-create the sense of unity that is implicit in the experience, despite the apparent disconnectedness of its individual impressions. Individual impressions must be given unity by the observer, and while in direct perception this is an unconscious process (a 'passive synthesis' in Husserl's terms), in literary description of a foreign place this unity must be won by rendering atmosphere, however immediately or gradually apparent.

A brief consideration of the concept of 'atmosphere' can help to contextualize Hofmannsthal's reflections on the composition of travel writing, but it also may apply to the descriptive space generated in his fiction. Atmosphere, so essential to the evocation of the exotic, is not a measurable or objective quality of a given space, though it is always situated within recognizable topographical or cultural boundaries. Atmosphere or ambience is the quality of space as felt and lived,[8] and its constitution requires the sense that various impressions belong to a place-specific whole, 'eine Welt für sich' ('a world for itself') as Hofmannsthal describes in the essay 'Gärten' ('Gardens') (GW, viii. 578). Not only gardens but also poems and paintings are described there in terms of a harmonious composition or arrangement; to perceive atmosphere is to recognize of the elements:

daß sie untereinander harmonisch sind, daß sie einander etwas zu sagen haben, daß sie in ihrem Miteinanderleben eine Seele ist, so wie die Worte [*sic*] des Gedichtes und die Farben des Bildes einander anglühen, eines das andere schwingen und leben machen.

(that they are harmonious among themselves, that they have something to say to one another, that they are one soul in their communal life, so that the words of the poem and the colours of the picture glow in one another, each moving the other and bringing each other to life.) (GW, viii. 578)

Hofmannsthal describes the notion of specifically literary atmosphere at length in the essay 'Shakespeares Könige und große Herren' (GW, viii. 45–46).

Georg Simmel—whose critique of modernity Hofmannsthal knew well—also offers an account of the constitution of atmosphere. The related notion of 'Stimmung' (atmosphere or mood) is considered, for example, in Simmel's discussion of landscape in the essay 'Philosophie der

---

[8] Hofmannsthal uses both terms: 'Atmosphäre', more frequently, and 'was die Italiener "l'ambiente", das Ringsherumgehende, nennen' ('what the Italians call "ambiance", that which wholly surrounds') (GW, viii. 579, 44–46, 43).

Landschaft' ('Philosophy of Landscape'). Reflection on landscape, first of all, is a modern phenomenon—a view also expressed in Rilke's essay 'Von der Landschaft' ('On Landscape'). Simmel shows how the unity that belongs to a 'landscape' is paradoxical, and due not to the object perceived but to its 'Stimmung' ('mood'). For although landscape is perceived as a unified whole, a landscape is really only a fragment of nature. Because, as an isolated part, it is opposed to nature's wholeness and infinite interconnectedness, landscape is characteristic of a modern way of experiencing nature. For Simmel a pre-modern relation to nature may be characterized by a religious sense of envelopment within a sacred whole (anticipating Freud's discussion of an '"ozeanische" Gefühl'), rather than an aesthetic objectification of what is only a part. Yet landscape, despite being only a part, is experienced as a unity; the unity perceived in a landscape is given by its atmospheric colour. Simmel argues that the unity that renders a landscape as a landscape (as opposed to a disparate assemblage of details cut off from the whole context), and its atmospheric colour, are two aspects of the same act of constitution on the part of the perceiving subject. Perception of atmosphere requires aesthetic synthesis on the part of the subject; this synthesis is made apparent, Simmel suggests, in painting, where the unity of a landscape is not only implicit in perception, but is actively produced by the painter. Atmosphere or 'Stimmung' must be understood, then, as the relationship between the observer and the observed, between the experiencing subject and the objects of experience. Atmosphere is then a quality of the whole complex that makes up the arrangement of a specific space, a task that Hofmannsthal, in the essay on gardens, compared to the work of the writer.

Like Simmel's discussion of *Stimmung* and its presentation in painting, and Hofmannsthal's own essay on gardens, Hofmannsthal's travel writings also reflect on how a unified sense of place can be presented; but here the spaces are explicitly exoticized. In 'Sudfranzösische Eindrücke', Hofmannsthal considers the disjointed nature of impressions of place, which he then renders in his 'Eindrücke' of southern France. Hofmannsthal presents an analogy between experiences of travel and a particularly memorable page from a Chinese picture book, with its various images incoherently assembled: 'Das Ganze hatte den seltsamen, sinnlosen Reiz der Träume. Ich glaube, so ungefähr sollten Reisebeschreibungen gemacht werden.' ('The whole had the strange, nonsensical allure of dreams. I believe that travel description should be composed something like this') (GW, vii. 589). But even in their incoherence, Hofmannsthal recognizes that as 'das Ganze' the impressions, however varying—in the picture there are flying dogs, red grape leaves, blue vases, a garden with geese and orchids, spiders, and sad-eyed monkeys, a river, a young woman threatened by bird-headed monsters—have a unified, dreamlike allure. Hofmannsthal then offers reflections on how the unified atmosphere of a place is communicated through manifold impressions. In Hofmannsthal's description—occasioned by a trip with his French tutor—the atmosphere of southern France becomes exoticized; this exoticization of place is evident not only from the Chinese picture-book analogy but in the comparison of southern France to an Egyptian landscape (GW, vii. 593).

As Simmel demonstrated of landscape, an exotic place is not simply given, but must be constituted through an 'eigentümlichen geistigen Prozeß' ('peculiar spiritual process') (GA7, 471). In exotic places a horizon of the unknown seems to surround whatever empirical details are noticed or selected for presentation. An ineffable 'Etwas' ('something'), as Hofmannsthal's narrator calls the secret intensity of van Gogh's images (GW7, 566), must be evoked through description of surrounding atmosphere, registration of vague or incomplete perceptions, distant horizons, and finally epiphanies provoked through contact with some special feature of a given locale. This process is necessary, though accomplished in different ways, in both *Reiseprosa* (travel writing) and fiction.[9] Some of Hofmannsthal's narrative essays have features of both genres, and thus cannot be judged according to the demands of objective reportage.[10] The essays discussed here are not merely travel memoirs, but evoke intensely mystical experiences that exceed description of empirically observable facts. These mystical epiphanies allow for re-enchantment of the experiencing subject.

Hofmannsthal's later travel writings aim to render both the sense of dreamlike allure and the palpability of real experience. But the problem of representing the experience of foreign places, transforming fragmentary and sometimes contradictory impressions into a whole, reflects also broader concerns about the self and its relation to past and present worlds. While the *Reiseprosa* depicts real experience, it also allows for the description of transformation of the self through a mystical moment or epiphany, in which the difference and distance of a foreign place in its present and past gives way to an intimate intensity felt by the observer. The novel *Andreas* is related to the *Reiseprosa* in depicting this transformation of self in episodes of travel. In all of these writings epiphany is occasioned by

---

[9] See Brenner (1989) for a discussion of the history of mistrust of the genre of *Reiseprosa* as fabricating or fictionalizing. Block (1987: 24–25) argues for the positive role of travel recollection, which aided Hofmannsthal's goal to create a sense of a unified existence out of apparently contradictory or unrelated impulses and materials.

[10] Some criticism of Hofmannsthal's travel writings stems from generic expectations that would separate fiction from non-fiction and put *Reiseprosa* in the latter category. For example, Nina Berman (1998: 14–15) accuses Hofmannsthal of 'fictionalization and reification of the environments and peoples he encounters' in northern Africa.

transport to an unfamiliar, but exotic or exoticized place; the epiphany promotes the feeling of a more unified state of being than had been felt in the familiar world of home. This epiphany might then be achieved in part through sharp contrast with the modern or familiar world of the protagonist or writer.[11] The modern self may well remain at the centre of the experiences provoked by *Fernweh*; but it is certainly challenged. This challenge is explicit in the reflections of Hofmannsthal's *Die Briefe des Zurückgekehrten*, a text which provides critical momentum for the fragmentation of the subject presented in *Andreas* and an important background for the reconsideration of European culture in Hofmannsthal's later travel writings.

FERNWEH, HEIMWEH, AND THE CRITIQUE OF MODERNITY: *DIE BRIEFE DES ZURÜCKGEKEHRTEN*

Fernweh is expressed in Hofmannsthal's early poetry, such as 'Reiselied' ('Travel Song'), 'Verse auf ein kleines Kind' ('Verses on a Small Child'), and 'Südliche Mondnacht' ('Southern Moonlit Night') (1897–1898) as a longing for far-off, timeless lands (SW, i. 341, 353, 358). But in *Briefe des Zurückgekehrten* a decade later, *Fernweh* expresses a response to, and a sharp critique of, modernity and the disenchanted way of life in modern Europe, and it is rooted in the narrator's depiction of real, but exoticized, places. The narrator issues a challenge to the modern European self and its access, through intellect and practical reason, to the essence of reality. As in the later *Augenblicke in Griechenland*, works of plastic (spatial) art will help to overcome a sense of alienation that is determined both by place and by time. The overcoming of alienation or disenchantment in both works requires contact with exoticized places: while the *Augenblicke* describes the 'ganz Orientalischen Duft' ('entirely oriental scent') of Greece, in the *Briefe* the colours in van Gogh's paintings are compared to the experience of colours in the sky by the Indian saint Rama Krishna (GW, vii. 629; SW, xxxi. 172). These Orientalizations, echoed in 'Die Idee Europa' ('The Idea of Europe') (1919), link Hofmannsthal's works with those of writers such as Dauthendey, who sought in the Orient a primal vitality foreign to modern European culture.

---

[11] Block (1987) discusses the relationship between the genre of travel writing and the self's relation to the past, but does not highlight the specific role of foreign places nor the critique of the familiar in juxtaposition to them; he does not discuss *Andreas*, but rather establishes a connection between Hofmannsthal's *Reiseprosa* and his larger project of 'self-revelation'.

In the *Briefe*, faraway places and their inhabitants are longingly described; and the feeling of *Fernweh* is central to the narrator's reflections:

> Ich sehnte mich, wie der Seekranke nach festem Boden, fort aus Europa und zurück nach den fernen guten Ländern, die ich verlassen hatte.
> (I longed, like a seasick man for solid ground, to leave Europe and return to the good faraway countries that I had abandoned.) (SW, xxxi. 168)

Returning to Germany after eighteen years, en route to his native Austria, the narrator of the *Briefe* feels alienated from the Europe of a new century. In contrast to the vitality and authenticity of exotic foreign places, modern European experience is felt as utterly disenchanted. The narrator finds comfort in memories of old Dürer prints viewed in his childhood, memories that prepare, however, for a specifically modern visual awakening. By the fourth of the letters, the narrator is shocked to discover van Gogh's paintings, which he sees by chance in a gallery in Holland. The densely lived experiences in foreign lands, and the sense of reaching to the essence of things, are expressed in the vivid colours of van Gogh's paintings, which were perhaps influenced by the latter's well-known interest in Asian art. Along with Cézanne and Gauguin, van Gogh's paintings would become a source for German writers seeking, through modern forms of abstraction, a more primitive and thus more authentic, mode of perception.[12] These painterly sources and the primitivism they provoke are discussed in greater detail in Chapter 5.

For the narrator, Europe is felt as an obstacle to self-realization: 'Ich möchte in mir selber blühn, und dies Europa könnte mich mir selber wegstehlen' ('I would like to blossom in myself, and this Europe could steal me away from myself') (SW, xxxi. 152). In contrast, the foreign places he experienced (among them North America, Spain, China, Indonesia, Uruguay, and the South Pacific) nurtured the movement and unity of the whole person, enlivened his senses: 'ich lebte...wo mein Denken und alle meine Nerven vom Leben so angespannt waren wie möglich' ('I lived...where my thoughts and all my nerves were as taut with life as possible') (SW, xxxi. 154).[13] The narrator describes a freedom

---

[12] See Lloyd (1991).

[13] The letter-writer's viewpoint is also expressed in Hofmannsthal's 1902 work 'Gespräch zwischen einem jungen Europäer und einem japanischen Edelmann' ('Conversation between a young European and a Japanese Nobleman'). Hofmannsthal writes, 'Der japanische Angler angelt mit Leib und Seele, saugt Flusslandschaft in sich; der Soldat, der Räuber ist ganz Schwert, bluttrunkenes Auge, gesträubtes Haar; der Büßende ist ganz Buße hinschmelzend unter eines Kindes Auge' ('the Japanese fisherman fishes with body and soul, soaks up the riverscape; the soldier, the robber is all sword, bloodthirsty eyes, wild hair; the penitent is wholly repentant, melting under the eye of a child'), whereas the 'Europäer in ihrer wulstigen Teufelserscheinung haben so etwas Unentschiedenes, Schlaffes' ('the

felt to be inaccessible in modern Germany. Yet he does not merely wish to forget his home; the foreign places where he lived had evoked an inward recollection of Germany; the foreign experiences impressed upon his inner soul 'spoke' of Germany. Yet the Germany they evoked was only an idea, not the one he finds upon return; it was a feeling 'vom innersten Wesen der Heimath' ('of the innermost essence of home') he had drawn from pictures, fables, and stories. The Germans of whom he dreamt were whole, undivided in themselves, unlike those he finds now: 'Sie waren eins in sich selber' ('They were one with themselves') (SW, xxxi. 156). One specific origin of his feeling of a Germanic home is discovered in memories of Dürer's pictures he had viewed as a child in Austria. The old world presented in those pictures, the feeling for forests, sky, and nature, gave a sense of an authentic and more magical relation to life for which he longs at present, and which seems graspable only in the vivid experiences afforded by vastly foreign and faraway places.

The narrator describes faces, speech, and vocal tone of the German people he finds upon returning to Europe. The Germans he describes are serious, hard-working people who have achieved much; but it does not give him any joy to be among them. They are disenchanted; and so the narrator's despair echoes what Hölderlin's Hyperion encounters in Germany: a people 'tiefunfähig' ('deeply incapable') of divine feeling. To Hofmannsthal's narrator German faces seem closed; there is no wholeness and unity of character to be read there, just as Hyperion claimed, 'ich kann kein Volk mir denken, das zerrißner wäre, wie die Deutschen' ('I can think of no people that would be so fragmented as the Germans'). Modern Germans fail to pursue life 'mit ganzer Seele' ('with the whole soul') (WB, i. 433). Hofmannsthal's narrator is no less severe in his critique: the modern Germans lack purity of character; the youth in them is mixed up with old age, and vice versa; politeness is coloured with coldness. He is especially distressed by the professional class and the motivation of social life by the pursuit of money—features of modern culture, which express the instrumental rationality Weber argued dominates disenchanted modernity and which are criticized in Hofmannsthal's later 'Die Idee Europa'. There Hofmannsthal argues that money has become the 'allgemeiner Endzweck' ('general final aim') and asks provocatively whether money has not replaced religion: 'hat das Geld ... nicht die Kraft, sich an Stelle Gottes zu setzen?' ('does money ... not have the power to take God's place?') (GW, ix. 50). Hofmannsthal's view echoes Simmel, whose *Philosophie des Geldes* Hofmannsthal had read in 1906, the year before he wrote

Europeans in their bulging devil's appearance have something so indecisive and slack about them') (SW, xxxi. 42).

the *Briefe des Zurückgekehrten*, and on at least two later occasions.[14] The impoverishment of the soul is due to the kind of abstraction that characterizes a society dominated by money. 'Geistige Krankheit' ('spiritual illness') is the diagnosis in 'Die Idee Europa' (GW, ix. 49) and in the *Briefe* a 'geistiger Geruch' ('spiritual smell') oppresses the narrator, which he can characterize only as 'ein europäisch-deutsches Gegenwartsgefühl' ('a European-German feeling of the present') (SW, xxxi. 158). Modern Germans live without a feeling of freedom, without a determined purpose, without greatness, but rather with the distance of irony and nervousness, cold and stale politeness. In their speech, in their tone of voice, he finds precariousness and uncertainty, abstraction. He asks:

> muß ich zurück nach Uruguay oder hinunter nach den Inseln der Südsee, um wieder von menschlichen Lippen diesen menschlichen Laut zu hören, der ... mir sagt, daß ich nicht allein bin auf der weiten Erde?
> (must I return to Uruguay or down to the islands of the South Seas to hear again the human sounds from human lips that ... say to me that I am not alone on the vast earth?) (SW, xxxi. 159–160)

The freedom and vitality he could feel in the marginal life of bandits, gold-diggers, penal colonists, the homeless in New York, sailors, and other vagabonds is devastatingly absent in the modern Germans who, for all their *Leistung* (accomplishment) lack a piety about life itself. He recalls the fable of the forest people who must flee their educated and propertied countrymen to live alone in the woods. *Fernweh* mixes with *Heimweh* as the narrator asks, 'Aber wo ist mein Wald, in dem ich zu Hause wäre?' ('But where is the forest in which I would be at home?') (SW, xxxi. 161).

The inner crisis that emerges in the fourth and fifth letters (entitled 'Die Farben' or 'Colours') has to do with the very structure of modern perception, the subject's grasp of reality. What will disturb Andreas is the difference between appearance and reality; but for the narrator of the *Briefe*, this is felt not as a stage of self-cultivation or *Bildung*, but as a fully exposed metaphysical crisis. The very essence of humanity and of the reality that the modern subject confronts has been voided by abstraction. Just as Simmel analysed the influence of money, Weber analysed the reduction of manifold human action to means-end purposivity and theoretical abstraction, displacing emotional or affective and traditional modes of thinking and being. Overly specialized and efficient, modern man is fragmented, and so the reality he confronts lacks ontological substance. In contrast, the letter-writer finds in non-modern cultures a resilient unity

---

[14] See Hoeber (1918: 475–477) and Frisby (2004: xxx–xxxiii), for discussions of Hofmannsthal's reading of Simmel's *Philosophie des Geldes*.

that promotes activity of 'the whole man'. The impoverishment of the
modern European way of life is extended to the very appearance of things
in the modern European context: they lack solidity. Glimpses of the abyss,
of non-life, of utter non-being, are felt in contrast to the vitality and reality
of van Gogh's presentation of the world. Van Gogh's renderings, with
their visible brushstrokes, movement, and vivid colour, reject any artificial
methods of perspective and lighting, but render the fresh vitality of things
primitively seen. What the narrator experiences in van Gogh's paintings is
akin to a religious perception of reality, as the narrator's comparison to
Krishna's experience of colours of the sky shows; it offers nothing less than
the possibility of a re-enchantment of the world. Both van Gogh and
Krishna seem to experience an enchanted perception expressed in terms of
colour. For the narrator of the *Briefe,* this re-enchantment is possible only
in the wake of a cultural crisis and the critical reflection on the culture of
home occasioned by the experience of the exotic. This re-enchantment is
imagined in *Andreas* as a stage in the natural evolution of a self exposed to
a foreign world and demands transformation of the individual.

DISTANCE, THE EXOTIC, AND *BILDUNG*: THE UNFINISHED NOVEL *ANDREAS*

Hofmannsthal's unfinished novel *Andreas* was begun in the same year as
the *Briefe* (1907) and illustrates the experience of travel to exotic places. In
the vein of a traditional *Bildungsroman,* which records an individual's
(usually young man's) development through the challenge of new and
different experiences, *Andreas,* set in the eighteenth century, charts the
title character's *Bildungsreise.* The minor nobleman from Vienna is sent off
by his parents on a journey to Venice, which brings unintended consequences. Andreas's own wish is to experience Venetian culture—it is
stated explicitly that the custom of wearing masks intrigues him—and it
is the mysteriousness of the Venetian atmosphere that initiates a process
of self-discovery.

But it is the differences, rather than similarities, between Hofmannsthal's novel fragment and the traditional *Bildungsroman,*[15] that
might help us to understand the relation of Hofmannsthal's text to his

---

[15] The differences of *Andreas* from the traditional *Bildungsroman* have been much
discussed. For example, Miles (1972: 3–12, 113–115) claims that the inward-oriented
development of Andreas's character is closer to Rilke's protagonist Malte than to Goethe's
Wilhelm Meister. Jacobs (1968: 40–41) also contrasts Andreas to Wilhelm Meister. Alewyn
(1960: 126) qualifies its relation to the *Entwicklungsroman.*

travel writings. Through travel, Andreas becomes disenchanted with life at home in Vienna. His most meaningful experiences are immediate shocks of fragmentation and epiphany rather than a gradual cultivation of his native possibilities. Like the narrators in the travel writing, Andreas experiences moments of epiphany that are connected to immediate experiences of place and to the exotic—or exoticized—nature of those places. Like the experience of Rilke's Malte, for whom Paris is the scene of disorientation, loss of self, and potential recovery, Andreas's loss of orientation in Venice exposes, and potentially resolves, his inner fragmentations.[16] That both characters are left without a clear vision of their progress or an unequivocal conclusion may have to do not only with the details of the respective genesis but also with the nature of the epiphanic experiences that constitute their most compelling moments. Hofmannsthal's notes refer to Baudelaire's sensation (from the prose poem 'Le Confiteor de l'Artiste') of exceeding infinity characteristic of the most intense experiences.[17] Andreas's experiences, like similar experiences in Hofmannsthal's travel writings and like those of Rilke's Malte, are concentrated in intense moments of perception or memory, irrespective of the historical progress on which the psychological and plot development of the *Bildungsroman* rely. Andreas faces the exigent task of finding both the centre and the boundaries of the self, a task that comes to light only through severe disorientation.

Andreas's desire to travel to Venice is linked to moments of *Fernweh* in his childhood past. It is in Venice that Andreas recalls not only his very recent experiences en route but also his boyhood longings for the faraway and magical, longings nurtured by his love for the theatre. He loved the theatre not only for its world of gestures and illusions but also for its evocations of unknown places and possibilities of experience. Andreas recalls a 'himmelblaue Schuh' on the stage between the uneven floor and the too-short curtain, which had provoked ecstatic pleasure. When the curtain was raised, the revelation of the whole forest scene and its princess was disappointing; it could not compare with the wonder of the fragmentary vision, its glimpse of the unknown: 'Der himmelblaue Schuh

---

[16] The relation to Rilke is also biographical: Rilke visited Hofmannsthal in 1907, the year he began *Die Aufzeichnungen des Malte Laurids Brigge* and Hofmannsthal wrote the first three-page draft, 'Venezianisches Reisetagebuch des Herrn von N. (1779)' for *Andreas* in Venice. See Chapter 5 for an analysis of Rilke's novel.

[17] Hofmannsthal quotes the fuller context: 'Il est de certaines sensations délicieuses dont le vague n'exclut pas l'intensité; et il n'est pas de point plus acérée que l'Infini' ('there are certain delicious sensations which, while imprecise, are not without intensity; and no blade has a keener tip than that of Infinity') (GWE/A, 181–182). Rilke also refers to Baudelaire in Malte.

war wunderbarer als alles' ('The heavenly blue shoe was more wonderful than everything') (SW, xxx. 40). Andreas's susceptibility to *Fernweh* is here suggested symbolically, but Andreas, in recalling this memory in Venice, is clearly aware of it:

> alles das war schön, aber es war nicht das zweischneidige Schwert, das durch die Seele drang, von zartester Wollust und unsäglicher Sehnsucht bis zu Weinen, Bangen, und Beglückung, wenn der blaue Schuh allein unter dem Vorhang da war.
>
> (all that was beautiful, but it was not the double-edged sword that penetrated the soul, of the tenderest lust and ineffable longing to the point of tears, torment, and delight, as when the blue shoe was there alone under the curtain.) (SW, xxx. 40)

The colour blue, like images of sea and sky, evokes the faraway and the possible beyond the familiar, actual world. This symbol of *Fernweh* prepares for the experience of disorientation in Venice, for Andreas's departure from the familiar world he understands.

Hofmannsthal's rendering of Venice as an exotic atmosphere[18] makes little use of description of the structure of Venice itself; the descriptive space includes the piazza, the dilapidated mansion of the impoverished count's family, the theatre across the canal, Nina's lodgings, the courtyards behind the houses, the church, and the nearby paths and bridge. The lack of any panoramic description of Venice in the novel fragment is appropriate, given the structure of the city, in which the winding canals, culs-de-sac, and mostly small, isolated piazzas allow for few sweeping views. Moreover, the narrative focus on isolated details reflects Andreas's attempt to make sense of his surroundings; Venice becomes the 'dream-theatre of his inner self'.[19] A more detailed description of Venice by Hofmannsthal can be found in other works, however, for instance the lyrical essay 'Erinnerung schöner Tage' ('Remembrance of Lovely Days') (1908), in which the glance and overheard laughter of an Englishwoman precipitate dreams and dreamy visions within the Venetian locale. Waking from such dreams, the narrator describes a feeling of transport evocative of *Fernweh*: 'Es war, als lichtete ein Schiff die Anker und ich müßte hastig fortgehen in eine fremde Welt' ('It was as if a ship had pulled up anchor and I had to go forth hastily into a strange world') (SW, xxviii. 168); the image of the ship lifting anchor had appeared in the poem 'Erlebnis' (1892). The narrative of *Andreas* implicitly relies upon the exotic atmosphere of Venice as

---

[18] On Hofmannsthal's choice of Venice as the setting for *Andreas*, see Alewyn (1960: 115); Miles (1972: 175–176).
[19] Miles (1972: 7–80).

described in the 'Erinnerung' essay; it is the Venice of the waning republic, a scene of façades, masks, and dilapidated Oriental beauty. The city is, as a fragmentary note about the Knight of Malta declares, a place 'der nicht völlig das Hier ist.—Für ihn Venedig Fusion der Antike und des Orients, Unmöglichkeit, von hier ins Kleinliche, Nichtige zurückzusinken' ('which is not entirely of the here and now—for him Venice as fusion of the ancient and the Orient, impossibility to sink back from here into the trivial, the paltry') (GW, vii. 298). In Hofmannsthal, as in other writers, the 'Orient' or the Asian is a marker for exoticization; and Venice as a scene of disorientation echoes the Oriental atmosphere of 'Tausendundeine Nacht' ('A Thousand and One Nights') a review of which Hofmannsthal wrote in the same year as he wrote the *Briefe* and began *Andreas*. This characterization of the Orient as disorienting and irreducibly mysterious is, of course, the basis for 'Orientalist' criticism; but exoticization need not signal affirmation of the subject through a symbolic conquering of the exotic place.

As in Mann's depiction of the city, Venice provides for Andreas an other-worldly atmosphere that seems to nurture illusion and dream, dissolution of an ordinary identity; it is, as for Mann's Aschenbach, half fairy-tale, half tourist-trap, but the Venetian experience for Andreas, however disorienting, aims towards education rather than collapse of self. Andreas does not wander through the labyrinth towards an ugly death, as does Aschenbach. And in contrast to Hofmannsthal's own character, the merchant's son in the story 'Das Märchen der 672. Nacht' ('The Tale of the 672nd Night') (1894), with whom Hofmannsthal compares Andreas in his notes for the novel (SW, xxx. 102), the disorientation is not final or fatal. Andreas's Venice is a site for perceptual confusions and disorientations; but unlike, for instance, Kafka's labyrinths, it is to foster (as the notes suggest) a re-emergence of self more whole than before.[20] Andreas's path towards unity of self, and the fragmentation which makes it necessary, can be understood through terminology Hofmannsthal had borrowed from William James: Andreas's 'anhedonia' or 'Verlust des Wertgefühles' ('loss of a sense of value') (SW, xxx. 115) might be healed through inspiration, mystical moments of sensing a deeper meaning, which escape rationality alone and which exceed reality as it is ordinarily experienced. While at work on *Andreas*, Hofmannsthal was reading not only Morton Prince's *Dissociation of a Personality*, which Alewyn demonstrated was the source for the Maria/ Mariquita figure, as well as Andreas's inner oppositions, but also James's

---

[20] In contrast to Tanner's (1992: 225) comparison with Kafka.

Varieties of Religious Experience. Despite the themes of fragmentation, self-loss, violence, and split personalities in the novel, it is not abnormality but, as Alewyn argued,[21] a restoration of the limits and unity of the individual that Hofmannsthal seeks for Andreas. This will require what James described as inner transcendence.

Venice is the site where these problems of the self might be best exposed. Hofmannsthal had visited Venice on many occasions (including travels through Italy in 1892, 1895, 1898, 1899, 1902, 1907, 1917, and 1924); and Venice served as the backdrop for several other works. There Hofmannsthal began (in 1907) the first three-page version of the novel, a first-person draft, 'Venezianisches Reisetagebuch des Herrn von N. (1779)' ('Venetian Travel Diary of Herr von N. (1779)') prompted both by the immediate surroundings and his reading of Philippe Monnier's book on Venice of the eighteenth century. Yet the significance of Venice in the further *Andreas* fragments can be understood only through its contrast both to Vienna—in Austria everything is common, and in its capital, the superficiality of social life obscures what is essential—and to the Carinthian landscape through which Andreas first travels. While Venice provokes an experience of fragmentation, the countryside is pastoral and enveloping. That Andreas allows himself to be swindled by the insidious (and ironically named) servant Gotthelff reveals not only his naive innocence but also his unreadiness for the harmony of self that the natural surroundings seem to symbolize. For Gotthelff's offences—symbolic of what James, in *The Varieties of Religious Experience,* calls 'natural evil'—alienate Andreas from the peasant nobility to which he feels drawn and from Romana, whose combination of purity and sensuous freedom (or the 'supernatural good') enchants him. Descriptions of the Carinthian topography, however, introduce the emerging motif of the work: Andreas's relation to himself can be established only through distance from home, through an orientation lost and re-established in the wider, radically unfamiliar world. His own fractured self must be brought into a harmonious balance, a fracture reflected outwardly in the opposition of Gotthelff and Romana, and inwardly through the divided personality of Maria/Mariquita, a mirror image of Andreas's own self. The customs of Venice of the eighteenth century provide a cultural context for the self-masking and theatricality of dissemblance that is at the centre of Maria/Mariquita's psyche and so allow it to reflect, beyond the isolated

---

[21] Alewyn (1960: 124). Despite his emphasis on split personality disorder in Hofmannsthal's novel, Alewyn argues that 'die rechten Grenzen und damit die rechte Brücke' ('the proper boundaries, and thereby the proper bridges') must be established 'zwischen Ich und welt' ('the I and the world') (126).

personality disorder of a particular individual, the problems of the self as such. But the very fragmentation of the self between present and past, the spiritual and the sensuous world, between authenticity and superficial society that troubles Andreas seems to reflect modern problems.

Andreas's experiences in the Carinthian valley, recalled after his arrival in Venice, give some indication of his own fragmentation: he cannot face himself and the exposure of his failures with the servant Gotthelff; he had not only failed to fend off evil but may be implicated in it himself. After Gotthelff's egregious misdeeds, Andreas himself feels unbearably exposed and escapes into the woods surrounding the farmstead:

> Zwischen den Stämmen war ihm wohler.... [E]r richtete seine Sprünge so ein, daß er sich jedesmal hinter einem starken Stamm verbarg, zwischen den Tannen waren schöne alte Laubbäume, Buchen und Ahorn, hinter jedem dieser versteckte er sich, dann sprang er weiter: endlich war er sich selber entsprungen wie einem Gefängnis.
> (Among the tree-trunks he felt better.... He aimed his leaps so that every time he landed he was hidden behind a broad trunk; among the pines were beautiful old broad-leaved trees, beeches and maples, and he hid behind each one, then leapt further: finally he leapt out of himself as if from a prison.) (SW, xxx. 71)

This apparent self-escape is, however, an illusion. A farmhand comes to bury the dog whose suffering had reminded Andreas of a childhood sin, his own abuse of animals. 'Das viele Herumlaufen ist unnütz, man läuft sich selber nicht davon' ('Running around so much is useless, one can't run away from oneself!'), he thinks (SW, xxx. 72). Only when he leaves for Venice, the imaginative merging with the flight of an eagle above is felt as an epiphany, marking dissolution of his former subjective state, and the possibility of renewal. His path towards unification, however, will first require a significant disorientation in Venice.

For the foreignness of Venice, and the strange occurrences he experiences there, provoke a radical de-centring of self. Venice exposes Andreas's inner oppositions, most essentially through the identification with the split personality of Maria/Mariquita whom he meets there. Andreas loses his sense of an ordered world, his sense of direction, and his capacity to understand and describe what has happened to him, as he falls in love with this dual person whose inner oppositions are fatally opposed. Yet Andreas also refuses any explanation of his confusing experience, preferring to savour the mystery of the dual appearance. Because he is himself inwardly fragmented, he accepts the mystery of Maria/Mariquita's outward fragmentation. The confusion of seeing first the mourning widow and then the expressive sensuous woman is mingled with the confusion of place:

ihm war zumut wie kaum je im Leben[,] zum erstenmal bezog sich ein
Unerklärliches aus jeder Ordnung heraustretend auf ihn, er fühlte[,] er
werde sich nie über dieses Geheimnis beruhigen können... die Localität
verwirrte sich ihm[,] er erzählte und sah[,] daß er nichts erzählen konnte, daß
er das Entscheidende von dem[,] was er erlebt hatte, nicht zu erzählen
verstand.... Er konnte sich nichts erklären, und doch wies er im Innersten
jede Erklärung zurück.

(for the first time something inexplicable came over him from out of every
order, he felt that he would never calm himself over this secret... the place
confused him[,] he told the story and yet saw that he could tell nothing, that
he did not understand how he could recount what was decisive in what he
experienced.... He could explain nothing to himself, and yet in his innermost soul, he rejected any explanation.) (SW, xxx. 91)

This attitude of acceptance, even protection, of the inexplicable comes at
the cost of subjective clarity and orientation. It reflects Hofmannsthal's
affirmation of James's notion of the 'sense of the exceedingness of the
possible over the real' (SW, xxxi. 138), but it also dispenses with what
Pratt condemned as the Orientalist 'relation of mastery' that could
be predicated between the travelling subject and his experiences in a
foreign place.[22] As a genuine stage in his *Bildung*, Andreas's disorientation
cannot be dismissed as merely an occasion for the exercise of self-reaffir-
mation, as another critic, following Said's claim that the Western mind
dramatizes foreignness in order to feel itself reinvigorated by conquering
it, has described Goethe's description of getting lost in the Venetian
labyrinth and Flaubert's disorientation in the labyrinthine alleys of
Cairo.[23] Andreas's experience of lostness in Venice also provokes his
recollections of the recent trauma in Carinthia. Like the merchant's son
in 'Das Märchen der 672. Nacht', who, though initially protected from
the outside world by his aesthetic severity, becomes endangered by over-
sensitivity to his servants (and so lack of boundaries), Andreas must learn
and establish his boundaries (lacking in exchanges with Gotthelff), and, to
prepare for Romana's ideal love, find his centre.[24] The lack of boundaries
and centre are, despite the novel's historical setting, reflective of the
modern crisis of the self, as, for instance, in the figures of Rilke's Malte

---

[22] Pratt (1992: 204).
[23] Zilcosky (2003: 45–46).
[24] See also Hofmannsthal's letter of 30 May 1893, to Edgar Karg von Bebenburg, which
expresses Hofmannsthal's worry about his own lack of boundaries, 'daß die Gedanken und
die Empfindungen der Bücher und der Menschen manchmal meine Gedanken und *Emp-*
findungen vollständig auslöschen und sich an ihre Stelle setzen' ('that the thoughts and feelings
of books and people sometimes completely extinguish my own thoughts and feelings and take
their place').

and Gottfried Benn's Rönne.[25] The modern nature of Andreas's crisis might also be compared to the breakdown experienced by the letter-writer of 'Ein Brief', for whom language and meaning have become destabilized. Hofmannsthal's direct confrontation with the modern, of course, is found in *Die Briefe des Zurückgekehrten,* which is, in that respect, closer to the critical depictions of modernity in Rilke and Benn. Disorientation in Venice is both topographical and social. While throughout the work familiar upper-class identifications serve to temper the anxiety associated with strange people and customs, they do not provide reliable guidance through the social idioms of Venetian culture, perhaps suggesting a critique of Andreas's tendency, like his father's, to rely on outward, merely social identifications (for instance trusting Gotthelff merely on the latter's mentioning of familiar aristocratic names). The half-dressed nobleman, the lottery designed by Zustina, the impoverishment and menial jobs of the noble family, and Nina's exotic suitors— she is an actress turned courtesan—give a confusing picture of local mores; Andreas is unsure what to mention in a letter home. The cultural scenery of Venice is presented through various means: masks, crumbling architecture, lush plants, birds, and flowers, the theatre and actors, all of which contribute to the decorous, though also dilapidated, exotic atmosphere, and exacerbate the confusion between *Sein* and *Schein.* The first person Andreas meets in Venice is the masked nobleman who had gambled away his clothes and appears in his undergarments and cape, an indication of the precariousness of identity and fortune. A severe sense of fragmentation is provoked through a series of doublings intertwined with Andreas's imagination: Nina is for a moment confounded with Romana; Nina herself is doubled through the good but unflattering likeness of her portrait; and the mourning widow Maria, a case of split personality, assumes the insolent and childish air of Mariquita, as she is named, among other nominations, in the notes. The appearance of this woman, whose duality first breaks through upon seeing Andreas, not only confuses him, but seems bound up with his fate. The dual figure Maria/Mariquita brings to mind a figure from Andreas's own ancestry, the double life of his uncle Leopold. Leopold's two lives come together symbolically at his deathbed scene, as Andreas imagines it: the legitimate, childless but noble wife enters through one door, and the illegitimate and peasant,

---

[25] In Rilke's *Die Aufzeichungen des Malte Laurids Brigge* (*The Notebooks of Malte Laurids Brigge*) Malte fears that might come through the open window and that he cannot hide from recognition by delinquent strangers, and suffers breakdown. See Chapter 5. Hofmannsthal had heard Rilke read from the novel in progress in Vienna in 1907. In Benn's drama 'Ithaka', Rönne despairs over a loss of 'Mitte'; and in the story 'Gehirne', he feels himself without 'Rind'. See Chapter 4.

but fertile, mistress and their children through another. This ancestral reference establishes an unconscious source of Andreas's fragmentation, also presented in Andreas's dreams. He dreams, for instance, that Romana fears him, and that he might in fact abuse her as Gotthelff did the servant.

The promise of a self reunified seems to be suggested in an alliance with the Knight of Malta, but this remains undeveloped in the most substantial narrative fragment. The Knight serves as a spiritual guide; he is not only himself exotic but made so further by experiences in India, China, and, in the notes, Persia and Japan; perhaps because of this wide experience, he is admired for feeling at home in the world. As a Christian knight and a Freemason, both experienced in the foreign and at home wherever he is, the Knight embodies a balance Andreas has yet to achieve. One result of the experience in Venice, and of this indirect exposure to still more radically foreign places through the Knight, is that Andreas outgrows his former existence in Vienna (SW, xxx. 119). The fragmentation in his own character is exposed, and his impressions need reorientation—'Gedanke, ob sich diese Steinchen im Kaleidoskop neu ordnen können' ('thought, whether these little gems in the kaleidoscope can arrange themselves anew')—but this possibility is suggested only through a dream of returning to Romana and the natural peacefulness she symbolizes (SW, xxx. 120).

Andreas's early projection of *Fernweh* in the theatre is fulfilled by the passage through disorientingly foreign places that results in an experience of self-estrangement. Andreas's momentary epiphany in Carinthia, finding himself at one with life and nature as he watches an eagle soaring, remains momentary; an inner transcendence seems to require distance from his former sense of self and submission to a new environment, which exposes, as in a mirror, his lack of boundaries. Only in Venice does the reader come to know, through Andreas's flashbacks, the events that had happened in the valley. While the rural Romana is at home in spiritual and bodily feeling, the Venetian personality of Maria/Mariquita is divided: Maria is ascetic and mystical, and Mariquita is driven by sensuality, rejecting truth and living only for corporeal pleasures. Romana as the symbol of unity of spirit and sensuous life then would represent a destination for Andreas, and, as an ideal love, that goal towards which his development points. While the novel is unfinished, it is clear that Andreas must venture into the unknown, through a wayward Venetian journey, in order to realize in himself a unity of spirit and sense. Hofmannsthal's novel presents the experience of exotic places as a challenge to the self, through which the latter would not merely be reaffirmed, but transformed.

VASTNESS, THE LABYRINTHINE, THE UNREACHABLE: TRAVEL WRITINGS IN NORTHERN AFRICA

The loss of orientation Andreas feels in Venice is echoed and further developed in Hofmannsthal's later travel writings, which have received relatively little recent scholarly attention.[26] Labyrinthine adventures in Northern Africa, which Hofmannsthal visited in 1925, also seem to hint at the transformation of self through its disorientation, but in the narrative essays of 'Reise im nördlichen Afrika', this transformation is not merely personal but occasions broader reflection on the traveller's own culture. Hofmannsthal's narrator describes experiences of North African cities, which invigorate his senses and provoke reflection on the experience of foreign places. Fez, with its ancient walls, houses, and narrow labyrinthine streets, evokes for the narrator a sense of the most ancient reality and is described as the secret of foreignness. The description is built up of layers of detail, anchored in the narrator's perspective from his dwelling at the edge of the city. A broad survey of the landscape, typically criticized in post-colonialist interpretation of travel writing,[27] is presented from this viewpoint, but spatial orientation is lost as soon as the narrator descends the garden steps and follows a servant through the city. In Saleh, the narrator, perched on a rooftop overlooking the city, discusses with two Frenchmen the foreignness of the local language. In the context of the description of the local scenery, the narrative turns to the French and German languages and their metaphysical qualities, including the sense in German of separation between embodied and spiritual aspects of experience, which emerged as a motif in *Andreas*. The narrative reflections on the German *Geist* conclude with a contrasting affirmation of the spatial experience in the exotic setting, evoking the vastness and light of the horizon—and thus of the distance itself—as a source for renewal. Along with a letter Hofmannsthal wrote to Ottonie Gräfin Degenfeld (March 17, 1925) about Marrakesh, in which the German impoverishment of the senses is contrasted to the vitality of the surroundings, these texts help to draw out the implications about exotic places of the earlier *Die Briefe des Zurückgekehrten*. While they may harbour some features of a colonialist attitude—the narrator mentions the French protectorate without critical

---

[26] Discussions of the later *Reiseprosa* can be found in: Block (1987); and Mattenklott (1991); Rovagnati (1994); N. Berman (1998).
[27] See, for example, Pratt's study of the surveying gaze of the colonialist writer (1992: especially 204–217).

evaluation of colonial occupation—all of these texts posit radical foreignness as opening up a primal experience, in contrast to which the modern European sense of reality and the Germanic disposition itself are criticized. If there is no critique of colonialist domination by Europeans, an interpretation of this lack must be balanced by recognition of the self-criticism these places provoke for the narrator.

In 'Fez', the contrast between the particular details of the city streets, people, marketplaces, houses, and gardens and the surrounding land- and seascape maintains the sense of *Fernweh* even as the narrator experiences the exotic locale with intense physical proximity. The loss of spatial orientation in the labyrinthine streets, the nearness of passing people and animals, and the sense of being enveloped by the city also render the narrator's submission to the radical foreignness of the locale. Throughout the essay, the physical position of the narrator is significant, moving from a position of overview to an immersion in which subjective control over spatial orientation is lost. At the outset, the narrator is standing on a high garden terrace at the house on the edge of the city, and so can render a broad description of the city and its surroundings. He then takes a walk through the city's dense, narrow central streets and alleyways, where the city life is seen up close. If the first moment suggests a position from which vast lands can be viewed and mapped out, as in a territorial survey, the second undermines this point of orientation and immerses the narrator in the local life, where his autonomy as a European visitor (and subject) must be compromised.

The contrast between minute detail of the immediate surroundings and the vast landscape beyond the city is striking, although it is presented through layered images of nearer to farther spaces as the focus expands. What seems, at first, to be a cartographical overview of the city and the mountainous landscape beyond it, is then balanced by descriptive registration of the minute details from the immediate locale with which the narrator has intimate contact. Starting from the point of view of his dwelling at the city's edge, the narrator's gaze follows the city wall, enclosing two hills covered with houses and securing the city against outside forces. The open space just outside the city, with its burial sites, isolated trees, and nomadic tents, provides a middle ground between the city and the mountains far beyond. Through a description of the Atlas Mountains in the distance and of the sky above them, the narrator highlights the vastness and suggests the unconquerability of the sky above the landscape. He describes:

> in der Ferne die weißschimmernde Gipfelkette des hohen Atlas, aber in
> solcher Ferne am Horizont, daß dieser Streif von Grau und Silber mit seiner

Last von leicht aufruhenden weißen Haufenwolken dem Himmel nichts von seiner Reinheit und Leere nimmt, nichts von seiner Höhe, aus der die klare kühle Nordostluft unablässig herabweht, durchschnitten vom ruhigen Flug der vielen Störche oder vom Flattern eines weißen Taubenschwarmes, über dem, ihn niederdrückend, die rostfarbigen Falken kreisen.

(in the distance the shimmering white peak of the high Atlas, but at such distance on the horizon that this stripe of grey and silver, with its burden of white cumulus clouds in light tumult, robs nothing of the purity and emptiness of the sky, nothing of its height, from which the clear cool Northeast wind incessantly blows down, intersected by the calm flight of many storks or the flapping of a white swarm of doves over which, bending down to it, the rust-coloured hawks circle.) (GW, vii. 641)

The distance of the mountains is emphasized with 'in der Ferne', followed by 'aber in solcher Ferne'. With this latter emphasis, the still more distant sky above the mountains is preserved in its purity and height. Thus, in sequence, descriptions of the city wall and what it encloses, then the hilly land surrounding the city, then the mountains, then the distant sky above the mountains, build a dilating chain of images from nearest to farthest and smallest to largest, all the spaces outside the city suggesting the emptiness of distance and a purity that increases with the distance. The narrator's description of three different kinds of birds that cross the sky— storks, flocks of pigeons, and falcons—provides continuity between the vastness of the sky and specific indigenous life. This detail then prepares for the return to description of the immediate surroundings, the terrace and garden of the house in which he is staying and his descent into the city.

That this description is nevertheless introduced by 'aber' ('but') as the initial word of the second paragraph rhetorically emphasizes the contrast between this sweeping gaze, allowed by the narrator's position on the terrace, and the disorientation felt by the narrator as he passes through the garden and house and enters the streets of the city. The particularity of detail is explicitly juxtaposed to the vast horizon. For when he descends from the highest terrace of the house, he notices the colour of the stones and even of their edges; he mentions orange trees, rose bushes, and stone fountains filled from within and overflowing in tiny blue rivulets of water. In proximity to these, the view of the distance is obscured:

so sehe ich von der unendlichen Durchsichtigkeit und Weite dieses vor Klarheit fast strengen Himmels nur mehr ein kleines Stück.
(So now I see only a small bit of the endless transparency and vastness of this sky almost severe in its clarity.) (GW, vii. 641)

And while the grand house had enclosed its 'genießenden Einzelnen' ('reveling individual') as if in a fortress, the visitor finds that the house is not impervious to the outside (GW, vii. 642). From the narrator's room, he is virtually exposed to the city life, for an acoustic oddity allows vivid perception of the sounds of the passing people and animals, as if they are entering the house itself. Thus, the play between vastness and proximity is continued in this compromise of the architecture of isolation. The sounds afford a physical involvement in, or at least reception of, the city that the dweller of his room cannot avoid. This detail aligns the narrator symbolically, not with the fortress of a closed-off household, but rather with the inescapable vitality of the city below.

The narrator's loss of spatial orientation as he walks through the city is accompanied by a diminution of subjective autonomy. Immediately in the street a horseman yells at him, 'als Warnung für den Fußgänger in seinem Weg' ('as warning for the pedestrian in his way') (GW, vii. 642)—the narrator thus referring to himself in the third person and as an anonymous object, rendering the subjective point of view only of the rider. A derisive and sharp glance is cast at him by an old man, who, riding a donkey, is spatially elevated in comparison. This metaphorically reverses the colonialist hierarchy and calls to his mind his presence as a foreigner: 'denn noch ist in dieser heiligen Stadt, dem Mekka des westlichen Islam, der Europäer das sehr Fremde' ('for the European is most foreign in this holy city, the mecca of Western Islam') (GW, vii. 643). The local inhabitants are thus not merely represented as parts of the scenery, or simply as victims of foreign occupation. Rather, their dislike of the European presence is registered, and so is the fact that the old Berber state was colonized by Islam. While Hofmannsthal's narrator nowhere calls into question the French rule of the protectorate, which gives the European traveller a sense of security, he does not erase the facts of history and of local resistance, referring to an event in which Europeans were killed there: 'aber es sind nicht mehr als zwölf Jahre, daß hier an einem Tage sämtliche 'Nazaräer' den Tod fanden; und ein Nachzittern davon ist in vielen Blicken, die uns streifen' ('yet it has been no more than twelve years that here one day many "Nazarians" came to their deaths, and an aftershock of that remains in many gazes upon us') (GW, vii. 643). The reference to this danger for European visitors registers the tension provoked by their presence; even if Hofmannsthal does not seem to regard this presence critically, he does not ignore its implications for the inhabitants.

The presentation of the city as labyrinthine suggests submission to the exotic surroundings and loss of subjective control. The narrator does not direct the route (as might a colonialist surveyor), but must rely on the servant, who is identified during the description of the walk as the guide ('der Führer') on whom he is dependent. The narrator proceeds without being able to identify everything he sees along the way:

> Aber schon hat sich aus der Öffnung eines Hauses heraus—oder ist es eine noch engere, noch finstere Gasse als die, in der ich meinem Führer folgt?— ein noch kleinerer Esel, auf dem zwei lachende kleine Kinder in blauen Leinenburnusses sitzen, hervorgeschoben. (GW, vii. 643)
>
> (But already in leaving the entrance of a house—or is it a still narrower, darker alley than the one in which I follow my guide?—an even smaller donkey on which two small children in linen burnouses sat, pressed on by.) (GW, vii. 643)

This uncertainty, here as to whether an opening is the door of a dwelling or another alleyway, is experienced repeatedly. In the following passage, the street, flanked by high walls, feels as if it is an enclosed room:

> Nun ist aber mein Führer, scharf links sich wendend, in ein Haus getreten; nein, es ist kein Hauseingang, sondern eine neue Gasse, ein neuer solcher Schacht aus den fensterlosen Mauern hoher uralter Häuser; sie treten nach oben hin zusammen, so daß das Gefühl, im geschlossenen Raum zu sein, sich noch verstärkt; zugleicht steigt diese Gasse an.
>
> (But now my guide, turning a sharp left, has stepped into a house; no, it is not an entrance to a house but rather a new alley, a new such tunnel made out of the windowless walls of high ancient houses; they come together overhead so that the feeling of being in a closed place intensifies; while this street continues to rise.) (GW, vii. 643)

These narrow streets, high walls, uncertain passageways, and the confused perception of exterior and interior space render the city as a labyrinth, not unlike the description Hofmannsthal gives in his review of 'Tausendu-neine Nacht'. Resonances between this essay and the travel writing have been suggested by post-colonial critics: imaginations of the Orient based on fiction, it is charged, are projected onto real spaces, as discussed in the Introduction.[28] While there is some merit to this critique, its basic presumption, that such spaces ought to be described in *Reiseprosa* as empirical facts, is problematic. This view neglects the constructed nature of experienced spaces, what Simmel called the 'Tätigkeit der Seele' ('activity of the soul') involved in the constitution of atmosphere as such (GA7, 133). Even in Said's account, any 'locales, regions, geographical sectors' are in an important sense 'not just there' but rather 'man-made'.[29] In Hofmannsthal's description, the feeling of being

---

[28] N. Berman (1998: 17–18) criticizes Hofmannsthal's writings on Africa on these grounds.

[29] Said (1979/2003: 4–5).

enclosed within the narrow space of the street extends to the city itself. There is an increasing sense of being enveloped within a larger whole. This is affirmed in a later passage with the repetition of the phrase 'mitten drin':

> Und so bin ich denn nach so wenigen Schritten mitten drin in dieser Stadt; wie sehr ist man und wie schnell mitten drin in ihr; wie schnell umgibt sie einen so vielgehäusig und geschlossen und ausgangslos, als wäre man ins Innere eines Granatapfels geraten.
>
> (And thus after so few steps I am in the middle of this city; how deeply and how quickly one is in the centre of it; how quickly it surrounds one, with so many houses and so closed and with no exit, as if one were caught in the middle of a pomegranate.) (GW, vii. 644)

The metaphor of a pomegranate 'exoticizes' the place and associates it with the sensuous and the forbidden, recognizable codes of the Oriental. But if there is anxiety about being closed in, the fruit metaphor is ambiguous, also suggestive of desire and life. The adjective 'ausgangslos' ('with no exit') expresses an awareness of the power of space to dominate subjective orientation, and along with the subjunctive 'als wäre' ('as if (one) were') and its corresponding metaphor, highlights the subjective element of perception.

The narrowness of the streets also enforces the narrator's physical proximity to the native peoples, as well as to their domesticated animals, such as horses and mules. When they pass by there is physical contact:

> und von oben her, wo sie sich wieder krümmt und scheinbar wieder in ein noch finstereres Hausinnere verliert, kommt mir auf einem schönen starken Maultier, das sie selber lenkt, eine verschleierte Frau entgegen. Die Straße ist so eng, daß fast ihr Steigbügel mich streift und daß um ein Nichts die Tücher und Schleier, in die ihre Gestalt gehüllt ist, mich berühren müßten.
>
> (and from above, where it bends over again and is apparently lost in an ever darker interior of a house, a veiled woman approaches on a beautiful strong mule, which she steers herself. The street is so narrow that her stirrup almost touches me and her robes and veil in which her figure is covered have to touch me. (GW, vii. 644–645)

And again:

> Von hier aus aber trägt mich die Welle der Gehenden und Reitenden, der kleinen Esel, die mich aus dem Weg schieben, der bettelnden Kinderhände, die mich leise anrühren, in einen ganz geschlossenen, ganz mit Menschen und Waren angefüllten Raum.
>
> (But from here I am carried by the waves of pedestrians and riders and the small donkeys, which shove me out of the way, the begging hands of children, which touch me lightly, into an entirely closed room packed full with people and wares.) (GW, vii. 645)

The touch cannot be avoided, but there is also no indication that the narrator would have preferred to avoid it. Instead, the richness of the physical experience is highlighted through bodily contact with native human beings and their domesticated animals. As when 'der Fußgänger' is yelled at by the rider, the narrator recognizes himself as an object obstructing the path. His perspective is not that of an abstract observer, since it is emphasized that he shares with the others a common embodiment, and is thus both subject perceiving and object perceived at once.

In the second of the African essays, a conversation between the narrator and two Frenchmen takes place on a rooftop above and overlooking the city. The discussion leads to a conversation about the French and especially German languages; whatever Eurocentrism is suggested by praise for these languages in the context of North Africa is tempered by the final descriptions of the beauty of the surroundings. The German language comes to be understood, it is implied, in the context of this discussion far from European soil, in the context of the very foreign environment of Saleh. While the essay provides far less intimacy with the exotic surroundings than the previous one, taken together they suggest that the cultural self-reflection of the narrator in the second essay is conditioned by exposure, described in the first essay, to the radical otherness of exotic place and the vision of vast landscapes beyond them. The motif of the necessity of the foreign for understanding 'das Eigene' ('the proper' or 'one's own') is familiar from Hölderlin—who is mentioned in the second essay and is quoted in 'Sizilien und wir' (GW, vii. 661)—and Hölderlin's famous letter to Casimir Ulrich Böhlendorff (see WB, ii. 940–942). The distinction between being (with which the French language is associated) and becoming (which is said to be celebrated by the German language) also calls up Hölderlin, who pondered theoretically 'Das Werden im Vergehen' ('Becoming in Dissolution') and its relationship to the feeling of life (see WB, ii. 641–646). His *Hyperion*'s travel between Germany and his native Greece, and Hölderlin's own sojourn in the exoticized France of Bordeaux, offered occasion for critical reflection upon the German *Geist*. In Hofmannsthal's essay, the German language is itself associated with the ontological vastness and depth suggested by *Fernweh*: 'Welche Weite! Welche Befruchtung aus der Dunkelheit!' ('What vastness! What fecundity from the darkness!') (GW, vii. 654). But this view of the German language is made relative, in the essay's last paragraph, to the exotic surroundings of Saleh, in a contrast highlighted by 'aber' and the description of the surroundings as reflections, 'wie gespiegelt' ('as if mirrored'):

Alles aber auch um uns sah in diesem wunderbaren Licht aus wie gespiegelt. Die Häuser uns zu Füßen, die hohen gelbroten Mauern drüben in Rabat, Tiere und Menschen am Ufer des Flusses, alles war völlig entkörpert. Die schmale Wolke in der Gestalt eines Fisches glühte purpurviolett. Ein Starenzug flog von ihr aus gegen Osten hin, und dort ging das Türkisblau in ein zartes Grün über. Das Ferne schien sehr nahe—das Nahe ungreifbar vergeistigt.

(But everything around us, too, looked, in this wonderful light, as if mirrored. The houses at our feet, the high ochre walls over in Rabat, animals and people on the banks of the river, everything was wholly disembodied. The thin cloud in the shape of a fish glowed violet. From it a flock of starlings flew Eastward, and there the turquoise blue merged into a soft green. What was distant seemed very near, and what was nearby ungraspably transformed.) (GW, vii. 654)

The exotic landscape seems spiritually elevated by an implicit relationship to being and becoming discussed by the narrator and his interlocutors. In this epiphany, symbolized by the eastward-shooting star, solid entities appear as if in transformation, and thus as 'entkörpert' ('disembodied'). The world for a moment seems 'in zauberhaftem Gleichgewicht' ('in magical balance'), and its beauty relies on the non-polarization of what is near and what is far (GW, vii. 654). By a paradoxical recognition of the intimacy of 'das Ferne' ('the distant'), what is one's own, 'das Nahe' ('the nearby') is transformed. Hofmannsthal's travel essays on Africa together then depict the experience of submission to exotic surroundings, which yields epiphany. This submission does not merely, as in *Andreas*, compromise the self's orientation in a promise of transformative *Bildung* of the individual, but presents an explicit opportunity for reflection on the narrator's own European culture. In other later writings, more painful aspects of *Fernweh* are revealed, as the essence of exotic places seem inaccessible to the modern traveller. This inaccessibility is distressing in light of the critique of modernity in *Die Briefe des Zurückgekehrten*; but the transformation that may be achieved in overcoming this distance is thereby heightened.

    In the third essay of 'Augenblicke in Griechenland', of which only a brief account can be given here, the narrator despairs over the inaccessibility of the past. Among the ruins the narrator feels alienated from the spirit of classical knowledge, even from an imagined appearance of the spectre of Plato. The narrator attempts to read Sophocles in order to find an access to that world, but finds the literary approach as unconvincing as the philosophical. Finding the ruins spiritually inaccessible, he turns to the museum, where he comes upon five ancient statues of goddesses: these provoke an epiphany he cannot resist. The narrator feels as if an inner vastness within him has been opened up. The experience of the epiphany itself is, significantly, described through metaphors of movement, distance, and travel:

In diesem Augenblick geschah mir etwas: ein namenloses Erschrecken: es kam nicht von außen, sondern irgendwoher aus unmeßbaren Fernen eines inneren Abgrundes. . . . Es war ein Verwobensein mit diesen, ein gemeinsames Irgendwohinströmen, eine unhörbare rhythmische Bewegung, stärker und anders als Musik, auf ein Ziel zu . . . es glich einer Reise.

(In this moment something happened to me: a nameless shock: it came not from without, rather from somewhere out of the immeasurable remoteness of an inner abyss. . . . It was a being-interwoven with this, a streaming towards somewhere in confluence, an inaudible rhythmic movement, stronger than and different from music, towards a goal . . . it was like a journey.) (GW, vii. 624–625)

With the metaphorical movement he feels in the statues, they become symbolic not only of the past they open up to him but of the distance that has been crossed. The narrator's own longing to dissolve into the unknown, to reach an undetermined distance, is stronger than his fear of self-loss and is projected onto the objects of his fascinated gaze. With this projection, the ordinary relation between the perceiving and feeling subject and the object of perception becomes reversed, a situation that bears a striking resemblance to that of the speaker of Rilke's 'Archaïscher Torso Apollos' ('Archaic Torso of Apollo') in the *Neue Gedichte* (*New Poems*). But the statues here are rendered as the agents of metaphorical movement and travel, agents of the *Ferne*. Their bodies are 'überzeugender als mein eigener' ('more convincing than my own'); he perceives 'eine Intention' ('an intention') in them. Despite the solidity of the statues, the narrator feels, as he describes in reference to one of the statues:

etwas Liquides an ihr, etwas Sehnsüchtiges, sie kommt irgendwoher und sie verrät, daß sie irgendwohin will. Sie ist auf einer Reise, sie landet in diesem Augenblick, will sie mich mitnehmen? Woher sonst diese Ahnung einer Abreise auch in mir, dieses rhythmische Weiterwerden der Atmosphäre, dieses mit festem Fuß wandeln an einem fremden breiten Fluß, Hinaufgleiten an einem niegesehenen gekrümmten Berg.

(something fluid in her, something of longing, she comes from some unknown place and betrays that she wants to go somewhere else. She is on a journey, she lands in this moment, does she want to take me along? From where else this intuition of departure in me too, this rhythmic expansion of the atmosphere, this wandering with a strong step into a strange broad river, flowing up on a never-seen crooked mountain.) (GW, vii. 626)

The persistent evocation of an 'Atmosphäre' of movement and travel suggests a sense of boundlessness. Nothing less than 'das Geheimnis der Unendlichkeit'—the secret of infinity, and thus of infinite distance from himself—is felt to be revealed by this experience of the Greek statues (GW, vii. 626). The connection between infinity and the direction of metaphorical travel is made explicit: 'Dies, was hier vor mir ist, mein Auge füllt, richtet mich irgendwohin, ins Unendliche' ('This which is before me fills my vision, turns me towards somewhere, towards infinity') (GW, vii. 627). The pleasure the narrator feels is an experience of self-forgetting, as if he is being thrown into the darkness; the narrator now feels in himself a sense of that lostness he had attributed to the wandering stranger met in the second essay; but he feels triumphant in this very loss. Of the statues, he states, 'Sie sind da, und sind unerreichlich. So bin ich auch' ('They are here, and are inaccessible. So am I too') (GW, vii. 627). The narrator's strength is won within the experience of self-loss, as he feels himself nearing the divine in a world re-enchanted by intimacy with the exotic past. The temporal dimensions of *Fernweh* in these reflections enlarge the possibilities of transformation when the distances are intuitively crossed in a moment of epiphany. Within modern European experience itself, however, as most sharply criticized by the narrator of *Die Briefe des Zurückgekehrten*, this re-enchantment is most difficult. This re-enchantment called up by the letter-writer through an experience of the vividness, simplicity, and vitality of exotic worlds, and found here in the narrator's epiphany before the statues of ancient Greek goddesses, links Hofmannsthal's writings to the work of Max Dauthendey, to which this study now turns.

THE RE-ENCHANTMENT OF THE WORLD IN DAUTHENDEY'S ASIA

Like Hofmannsthal somewhat closer to home, Dauthendey was a seasoned traveller to far-off and 'exotic' lands, and his descriptions, however lyrical, impressionistic, or at times relying on clichéd images of the exotic, emerge from observation and intuitive reception of the places he depicts. In Dauthendey's narratives in *Lingam*—set in Bombay, Ceylon, Jaipur, Burma, Penang, Singapore, China, and Japan—events such as murder, revenge, and accidental death are connected to exotic or exoticized features of places; and yet the places remain alluring for the reader despite the suffering depicted there. The characters' fates and perspectives are connected through imagery to surrounding cultural and physical geography; religious symbolism gives a spiritual aura to the events, and often lyrical descriptions of native bodies, local dress, flora and fauna, weather, natural elements, and cities and surrounding landscapes contribute to the mysterious vitality of the settings. The descriptions are, however narratively framed, grounded in the author's travel, while realistic presentation of specific cities, towns, streets, and their natural surroundings is mingled with exoticizing and spiritualizing metaphors, such that the stories have the allure of *Märchen*.

A contrast with Hermann Hesse's *Aus Indien* (1913), a collection of travel essays that describes many of the same places and cultures, can serve to illustrate the modes of enchantment in Dauthendey's narratives in *Lingam* and *Geschichten aus den vier Winden*. Although both authors rely on Orientalizing images, and both reflect on the realities of European colonialism, the observations of Hesse's narrator remain rooted in a tourist's perspective—for the most part without the transformative epiphany characteristic of Hofmannsthal's travel writings—while Dauthendey's fiction allows the narrator to present these worlds with intuitive sympathy, shifting the focus from the European to (imagined) indigenous Asian perspectives.[30] Both Hesse and Dauthendey, while not immune to postcolonialist critique,[31] offer critical reflection on the experience and construction of the exotic by Europeans and on the realities of colonialism for the colonized peoples. Yet while Hesse tends to emphasize the disillusionment of the tourist who fails to find a projected *Wunschraum*, in Dauthendey a vital, enchanted alternative to the European sense of reality is offered through imagining the same places from a radically different perspective. While such imagining invites criticism of the presumptions about the Asiatic 'other' on the part of the European, this vital shift in perspective brings Dauthendey's writings close to the enchantment expressed by Hofmannsthal.

Despite clichéd images, Dauthendey's Asia differs from prevailing European idealizations of Asia, characterized (as in Mann, for instance)

---

[30] Reif (1975) criticizes the similarity of Dauthendey's images of Mexican natives in *Raubmenschen* to Hesse's images of native Asians, arguing that Dauthendey achieves 'kaum mehr als ein sentimentalisches und ziemlich allgemeines Bild' ('hardly more than a sentimental and rather general picture') of indigenous people (45); but Reif's study does not consider the texts in which Dauthendey, more innovatively, describes Asia, and thus fails to note the striking differences between the authors' descriptions. *Lingam* is praised as Dauthendey's best prose writing but is not discussed further (41).

[31] A critique of Hesse's *Aus Indien* is given in Zilcosky (2003); for example, 'Hesse's view [of India] relieves him of a sense of alienation . . . Hesse has gained a sense of property . . . India satisfies his exotic longings . . . by paradoxically transforming it into his (and "our") long-lost Germanic home' (28). Reif (1975) associates Hesse's text with 'eine sehnsuchtsvolle Hinwendung zu einem paradisischen Urzustand' ('a turn driven by longing towards a paradise of an original state') but also acknowledges 'kolonialkritischen Komponente' ('components critical of colonialism') (42, 44).

by raw power, sensuous luxury, and inertia. Far from presenting a mono-lithic 'Orient' in which various cultures are interchangeable, Asian cul-tures are, first of all, differentiated in Dauthendey's stories, as they are for Hesse; specific religions, landscapes, weather, and cultural traditions serve to differentiate the settings and the outlook of the characters. Dauthen-dey's narrator thus presents not merely the tourist's or philosopher's Asia—as a monotonous, other-worldly garden of sensuous pleasure or spiritual contemplation—although there are hints, too, of such idealiza-tions of the Orient. The Asia of *Lingam* is constituted by the juxtaposition of various cultures and various places, and is given from the point of view of characters in radically different social and cultural situations. While in Hesse's *Aus Indien*, as in Hofmannsthal's writings on Africa, the natives constitute merely part of the scenery, Dauthendey's fiction allows the native characters to be depicted in complex situations of life in which colonial or touring Europeans play, for the most part, a marginal role. In toil, strife, triumph, helplessness, or old age, they experience the effects of class division and poverty, misfortune, exploitation, or unfulfilled desires. While the narrator's use of dehumanizing images of native inhabitants—they are persistently compared to animals, plants, and inanimate objects—is problematic and ripe for post-colonial critique (as are the naturalizing metaphors for the colonial presence), Dauthendey's sympathetic presen-tation of both native perspectives and their struggles is innovative. Most often natives, not the European visitor, serve as the protagonists of Dauthendey's stories, and by imagining their experiences, Dauthendey's narrator presents for the European reader compelling alternative visions of the world. This approach, of course, is not without ethical risk. Dauthendey narratively evokes a range of perspectives radically different from those available within his own culture, without supplying adequate cognitive stock by which the reader might judge the credibility of such evocations. The failings, limitations, or idiosyncrasies of a particular character (gullibility, superstition, infidelity, for instance), may easily be read as emblematic for his or her respective culture, where no competing native voices intervene. Undoubtedly problematic, Dauthendey's fiction, like Hofmannsthal's writing, nonetheless transcends mere 'exoticism' in the depictions of places alluringly distant from modern Germanic culture, by suggesting in these alternatives a re-enchantment of the world. While Hofmannsthal's narra-tor of the *Briefe* praises from the point of view of an observer 'exotic' peoples for their richness of perception and for the intensity of their actions, and contrasts these to the ironic, ambivalent, and abstract character of the modern German, in Dauthendey's *Lingam* the concrete simplicity, authenticity, and vitality of the imagined native perspective enchant the reader directly.

Since Dauthendey is a considerably lesser known author than Hofmannsthal, and is, along with Kubin, the least known author whose works are discussed in this study, some biographical detail must be provided as a background to his works. Aside from Hesse, no modern German author seems to have been as attracted to faraway and exotic places, and to have profited as much from *Fernweh*, as Dauthendey. Having already travelled almost incessantly during the preceding decade throughout Europe, Russia, and North America, Dauthendey travelled through the Far East in 1905–1906. During this trip, arranged expressly for the production of literary writing, he visited India, Burma, Malaya, China, and Japan, among other places; these experiences formed the basis of, and provided the settings for, a now little-discussed work of 1909, *Lingam: Zwölf asiatische Novellen* (*Lingam: Twelve Asian Novellas*). They also resulted in many other works, including his then much-read book of 'Japanese' love stories, *Die acht Gesichter am Biwasee* (*Eight Faces at Biwasee*) (1911), poetry, lyrical travel journals, *Märchen*, and letters, many of which evidence Dauthendey's affinity for Asia and its radical differences from European culture. His renderings of Asia suggest places of enchantment and vitality that sharply contrast with the modern Europe criticized in Hofmannsthal's *Briefe*. Dauthendey's enthusiasm for exotic places was tempered when, after returning to South-east Asia in 1914, he was interned in Java (as a German citizen) at the outbreak of the First World War; he died there in 1918 of malaria. The popularity of *Lingam* (by 1923, 13,000 copies had been printed) and the even more successful *Biwasee* work is suggestive of the German reading public's fascination with exotic places at the time; but, like Hesse's *Aus Indien*, it also reflects early twentieth-century interest in Asian cultures in particular, of which Hofmannsthal was also enamoured despite never having travelled to Asia.

While Dauthendey's other works are compelling, *Lingam* is unique in offering a diversity of Asian settings and cultures within a single group of texts, and so, along with a story from *Geschichten aus den vier Winden* (*Stories from the Four Winds*), will be the focus in this study. The stories in *Lingam* are individuated, but tonally unified by their presentation of the perspective not of tourists but natives or inhabitants, and by their magical aura; although problematic in the ways aforementioned, these features generate the sense of an intimate passage through foreign worlds. *Lingam* is, then, distinguished from the *Reiseprosa* of Hofmannsthal and Hesse not most prominently by fictionalization, but by point of view. Although Dauthendey's narrator is objective, the point of view merges with that of the native protagonists, with few exceptions. Yet the presumed reader is not a native of those places, since the narrator comments on features that would be unremarkable, since so familiar, to the native: the look, smell, and feel of the surroundings, the appearance of inhabitants, their clothing and bodies, the colour of their skin, their everyday habits, local rituals, and native beliefs so strikingly different from that of the foreign observer. The narrative voice thus aims to bridge cultural and geographical distances between the native protagonists and the presumed European reader. This differentiates the work from both Hofmannsthal's writings and those of Hesse, both of which offer the perspective of the Germanic traveller as he confronts a foreign world. The traveller's perspective is, however, presented in Dauthendey's story 'Himalajafinsternis', from *Geschichten aus den vier Winden*.

Understanding how the diverse stories of *Lingam* constitute a unified text, however loosely, and how the overall relation to the exotic is established in them, will help to establish the means by which they provoke enchantment for the reader. Like some of Hofmannsthal's fiction and travel essays, the stories must establish the atmospheric allure of the exotic settings. But here this allure must be sustained even through the depiction of acts of violence and disastrous fates; for Dauthendey's Asia is not idealized. The tension between allure and suffering within the stories seems to be an expression of the very *Fernweh*—the painful allure of the *Ferne*—which motivates them, and of the dangers also lingering in the mystery of unknown places. Yet *Lingam* as a whole, despite admittedly problematic imagery and the risks of assuming points of view of natives, transcends mere exoticism.[32] Dauthendey's work expresses a post-Enlightenment vision: not an overcoming of cultural differences in favour of a universal human truth, as Klaus Börner has argued is characteristic of Dauthendey, but the attempt to experience the universally human through these differences, is most attractive in his work.[33]

While Hofmannsthal had 'exoticized' some settings within Europe, Dauthendey's settings are already recognized by the European reader as exotic, and Dauthendey relies on the implicit contrast between the Asian settings and European experiences of everyday life. In the stories set in India, for example, the unashamed acceptance of, and reverence for, the naked body and human sexuality are highlighted, contrasting sharply with Western European mores. Vital bodily experience—presented through description of the naked body itself, sexual desire, labour, dance and other movement, physical sensations, and closeness to animals—is implicitly contrasted to the European's more abstract approach to the physical

---

[32] In contrast to Klaus Börner's (1997: 186) dismissal of *Lingam*.

[33] In Börner's (1997: 192) view, Dauthendey's sensitivity to foreign cultures yields to a transcendence of cultural differences, expressing 'archetypischen Universalismus' ('archetypical universalism').

world, according to a world-view that tends to render bodily experience either insignificant or problematic.[34] This vitality of the body in exotic places is also registered by Hofmannsthal's letter-writer of the *Briefe des Zurückgekehrten*: Addison's adage (which Hofmannsthal often quoted) that the 'whole man' that must move 'at once' refers to the physical vitality lacking in the intellectual and abstract modern European character. In Dauthendey this lack of vitality of the European is symbolically presented. In 'Der Garten ohne Jahreszeiten,' for example, the Europeans are depicted as fully clothed in white, like ghosts, which confuses the provincial native; and in the same story, as in others, naked brown skin of the natives is repeatedly and affirmatively highlighted. The sexuality of the married couple is treated in a decidedly non-European way. The points of view presented by the narrator differ significantly from the European world-view, if that can be characterized by suppression or regulation of sexual, physical, and emotional feeling in favour of the rational intellect as the bases for judgment and action.

In Weber's analysis of the disenchanted world-view of modern Europe, he describes the rejection of 'alle magischen Mittel der Heilsuche als Aberglaube und Frevel' ('all magical means of healing as superstition and sacrilege') and the explanation of all events, even when in religious terms, according to a total and systematic, rational vision of the world (GA, i. 94). While the modern European would reject, accordingly, the belief that inexplicable supernatural powers intervene in human fate, *Lingam*'s characters, and the fates they endure, are profoundly influenced by this 'enchanted' outlook, also described in anthropological terms in Lévy-Bruhl's characterization of so-called 'primitive' mentality. With only a few exceptions, where the narrator comments about the Oriental or Asian acceptance of the supernatural and the magical, the narrative tone merges with this acceptance, and the plots develop in harmony with it. Aspects of Asian religions and mythology are present, too—for example, the Hindu symbol of sexual union gives the collection its title. In some stories the religious or supernatural is dominant: Dalar is inspired by violent images of the vengeful goddess Kali in the first story; Buddhist reverence for Kimgun's infant son, and the revenge of the golden tiger for his haughtiness, dominate a later one; and the Malay superstition that damage to a person's image will be inflicted upon his or her body is realized in the story set in Penang. In these stories the intervention of the divine is magical, that is, not explicable according to a rational, scientific

---

[34] The body and sexuality are also highlighted in some 'exoticized' European settings, such as the peasant mountain culture in Musil's 'Grigia', where it is implicitly contrasted to the decadent sexuality of more modern Northern Europeans. See Chapter 4.

account of reality as a whole. The supernatural or religious not only plays a role in many of the plots but also provides a guiding tonality to the narrator's idiosyncratic use of imagery. Hesse, too, while criticizing the modernized expression of Asian religion, praises their 'Lebensstrom und magische Atmosphäre' ('life current and magical atmosphere') as 'das einzige, um was wir diese armen und unterworfenen Völker ernstlich beneiden dürfen' ('the only thing that we can seriously envy of this poor and downtrodden people') (SW, xiii. 283).

The unity of Dauthendey's *Lingam* relies in fact upon the diversity of its cultural geographies, and so a survey of its settings must be given. The first three stories take place in Bombay. The streets of that city, with its traffic of people, rickshaws, and animals, its workshops open to the street, public washing in the fountains, and its temples, situate a tailor's brewing revenge in 'Dalar rächt sich' ('Dalar Gets Revenge'). For an imagined infidelity, Dalar abandons his wife to a life of poverty, leaving for a religious community in the mountains while she must contend alone with their debts. In Bombay, too, the street-magician Walai is unable to compete with an Englishman's compliments to a dancer with whom he falls in love; instead of money, he offers his beloved young son in a gruesome sacrifice by the same sword with which they had entertained the tourists. A wealthy villa and its gardens in 'Unter den Totentürmen' ('Under the Towers of the Dead') where dead Parsi are laid out for vultures, situates a rich young Parsi's misfortune in marriage to an intellectual woman ill-suited to a traditional union. In Jaipur, an orphaned boy who exercises the noble's favourite elephant as the city is being prepared for a visit by the Prince of Wales, imagines being able to bring rain to the draught-stricken region and reverse his parents' deaths caused by servitude and poverty. Here, as in the previous stories, colonial relations and gross class and caste divisions, or problems of modernization, are marginally presented, but serve as poignant sources of suffering. In the Calcutta of 'Eingeschlossene Tiere' ('Captive Animals') the English daughter of a botanist hides with a young Indian worker at the zoological garden to avoid being brought back to England from the colony; she experiences the frightening yet magical metamorphosis of the park at night, the description of which seems to express the deep mysteriousness and primitive animality attributed to the foreign world to which she has become attached. In 'Der Kuli Kimgun' ('The Coolie Kimgun') the title character travels to the capital port city of Burma to participate in the salvage of a famous bell dropped into the sea by colonists; through a stroke of luck he marries a wealthy girl, but their deformed and revered son is eaten by a tiger in the golden Buddhist palace, as if to avenge the coolie's attraction to gold. In the Ceylon of 'Der Garten ohne Jahreszeiten' ('The Garden Without Seasons'), a young mountain couple is brought in turns by the colonial garden manager to the capital; each is corrupted there by the commercial city life and exploitation by colonists and tourists, but is redeemed by the inexplicable resilience of their love. In 'Im blauen Licht von Penang' ('In the Blue Light of Penang'), the wife of a photographer unknowingly stabs the courtesan's photo, which had been sewn into her husband's housecoat for good luck; the blue light cast over the city plays a role in the fates of all characters. In the Canton of 'Der unbeerdigte Vater' ('The Unburied Father'), a young girl's wish to be able to bury her father brings about an earthquake. Also in China, the horoscope of the young friend of an astrologer is shared with the young kaiser; the fate of both are unfolded in a Mandarin club, which houses an artificial landscape garden and female singers crippled by bound feet. In a Japanese garden house, the Christian notion of the resurrection of the flesh is interpreted by an elderly man, who at 105 presents a feigned youth and revitalized desire to the wife of the tea-house owner across the street. While some of these stories seem to rely as much on cliché as on observation, others give remarkable detail—regarding specific streets in a given city, particular mountains or valleys, and local flora and fauna— even as the settings are 'exoticized' through metaphor. Rather than merely fragmented impressions from separate worlds, these stories build up a tonally unified presentation through their evocation of an enchanted reality, which radically defamiliarizes, and 're-enchants,' the world as it is understood by the European reader.

ENCHANTMENT AS CRITICAL DISTANCE FROM MODERN EUROPE

Dauthendey's 'Eingeschlossene Tiere' is the only story that features a European as protagonist. Perhaps because of this fact, the story achieves the most explicit reflection of *Fernweh* and the hope for re-enchantment of the world through the exotic experience. The enchanted world of India is directly contrasted to the English origins of the protagonist, and then offers a critical juxtaposition between Asian enchantment and European modernity. The transformation of a zoological park by the fall of evening expresses the inner desires and fears of the English girl Esthe (Dauthendey probably had the name 'Esther' in mind) as she confronts an impending departure from India. As the daughter of a colonial botanist brought up in and accustomed to India 'wie eine Koralle am Meeresgrund' ('like a coral on the sea floor'), Esthe suffers from anticipatory *Fernweh* as her father prepares for their return to England (L, 69). Yet her youth and her femininity distance her from a traditionally masculine colonial perspective, and both seem to play a role in her reception of the foreign world of India, since they are traditionally associated with the imagination. Esthe decides to be seduced by an Indian boy as justification for staying in the colonies; this plan draws Esthe to her friend Todor who works at Calcutta's zoological garden, where she is intent on spending the night. The sudden insertion of the present tense in an early paragraph—'Es ist Sonntagnachmittag' ('It is Sunday afternoon')—signals an adoption of the girl's point of view, with her panic about the next morning's departure from the hotel, and her secret calculations (L, 70).

The description of the botanical garden reveals Esthe's deep longing for the vitality of the natural surroundings, and for the sensuality of the native culture she imagines as bound together with it. Her affinity with the animals in the garden, and her desire to hear them at night, calls up a sense of primitive and unconscious forces. She tells Todor:

> Ich möchte im Finstern an den Käfiggittern entlang gehen und die Tigeraugen sehen, wenn sie grün und gelb auf mich losstürzen; die großen fliegenden Hunde, die tagsüber schlafen und kopfüber an den Bäumen hängen, möchte ich nachts aufwachen sehen und möchte sehen, wie die Schlangen sich nachts am Glas der Aquarien elektrisch reiben. Und vor allem habe ich Appetit nach dem verruchten Gebrüll der Heulaffen, die im Mondschein klagen sollen, als ob sie sich gegenseitig erdrosselten, und dann muß ich die Signalpfiffe der großen Trompetennachtigallen kennen lernen.
>
> (I would like to walk along the cage bars in the twilight and see the tigers' eyes when they dart at me all green and yellow; the great flying dogs that sleep all day and hang upside-down from the trees, I want to see them awaken at night, and want to see how at night snakes grate electric on the aquarium glass. And above all I want to hear the mad shrieks of the hyenas which are supposed to wail in the moonlight as if they were strangling each other, and then I have to get to know the song of the great trumpet nightingales.) (L, 73)

Esthe asks Todor to procure the keys to the snake and tiger houses. An imagined liberation of these animals expresses both sexual and other primitive desires she aims to feel unleashed. But it also symbolizes the dangers of crossing social and sexual boundaries that she and the boy do not fully understand. Later in the story the tiger and snake are identified with Todor himself in Esthe's imagination as she calls out after him, confirming her sexual desire for him as the basis of her sympathy with animal nature.

Esthe's relation to the outside world, and to European social expectations, are quickly forgotten as twilight sets in and obscures all markers of orientation. The broad-leafed *Schlingpflanzen* (vines) under which she rests with Todor create a virtual enclosure, and a sense of interiority separate from the familiar world.

> Draußen verschwanden mit einem Male die rotsandigen Gartenwege in der plötzlichen Tropendämmerung.... Aus dem plötzlich grauen Abendlicht drang jetzt das langausgestoßene Geheul der wilden Tiere.
>
> (Outside all at once, the sandy red garden paths disappeared in the tropical twilight.... From the suddenly grey light of evening irrupted the long-suppressed howling of wild animals.) (L, 74)

This interior not only offers a feeling of privacy for Esthe's refuge with Todor but also a symbol for the imagination through which the garden world will be transformed. The descriptions of the park at dusk and in the darkness, with animal sounds and smells transformed into vivid correlatives for the girl's own feeling, present images that stand in for the exotic imagination itself. Here the exotic park at night, with its sounds and smells of Asian animality, is inseparable from the sensual 'darkness' associated with feminine sexuality:

> Die Luft des Gartens begann wütender nach Tierhaut und Tierschweiß zu riechen. Esthe gruselte es angenehm bei dem wilden Geruch.... Alle Bäume verschwanden jetzt, als gingen sie alle aus dem Garten, und Ströme von Düften wanderten wie fremde lebendige Wesen durch die Dunkelheit. Auch alle Farben begannen zu wandern. Der Scharlach der Kakteenblüten war pechschwarz geworden, die blauen Mandarinenblüten leuchteten weiß, die Yuccapalmen glizterten wie Fischgräten und Fischgerippe und die Palmyraschäfte wie große weiße Elefantenknochen.
>
> (The garden air began to reek furiously of animal sweat and skin. Ester shuddered pleasantly at the wild scent.... All of the trees disappeared now, as if they all left the garden, and rivers of scent wafted through the darkness like strange living beings. Even the colours began to wander. The scarlet of the cactus blossoms had become jet black, the blue mandarin blossoms glowed white, yucca palms glittered like fish scales and fins, and palm shafts like great white elephant bones. (L, 75)

The pungent smells and ghostly colours transform a familiar but exotic collection of botanical species into vital and moving beings. Non-sentient plants become animated, as if the most primitive form of material life—and in correlation with them, the most primitive aspects of the human soul—were taken up into higher forms of vitality. The boundary is blurred between basic material life and animality, a description of which is attended by hints of danger:

> Die Dunkelheit gab den Bäumen klumpige Beine und den Büschen gedunsene Leiber, daß sie Molchen glichen; die Nachtfarbe verwandelte die Welt der Pflanzen in eine Tierwelt. Die Erde vor Esthes Füßen dünstete einen

bittern Schweiß aus, den das Mädchen wie ein Gift auf der Zunge schmeckte.

(The darkness gave the trees lumpy legs and the bushes bloated bellies so that they looked like newts; the night colour transformed the world of plants into an animal world. The earth at Esther's feet steamed a bitter sweat, which the girl tasted on her tongue like a poison.) (L, 75)

As Esthe, after Todor's departure, makes her way through the foliage, shapes of exotic flowers and leaves are felt on her fingertips. Her dreamlike experience suggests a total defamiliarization, a submission to the world of strange, enchanting, but also frightening forms, as the tactile sensation takes the place of visual orientation and renders Esthe vulnerable to her contact with the exotic world:

Esthe stand vor der Bank auf und tastete sich durch die Laube. Sie griff nach den weißlichen Tuberosen; die fühlten sich wie glatte, schleimige Augäpfel an, die sich unter ihren Fingerspitzen bewegten. Sie griff in die Schlingpflanzen, die waren wie das Gekröse und Eingeweide eines frischgeschlachteten Tierleibes, lauwarm und weich. 'Todor!' rief das junge Mädchen. Todor aber schien verschwunden.

(Ester stood up on the bench and felt her way through the arbour. She grasped for the white tube roses; they felt like smooth shiny eyeballs, which moved under her fingertips. She grasped in the creepers, they were like intestines and entrails of a freshly slaughtered animal corpse, lukewarm and soft. 'Todor!' cried the young girl. But Todor seemed to have disappeared.) (L, 76)

Soon Esthe's perceptual experience is inseparable from the surroundings perceived. Descriptions of the cries of caged animals in the night seem to be expressions of human feelings. Already familiar with India, Esthe finds in the night-time transformation an access to a still deeper recess of the mysterious foreign that seems to beckon her. The metaphoric identification of the cries with human longing suggests some drive for freedom that is bound up both with sexual desire and with *Fernweh* itself.

Esthe kannte wohl die indischen Nächte voll Zikadengerassel und Affengeschrei; auch die Schreie der Schakale und das Gelächter vieler wilder Nachtvögel hatte sie gehört, aber diese langen, qualvollen Stoßseufzer eingeschlossener Tiere, welche die Luftwellen aufregten, daß die Blätter im Dunkel zischelten, diese inbrünstigen Sehnsuchtsschreie, ... die geschüttelt wie Ketten unter dem Freiheitsdrang wahnsinnig gewordener Bestien rasselten, das hatte Esthe noch nie gehört.

(Esther knew well the Indian nights full of rattling cicadas and the apes' cry; she had also heard the cry of the jackals and laughter of many wild night birds, but this long, torturous groaning of captive animals, which agitated the airwaves so that the leaves hissed in the darkness, this fervent cry of longing... that shook like chains under the beasts grown mad with the drive for freedom, this Esther had never heard.) (L, 77)

Not only Esthe's feelings but also her physiological states are confounded with images of this plant and animal world. Her heart's leaps are compared to a panther, its rolling like an enormous snake—two images also identified with Todor—and her heart is also compared to a solidly rooted plant that cannot move from its origins. The animals' cries are compared to her own inner voices:

> Und alle die Schreie in dem finstern Garten, die aus den Tierkehlen platzten und der Luft weh taten, wurden in Esthe wie ihre tausend eigenen Stimmen. Alles, was im Garten an Wildheit wucherte, an Inbrunst und Leidenschaft, wurde zu Esthes Herz. Ihr Blut ging alle Tierverwandlungen durch, als wollte es fort aus ihrem Leib, vielgestaltig in die Nacht stürmen; wie die Raubtiere, die ihre Haare an den Gitterstäben reiben und ihre Tatzen durch die Eisen drängen, drängte das Blut nach einer unbekannten Freiheit.
>
> (And all the cries in the dark garden that burst from the animals' throats and wounded the air became in Esther like her own thousand voices. Everything rampant in wildness in the garden, in fervency and passion, went to Esther's heart. Her blood went through all the bestial metamorphoses, as if it wanted out of her body, to storm the night in many forms; like the predators, which rub their fur on the cage bars and drive their claws through the iron, the blood strove for some unknown freedom.) (L, 77–78)

The physiological rendering of these images suggests that Esthe's desire for an unknown freedom comes from the deepest and most basic sources of her vitality. This longing—animalistic, primitive, sensuous, and yet basically human—brings together deep bodily forces and spiritual feeling. Animal life, like the vultures in 'Unter den Totentürmen,' the tiger in 'Der Kuli Kimgun,' and the snake in 'Im blauen Licht vom Penang,' participates in and becomes symbolic of human fate and experience. By highlighting the English girl's intimate imagination of this participation, 'Eingeschlossene Tiere' seems to serve as an account of *Fernweh* itself, and as such provides means to understand its function in *Lingam* as a whole. These—to the modern European writer and reader—remote spaces of the world become metaphoric for what Bachelard calls the inner space, 'l'espace du dedans', of the human imagination.[35] The zoological garden becomes an enchanted world of exotic and sensuous vitality, expressing both the world of her childhood Esthe does not want to leave, and the break into the unknown provoked by her emerging adolescent desire. The world she experiences in the park at night, above all,

---

[35] Bachelard (1957: 186).

spatializes the richness, ambivalence, and mystical nature of her deepest feelings; it symbolizes a wholly different order of life, mind, and relationships than Esthe imagines will be found in the English homeland to which is to return.

The enchanted worlds of *Lingam* are constituted through description of experiences similar to those recalled and longed for by the narrator of Hofmannsthal's *Briefe*: the purity of human desire or purpose, unrepressed bodily sensuousness or awakening sexuality, shared vitality and feeling with plant or animal life, the sense of a participation of nature in human feeling and experience. The unity underlying the diverse settings in *Lingam* is established by the enchanted tonality of place rendered by means of narrative intimacy with the alluring and frightening differences of foreign worlds; in all of them there is a sense of supernatural or magical forces at work in human fate. *Lingam* thus offers the reader an alternative to the familiarly rationalized world, a release from the intellect's suppression or exclusion of more vital human feeling.

ENCHANTMENT AND DISILLUSIONMENT IN DAUTHENDEY AND IN HESSE'S *AUS INDIEN*

Dauthendey's collection of stories *Geschichten aus den vier Winden* (1915) does provide a narrative description of Asia, among other places in Europe, from the perspective of the traveller, a perspective presented, then, by all three authors discussed in this chapter. Both Dauthendey's 'Himalajafinsternis' from that collection and Hesse's *Aus Indien* depict a traveller's ascent of the Pedrotallagalla, the highest peak on Ceylon (now Sri Lanka), in which both disillusionment and enchantment are experienced. In Dauthendey's story the narrator is taken by rickshaw-pullers to a Tibetan temple in Ceylon, 'der...nach langen Fahrten, auf verschlungenen Wegen erreicht wird' ('which is reached after a long journey on winding paths') (GVW, 48). The narrator is disappointed in his experience of the temple, but at night is haunted by a woman who, along the way, had inadvertently sold him an amulet to which she has a superstitious attachment. This story of Dauthendey's is closest to Hofmannsthal's and Hesse's writings not only in presenting the European traveller in exotic places but also in reflecting explicitly on the experience of travel itself and the constitution of the 'exotic'.

Dauthendey's narrator of 'Himalajafinsternis', told in the first person, reflects on the difficult relation of travel to the *Fernweh*, which may provoke it. The discovery of far-off and different places can neutralize the magic of a long-nurtured expectation. The traveller then experiences the paradoxical situation, mentioned in the introduction to this chapter, that travel limits the imagination:

> Das ist der Fluch und zugleich die Wollust des Reisens, daß es dir Orte, die dir vorher in der Unendlichkeit und in der Unerreichbarkeit lagen, endlich und erreichbar macht. Diese Endlichkeit und Erreichbarkeit zieht dir aber geistige Grenzen, die du nie mehr los werden wirst.
>
> (That is the curse and at the same time the excitement of travel, that places which were once infinitely far and inaccessible to you become finite and accessible. But this finitude and accessibility draws boundaries in your soul that you will never erase.) (GVW, 43)

The mere imagination of far-off places is open-ended and unlimited. But actual travel, in which vague expectations are replaced by first-hand experiences, limits through actuality what in fantasy was limitless and endlessly changeable. Dauthendey's narrator, a seasoned traveller, like the author himself on his way through India, argues that one who has travelled much is more bound to the earth than one who has never travelled, implying that travel has limited his imagination: 'Die Flügel der Geistigkeit werden ihm von der Wirklichkeit beschnitten' ('The wings of spirit are clipped by reality') (GVW, 44). Thus, the story reflects on the possibility of the traveller's disillusionment, also a frequent subject of Hesse's travel narratives. Hesse writes of the traveller's fairy-tale inspired expectations:

> Der Europäer, der mit anderen als geschäftlichen Absichten nach den malayischen Inseln fährt, hat stets, und auch wenn er gar nicht auf Erfüllung hofft, als Hintergrund seiner Vorstellungen und Wünsche die Landschaft und die primitive Paradiesunschuld einer van Zantenschen Insel.
>
> (The European who with other than commercial aims travels to the Malaysian islands always has the landscape and primitive paradisal innocence of an island from out of van Zanten as the background of his imaginings and wishes, even if he hopes for no fulfilment.) (SW, xiii. 238)

But Hesse recognizes these expectations as mere projections: 'wenn ich über sie nachdenke, so stellt sich heraus, daß nur ganz wenige richtig 'exotische' dabei sind' ('when I reflect on them, it occurs that only very few of them are really "exotic"') (SW, xiii. 280). Disillusionment arises in the conflict between the expectation of the 'exotic' nurtured in *Fernweh* and a finally experienced actuality; reflecting on their disappointment, the narrators of both authors become conscious of the exotic as a constituted quality rather than an objective feature of places.

Like Hofmannsthal and Hesse, Dauthendey's narrator reflects on the nature of expectation and its role in experiencing foreign places. He relates how he had imagined the Himalayas before his travel there, based on memories of the Dolomites and the Swiss Alps, comparisons also made by Hesse in *Aus Indien*. Based on his experiences in mountainous Europe, Dauthendey's traveller had imagined an 'Erdsinken immer nur tief in weißen Schnee und unter ewig eisigblauem Himmel' ('a valley always only ever deep with white snow and under a perpetually ice-blue sky') (GVW, 45). The reality, however, is different; he sees the earth in gloomy shades of grey, and as it is February, fields of fog rise from the valleys in graduated shades, changing with shadow and illumination. Yet it is the religious culture which disappoints him; having imagined a holy and magical aura in the Tibetan temple, upon reaching it he finds a simple white structure, at the entrance of which is an attendant boy turning a prayer mill, each turn counting for 'das . . . Ablesen der tausend Gebete' ('the reading off of a thousand prayers') (GVW, 48). This machine is not the only encroachment of modernity: on the walls there are, alongside religious images, photographs, postcards, and prints from English magazines, of English, German, French, and Russian princes and generals, and sketches of newly invented machines; the pictures, the narrator claims, are regarded as holy by the Tibetan priests, creating a grotesque 'Wirrwarr von zeitlosem Spuk' ('clamour of timeless haunting') (GVW, 48).

Dauthendey's description of the mountain landscape in 'Himalajafinsternis' ('Himalayan Darkness') however, allows for the possibility that disillusionment is not final; although travel may limit the imagination, it can also liberate it. There are experiences that can break through the 'Wirklichkeit des Reisens' or the merely empirical, and thereby limited, reality of foreign places. This may occur if one is able to yield—like Hofmannsthal's narrator in his moments of epiphany—to experiences of the infinite ('unsterbliche Erlebnisse heimbringen' ('to bring home immortal experiences')). This may happen when the traveller feels intimately connected to the people he encounters in travel,

wenn sich das Schicksal des Reisenden mit Menschenschicksalen fremder Orte so verknüpft, daß der Ort, die Landschaft, das Gesehene ganz an Bedeutung verlieren, ins Nichts sinken, und das am eigenen Schicksal erfahrene Zeit, Ort, und Wirklichkeit überragt.

(If the fate of the traveller so connects with that of people from a foreign place, so that the place, the landscape, what is seen there loses all its meaning, sinks into nothing, and the time, place, and reality of one's own fated experience towers above.) (GVW, 44)

The narrator experiences a magical disorientation when visited by the ghostlike 'ewige Witwe' as she attempts to retrieve her amulet without being seen. While the narrator's visit to the temple failed to induce a feeling of enchantment, such an effect results from the encounter with a woman whose superstitious beliefs transform him. At night he is haunted by sounds and movements in his hotel room and on the balcony, and then wholly disoriented by the incense she blows into his room. Only later, when he discovers the amulet missing, he realizes that he had been visited by the widow who had awakened in him a sense of mysterious forces, a sense evoked during the narrator's nighttime ride to a mountain peak to watch the sunrise with the other hotel guests. The abyssal depths of the Himalayan valleys, and the intensity of the twilight, bring to the narrator's mind the experience of disorientation he had experienced in his room when, after a window had been broken, a sweet and drug-like incense had seeped in. For the modern person, Dauthendey's narrator claims, such experiences, albeit rare, are equivalent to religious experiences, for instance the experience of earlier, naive people at the altar, receiving their gods (GVW, 45). Freud's notion that in a primitive element of the psyche (though he attributes it to infantile experiences of feeding at the mother's breast and to erotic love) remains 'das ozeanische Gefühl' could explain the possibility of such enchantment for the European foreigner (WA, ii. 369).

Hesse, too, while disappointed by his encounters, points to the magical atmosphere provided by Asian religions in contrast to the intellectualized and individualistic culture of the Northern European, who experiences enchantment 'nur selten, etwa beim Anhören einer Bachmusik' ('only seldom, as when listening to the music of Bach') (SW, xiii. 281). While the cultural encounter in the temple disappoints him, Dauthendey's narrator is astonished by the disorientation he experiences; and this disorientation—like Esthe's in the zoological garden and Andreas's in Venice—becomes the condition for enchantment. This disorientation is reflected in description of the landscape, when the narrator loses a sense of direction, of right and left, as well as up and down. The mountains seem to be flying, then sinking; the narrator then describes them in starlight and moonlight, 'als wäre der Himalaja eine Gedankenwelt geworden, in der sich fluchtartig Bilder und Eindrücke, Wirklichkeit und Unwirklichkeit jagten' ('as if the Himalayas became a world of thought, in which images and impressions, reality and unreality fleetingly raced') (GVW, 46). The sense of geographical unreality gives the narrator some intuition of transcendence, of the widow's connection to the beyond, since the amulet she is desperate to retrieve is believed to ensure the fidelity of her late husband in the next life.

Hesse's *Aus Indien* also presents experiences of disillusionment and enchantment in the same places featured in Dauthendey's stories. The essays that make up *Aus Indien* recount travels through South-east Asia, including descriptions of Singapore, Penang, Ceylon, and Sumatra. Like the main authors discussed in this chapter, Hesse reflects upon the relations between Europeans and the indigenous peoples of the places he visits; but in contrast to Hofmannsthal's apparent acceptance of the French protectorate in Northern Africa, Hesse regards the colonial relationship between the Dutch and English colonists and their subordinated peoples critically, and this criticism is the main cause of the narrator's disillusionment. While not calling for the eradication altogether of colonial power, Hesse, like Dauthendey, registers the negative effects of colonialist exploitation upon the native peoples and their culture, and Hesse refers repeatedly to the violent suppression of natives by Dutch colonists. His criticisms, along with references to the novel by Multatuli (Eduard Douwes Dekker), *Max Havelaar oder die Kaffeeversteigerungen der Niederländischen Handelsgesellschaft* (*Max Havelaar or the Coffee Auction of Dutch Commercial Trade*), which exposed colonial exploitation of Java by the Dutch, emerge as a theme of his travel narratives, even if a peripheral one (Hesse, SW, xiii. 241, 249, 242, 253). Hesse's appreciation for native peoples—in particular the Chinese in whom he finds a refined and noble aesthetic sensibility (he discusses Chinese music, dress, and architecture) and the Malay people in whom he finds social harmony and unwavering benevolence—does present Orientalizing images, and this appreciation is mixed with a critical perception of the corruption of indigenous cultures within the context of colonialism.

What links Dauthendey and Hesse are not only that they travelled to and depicted the same places, but that they both reveal the 'exotic' as to some extent a fabrication of the Western imagination and European trade. In 'Himalajafinsternis' just described, Dauthendey's narrator finds in the Tibetan temple absurd appropriations of Western culture by the priests, who smoke Western cigarettes and drink English beer as they superstitiously revere photos of Western rulers and machines. Hesse similarly expresses disillusionment, for example, in describing the colourful 'Oriental' costumes of Malays in Singapore, which are in fact produced in Europe. The effect is 'wahre Karikaturen von Trachten,' costumes 'viel greller, viel indischer, jubelnder, wilder, giftiger, als sie je in Asien gesehen worden waren' ('real caricatures of national costume, much gaudier, much more Indian, exuberant, wilder, more poisonous, than they had ever been in Asia') (SW, xiii. 219). And the visit to a Buddhist temple in 'Tagebuchblatt aus Kandy' ('Diary Entry from Kandy') presents a tourist hounded by requests for money by priests who no longer even read Sanskrit, and participants in the service taken advantage of: 'Der Buddhismus von Ceylon ist hübsch, um ihn zu photographieren und Feuilletons darüber zu schreiben; darüber hinaus ist er nichts als eine von den vielen rührenden, qualvoll grotesken Formen, in denen hilfloses Menschenleid seine

Not und seinen Mangel an Geist und Stärke ausdrückt' ('The Buddhism of Ceylon is pretty to photograph and to describe in feuilleton articles; but beyond that it is nothing other than one of the many placating, torturously grotesque forms in which helpless human suffering expresses its need and its lack of spirit and strength') (SW, xiii. 274–275). In another passage Hesse writes still more critically:

Ich lernte sogar, mich über Indien lustig zu machen, und ich schluckte die scheußliche Erfahrung, daß der seelenvolle, suchende Beterblick der meisten Inder gar nicht ein Ruf nach Göttern und Erlösung ist, sondern einfach ein Ruf nach Money.

(I even learned to make fun of India and I made the dreadful discovery that the soulful, needy, beggar gaze of most Indians is not a cry to the gods and for salvation at all, but simply a cry for money.) (SW, xiii. 264)

Hofmannsthal, of course, does not account for this aspect of colonized Asia when he juxtaposes the ancient culture to disenchanted modern Europe in 'Die Idee Europa', although he cites criticism of its Europeanization; but Hesse pointedly reveals that even the children 'kokettieren sogar sehr gerne und lernen den bettelnden Ruf nach Money als erste englische Vokabel, oft noch, ehe sie Singhalesisch können' ('enjoy their coquetry and learn how to beg for money as the first English syllables, often before they can even speak their own tongue') (SW, xiii. 270). Yet while Hesse straightforwardly criticizes both colonizers and colonized, registering the disappointment of the traveller who finds a fabricated 'Orient' and natives caught up in exploitative commerce, his narrator never attempts to imagine the native perspective. A description of being pulled by a coolie through Singapore is perhaps symbolic of the traveller's position: Hesse's narrator describes the coolie's naked back and body, but never imagines the point of view of one pulling the rickshaw, nor does he express sympathy for his labour (SW, xiii. 218). There are, too, Orientalizing descriptions, for instance of the 'Kindlichkeit der meisten Malayen' ('childishness of most Malays') of their 'Kindergesichter' ('childish faces') of Japanese prostitutes who sit on the roadside wall 'wie fette Tauben' ('like fat doves') (Hesse, SW, xiii. 238, 282, 216).[36] Some of the descriptions include problematic racial generalizations, such as when the narrator evokes, in a list of the difficulties of travel, 'die Grausamkeit der Chinesen, die Verlogenheit der Japaner, das Stehlen der Malayen und andere große und kleine Übel des Ostens' ('the cruelty of the Chinese, the dishonesty of the

[36] Said (1979/2003: 40) describes this characterization of the 'Oriental as irrational, depraved (fallen), childlike' in contrast to which the European is assumed to be 'rational, virtuous, mature'.

Japanese, the stealing on the part of Malays, and other great and trivial
maladies of the East') (SW, xiii. 243).

Yet there are also moments in Hesse's narratives, like Hofmannsthal's
and Dauthendey's 'Himalajafinsternis', in which the European traveller is
disoriented or disadvantaged. Just as Hofmannsthal's describes disorientation while walking through the labyrinthine alleys of Fez, and Dauthendey's
narrator in 'Himalajafinsternis' is drugged by the native widow who
haunts him, Hesse describes experiences of helplessness. In 'Indische
Schmetterlinge' ('Indian Butterflies'), Hesse's narrator, in danger of running out of money, is pursued by an Indian seller of rare butterflies, who
stalks him persistently through the city of Kandy, waiting at his hotel every
morning and evening, following and hounding him until he finally gives
in. While Hesse often embraces a tourist's fantasies—one essay, appropri-
ately entitled 'Augenlust' ('lust of the eyes') is devoted to an imaginary
shopping spree in Singapore—he also describes other experiences in which
the self-certain subject seems to be called into question.

This occurs especially in Hesse's reflections on landscape, and his
experiences of epiphany within the primal forests, which bring his writings
in the range of the enchantment presented by Hofmannsthal and
Dauthendey. While in *Lingam* Dauthendey evokes a sense of magical
reality on the basis of cultural beliefs and rituals and in specifically
cultivated environments, such as gardens, and in 'Himalajafinsternis'
draws implicit parallels between the depths of the Himalayan twilight
and the experience of transcendence induced by his contact with the
widow, Hesse finds some sense of enchantment in the force of nature
that is indifferent to humanity. What is perhaps most striking in Hesse's
descriptions is that the narrator repeatedly turns to the power and force of
nature in the wilderness of South-east Asia, commenting on the seemingly
limitless power of nature to overrun cultural progress with its persistent
life-force and fertility: 'Hier gärt die Natur ohne Pause in erschreckender
Fruchtbarkeit, in einem rasenden Lebens- und Verschwendungsfieber, das
mich betäubt und beinahe entsetzt' ('Here nature seethes constantly with
an alarming fecundity in a frenzied fever of life and waste, which stuns and
nearly repulses me') (SW, xiii. 240). Hesse's sense of nature as an original
unity bears traces of a Schopenhauerian appropriation of Indian spirituality; he recognizes 'die Quelle des Lebens ... in welcher alles seinen Anfang
nahm und welche die ewige Einheit der Erscheinungen bedeutet'
('the source of life in which everything had its beginning and which
signifies the perpetual unity of appearances') (SW, xiii. 232). He points
to these regions as the original source of not only of humanity but also of
nature itself and its appearances. His near mystical appreciation of the
Asian *Urwald*, however, leads to an underestimation of the effects of

European presence. The narrator believes (unfortunately incorrectly) that the penetration of the wilderness by the Dutch colonial lumber trade will be ineffectual against the massive jungle's constant regeneration. Hesse's point of view, however, complicates readings that would pose the European as winning 'the traditional exotic struggle between man and nature'; it significantly departs from what Pratt has described as the 'solemnity and self-congratulatory tone' of the European traveller's imperialist survey of exotic scenes.[37]

In one essay, 'Waldnacht' ('Forest Night'), the symbolic stance of the European traveller as collector and hunter—his party has spent the day in the *Urwald* hunting, taking photographs, and collecting butterflies—gives way to a sense of immersion in the overpowering wilderness, not unlike Esthe's imaginative immersion in nature in Dauthendey's 'Eingeschlossene Tiere'. The transformation described by Hesse's narrator is here, however, explicitly paralleled by reflections on the colonial suppression of the natives. At night the narrator listens to the forest outside his bamboo hut and imagines the immense power of nature:

> Da draußen war es kaum um einen Schatten heller als zwischen meinen Bambuswänden und Bastmatten, aber man spürte die wilde Natur draußen gären und kochen in ihrem nie unterbrochenen geilen Treiben und Zeugen, man hörte hundert Tiere und atmete den krautigen Geruch von üppigem Wachstum.
>
> (There outside it was hardly a shade brighter than it was between my bamboo walls and raffia mats, but one could sense the wild nature out there seething and boiling in its incessant lustful breeding and procreating, one could hear a hundred animals and breathed the herbaceous smell of sumptuous growth.) (SW, xiii. 248–249)

The narrator then reflects upon the relation to this wilderness of the unprotected natives and the colonizing Europeans in their huts. He thinks of the Dutch who violently suppressed the natives, shooting them down three years before, in order to progress with their lumber trade. The narrator imagines the souls of the dead, feared by the natives, whereas the colonists are unconcerned: 'wir Weißen schreien ruhig und herrisch kalte Befehle und sehen die dunkeln uralten Eisenholzbäume ohne Rührung fallen' ('we whites should calm and lordly cold commands watch emotionless the dark ancient ironwood trees fall') (SW, xiii. 249). The narrator presents this juxtaposition without further comment, but it is followed by an intriguing report of a dream, wherein the narrator is passively nurtured by the natural surroundings. He imagines himself as a

---

[37] Pratt (1992: 208); Zilcosky (2003: 28).

crying child, whose mother sings to him in the native language, symbolic
of the *Urwald*:

> In blassen Halbgedanken dämmerte ich ein, hing müde schwüle Stunden
> zwischen Traum und Wirklichkeit. Ich war ein Kind und war am Weinen,
> und eine Mutter wiegte mich mit Gesumse, aber sie sang Malayisch, und
> wenn ich die bleischweren Augen öffnen und sie ansehen wollte, so war es
> das tausendjährige Angesicht des Urwaldes, das über mich gebeugt hing und
> mir zuflüsterte. Ja, hier war ich am Herzen der Natur; hier war die Welt
> nicht anders als vor hundertausend Jahren.
>
> (I dawned in pale half-thoughts, oscillated sleepily for sultry hours be-
> tween dream and reality. I was a child and crying, and a mother rocked me
> with a lullaby, but she sang in Malay, and when I opened my lead-heavy eyes
> and wanted to look at her, it was the millennia-old face of the jungle that bent
> over me and whispered to me. Yes, here I was in the heart of nature, here the
> world did not differ from that of a hundred thousand years ago.) (SW, xiii. 249)

With this reflection the narrator diminishes the importance of the European presence, but also takes comfort in the power of nature to drive back
the colonists: 'Man konnte Drahtseile an den Gaurisankar nageln und den
Eskimos ihre Fischjagd mit Motorbooten verderben, aber gegen den
Urwald würden wir noch eine gute Weile nicht aufkommen. Da fraß
die Malaria unsere Leute, der Rost unsere Nägel und Flinten.' ('One could
nail steel cords to the Gaurisankar and ruin the Eskimos' fishing with
motor boats, but we would not be able to rise against the jungle for a long
time. There malaria devoured our people, the rust our nails and flint')
(SW, xiii. 249). The narrator seems to hope for the eventual diminution
of colonial presence by the more overwhelming and timeless power
of nature. In the onset of a storm, Hesse's narrator feels a rare sense of
enchantment. Just as Dauthendey's narrator in 'Himalajafinsternis' accepts an enchanted view of reality, and Hofmannsthal's Andreas rejects
'jede Erklärung' in face of the inexplicable, Hesse embraces the experience
of the incomprehensible and feels no fear of the storm:

> Es kam mir nicht einen Augenblick sinnlos vor, daß ich im Süden des
> Sumpfurwaldes von Sumatra stehe und einem tropischen Nachtgewitter
> zusehe, ich empfand auch keinen Augenblick eine Ahnung von Gefahr,
> sondern ich fühlte voraus und sah mich noch hundertmal, an weit von
> hier entfernten Orten, einsam und neugierig stehen und dem Unbegreiflichen
> mit Verwunderung zusehen, dem das Unbegreifliche und Vernunftlose in mir
> selbst Antwort gab und sich verbrüderte.
>
> (It did not for a moment seem crazy to me that I was standing in the
> southern marshy jungle of Sumatra and watching a tropic night storm, and
> I felt for no moment a sense of danger, rather I looked to the future and saw
> myself a hundred times in places far from here, standing lonely and inquisi-

tive and watching the incomprehensible with wonder, the very same that was answered by and brother to the incomprehensible and irrational within myself.) (SW, xiii. 250)

Hesse's acceptance of the ungraspable is echoed in Hofmannsthal's hopes for a new European reality, inspired by Asia and its 'Welt von Mysterien und ganz ungreifbaren allerwirksamsten Lebendigkeiten' ('world of mysteries and entirely ungraspable, most effective vivacities') (GW, ix. 52).

CONCLUSION

Like Hesse's 'Orientalizing' descriptions, Dauthendey's imagery is not unproblematic. The metaphoric means by which places are exoticized is also extended to descriptions of native people. Their 'Orientalness' is presented through metaphoric identification with recognizably Asian images of plants, animals, and other objects. The courtesan in Penang sleeps naked in her open housecoat 'wie das Fleisch einer geschlitzten Mangofrucht in rotgelber Schale' ('like the flesh of a slit mango in its red-golden skin') (L, 136). Walai watches the coolie dancer 'wie ein Tiger, der blutunruhig durch die Wimpern blinzelt' ('like a tiger squinty blood-thirsty through its lashes') (L, 29). The dancer's breasts are like 'zwei kleine Seidenkissen' ('two small silk cushions') (L, 30). The Chinese singers with bound feet 'trippelten mit den Füßen kurz wie Ziegen aufstoßend herein' ('scuttled and pushed their way in with feet as blunt as goats') (L, 185). The tea-house owners in Japan 'kicherten, wie Mäuse, die über ein Stück Speck hüpfen' ('giggled like mice leaping in joy over a piece of bacon fat') (L, 196). Todor accompanies the English girl through the garden 'wie ein brauner Käfer' ('like a brown beetle') (L, 71) (although she is also compared to 'ein geblendetes Insekt' ('a dazed insect') later in the story, and yells for help 'wie eine Krähe' (like a crow') (L, 79, 78)). Kimgun is compared to a gazelle, a hare, and a monkey. In addition to this Orientalist imagery, *Lingam* also relies upon recognizable images of the Asian already well-known to European readers and perhaps clichéd: elephants in India, Chinese astrology, the Japanese reverence for the very old, a child eaten by a tiger, the golden temple of the Buddha, and other such motifs seem to appeal to a tourist's postcard vision of Asia. Hofmannsthal's narrator in 'Fez' presents the European perspective with some similarly problematic descriptions of natives—one native riding past on a donkey is described as having 'wulstige Riesenlippen, eine knollige Nase, eine ungeheuerliche Perücke von krausem Haar, und quer über die ganze Wange eine Narbe, tief, gräßlich und überlebensgroß wie das ganze

Gesicht' ('giant, rubbery lips, a bulbous nose, a monstrous head of course hair, and across his whole cheek a scar, deep, hideous, and larger than life, like his whole face') (GW, vii. 644). While this description is highly problematic in its unflattering exaggeration and racially insensitive caricaturing, elsewhere the narrator also regards other non-Europeans as beautiful and aristocratic (GW, vii. 643). Hesse, too, describes the Malay children as beautiful and praises the Chinese aesthetic in respect to the simplicity of clothing and architecture, and the complexity and harmony of music. Despite problematic imagery and description, in Dauthendey, Hofmannsthal, and Hesse, the overall presentation of exotic places provokes critical self-reflection on European ways of being and perceiving.

It must also be noted that while the colonial presence is nowhere affirmed in Dauthendey, it is naturalized in some images. Where colonists are described through plant and animal imagery, the effect is not Orientalization, but naturalization, of their presence. They seem then to belong to the local environment, and the violence of colonial occupation goes unregistered, as when Kimgun sees English ships, compared to turtles in the river: 'Von seinen Palmen sah er schon von weitem die englischen Verdeckdampfer, die zweistöckigen, die wie Riesenschildkröten den Fluß hinauf und hinab schwammen' ('From its palms he already saw from afar the English steamboats, the double-decked ones, which swam up and down the river like giant turtles') (L, 85). In another image, the dresses of Englishwomen are compared to blooming Asian trees (L, 119). Nevertheless, the marginalization of the European in most of the stories lends them an outsider status and quietly implicates their role in Asia as tourist and exploiter. Similarly, Hofmannsthal's narrator acknowledges his own difference as an outsider and his unwelcome presence as a European in the French African colony (GW, vii. 643). While neither author, in contrast to Hesse, offers an explicit critique of the colonial presence, the colonial hierarchy and symbolic subject-position is at least imaginatively overcome by the experience of submission to the foreign places or perspectives. Hofmannsthal's narrator in 'Fez' will lose any overarching orientation, and be led somewhat helplessly through the city in which he feels enveloped. In Dauthendey's work the marginalization of colonial presence shifts the focus of the European reader from the colonial perspective to the native psychology, religion, and local atmosphere, even if those must still be imagined by a European author. Some metaphors are undoubtedly problematic, yet others serve to displace the Western view of reality. The description of place via animating and enchanting metaphors serves not only to 'Orientalize' the setting for the reader but also to distance the reality presented in the stories from European visions of the world. This not only renders the settings lyrical and alluring, but gives an access for the

European-German reader to a radically different sense of reality that in some important respects reflects critically on European and particularly German culture, which Hofmannsthal, like Dauthendey, regards as sensually impoverished: the vital colour of other topographies is compared to 'unserer grauen und braunen Welt' ('our grey and brown world') (GW, vii. 593).

In Dauthendey's *Lingam* the depiction of bodily experience expresses a physical vitality repressed in German culture. The magical intervention in reality, and the simplicity, sincerity, and authenticity of the protagonists' feelings, also contribute to the enchanted atmosphere. Even in the violent stories, such as 'Dalar rächt sich' and 'Der Zauberer Walai', the clarity and singularity of purpose with which even a violent and horrible deed is executed, evince the piety of life that Hofmannsthal's narrator of the *Briefe* so longingly praised in contrast to the cold, ambivalent, and calculating decorum of the modern German. While disturbing, even the opening stories of *Lingam* present a drastic contrast to the modern European intellect that, despite their tragic consequences, evoke at some level admiration for the intensity of feeling they express.

It has been argued, as of Dauthendey and Hofmannsthal, that Hesse's travel writings support the colonialist subject by presenting the traveller symbolically appropriating a foreign world. The description of reaching the peak of Pedrotallagalla, in an essay named after that mountain, is criticized for presenting a monarchical view over a territory surveyed; for when he reaches the top Hesse's narrator surveys the view as if symbolically reiterating the European claim to territory, to a 'zweite Heimat' ('second home') in the East.[38] Yet even here critics have failed to note the ways in which Hesse's narrative undermines any symbolic appropriation: 'Diese große Urlandschaft sprach starker zu mir als alles, was ich sonst von Indien gesehen habe … aber es war mir immer fremd und merkwürdig, niemals ganz nah und ganz zu eigen' ('This great primordial landscape spoke more strongly to me than everything I had seen so far in India … but it was always foreign and peculiar to me, never quite close and never quite my own') (SW, xiii. 277). Hesse explicitly criticizes the drive to imagine a 'zweite Heimat' in the Orient:

> Wir kommen voll Sehnsucht nach dem Süden und Osten, von dunkler, dankbarer Heimatahnung getrieben, und wir finden hier das Paradies. . . . Aber wir selbst sind anders, wir sind hier fremd … wir haben längst das Paradies verloren, und das neue, das wir haben und bauen wollen, ist nicht

---

[38] Zilcosky (2003: 28).

am Äquator und an den warmen Meeren des Ostens zu finden, das liegt in
uns und in unsrer eigenen nordländischen Zukunft

(We come full of longing to the South and the East, driven by a dark,
thankful idea of home, and we find paradise here ... but we ourselves are
other, we are strangers here ... we lost paradise long ago, and the new one
which we must and want to build is not to be found on the equator and on
the warm seas of the East, but lies in us and in our own Northern future.)

The inspiration drawn from exotic places is not destined to bring about
their appropriation, but, as in Hofmannsthal's discussion of Europe, to
produce a revitalization of home and alternatives to dominant modern
forms of consciousness. The rendering of foreign places as mysterious or
ungraspable must be subjected to critical analysis; but it need not signal an
automatic, unreflective complicity with the exploitation of such places and
their peoples, as Said has argued. Rather, this rendering can also represent
a non-appropriative longing for senses of reality that evade the modern
'sentiment of rationality' (James) and the 'disenchantment of the world'
(Weber) to which its exclusion of difficult feeling, paradox, and all manner
of vagueness eventually leads. For Hofmannsthal Asia—'Bewußt seines
erhabenen inneren Erbes, jener Erstgeburt des religiösen Denkens'
('Aware of its sublime inner heritage, the first birth of religious
thought')—was a possible ideal for a critical reinvigoration of European
culture (GW, ix. 51). Dauthendey's experienced vision of Asia confirms
Hofmannsthal's sensibility through the enchanted imagination of difference, even if Dauthendey's depictions are far from ideal. While Hesse's
travel writings express much disillusionment, they also invoke moments
of enchantment that merit some comparison to Dauthendey and
Hofmannsthal. All of these places described in the writings discussed
here are exoticized through the longings of *Fernweh*, through travel to
and imaginative enchantment with worlds strange to the modern German
consciousness.

2

Infectious-Erotic Topographies

Mann's Der Tod in Venedig *and* Der Zauberberg *and Zweig's* Der Amokläufer

The exotic evocation of geographical and historical spaces has functioned in modern literature as a medium of contest between metaphysically opposed aspects of human nature. Exotic spaces promote contests between decadence and morality, inclinations towards life and death, primitive impulses and the refinements of civilization. Places that are exoticized by evocation of historical-literary associations and architectural singularity (such as Venice), or of their perceived grandeur and inhospitality (the Swiss Alps), or of radical cultural and climatic difference from Europe (the East Indies) have functioned in literature to engage problems of individual and national identity, to test the boundaries and stability of the self. The exotic topos offers a radical break from an ordinary sense of familiarity with the surrounding world. It serves to destabilize the presumed separation between the familiar and the foreign, potentially demonstrating the fragility of individual autonomy, and suggesting deep roots of the primitive within a supposedly civilized psyche. Yet the exotic atmosphere of the settings to be discussed in this chapter is constituted more dramatically and specifically through their associations with sexual desire and pathological contagion, both forms of intimate and potentially threatening interchange between self and others. Leading to the downfall of three German protagonists, this interchange also challenges the metaphorical or real 'colonial' divisions that may govern relations between Western Europeans and historically subordinate others, a consideration of which ought to present a counterweight to post-colonial or Orientalist interpretations of these texts.[1]

---

[1] Yahya Elsaghe, for instance, presents the symbolic geography of *Der Tod in Venedig* as at least implicitly anti-Semitic, xenophobic, misogynistic (1997: 25–32), and racist (2000: 39). Nancy Nenno (1996: 305, 314) associates *Der Zauberberg* with colonialism. Alexander Honold (1999: 167–174) traces the symbolism of the mountain within the context of German colonialist discourse. In comparison, Zweig has received scant attention; Ganeshan's (1975: 294) account of *Der Amokläufer* and related essays, while sympathetic

For while the symbolic topographies may rely upon problematic oppositions between the German or Western European and a foreign 'other', as well as on the exoticization of illness and potentially dangerous sexuality, these also shift as the protagonists' sense of self and vision of the world deteriorate. These texts develop 'a more complex and transgressive relation between the poles of the colonial dialectic' than simple opposition.² They generate insight about the human condition—about the self, its communication with otherness, and the otherness 'within', symbolized here by exoticized eros and illness—that do not respect this polarization.

FRAGILE BOUNDARIES: THREE INFECTIOUS-EROTIC TOPOGRAPHIES

Thomas Mann's *Der Tod in Venedig* is perhaps the most representative text in which sexuality and pathological contagion are drawn together through the exotic location. For Aschenbach's moral and physical collapse is explicitly intertwined with the representation of Venice as enchanting, sexually beguiling, and infectious, as overtaken by an Asian pestilence; its exoticization is intertwined with Aschenbach's sexual obsession with the Polish adolescent Tadzio. In being transported to Venice, Aschenbach experiences a confusion and loosening of his ordinary sense of self, with his Germanic-Prussian habits and classical aesthetics, and the release of repressed elements of his psyche. The *Fernweh* provoked by the appearance of a stranger in the Munich cemetery foreshadows his eventual psychological alliance with aspects of the Venetian city as he pines for the unapproachable Tadzio, leading to the collapse of his aesthetic principles and will. While Mann finds in Venice a setting already long associated with ambiguity—it is a city, as Georg Simmel wrote in 1907, 'wo all das Heitere und Helle, das Leichte und Freie, nur einem finstern, gewalttätigen, unerbitterlich zweckmäßigen Leben zur Fassade diente' ('where everything cheerful and bright, the light and free, serves only as a façade for a dark, violent, mercilessly instrumental life') (GA8, 259)—the narrative presentation of Venice also exoticizes the city in ways that correlate to Aschenbach's downfall.

In contrast to Mann's works, Stefan Zweig's *Der Amokläufer* is set for the most part outside Europe, but the tension between the exotic and the

to Zweig's "nicht mehr eurozentrisch" point of view, presents them from the perspective of colonialism.

² R. Berman (1998: 14).

European is maintained by the narrative shifts in setting and the ethni-cities of the conflicting characters, and the novella constructs a similar triangulation of exotic place, sexuality, and disease. Narration of the main events occurs on a ship returning to Europe from the East Indies, where the German doctor has spent seven years in a remote colonial practice among the natives. His conflict with an Englishwoman ends tragically; after failing to seduce her in exchange for his help, he finds her dying from acute infection and bleeding after a botched abortion in the squalid Chinatown section of the capital city. The lustful madness unleashed in the doctor, and his consequent violence towards the woman and her native servant, are attributed by the doctor to local climatic conditions, suggesting his submission to the irrationality of the foreign surroundings, to a native infection. Under the pressure of exotic influences, the bour-geois German self, and here the position of the European as cultural superior, breaks down.

While the cultural geography of *Der Tod in Venedig* is a familiar theme in recent scholarship,[3] and the exotic features of *Der Amokläufer* are readily conjured for the European by the tropical Asian and colonial atmosphere, similar structures can be seen in Mann's *Der Zauberberg*, despite the stark contrasts between the Alpine setting, Venice, and the Far East. Like Aschenbach's travel to Venice and the doctor's arrival in the colonies, the Alps offer, first of all, a defamiliarizing landscape for Hans Castorp. This defamiliarization is explicitly linked to space through narra-tive commentary on Castorp's approach to the Alpine sanatorium. Although this landscape does not evoke the exotic in the way that Venice and Asia do (since the mountains evoke a realm of sublimity indifferent to the surrounding European 'Flachland'), it becomes constructed as an exotic space, rendered so through sexual and corporeal imagery. All of these settings present protagonists vulnerable to infection within a con-fined atmosphere: the sanatorium high up in the mountains confines Castorp; the quarantine city of Venice confines Aschenbach; and the doctor feels exiled to a remote district station surrounded only by 'Wald, Plantagen, Dickicht und Sumpf' ('forest, plantation, jungle and swamp') (A, 88). Like the more readily exoticized settings, the Alps, centred in Europe but vertically removed from the 'Flachland', serve as a space within which the European, and in particular German, cultural identity can be contested. It will be shown that the 'Zauberberg' constitutes neither principally a 'blank space' for the projection of identity struggles,[4] nor an unequivocal symbol of Eastern solitude 'transplanted onto the

---

[3] Most recently by Elizabeth Boa (2006).
[4] As Nenno (1996: 308, 313) argues.

mountain',[5] but a site for contest between opposing forces of life and death, Occidental and Oriental sensibilities. The exotic rendering of the Alpine space depends upon specific geographical features,[6] such as the elevation, peculiar weather, and topographical shape, all of which take on symbolic meaning.

The exotic space of the 'Zauberberg' is constructed not least of all through the description of the Berghof itself as fostering illness and its erotic attractions. The sanatorium is a highly charged and confined atmosphere that promotes sexual licentiousness in the context of international exchange. The architecture of the Berghof plays a role, with its communicating balconies, social rooms, and basement chambers in which research into the human body and the psyche represent ventures into regions of the alluring unknown. Further, Castorp's gradual detachment from the habits of his civilization, and his acclimatization to the Berghof environment, are expressed through explicit contrast between Western and Eastern sensibilities evoked through the presence of foreigners. The Western European outlook is associated with health, rationality, efficiency, and Enlightenment humanism, and the ordering of time and space to human dimensions, while the Eastern and Asian are associated with the irrational and sensual, with illness, lethargy, barbarism, intoxication, and the vastness of unconquered space and monotonous time. Yet the deepest resonances with the exotic are promoted through descriptive confounding of images of exotic physiognomies (those of the Slavic Chauchat and Hippe and the colonial Dutchman Peeperkorn) with those of landscape, and, in the 'Schnee' chapter in which Castorp experiences an apocalyptic vision, by the blending of images of the winter mountains with exotic images of desert and sea.

In these exoticized places, and under the strain of sexual desire and illness, the German bourgeois self breaks down. Rather than being wholly abandoned, the scientific or professional expertise of the protagonists, signifying both their bourgeois status and their alliance with a Western world-view, is enlisted in spiritual displacement and deterioration. Hans Castorp uses his scientific knowledge, including his engineering studies, in analysing parts of Clawdia Chauchat's body. Zweig's doctor is sought out by the Englishwoman for his medical expertise, and he is sent for from the abortionist's in hopes that he might be able to save her. The celebrated writer Aschenbach attempts to justify his homosexual paedophilia through reference to classical aesthetics, and he writes exquisitely on the beach

---

[5] As argued by Engelberg (1999: 106).
[6] On this point I differ from Rau (1994: 96), who presents the settings as geographically neutral.

enraptured by Tadzio's presence. In these ways the protagonists do not simply abandon the achievements of their civilization for the foreign object of desire; rather, their intellectual resources are vulnerable to collaboration with what are experienced as dangerous and anti-rational impulses. When coupled with the motif of pathological contagion or infection, this points to the evocation of latent primitivism within the 'civilized', Western psyche, perhaps most repressed by the German sensibility.

In these works erotic desire, some kind of infection, and the exotic setting constitute the conditions of possibility for moral and psychological breakdown. All three protagonists, in an exotic or exoticized place, submit to lascivious pursuits linked to disease and death and promoted by the surrounding atmosphere. In each case this submission suggests that European, and particularly German, rationality gives way to the seduction of uncontrollable forces. All three protagonists become vessels for primitive impulses of life and death that transgress the boundaries of the individual self and break down rational autonomy. Aschenbach's idealizing aesthetics collapses in the face of Tadzio's physical beauty and the desire it provokes. Both Castorp's character and, it is implied, his civilization are revealed as vulnerable to primitive forces and to decadence. The sexual madness that afflicts the isolated doctor in the tropics ends in his own downfall, just as it mirrors the violence of colonial possession. By rendering such transgression and breakdown, this literature goes against the grain of whatever triumphant aspect of 'Orientalism' through which, according to Edward Said, European culture bolstered its sense of self through the projection of its repressed aspects as radical difference.[7] For whatever underground self might be represented by primitive forces, it is in these texts ultimately inseparable from any apparent and familiar sense of self. Modernism, at least since Nietzsche and Schopenhauer, seems to be characterized in part by this insight.

Desire and infection are both spatial conditions potentially exoticized, in so far as both have to do with communication across the boundary between self and something 'other'; both indicate a transgression of a presumed physical barrier between an inner self and the unknown elements of the outer world, a lack of control over the unbounded world without. They are both, as Foucault writes in his study of the epidemic, 'a problem of the threshold'.[8] In desiring another, one is driven to cross boundaries, and this can pose a threat to any aesthetic, metaphysical, or cultural position that may exclude what that other represents; since desire

---

[7] Said (1979/2003: 3).   [8] Foucault (1989: 25).

respects no political, ethnic, or social divisions, it can threaten cultural identity. The protagonists in these works are all also afflicted by a contagious or symbolic infection that is caught up with their desire. Erotic transgression and contagious illness have been linked together since at least Sophocles' *Oedipus Rex*, with its background of the plague in Thebes.[9] Compromise to the physical body has been long associated with moral decay; thus any feared illness, Susan Sontag has argued, 'will be felt to be morally, if not literally, contagious'.[10] Like desire, the disease or pathology suffered by the protagonists here indicates a porous relationship to surroundings; contagion in particular evokes an inability to keep the effects of foreign influences at bay, revealing the fictitious nature of any absolute boundaries guarding a self or a familiar culture.[11]

Sontag's view is that all fatal and particularly incurable diseases become powerful metaphors; this is true of the pathologies evoked in these texts—cholera, amok, and tuberculosis. In Europe of 1911, cholera, though calling up the devastations of centuries past and waning since the nineteenth century, was current; when Mann visited Venice and wrote *Der Tod in Venedig*, plague had arrived, and was, as in the novella, hushed up by the city authorities.[12] Yet the imagery of contagion in *Der Tod in Venedig* evokes pre-modern speculation about the plague and anxiety about its potential devastations. Daniel Defoe's 1721 *Journal of the Plague Year* recounts attempts to identify the cause of the plague: polluted or foul air, corrupt fruits, contact with the infected, and foreign imports are mentioned among the possible sources.[13] Amok, in contrast, drew the interest of Europeans through colonization of Asia, and might have been brought to Zweig's attention through his travels in India. The word 'amok' is of Malay-Indonesian origin, adopted in South India, Java, and Malaya since at least the sixteenth century to describe outbreaks of feverish, frenzied, homicidal madness. Spontaneous amok in individuals (as distinct from frenzied military ambush) was attributed to malarial infection.[14] Tuberculosis, all too familiar in modern Europe, was treated at the sanatorium in Davos, which Mann visited with his ailing wife. As a metabolic consumption, tuberculosis is associated, as it is in Mann's novel,

---

[9] The plague is the basis of René Girard's (2005: 87–88) interpretation of Sophocles.

[10] Sontag (1989: 6).

[11] The etymology of contagion and infection, and their links to culture, are discussed in Sontag (1989: 72); Pernick (2002: 858–860); Lund (2003: 48–49); Weinstein (2003: 109–112).

[12] See Leppmann's (1975: 69–70) account of the epidemic in Venice and public reaction to it.

[13] Defoe (1992).

[14] The cultural history of amok is presented in Simons and Hughes (1985); Spires (1988); and Vogl (2005).

with intensity of life at the border of death, with a burning and death-directed sexuality; thus, in the nineteenth century it came to symbolize what Foucault calls the 'lyrical core of man'.[15] The presentation of tuberculosis in *Der Zauberberg* not only draws upon Romantic and Nietzschean affinities for illness as provoking insights of genius but also reflects the medical science of its time, according to which the illness is attributed to both biological and cultural causes.[16] Like erotic desire, illness is exoticized in all of these texts, taking on the larger metaphorical and spatial associations of contagion and infection: uncontrolled circulation of dangerous influences, compromise of boundaries between individuals, and the external stimulation of latent inner pathology.

THE INFECTIOUS-EROTIC IN
DER TOD IN VENEDIG

Infection, desire, and exotic space collaborate in the crisis of Mann's novella *Der Tod in Venedig*. The psychological and physical events are deeply intertwined with the details and atmosphere of the setting. While the treatment of Venice as an exotic location is well grounded in literary history, Mann's novella is unique in posing the exotic Venetian city as a site for both epidemic and singular sexual obsession. The double exposure to the sexual allure of the Polish boy Tadzio and to infection with cholera from India functions not only to break down Aschenbach's moral and intellectual sensibilities but also to implicate his Germanic-Prussian understanding of reality as inadequate in the face of primal forces of life and death. Similar implications about the European self will be seen in *Der Zauberberg* and in Zweig's *Der Amokläufer*. In Mann's novella the travel to Venice from Munich already has a significant defamiliarizing effect, preparing Aschenbach for the fatal attraction of the exotic in Venice itself.

Like the beginnings of *Der Zauberberg* and *Der Amokläufer*, the opening of *Der Tod in Venedig* focuses on the experience of spatial defamiliarization, which anticipates a polarity between the German setting and a Venice associated with Oriental influences. Munich is unusually warm and sultry in the May of an unspecified year, when Aschenbach decides to take a walk. This 'falscher Hochsommer' ('false high summer') of August weather in the springtime points to Aschenbach's eventual arrival in Venice, with its damp heat and its resplendent façades hiding decaying interiors (FA2.1, 501). Such climatic irregularity is a major motif in *Der*

---

[15] Foucault (1989: 211).   [16] Engelhardt (1996: 326, 335, 344).

Zauberberg, as it persistently confuses Hans Castorp and the Berghof residents who might still have usual expectations of the natural world; and the sultry weather of the Asian tropics is indicated as contributing to the doctor's affliction in *Der Amokläufer*. In Mann's novella this false summer serves to stimulate Aschenbach's *Fernweh* for a tropical locale, and it anticipates the plague that, denied by the city authorities, will spread through Venice. The sultry weather foreshadows not only Aschenbach's trip south but also the weakening of that exacting will, for it makes Aschenbach feel 'müde' ('tired')—a characteristic fatigue experienced as an Oriental affliction by all three venturers into exotic regions considered in this chapter. This fatigue compromises what Hans Castorp will affirm is a particularly German phlegmatic efficiency, and it precedes the Amokläufer's feverish breakdown. Although the tram should take Aschenbach back directly, 'in gerader Linie' ('in a straight line') (FA2.1, 502), he is held up at the North Cemetery, where he encounters a stranger who has been associated with the diabolical-Dionysian.[17] Dionysus, like cholera, is said to originate from the East; and the association is not only coincidental, for a strange outbreak of illness is also the backdrop for the Bacchic festival in Euripides' *The Bacchae*.[18] The exotic stranger gives Aschenbach's thoughts 'eine völlig andere Richtung'—towards the exotic south (FA2.1, 502). Aschenbach begins to fantasize about a tropical landscape:

> er sah, sah eine Landschaft, ein tropisches Sumpfgebiet unter dickdunstigem Himmel, feucht, üppig und ungeheuer, eine Art Urweltwildnis aus Inseln, Morästen und Schlamm führenden Wasserarmen,—sah aus geilem Farrengewucher, aus Gründen von fettem, gequollenem und abenteuerlich blühendem Pflanzenwerk haarige Palmenschäfte nah und ferne emporstreben.
>
> (he saw, saw a landscape, a tropical swampland under a thick hazy sky, moist, lush, and monstrous, a sort of primordial wilderness of out islands, morasses, and muddy alluvial channels—saw far and wide hairy trunks of palm trees thrusting upwards from rank jungles of fern, among fat, fleshy, and adventurously blooming plants.) (FA2.1, 504)

The description is highly sensuous and yet also disturbingly devoid of the marks of civilization. The vision includes further images of malformed trees and large milky-white flowers, high-shouldered birds with strange beaks, a tiger crouching in the swamp. Through free indirect speech, the narrator presents Aschenbach's attempt to dismiss this vision as 'Reiselust' ('desire to travel') (FA2.1, 504), but it proves more significant: 'Fluchtdrang war sie... diese Sehnsucht ins Ferne und Neue, diese

---

[17] For instance, in Sheppard's (1990: 94–95) account.
[18] See Girard's (2005: 135) account of epidemic in *The Bacchae*.

Begierde nach Befreiung, Entbürdung und Vergessen' ('This longing for the faraway and new . . . this lusting after liberation, unburdening, forgetting, was an urge to escape') (FA2.1, 505–506). Thus, it is *Fernweh*, a flight from the comfortable German *Heimat*, which drives the protagonist southward.[19] Aschenbach does not get to Venice by way of a direct route. Rather, he first ventures towards an intermediate destination, which fails to satisfy his need for the 'Fremdartige und Bezugslose' ('foreign and unrelated'). On the island of Pola (the name of which is homophonous with Tadzio's Polish nationality), Aschenbach is disturbed by an inner longing for a still unspecified destination: 'ein Zug seines Innern, ihm war noch nicht deutlich, wohin' ('an inner impulse, it was not yet clear to him, where to') (FA2.1, 516). Aschenbach soon realizes that Venice is the sole possibility: nowhere else 'über Nacht' ('overnight') could he reach 'das Unvergleichliche, das märchenhaft Abweichende' ('the incomparable, the fabulously divergent place'). To get to Venice he will travel overnight, through the darkness, metaphorically suggesting a furtive passage. In four unusually short sentences, the narrator suggests Aschenbach's hasty rationalization, hinted at by the clip phrasing, in contrast to a usually highly elaborate verbal style: 'Aber das war klar. Was sollte er hier? Er war fehlgegangen. Dorthin hatte er reisen wollen' ('But it was clear. What did he want here? He had gone the wrong way. There he had wanted to go') (FA2.1, 517). This rare rhythmic truncation will be echoed at essential points of Aschenbach's development, emphasizing two sides of his feverish 'infection': his erotic rapture as 'Tadzio badete' ('Tadzio bathed') (FA2.1, 539); and his last visit to the beach where he collapses from cholera infection: 'Es war unwirtlich dort' ('It was inhospitable there') (FA2.1, 590). Zweig's *Der Amokläufer* will employ a similar contrast, when the elaborately lyrical description by the frame narrator is interrupted by the choppy, stilted speech of the febrile doctor.

Aschenbach's travel to Venice by ship echoes the experience of disorientation from the Munich cemetery. The description anticipates narrative exoticization of the locale. Occupied by strange and carnival-like figures (including a hunchbacked sailor, the drunken captain, the ticket-taker compared to a circus director, and the made-up old dandy), the ship provokes a dream state of alienation from objective reality. Like a ship of fools, the passengers' oddity seems correlate to the disorientation of floating on the vast, elemental sea. While the colourful figures are striking, the formlessness of the sea against which they are contrasted is more closely related to Aschenbach's feeling; it gives Aschenbach, despite his

---

[19] Boa (2006: 26) associates this novella with a turn away from *Heimat* literature.

aesthetic rigour, a feeling of de-individuation. This feeling of loss of self in the face of the immensity of the sea is expressed in similar terms in the other works discussed in this chapter. The frame narrator of *Der Amokläufer* describes a dissolution of the self's boundaries on the deck of the 'Oceania'; contemplating the sky and sea, he feels fused with them. The narrator of *Der Zauberberg* describes Hans Castorp's lostness in the Alpine snowstorm, as well as his recollected experience of walking on the seashore, as a submission to the vastness of undifferentiated space. The imagery of *Der Tod in Venedig* affirms this sense of formlessness in an enveloping cosmos: 'Unter der trüben Kuppel des Himmels dehnte sich rings die ungeheure Scheibe des öden Meeres' ('Under the gloomy dome of the sky stretched all around an enormous disk of desolate sea'). Even more than the strange passengers, exposure to the formless sea, with its vast unbroken horizon, weakens Aschenbach's composure:

> Aber im leeren, im ungegliederten Raume fehlt unserem Sinn auch das Maß der Zeit, und wir dämmern im Ungemessenen.
>
> (But in empty, unarticulated space, our sensibility also lacks a temporal measure, and we enter the twilight of the immeasurable.) (FA2.1, 520)

This relationship between monotonous space and loss of temporal measure becomes a major theme of *Der Zauberberg*. In this sentence the 'Aber' and the use of the first-person plural—'wir'—suggests a narrative irony, a critical register of Aschenbach's loss of self-individuation, as a sign of submission to the nihilistic cosmic will, which becomes thematic in the dream vision of Castorp's experience in the Alpine snow. Hints of Aschenbach's downfall are given in his 'Gefühl des Schwimmens' ('feeling of swimming'), a loss of firm grounding in the coordinates of an objective reality, and by the 'verwirrten Traumworten' ('confused dreamwords') and contorted images with which his consciousness is lulled into sleep (FA2.1, 519, 520). This loss of firm grounding is also felt in Venice itself, with its labyrinth of canals; Emerson wrote of Venice, 'It is as if you were always at sea.'[20]

As Aschenbach approaches San Marco, Venice will appear as 'die unwahrscheinlichste der Städte' ('the most improbable of cities'). The ship's passage towards this central Venetian square provides a mixed composition of fantastical architecture: the Republic, the Palace, the Bridge of Sighs, the columns with lions and saints, the projecting side 'des Märchentempels' ('the fairy-tale temple') as the narrator calls St. Mark's church, a view of the gate, and, perhaps ominously, the enormous town clock (FA2.1, 522). An ambiguous image of Venice is given

---

[20] Emerson's (1958: 72) journal entry for 3 June 1833.

through its literary exoticization: the city is presented with disorienting strangeness, as magically alluring and ornate. Although he is fascinated by the majesty of it, Aschenbach is also disgusted by the gritty details, in particular by its native inhabitants. In order to arrive at his hotel, he must take the coffin-like gondola, 'sargschwarz lackierte' ('lacquered coffin-black'), an association echoed in Zweig's novella as the vessel 'Oceania' is repeatedly referred to as a 'Sarg'. Aschenbach experiences the gondola ride as distressing:

> Wer hätte nicht einen flüchtigen Schauder, eine geheime Scheu und Beklommenheit zu bekämpfen gehabt, wenn es zum ersten Male oder nach langer Entwöhnung galt, eine venezianische Gondel zu besteigen?
> (Who would not have had to fight off a passing shudder, a secret shyness and unease, in stepping into a Venetian gondola for the first time, or after enough time had passed that it no longer seemed ordinary?) (FA2.1, 523)

Aschenbach reclines in soft velvet, for the seat in a gondola is 'der erschlaffendste Sitz von der Welt' ('the slackest seat in the world'), an evocation, with the root 'schlaf', of the fatigue experienced at the Munich cemetery. There are Oriental overtones in this devitalization, as can be seen in all of the works discussed in this chapter: through the Asiatic cholera this fatigue will overwhelm Aschenbach; in *Der Zauberberg* inertia and sloth are explicitly identified as Oriental; in *Der Amokläufer* the state of amok is introduced by 'eine Art Tropenkrankeit' ('a sort of tropical illness') that provokes a 'kraftlose Nostalgie' ('powerless nostalgia') (89–90). Although Aschenbach will protest the gondolier's direction—they are moving seaward through a haze—the narration fuses with Aschenbach's point of view, indicating his submission to the obscurity and 'Ungefähr', which his literary morality rejects: 'Wie still und stiller es um ihn wurde! Nichts war zu vernehmen, als das Plätschern des Ruders' ('How silent it was and how the silence grew around him! One could perceive nothing but the splashing of the oar') (FA2.1, 524). Aschenbach's sinking into the lulling softness of the gondola ride is also a microcosmic image of Venice itself a 'gesunkene[n] Königin' (FA2.1, 543). The image of a 'sunken queen' draws upon the former political and cultural glory of Venice. But with its infrastructure decaying and its population and visitors exposed to the plague, the sinking of Venice is analogous to Aschenbach's impending collapse. The narrator's lyrical emphasis on the façade, decay, and sinking exoticizes Venice in concrete, physical terms.

The exotic setting becomes a site of contest between opposing forces of human nature. Venice will nurture Aschenbach's exaltation and self-destruction, his self-abandon to both surging vitality and fatal disease. He experiences a heightening of his artistic sensibilities, and a gradual and complete loss of form. The structure of the city itself allows for both hiding and exposure, isolation and traffic with the foreign, and presents both the beautiful façade and the decaying or empty interior, aesthetic form and the sensual formlessness of the sea. In Aschenbach's last vision of Tadzio waving from the sea, these oppositions seem to collapse.

The structure and history of the city are important. Venice is made up of myriad alleys, innumerable and indistinguishable bridges and piazzas; seawater courses through the city via 'das trübe Labyrinth der Kanäle' ('the murky labyrinth of canals') (FA2.1, 542) threatening to sink the city. These features and their metaphorical associations—disorienting, endangering, and elemental—give Venice a charged atmosphere. Venice has long associations with furtive sexuality[21]—at its cultural height, carnival was celebrated six months a year. The canals, too, provide a mirroring image of the façades of crumbling palaces, an ontological deception. Simmel certainly describes it in those terms:

> Denn dies ist das Tragische an Venedig, wodurch es zum Symbol einer ganz einzigen Ordnung unsrer Formen der Weltauffassung wird: daß die Oberfläche, die ihr Grund verlassen hat, der Schein, in dem kein Sein mehr lebt, sich dennoch als ein Vollständiges und Substantielles gibt.
>
> (For that is what is tragic about Venice, through which it becomes a symbol of an entirely singular order of our forms of world understanding: that the surfaces, which have abandoned their ground, the appearance, in which no being resides, present themselves nonetheless as something complete and substantial.) (GA8, 261)

Venice seems to contest the mature Aschenbach's philosophy of classical simplicity and order, his rejection of any psychological analysis of the emotional life, his expulsion of any sympathy with the abyss; but in fact Venice exposes the 'Romantic leanings' not only of its author but its protagonist.[22] While the artistic heritage of Venice and its seascape satisfy Aschenbach's demand for beauty, and provide the conditions for an idealizing Apollonian admiration of Tadzio, the sensuous reality of Venice provides a striking contrast. Its architecture is fantastical rather than classical. Decay and filth seep in from behind the façade. While Mann himself might have in mind the Nietzschean opposition between Apollonian beauty and Dionysian suffering,[23] Aschenbach consciously inherits a

---

[21] See Tony Tanner's (1992: 5) register of literary accounts of Venice as 'saturated with secret sexuality.'

[22] Robertson (2002a: 98).

[23] Cf. Sheppard (1990: 94), who argues for the 'monofocal' Dionysian mythology, as influencing both the symbolism of the figures and the motives for Aschenbach's naturalization of them. A more simplistic account is given in Giobbi, who separates Nietzsche's

literary idea of Venice, as a reference to a Venetian sonnet by Platen suggests. Aschenbach inherits, then, a Venice already saturated with Romantic and mythological associations.[24] With its history of masquerade and secret societies, intrigue, crime, its status as a harbour and centre of commerce with the East—it was also a point of departure for pilgrims and crusaders—its openness to foreign influences and African winds, and its loss of power since the victory of Napoleon, the city contrasts with Aschenbach's literary rejection of scepticism and mistrust.[25] The image of post-Romantic Venice has appeared in literature—since at least Byron's 'Ode to Venice' (1816)—as a theatre of decline and disorder, sensuality, sin, and death. Moreover, Venice has been associated with deviant—and in the post-classical age that describes homosexual—longings,[26] which at first, given the beauty of the surroundings, seem quite reasonably integrated into Aschenbach's elevating, Platonic theory of *eros*.

The dual setting of the Lido and the city of Venice offers a setting for the play between opposing forces of form and formlessness that mirror aesthetic admiration, on the one hand, and submission to disease and lust, on the other. Disease and unrestrained sexual desire are both associated with the breakdown of proper boundaries (and thus form) in the Platonic world-view on which Aschenbach ostensibly relies; love itself is considered, in Plato's dialogue *Phaedrus*, a kind of madness akin to disease that must be resisted by the rational part of the soul. Aschenbach's aesthetic admiration of Tadzio's form then serves as an intellectual façade obscuring a brewing crisis. With Aschenbach's first viewing of Tadzio swimming, the sea, in its beauty, takes on a mythological cast: he imagines the boy rising from the sea as in a poetic tale 'vom Ursprung der Form und von der Geburt der Götter' ('of the origin of form and of the birth of the gods') (FA2.1, 540). This shimmering splendour of the sea will be sharply juxtaposed to the sordidness of inner Venice, but the duality of sea and city seems to collaborate in Aschenbach's disorientation, his oscillation between Prussian composure and classical form and Eastern decadence. While the Lido and Venice might signify, respectively, an outpost of Western civilization and the Oriental feminine site of decadence, the experience of the sea from the Lido is also 'Orientalized', as submission to vast spatial monotony and entrancement with the void.

concepts, such as when Tadzio is associated with the Apollonian and Venice with the Dionysian (Giobbi 1989: 56–57). Cf. Robertson (2002a: 104), who argues for the 'precarious balance between two forces.'

[24] Pabst (1955: 345); Petriconi (1958: 86).
[25] See Mann's (1983: 115) notes in Reed's edition.
[26] See Aldrich (1993); Brinkley (1999: 2f).

Aschenbach is aware of the seductive nature of the sea, but at first he is able to justify allowing his gaze again to get lost in it, with reference to his work. The unarticulated space with its wide horizon, he reasons, provides a rest from the demanding complexity of his writing; its formlessness is associated with the void that Aschenbach compares to the perfection of art. He overlooks any association this formless monotony might have with imagined Oriental sensibilities, with anonymous submission to the vastness of monotonous space, an association that becomes explicit through Settembrini's warnings to Castorp in *Der Zauberberg*, to be discussed later in this chapter.

Aschenbach's reasoning and view are interrupted by the entrance of Tadzio into his field of vision:

> Wie er nun aber so tief ins Leere träumte, ward plötzlich die überschnitten, und als er seinen Blick aus dem Unbegrenzten einholte und sammelte, da war es der schöne Knabe.
>
> (But as he now dreamily gazed so deeply into the emptiness, it was suddenly intersected, and as he retrieved his vision from the boundless and focused, there was before him the beautiful boy.) (FA2.1, 536–537)

The elemental horizontal sea is visually contrasted with an interrupting, and in that sense incongruent, vertical form, perhaps challenging Aschenbach's equation of nothingness and perfection, but certainly associating Tadzio, ominously, with the abyss, according to the terms of *Der Zauberberg*, with an Oriental vastness. The self-dissolution hinted at in images of the monotonous sea on Aschenbach's approach to Venice is evoked again, as the passion Aschenbach develops for Tadzio leads to drastic self-abandonment. This anticipates Castorp's longing for Clawdia Chauchat, with her origins in what seems to Castorp an unchartered vastness beyond the Caucasus. While Castorp's obsessive loves for Pribislav Hippe and Clawdia Chauchat are explicitly diagnosed as surrender to Eastern-Asian influences, alignment of the Polish Tadzio with the Eastern-Asian exotic, as well as with a colonized people, is here an implicit subtext.[27]

While Aschenbach is an admirer of Prussian sensibilities, he sympathizes with Tadzio's national identification. Aschenbach hails from Silesia, is half-Slavic from his mother's side, and finds himself in accord with Tadzio's hostility towards the Russian tourists at the Lido hotel. Although Tadzio's Slavic ethnicity is linked to that of Aschenbach's own sensuous and fiery mother from Bohemia, Mann avoids any stereotypes

---

[27] See Robertson (2000a: 134–135).

of decadence when describing the Polish family, including Tadzio.[28] The desexualized presentation of the girls and women allows for Tadzio to be foregrounded as innocently coquettish and for an implication of Aschenbach's homosexual gaze. Thus, Aschenbach presents an ambiguous counterpart to the feminized Tadzio, a young boy of a subjugated nationality, with delicate health, aware of being the object of the older man's attention. Aschenbach's sympathy for Tadzio is in part a projection of solidarity by the fallen 'Autor' upon the weaker other, as Aschenbach himself confronts his own marginalizing homosexuality. The reference to Platen, a German poet highly sympathetic to the Polish plight in the nineteenth century, is also suggestive. One of Platen's *Polenlieder,* for example, 'Wiegenlied einer polnischen Mutter' ('Lullaby of a Polish Mother') (1831), is a lullaby for a boy orphaned by his father's death in the Polish uprising; Tadzio is attended entirely by women, with no father ever mentioned, and despises the Russians in his midst. Platen's images of 'Pestilenz' and a menacing 'Tigertier' in that poem[29] are highly resonant with the novella's Asian-Oriental motives, including Aschenbach's vision of a tiger crouching in the swamp at the Munich cemetery and the Indian origin of plague—'Erzeugt aus den warmen Morästen des Ganges-Deltas . . . in deren Bambusdickichten der Tiger kauert' ('Nurtured in the warm morasses of the Ganges delta . . . in the bamboo jungles of which the tiger crouches') (FA2.1, 578). While Oriental influences are associated with seduction, decadence, and contagion, and Tadzio's Slavic origins potentially align him symbolically with those, he is not a carrier but the victim of disease, and ultimately of the older German's moral weakness and unleashed desires.

Both reflection and agent of Aschenbach's crisis, Venice provides the conditions in which it unfolds and seems to collaborate in his downfall. Hints of physical decay seem to be morally infectious, drawing him in, suggesting a link between the atmosphere, moral decay, and the immanent epidemic. The uncomfortably sultry and thick air, filled with local smells from houses, shops, food stalls, and perfumes, oppresses him. But the atmosphere is both stimulating and lulling.

Je länger er ging, desto quälender bemächtigte sich seiner der abscheuliche Zustand, den die Seeluft zusammen mit dem Scirocco hervorbringen kann, und der zugleich Erregung und Erschlaffung ist.

---

[28] Fieguth (1995: 134–138) situates Mann's presentation of the Polish Tadzio within the context of shifting German stereotypes of Poles, including their association with decadence, at the turn of the century.

[29] Platen, in Kozielek (ed.) (1989: 205–207).

(The longer he walked, the more oppressed he was by the appalling condition sometimes brought on by the sea air in combination with the Sirocco, and which provokes excitement and exhaustion at once.) (FA2.1, 541–542)

This dual experience of excitement and dimming of energies characterizes the infectious-erotic coupling in all of the texts discussed in this chapter. While perspiring and feverish, bothered by beggars and the odour of the canals, Aschenbach sits down in the forgotten, empty 'Platz' that recalls for the reader the 'leere Halteplatz' ('empty tramstop') at the Munich cemetery. It is at this little square that Aschenbach will experience, in the final chapter, his 'Erkenntnis bei der Cisterne' ('Knowledge at the Cistern'),[30] the speech modelled on Plato's *Phaedrus* in which his aesthetics of love, which had justified his growing obsession with Tadzio, falls apart; here Aschenbach renounces higher ideals. The Platonic reference not only provides conceptual structure and imagery for Aschenbach's idealizing aesthetics; it also suggests that the fallen republic of Venice, as the site of Aschenbach's struggle, is a modern analogy for the human soul 'writ large', as the ideal republic served for Plato's Socrates. Like the human soul, Venice is the site for the division and struggle between reason and sensuality, here geographically symbolized by Western Europe and the exoticized East. The duality of the physical setting, with the Lido hotel and the city itself, collaborates in Aschenbach's downfall by aiding his self-delusion. With the hotel beach at the Lido and its pristine seascape, Aschenbach can watch Tadzio play, separated from the sordid city and its dark majesty. Aschenbach is enchanted by the charm of Venice, of the dual possibilities of seascape and city, combining 'die Reize eines gep-flegten Badelebens an südlichem Strande mit der traulich bereiten Nähe der wunderlich-wundersamen Stadt' ('the allure of a pampered life of a bathing resort on a southern beach with the familiar accessible proximity of the strange-wonderful city') (FA2.1, 550). While he contemplates Tadzio on the beach and in the dining-rooms, Aschenbach sees Tadzio 'überall' ('everywhere'): in the ground-floor rooms of the hotel, in the boat to the city, in the piazzas, 'und oft noch zwischenein auf Wegen und Stegen' ('and often even in between, in alleys and on footpaths')—and here the ironic distance of the narrative voice recalls that at the Munich cemetery—'wenn der Zufall ein Übriges tat' ('when chance played a part') (FA2.1, 551). While Aschenbach is able to see Tadzio everywhere, he maintains a mental bifurcation, based on the separation of the civilized (European) bathing resort and the (Orientalized) sordid city, which allows Platonist exaltations to obscure his brewing sexual obsession. While the

---

[30] Mann's working notes in Reed (ed.) (1983: 120).

beach affords a constant view of Tadzio bathing in the pristine element, in the city he can follow Tadzio furtively through the infected labyrinth that smells ominously of carbolic acid.

With his constant proximity to Tadzio, Aschenbach's passion and exaltation of his passion grow in tandem, along with the threat of plague. Tadzio playing on the beach provokes the first 'Phaedrus' speech, Aschenbach's reflections on Platonic love that justify *eros* as the anamnesis, through a vision of beauty, of the forms. The narrative inserts in the speech—'Stand nicht geschrieben, daß' ('Was it not written that'), 'heißt es' ('supposedly'), 'ja' ('after all'), and finally 'So dachte der Enthusiasmierte' ('So thought the enthusiast')—serve to qualify and distance the narrative voice from Aschenbach's application of Platonic theory. Aschenbach, enraptured by the analogy of Phaedrus and Socrates, feels himself to be experiencing a Platonic vision of truth itself and is thus inspired to write. A (mere) page and a half of exquisite prose results—as it had for Mann on the same beach near the ten-year-old Wladyslaw Moes[31]—and yet at the closure of this paragraph and of the scene (the next starts on the following day), Aschenbach feels 'zerrüttet' ('broken') as if guilty of some debauchery (FA2.1, 556). Aschenbach is unable to hold back from the sensuous provocation that is to stimulate anamnesis. What Aschenbach has experienced is not a true 'recollection', but a highly inspired exaltation of the very passions that prompt his impending breakdown.

The second evocation of Plato's *Phaedrus* is the only directly quoted monologue in the text; here Aschenbach admits his collapse, acknowledging the failure of classical 'Form und Unbefangenheit', which has not prevented his contact with the abyss, the illicit, debauchery (FA2.1, 589). This dark insight takes place in the same desolate square with the cistern, in a scene that brings together in one locality, and in an uneasy synthesis, the oppositions of hiding and exposure, isolation and infection by the foreign (love and cholera), the contrast between façade and interior reality, and the collapse of form into formlessness. Aschenbach follows Tadzio through the labyrinth of streets, losing his bearings ('Mit versagendem Ortssinn') and even the basic directions of the compass ('der Himmelsgegenden nicht mehr sicher') (FA2.1, 586, 587). While the earlier moments of loss of temporal sense indicated stages of self-abandonment, the loss of spatial directionality is more severe, indicating an impending collapse.

In the Venetian labyrinth, Aschenbach loses his position as the modern self-assured subject, the point of anchor for surveying the knowable world. As he follows the Polish family, hiding behind the wells and in the

---

[31] Brinkley (1999: 2).

distorted angles of the little streets, Aschenbach gets lost in the alleys, unaided by the bridges and squares that 'zu sehr einander gleichen' ('look too similar to each other') (FA2.1, 587). When he loses track of Tadzio and abandons his search, Aschenbach, feverish and quivering, quenches his thirst with the strawberries he must realize could be infected, thus participating in his own annihilation. Along a quiet, abandoned, dirty square, Aschenbach notices one house in particular that appears palace-like, with its Gothic windows, but behind which 'die Leere wohnte' ('emptiness dwells') (FA2.1, 588), an image that evokes the hollowing-out of the artist's soul, as well as the ultimate emptiness of that 'Oriental' vastness the sea vision had offered. The lion balconies of the edifice recall the 'apokalyptische Tiere' ('apocalyptic animals') on the Munich cemetery chapel, seen from the empty 'Halteplatz'. These cross-resonances between the Munich and Venetian settings confirm the significance of place in Aschenbach's downfall, as spatial correlates to his inner crisis.

The description of the city is inseparable from Aschenbach's state of deceptive intoxication; he inwardly colludes with the authorities to keep 'dieses schlimme Geheimnis der Stadt, das mit seinem eigensten Geheimnis verschmolz' ('the dark secret of the city, that fused with his ownmost secret') (FA2.1, 565). He perceives correlations between the homicidal social chaos erupting in the city and his own criminal intentions:

> Aber zugleich wandte er beständig eine spürende und eigensinnige Aufmerk-
> samkeit den unsauberen Vorgängen im Inneren Venedigs zu, jenem Aben-
> teuer der Außenwelt, das mit dem seines Herzens dunkel zusammenfloß und
> seine Leidenschaft mit unbestimmten, gesetzlosen Hoffnungen näherte.
>
> (But at the same time, he kept turning his inquisitive and persistent
> attention to the unseemly events unfolding inside Venice, to that adventure
> of the outside world in its dark confluence with that of his heart, and which
> nourished his passion with vague, lawless hopes.) (FA2.1, 569)

Dizzy with choleric fever, the confusion in Aschenbach's experience becomes ever more tragically explicit. He is beset by a feeling of dread, which confuses his psyche with the world:

> einem Gefühl der Ausweg- und Aussichtslosigkeit, von dem nicht klar
> wurde, ob es sich auf die äußere Welt oder auf seine eigene Existenz bezog.
>
> (a feeling of hopelessness and loss of perspective, and it was not clear
> whether that referred to the outside world or to his own individual exis-
> tence.) (FA2.1, 590)

This loss of separation from the external world—also experienced in Castorp's 'Schnee' vision and on the deck of the 'Oceania' in *Der Amokläufer*—reflects Aschenbach's experience of infection and desire in so far as both obliterate the boundaries of the self. Corroding his sense of propriety and form, inner and outer realities merge in the final pages of the novel. Descriptions of the seascape before him are indistinguishable from those of his collapse, of his perceptions of dying from the Asian pestilence. The description of the last vision of Tadzio calls up Aschenbach's capitulation to the abyss. On a sandbank Tadzio is separated from the 'Festlande' ('solid land') by the wide strip of water and stands majestically 'dort draußen im Meere, im Winde, vorm Nebelhaft-Grenzenlosen' ('out there in the sea, in the wind, before the nebulously boundless') (FA2.1, 592). Here form, in Tadzio's sculpturesque figure, merges with the formless, the limitless and hazy vastness; Tadzio is separated from those on firm land and is one with the homogeneous element, with formless, monotonous space. This merging signals the death of Aschenbach's individuation as an autonomous self who, as an artist, gives form to the world he presents. Aschenbach's death is also the death of his art, evoked by the 'scheinbar herrenlos' ('apparently abandoned') black-draped camera on the beach (FA2.1, 590).

The illicitness of Aschenbach's love for Tadzio and his infection with cholera are metaphorically intertwined, as they both reflect submission to Venetian temptations and deceptions. Cholera and desire are also symbolic of the moral dangers of the exotic: Aschenbach's pursuit of Tadzio, his hopes for sexual consummation, and his decision not to inform Tadzio's family of the plague recklessly subordinate the other's welfare to his own obsessive lust. But Aschenbach's death also brings a collapse of this pursuit and serves as an implicit critique of the pretensions of its intellectual and aesthetic justifications. If Aschenbach had also appropriated Tadzio for his aesthetic vision, this aesthetics is disturbingly precarious. The striking presence of the camera in the final scene seems to preclude any resurrection of the Platonic, transcendental vision.[32] While Platonic contemplation of beauty characteristic of Aschenbach's vision as an artist offers a unification of the desiring soul with the ideal, the lone camera symbolizes an abandoned voyeurism. The camera's reproduction of the visual recalls Plato's indictment—in *Phaedrus*—of writing as mere mimesis.[33] Aschenbach is, after all, not only artist and author but 'der Schriftsteller' ('writer') (FA2.1, 501, 511, 555). Simmel's description of Venice could be applied to the modern camera and strangely summarizes Plato's rejection of writing and of mimesis in general:

---

[32] Here I differ from Boa's (2006: 32–33) view that the Platonic vision is reinstated at the novel's end.

[33] Plato, *Phaedrus*, 275d–e.

die Erscheinung lebt wie in ostentativer Abtrennung vom Sein, die Außenseite erhält von ihrer Innenseite keinerlei Direktive und Nahrung, sie gehorcht nicht dem Gesetze einer übergreifenden seelischen Wirklichkeit, sondern dem der Kunst, das jenes gerade zu dementieren bestimmt scheint.

(appearance lives as if in ostentatious divergence from being, the external aspect receives no directive or nourishment from its inner side, it does not respect the laws of an overarching reality of the soul, but rather that of art, which seems determined precisely to deny such.) (GA8, 259)

In the Platonic view, poetic inspiration without reason, mimesis without the essence of what is thereby represented, both agitate and appeal to the lower parts of the soul. The novella suggests that the draw of the sensuous, of the unbounded and transgressive is, for all Aschenbach's allegiance to form, inevitable.

Infectious-erotic Venice becomes a site both for the confrontation with otherness and for the tragic merging of contradictory, but necessary, human impulses. Uniquely promoted by the Venetian space, the ambiguity of the exotic, both desirable and threatening, remains unresolved at the novel's conclusion. While the beauty of Aschenbach's final illusion lingers—his seeming to move, with Tadzio, 'ins Verheißungsvoll-Ungeheure' ('into the promising and monstrous') (FA2.1, 592)—the final paragraph, with its terse, empirical report of Aschenbach's death, admits its lyrical sublimation only as Aschenbach's private, illusory experience.

SEXUALITY, ILLNESS, AND COLONIAL AGGRESSION IN *DER AMOKLÄUFER*

Stefan Zweig's *Der Amokläufer* also features a German bourgeois protagonist in an exotic locale whose death is provoked by an illness inseparable from erotic obsession. Thus, the text can be profitably compared to Mann's novella and, as will be seen later in this chapter, to his novel *Der Zauberberg*. Since much of Zweig's story is set in the East Indies and involves aggressive treatment of natives, it affords, additionally, an examination of a colonialist relation to the exotic foreign that might be implied, if more subtly, in Mann's works.[34] Like the author Aschenbach and the would-be engineer Hans Castorp, the unnamed protagonist of *Der Amokläufer* submits to a locally nurtured disease, in his case the attack of amok. Running amok is attributed to a kind of tropical 'infection' and to local

---

[34] Nenno (1996) and Robertson (2000a).

climatic conditions, and the German doctor's affliction and consequent breakdown serve, more symbolically, to expose the moral and cognitive fragility of the civilized European. That it takes on a particularly sexual, rather than homicidal, form in *Der Amokläufer* allows for the suggestion of release of repressed elements of the 'civilized' European psyche, and links this novella closely with Mann's works. Although the text has been relatively neglected by scholars, Mann himself recognized Zweig's novella as 'meisterhaft' ('masterly').[35]

In *Der Tod in Venedig* and *Der Zauberberg*, the initial travel to a historically or symbolically exotic place is narratively highlighted; this is also the case with Zweig's work. Like Aschenbach's trip to the Munich cemetery and subsequent, indirect route to Venice, and Castorp's progress by ship and train to the Swiss Alps, the doctor's departure to the East Indies plays an important role in foreshadowing the destabilization of his character. In all three works, the narrative's focus on passage to the respective destination functions to reveal psychological change. In all cases the transition is one of uneasiness or distress: Aschenbach feels disturbed by the old dandy on the ship and helpless while being rowed seaward in the gondola; Castorp is confused about the direction in which the train travels and the fact that he has arrived; and the doctor, most violently, is robbed in the port at knifepoint before departing. Each protagonist then arrives more vulnerable to the effects of spatial defamil-iarization, described theoretically in *Der Zauberberg* (discussed in the next section), and to exoticization. For all three protagonists, the travel requires passage by ship over water, evoking both psychic depths and an uncon-trollable and primitive element of nature, as well as potential associations with death and the classical underworld.

In contrast to that of Mann's protagonists, the Amokläufer's travel is not provoked by internal pressures of *Fernweh* (as induced in Aschenbach by the stranger's appearance in the cemetery) or incipient illness (the three-week Alpine trip is ordered by Castorp's doctor), but rather by the external factors of economic exile and professional stigmatization. The doctor's career in Germany had ended through potential scandal, involving a woman for whom he stole money from the hospital that employed him. Thus, the doctor begins his journey to the East Indies already morally compromised and dependent on the Dutch government, which has hired him for a remote colonial practice. That he is not only a transgressor, but will also become victim to foreign circumstances, is fore-shadowed by his being robbed in Rotterdam where he is to board the

---

[35] Mann's letter to Zweig, 2 February 1923, first published in Jonas (1981: 104).

ship. He not only starts off his journey penniless, but with his bourgeois autonomy, his self-determination, and professional dignity, in question. The fact that he is first encountered by the narrator on a returning ship, in a dark corner of the deck evading other passengers, signals from the outset the failure and perhaps catastrophe of the experience he will recount.

In formal terms, *Der Amokläufer* is of the same genre as *Der Tod in Venedig*. Yet three narrative features of the work set Zweig's novella apart from that of Mann. The first concerns the narrative structure itself. The story is told by a first-person 'frame' narrator who appears in the story as a tourist returning home to Europe, whereas Mann's omniscient and often ironic narrator does not personally appear. Secondly, there is a double narration, for the principal inset story of Zweig's work is told also in the first person by the doctor-stranger to the frame narrator, a tourist on the ship bound for home. Thirdly, the central events do not unfold contemporaneously with the narration but are past events reported. Yet the doctor's story itself, and the fact that he reports the events in a state of lingering psychological disturbance, has a significant effect upon the frame narrator. The latter's narration consequently affords no ironic and little objective distance, as in Mann's works. The narrative figure functions not merely to provide authenticity and intimacy to the doctor's story, and to suggest links between that story and society in general, as David Turner argues in defending the importance of the frame narrator;[36] still more significantly, he provides a vulnerable, but 'uninfected', self against which the doctor's downfall can be measured. In deciding to confess his story in the first person rather than impersonally, the doctor explicitly revokes his social and cultural position as a doctor and man of science, and assumes the pose of the patient: 'ich ziehe mich nackt aus und sage: ich' ('I strip myself naked and say: I') (A, 86). The frame narrator doubles this first-person perspective.

The doubling of first-person narration contributes to the questioning of first-person subjectivity itself. Both the main frame narrator and the stranger-doctor he meets describe their own submission to exotic forces beyond the control of the individual self. The parallels between the frame narrator and the stranger who speaks to him are then more significant than have been recognized in the scholarship. They share not only a common means of travel and distaste for the social life of the ocean-liner passengers, as Turner points out;[37] in addition, they are also both Germans and

---

[36] Turner (1981: 118) argues for these traditional functions for the frame narrator but also for a more interpretive function, providing 'a sympathetic bridge between their world and ours, introducing unexpected and sometimes uncomfortable links' between them.
[37] Turner (1981: 124).

profoundly affected by their respective exotic surroundings. Although the narrator remains healthy while the doctor-stranger has succumbed to madness, the atmospherically induced illness in Asia is foreshadowed by the experience of the narrator on the ship just before he meets the stranger. The narrator's description of the atmosphere reveals that he is overwhelmed by the effects of sea and wind, the night sky over the ship, the moonlight and the light of the Southern Cross in the sky.

The frame narrator, en route to the Naples harbour from Calcutta, seeks solitude, which would enable him to put into order the impressions garnered from recent travels. In stark contrast to the doctor whom he will meet on the deck, his attitude about his travels suggests a personality intact. The frame narrator is able to assimilate foreign influences, arrange impressions in his memory, and appropriate them for his own imagination. In this manner, a distinction is initially highlighted between the outer world, with its diverse impressions, and the inner narrative self with its sense of unifying order. Yet the narrator's description of this desire for solitude is also ambiguous, in that it also evokes the power of the exotic impressions, and their tension with the predatory curiosity of the traveller:

> Ich hatte eine neue Welt gesehen, rasch ineinanderstürzende Bilder in rasender Jagd in mich hineingetrunken. Nun wollte ich mirs übersinnen, zerteilen, ordnen, nachbildend das heiß in den Blick Gedrängte gestalten.
>
> (I had seen a new world; I had drunken in images that wildly tangled with each other as they raced through my mind. Now I wanted to be able to think them over, arrange them, categorize, and recompose the forms that had pressed themselves on my vision.) (A, 75)

The suggestion 'in rasender Jagd' will correlate to the stranger's description of his rabid pursuit of the Englishwoman.

Moreover, the narrator already feels uneasy amongst the nervously chattering and promenading passengers, just as the doctor is on board in self-imposed social exile. The narrator's cabin offers little comfort, as it is cramped, hot, and noisy, and located in the middle of the ship, where the ventilator and engine are disturbingly audible. Foreshadowing the revelation of the presence of the Englishwoman's sarcophagus on board, the cabin from which the narrator escapes onto the deck is compared to a grave and a coffin. Its atmosphere is contrasted to the fresh air on deck:

> So flüchtete ich, kaum daß ich den Koffer in das muffige Grab aus grauen Traversen verstaut hatte, wieder zurück auf Deck, und wie Ambra trank ich, aufsteigend aus der Tiefe, den süßlichen weichen Wind, der vom Lande her über die Wellen wehte.

(Hardly had I stowed my luggage in the dingy girders of the stuffy tomb, I climbed back up from the depths to the deck and drank in the sweet gentle wind blowing over the waves from the land, as if it were ambrosia.) (A, 75)

Several details then foreshadow the events to be recounted by the stranger. The latter is forced to leave the colonies and follows the Englishwoman's corpse onto the ship in order to protect her secret abortion from being discovered in autopsy by Dutch officials. The narrator here uses the verb 'flüchtete', and the cabin, beneath water level, is associated with meta-phorically suggestive depths ('Tiefe') and the grave ('Grab') (later also 'Sarg') (A, 76). In the cabin he loses spatio-temporal orientation: 'ich brauchte Minuten, um mich an Zeit und Ort zurückzufinden' ('I needed minutes to reorient myself in time and space') (A, 76). In contrast, the wind over the waves is sensually described, as sweet and soft, compared to ambrosia, evocative of eternity.

Description of the sky above an open sea after midnight, and of the 'Oceania' ship itself, prepare a parallel for the loss of self on the part of the narrator that will correlate to the stranger's story. This parallel will implicitly justify the narrator's sympathy with the stranger despite the latter's raving descriptions of morally questionable acts. Feeling rocked by the ship's movement, looking up at the Southern Cross in the sky, the narrator describes a state of enchantment:

Ich stand und sah empor: mir war wie in einem Bade, wo Wasser warm von oben fällt, nur daß dies Licht war, das mir weiß und auch lau die Hände überspülte, die Schultern, das Haupt mild umgoß und irgendwie nach innen zu dringen schien, denn alles Dumpfe in mir war plötzlich aufgehellt.

I stood and looked above: it felt to me as if I were in a bath, where warm water falls from above, only it was light that spilled white over me and tepid into my hands, pouring mildly over my shoulders and head and somehow seemed to penetrate inside, for everything sombre in me was suddenly illuminated. (A, 77)

The Southern Cross reminds the reader of the passage through tropical seas, and the sky over the exotic Southern ports the ship has visited (Australia, Singapore, Calcutta are mentioned). It foreshadows the imagi-native return to the South-east Asian tropics through the stranger's re-collections. The narrator compares the starlight to a bath into which he is submerged, suggesting a physical, as well as spiritual, sense of submission to a cosmic element, much like Aschenbach's entranced disorientation on the ship to Venice. As in *Der Tod in Venedig*, suggestions of the exotic are given through description of smells, which, unlike the 'Bilder' from the tourist's travels, evade any subjection to mental arrangement. The air is intoxicating, smelling of fruits and scents of far islands.

Ich atmete befreit, rein, und jäh beseligt spürte ich auf den Lippen wie ein klares Getränk die Luft, die weiche, gegorene, leicht trunken machende Luft, in der Atem von Früchten, Duft von fernen Inseln war.

(I breathed freely, purely, and suddenly delighted I felt the air on my lips like a clear drink, the soft, effervescent, easily intoxicating air, in which there was the scent of fruits, the fragrance of far islands.) (A, 77)

The air is described again in terms of fluidity, like a clear drink, which intoxicates, and so cannot be appropriated by the touristic collector of images. Rather than ordering these impressions, the narrator longs to lie down, to submit to the dreaming the intoxicating vision induces:

Nun, zum ersten Male, seit ich die Planken betreten, überkam mich die heilige Lust des Träumens, und jene andere sinnlichere, meinen Körper weibisch hinzugeben an dieses Weiche, das mich umdrängte. Ich wollte mich hinlegen, den Blick hinauf zu den weißen Hieroglyphen.

(Now, for the fist time since I stepped onto the planks, the sacred delight of dreams overcame me, and that other more sensual pleasure of giving in with my body, womanlike, to the softness surrounding me. I wanted to lie down and gaze up at the white hieroglyphs.) (A, 77)

The feminine rendering of this desired submission ('meinen Körper weibisch hinzugeben')—so different from the doctor's initially aggressive pursuit, but much like his later self-sacrifice for the woman's secret—is coupled here with a sense of the mysteriousness of the night sky. The stars, with their yellow light—a colour repeatedly associated with the Asian natives in the novella (A, 89, 103, 121, 126)—are compared to white hieroglyphs. The narrator's experience of the natural surroundings bears some comparison to Hans Castorp's first outing into nature in *Der Zauberberg*. Whereas the 'Bildmäßigkeit' ('pictorality') of Hans Castorp's first intimate viewing of the Alpine landscape is displaced by the 'Urbild' ('primal image') of an early and primal longing, here the narrator's touristic 'Bilder' ('pictures') are displaced by the hieroglyphic stars that cannot be cognitively read. If the European model of the self can be characterized by a self-grounded centre of rationality from which the universe is given order—through conceptual identification, taxonomical assignment, or cartographical mapping—the description here suggests at least a temporary usurpation of that centre. Rather than the light of reason, the narrator is overwhelmed by the light from the moon and stars, which seemed to burn 'wie aus einem geheimnisvollen Innen' ('from some mysterious interior') (A, 77). The coupling of yellow and white in this description of the stars and starlight will be reiterated in the doctor's description of the Englishwoman at the ball: she wears a yellow dress and her exposed shoulders are white as ivory, associating her with the

Asian locale. Light is also a significant metaphor in Mann's *Der Zauber-berg*. During his 'Schnee' outing, Castorp, too, is captivated by a blue light from the snow, rendered exotic by the superimposed images of Chauchat's and Hippe's 'Kirgisenaugen' ('Kirghistani eyes'). These cross-references are made here too: the narrator's sky is 'stahlblau hart' ('steel-blue strict') much like the Englishwoman's cold gaze that drives the doctor mad: 'hart, be-herrscht... ein Gesicht mit grauen englischen Augen' ('hard, mastered... a face with grey English eyes') (A, 95).

While the enchanting light suggests surrender to the elements, organic metaphors used to describe the ship likewise situate the narrator within a context of animate forces that exceed the self. In his room at midnight he hears:

> nur die Maschine, das atmende Herz des Leviathans, stieß keuchend den knisternden Leib des Schiffes vor ins Unsichtbare.
> (Only the engine, the breathing heart of the leviathan, throbbed as it thrust the creaking body of the ship forward into the invisible.) (A, 76)

The ship is soon described as an enormous plough, which, through its rocking progress through the water, becomes indistinguishable from the element itself.

> Immer wieder hob, immer wieder senkte sich der Pflug in die schwarzflu-tende Scholle, und ich fühlte alle Qual des besiegten Elements, fühlte alle Lust der irdischen Kraft in diesem funkelnden Spiel.
> (The plough rose ever again and sank ever again into the black-flooding soil, and in that sparkling interplay I felt all the agony of the vanquished elements, all the delight of the earthly force.) (A, 78)

The machine of the ship and the element through which it passes are personified, and soon the sense of self dissolves into this spatial context. The narrator's sympathy with the sea 'conquered' by the ship evokes a critique of colonial domination relevant to the Asian setting. The narrator, just before meeting the stranger in a dark corner of the deck, loses the distinction between himself and his surrounding atmosphere:

> Unten fühlte ich die Wasser leise rauschen, über mir mit unhörbarem Klang den weißen Strom dieser Welt. Und allmählich schwoll dieses Rauschen mir ins Blut: ich fühlte mich selbst nicht mehr, wußte nicht, ob dies Atmen mein eigenes war oder des Schiffes fernpochendes Herz, ich strömte, verströmte in diesem ruhelosen Rauschen der mitternächtigen Welt.
> (Below me I felt the water rushing quietly, above me the inaudible reso-nance of the white torrent of this world. And gradually this rushing swelled in my own blood: I no longer felt myself, did not know whether this breathing was mine or if it was the ship's distantly throbbing heart, I streamed, poured away into this restless rush of the midnight world.) (A, 78)

The narrator can no longer distinguish between his own body and the ship's movement, his breath and the ship's engine, and between himself and the elements of starlight and water. This self-dissolution in the atmosphere is interrupted by the doctor-stranger's cough from a dark corner. While they sit together in the dark, the light from the Southern Cross obscures all but their silhouettes. There is reference throughout this initial narrative to the tropical air and its oppressive, confusing humidity (A, 80, 81).

With this powerful description of the frame narrator's initial experiences, there is no question of objective narration. His curiosity about the stranger's story is compared to an inflamed passion, 'die nicht viel geringer ist als jene des Besitzenwollens bei einer Frau' ('not much less than a woman's possessiveness'), a comparison that will be explicitly paralleled by the stranger's mad lust for the Englishwoman (A, 81). In wanting to discover the stranger's secret, the narrator is pulled by an unknown force as if against his will: 'Irgend etwas zog mich, verwirrte mich . . . Schritt für Schritt, widerwillig und doch gezogen, gab ich mir nach' ('Something drove me on, confused me . . . step by step, reluctantly and yet enticed, I gave in') (A, 81–82). If his formal position is merely that of a 'frame' narrator, this is not justifiable in terms of the lesser intensity of his experiences, but rather only by their relative lack of objective consequences in the story as a whole.[38] The vulnerability of the frame narrator to atmospheric influences generalizes the very particular experience of the doctor. But it also demonstrates the vulnerability of the self as such, and the porosity of its boundaries, affirming, at the same time, the magical and beguiling power of the tropical-Southern exotic atmosphere.

The double narration and its necessary temporality contribute to the unique narrative space of the text. The interweaving of the doctor's reportage with that of the frame narrator (who reports the doctor's pauses, his drinking from the whisky bottles, the chime of a clock indicating the passage of the hours, features of the night weather) necessitates the repeated juxtaposition of the Asian setting with that of the ship on its progress towards Naples harbour. That harbour, from which the narrator will read the news of the stranger's death, is itself symbolically midway between Northern Europe and the exotic Eastern colonies. This structure is familiar from *Der Tod in Venedig*, where the refined hotel on the Lido provides for Aschenbach an intermediate space between his native Germany, and the sober habits of his everyday life there, and exotic

---

[38] Turner (1981: 128) questions the adequacy of the notion of 'frame' narration, but the figure in question in *Der Amokläufer* fulfils a more specific function than he accounts for. Turner argues that the 'encounter itself initiates a humanizing process' and enacts 'human values.'

Venice, fallen to debauchery and criminality as the cholera infection overtakes the city.

The colonial setting itself is nowhere described objectively, but through the eyes of one already infected through an extended sojourn there. The doctor's first characterization is negative, evoking the collapse of civility he has experienced in exile there. The region is described with verbs ('auffrißt', 'saugt') that suggest a devouring animal:

> das Schämen habe ich verlernt in dieser dreckigen Einsamkeit, in diesem verfluchten Land, das einem die Seele auffrißt und das Mark aus den Lenden saugt.
>
> (I forgot all shame in this filthy isolation, in this accursed country that tears the soul out of one and sucks the marrow from a man's loins.) (A, 86)

In another passage the East Indies region is symbolic of death:

> ich wußte, daß die Grabkreuze auf diesen Fieberplantagen dreimal so schnell wachsen wie bei uns, aber wenn man jung ist, glaubt man, das Fieber und der Tod springt immer nur auf die andern.
>
> (I knew that on these fever plantations the crosses on the graves multiply three times as fast as at home, but when one is young, one thinks that fever and death always only affect others.) (A, 88)

This characterization is explicitly contrasted to the tourist's experience of 'Indien'—as the doctor vaguely refers to the Dutch colonies—with its temples and palm trees easily romanticized, and with the doctor's initial curiosity about the exotic surroundings. Upon arrival the doctor had planned to study the languages, diseases, religious texts of the region, and even the psychology of the natives. He longs to be, as Aschenbach and Hans Castorp are initially presented, a civilizing force, a 'Missionar der Menschlichkeit, der Zivilisation' ('missionary of humanity, of civilization') (A, 86). Like Mann's Mynheer Peeperkorn, he takes interest in native poisons and weapons (A, 88). But soon he is overtaken by lethargy, similar to Castorp's Orientally characterized 'Stumpfsinn' ('mindlessness'), and is similarly cut off from his European nature. The climate and the hot and humid forests are implicated:

> Aber in diesem unsichtbaren Glashaus dort geht einem die Kraft aus, das Fieber—man kriegts ja doch, mag man noch so viel Chinin in sich fressen— greift einem ans Mark, man wird schlapp und faul, wird weich, eine Qualle. Irgendwie ist man als Europäer von seinem wahren Wesen abgeschnitten.
>
> (But then in this invisible glass house one's strength seeps away, the fever— and one gets it of course, one can gobble up only so much quinine—cuts to the marrow, one gets indolent and lethargic, soft as a jellyfish. Somehow one is cut off from one's true nature as a European.) (A, 86–87)

Not only the lethargy, but the references to fever and to quinine suggest malarial infection. In the doctor's account, this is especially dangerous for Europeans, who quickly deteriorate in the region, losing their composure, taking up drink, opium, fighting, submitting to bestial behaviour, and madness. Although homesick for Europe, to the point of a furious, feverish sickness (A, 89), they are eventually, like Hans Castorp, unable to return home. They have submitted to chronic sluggishness and, in respect to Europe, have become 'vergessen, fremd' ('forgotten, strange') (A, 87).

The doctor's self-diagnosis as 'amok' can be read as a symbolic infection or even contagion despite the fact that the precise aetiology of the syndrome is not known. While the origin of the illness remains a mystery, a 'furchtbare Geheimnis' ('horrible secret') (A, 106), the references to fever, malaria, and comparisons with rabies—'eine Art menschlicher Hundswut', 'Schaum tritt dem Laufenden vor die Lippen, er heult wie ein Rasender' ('a kind of human rabies', 'foam forms on the lips of the runner, he howls like a lunatic') (A, 105, 106)—carry associations of pathogenic infection. Just as the cholera originates from India in *Der Tod in Venedig*, the tropical climate is here associated with deathly disease. Vague but persistent accounts of climatic influences—'Irgendwie hängt es mit dem Klima zusammen, mit dieser schwülen, geballten Atmosphäre' ('Somehow it has to do with the climate, with this sultry, oppressive atmosphere') (A, 106)—present the surrounding atmosphere as infectious. The frame narrator and the doctor both acknowledge the cultural history of the disease. The running 'amok' of Malays is usually homicidal rampage, and the doctor provides the frame narrator with a precise description of its stages, from normalcy to 'stumpf' indifference, followed by a sudden outbreak of rage, running in a murderous frenzy until he is killed. The runner amok may be wholly capable of rational discussion, even though he has lost self-control, and takes on a feverish and vacant expression. While such outbreaks of madness are not unknown in modern Europe—the motif is presented in Georg Heym's 'Der Irre' ('The Madman')—the Malay syndrome follows a particular course, which in most respects characterizes the doctor's case.

This renders rather dubious the claim by Ganeshan that there is nothing 'Indian' about the story but the general mood and humidity. While Ganeshan claims that 'Indien ist hier die äußere Kulisse für ein europäisches Schicksal' ('India is here the foreign backdrop for a European fate'), the particular climate, the cultural associations of running amok, as well as the estrangement from European circumstances and the treatment of the natives by colonial Europeans, are integral to the novella's meaning.[39] Just as the particularity of locale in Mann's works is essential—Venice is not interchangeable with other cities, and, as will be seen in the next section, the Alpine setting cannot be seen as a blank or neutral space in *Der Zauberberg*—here the tropical East Asian setting takes on a hermeneutic function. The specific features of the exotic space in each case allow for a trial of individual and European identity.

Several details, however, distinguish the doctor's illness from that which would typically affect the native. The doctor's rage is not a homicidal but a sexual pursuit. This allows for the implication that the sources of madness, though erupting within the exotic context, reach deep into the familiar unknown of the European psyche. This links the doctor's affliction to those of Castorp and Aschenbach, whose author reflects on Freud's view of the psyche with reference to the 'Asian' vastness of the unconscious (Mann, GW, ix. 486). It also affords an at least implicit critique of possessive-colonial relations by exposing, and then inverting, their violence. While the doctor has become accustomed to, and tired of, the 'slavishly' submissive native women, his rage is ignited by the English-woman's haughty rejection. But it is this colonial attitude of domination—reiterated in his outrage that her native boy servant obstructs the path of a European man and doctor—which renders his downfall inevitable. The fact that the doctor himself had studied the disease (A, 105) that then overcomes him is also suggestive: the scientific attitude of the rational European also offers no protection against this mysterious affliction. In his research the doctor had failed to discover the origins of the disease; the European is unable to penetrate the mystery of this illness, its resistance to the light of scientific scrutiny.

This surely reflects Zweig's view, expressed in an essay of 1910 about his travel to India, that the European can never overcome the 'unüberwind-bare Fremdheit' ('indomitable foreignness') of the region and its inhabitants (BMBS, 260). While Said criticizes renderings of non-European places as 'exotic' and thus mysterious and unknowable, implicating them in justifications for colonialism, recognition of irreducible difference can serve, alternatively, as a basis for respect or appreciation. Zweig's own testimony, in letters and feuilleton articles, is interesting on this point: he expresses distress at being treated with respect as a European; he is critical of Europeanization of Indian cities; and overcomes a Eurocentric 'imaginative geography' by coming to view 'Europa längst nicht mehr als die ewige Achse unseres Weltalls' ('Europe, for a long time, no longer as the perpetual axis of our universe') (WG, 173). Zweig's protagonist's views

---

[39] Ganeshan (1975: 307).

clearly do not reflect his author's; but the protagonist's attitude changes at least to some extent, when he must rely on the native servant to help protect the Englishwoman's secret. More radically, his disease will eventually put him in the position of the 'native' runner amok, with self-sacrifice as its consequence, as he accompanies her lead-wrapped corpse into the sea.

In all of the works discussed in this chapter, the object of obsessive desire is not wholly other, but a European, with some significant connection to the Asian-Eastern exotic. In *Der Zauberberg*, the Russian roots of Clawdia Chauchat and her French surname by marriage serve as a reminder of the Eurasian complexity of her origins. Pribislav Hippe is a mixture of German and Slavic 'races'. Tadzio, an aristocratic Pole, despises the Russians in his midst, expressing a tension between the Eurasian oppressor and the Western Europe of his family's holidays and refined social habits; but he is also pursued by the German writer through the complex of sympathetic and possessive responses to his beauty. The Englishwoman of *Der Amokläufer* is exoticized more symbolically through a double association with North-western Europe (and America, where her Dutch husband has been doing business) and with the Asian tropics. Left alone by her husband in the colonies, she has had what the doctor imagines must have been a passionate sexual affair. The doctor's imagination of her passion—'nackt wie ein Tier und vielleicht stöhnend vor Lust... ich war besessen von der Idee, sie zu erniedrigen... sie zu besitzen' ('naked like an animal and perhaps groaning with desire... I was possessed by the idea of humiliating her... possessing her') (A, 99)—echoes the colonial metaphors of contemporaneous psychology, for which feminine sexuality is yet unexplored as a 'dark continent', in Freud's terms (WA, i. 39).[40] The doctor's attempt to subordinate the woman, with her coldness and pride, is implied through imagery that associates her with the colonized: the presence of her native servant-boy; her yellow dress and exposed shoulders 'wie mattes Elfenbein' ('like matte ivory'); and the squalid Chinese house in which she is found naked, bleeding, and febrile (A, 111).

What the doctor finds in the Englishwoman is not merely a fellow European, but a challenge to his own status as a colonial superior. The doctor is accustomed, by virtue of being a lone European in the native provinces, to being treated with slavish deference, and, by virtue of being a

---

[40] Freud uses English in the original. R. Berman (1998: 149–153) points out that Freud, in his critique of psychology, in fact dismisses this much-cited colonialist metaphor, which would make feminine sexuality opaque to science.

doctor, to acknowledgment of professional authority. Moreover, the native women are reportedly submissive in respect to his sexual desires:

> Denn diese Mädchen hier, diese zwitschernden kleinen zierlichen Tierchen, die zittern ja vor Ehrfurcht, wenn ein Weißer, ein 'Herr', sie nimmt... sie löschen aus in Demut, immer sind sie einem offen, immer bereit... zu dienen.'
>
> (For the girls here, these twittering little fragile animals, who tremble with awe if a white man, a 'master,' takes them... they extinguish themselves in humility, they are always open to one, always ready... to serve.) (A, 100)

His description of the native women as animalistic and slavish starkly contrasts to the Englishwoman's impersonal demeanour, her refusal of his advances, and above all her 'Befehl' that he not follow her (A, 102). Yet she is the one whom he wants to 'colonize': while the native women are 'immer... einem offen', her sexuality is untouchable, closed off, and mysterious, and provokes his possessive desire. Her calculating and haughty distance strikes him as insubordinate. Her absolute refusal of his offer for sexual relations in exchange for his help in obtaining an abortion is enraging, for she laughs at him. In response, he feels for her 'eine Art gewalttätiger Gier' ('a sort of violent lust') (A, 98). Her Englishness is foreign to the doctor, but so is her status as another colonial European, whose ties to the tropical region are very different from his own. While the doctor's treatment of the native servant, for instance, is violent, hers is humane, trusting, and almost familial. As a foreigner within the foreign environment, she upsets the doctor's colonialist assumption of a masculine European distance and superiority. This upset leads to reversal, for the doctor's will then deteriorates from native infection; his passion overcomes and leads to his denigration, and he sacrifices himself to keep her secret. This reversal aligns him, after all, with the faithfulness of the native servant-boy and with the slavishness he attributes to natives in general. A similar reversal operates in *Der Tod in Venedig*: while Aschenbach is disgusted by the native Venetians, the singer, and the old dandy on the ship, he gradually aligns himself with what they symbolize: sordid duplicity, grotesque emotionality, and cosmetic pretensions of youth.

When the Amokläufer ventures into the Chinatown section of that city—with its opium dens, thieves' nests, and bordellos (A, 120)—in order to rescue the Englishwoman from a back-alley abortion, he resumes the role of doctor he had abandoned during his pursuit. The woman's bleeding and feverish body is no longer an object of desire but of medical urgency. His expertise is sharply contrasted to the injurious 'Chinesin', herself a foreigner within the foreign context of the East Indies. Yet her presence ironically mirrors his own failures, for while the Chinese abortionist has fatally wounded the patient in a dangerously unclean environment, the doctor has in effect driven her there, and, without even clean water at hand, is helpless to save her from both the bleeding and the fever, which together prove fatal. The doctor's subsequent resolve to keep the Englishwoman's secret even at the cost of his career and eventually his life, suggests that he has not emerged from the amok madness, which is held to end in the amok runner's death. Rather, the doctor's former and professional identity is absorbed by his disease. The vulnerability of the frame narrator to the overwhelming effects of the exotic atmosphere confirms this radical compromise as a potentially generalizable statement about European identity itself. But the frame narrator's submissive absorption of the surrounding environment also provides a contrast to the doctor's initial colonialist, aggressive attitude, so that the reader encounters two different European responses to the exotic.

CONSTRUCTIONS OF EXOTIC SPACE IN *DER ZAUBERBERG*

Zweig's novella maximizes the significance of the colonial setting and the association of the exotic with desire, irrationality, disease, barbarity, and death. The exotic setting of *Der Tod in Venedig* is likewise intimately related to Aschenbach's collapse, the 'deconstruction' of the German bourgeois subject he represents and of the ideals of European civilization invoked by Platonic philosophy.[41] Mann's use of the exotic setting is aided by inheritance of literary and cultural renderings of the city, and by the specific characteristics of its physical history, location, and structure. In *Der Zauberberg*, however, the exotic locale must be more deliberately constructed through images of the desired, mysterious, and potentially threatening foreign, superimposed onto the ostensibly neutral Alpine setting. Through its exoticization, space becomes a primary motif in the novel.

Like Aschenbach's progress towards Venice, and the doctor's arrival in the Far East, Castorp's travel to the Berghof is described in detail, with explicit reflection upon the experience of defamiliarization provoked by the fact of change in place, the landscape through which he travels, and the surroundings in which he finds himself upon arrival. A serpentine progress

---

[41] As Boa (2006: 32) also maintains.

is described, with a degree of detail that seems laborious in comparison to the lack of detail concerning the traveller himself.

> Es geht durch mehrerer Herren Länder, bergauf und bergab, von der süddeutschen Hochebene hinunter zum Gestade des Schwäbischen Meeres und zu Schiff über seine springenden Wellen hin, dahin über Schlünde, die früher für unergründlich galten.
>
> (The journey led through many landscapes, up and down the mountains, descending from the south German high plain to the shores of the Swabian Sea, and by ship across its leaping waves, passing over abysses that were once thought to be unfathomable.) (FA5.1, 11)

The details here already begin to describe the topography in metaphorical terms. In contrast to the 'Hochebene' or plateau of southern Germany (itself metaphorically suggestive of a stable, unsurprising vista at a moderate but not drastic elevation), the mountain terrain, evoked within the narrative sweep of a single sentence, is reached by traversing elevations and depressions and crossing by ship over unstable waters and abyssal depths once thought unfathomable. Crossing over water in all three texts discussed in this chapter highlights the difference from familiar German territory and the parallel voyage into the depths of the self. The passage up and down the mountains disallows any identification of the Alpine destination as an unequivocal symbol for spiritual elevation. The image of abyssal depths, which are presumably now fathomable, anticipates, too, the probing of Castorp's psychic depths at the Berghof, and other ventures into the once unknown. The ascent veers towards seeming endlessness, provoking an anxiety in Castorp that is exacerbated by the passing view of crevices and gorges between the peaks.

The role of landscape in the constitution of experience, and particularly the experience of temporality, is highlighted through an imagined 'Strandspaziergang' ('walk on the beach'). Having described the inner changes in Castorp, in particular with respect to his sense of time, the narrator turns to a reflection on landscape. Here the Alpine surroundings and their effect on Castorp are described indirectly, through the analogy with the experience of strolling by the sea, of which the snowy Alps reminds him. This 'landscape' described is a seascape, the monotonous vista of which fosters perceptual confusion through dissolution of ordinary spatial perspective:

> Es gibt auf Erden eine Lebenslage, gibt landschaftliche Umstände (wenn man von 'Landschaft' sprechen darf in dem uns vorschwebenden Falle), unter denen eine solche Verwirrung und Verwischung der zeitlich-räumlichen Distanzen bis zur schwindeligen Einerleiheit gewissermaßen von Natur und Rechtes wegen statthat.... Wir meinen den Spaziergang am Meerestrande.

(There is a situation in life on earth, situations of landscape (if one may speak of 'landscape' in the case we have in mind), under which a certain confusion and obliteration of spatio-temporal distances to the point of vertiginous homogeneity is more or less natural and right. . . . We mean a stroll on the seashore.) (FA5.1, 824)

The narrator invites the reader to imagine a beloved seascape, and then addresses the sea directly, describing an imaginary walk among the dunes. The spatial experience has direct bearing on the experience of time. The vastness of the spatial monotony of the water and waves and the seemingly endless horizon give the impression of unmeasured space in which time is no longer felt: 'in ungemessener Monotonie des Raumes ertrinkt die Zeit, Bewegung von Punkt zu Punkt ist keine Bewegung mehr, wenn Einerleiheit regiert, und wo Bewegung nicht mehr Bewegung ist, ist keine Zeit' ('time drowns in the immeasurable monotony of space, movement from point to point is no longer movement when uniformity reigns, and where there is no longer movement, there is no time') (FA5.1, 825). The capacity of monotonous space to swallow up time, to shelter one in eternity gives space a prominent role in Castorp's transformation. That the 'Strandspaziergang' is linked to the Alpine landscape is powerfully evident in the 'Schnee' chapter (to be discussed shortly), in which the snowy mountains evoke images of the sea. The snowy Alps and the vast sea have common metaphysical associations—'die Urmonotonie des Naturbildes war beiden Sphären gemeinsam' ('the primordial monotony of nature's image was common to both realms')—and these will be Oriental (FA5.1, 711).

The analogy between the snowy Alpine landscape and the 'Strandspaziergang', in respect to the monotony of time and the vastness of unarticulated space, is associated with an Eastern and Asian sensibility. Spatial defamiliarization and gradual alienation from his home render Castorp— and the civilization for which he stands—vulnerable to the exotic. Elements that are not only foreign but also alluring and mysterious, render the atmosphere of the Berghof and the surrounding landscape as an exotic place. That the seductiveness of the exotic is explicitly linked to illness and death makes it also dangerous, both physically and spiritually. More drastically, the struggle within Castorp's soul is also represented, through the pedagogical speeches of Settembrini and more implicitly, as a struggle for Western civilization itself. Chauchat represents one of many foreign influences, but her Slavic association with the Asian is particularly threatening, evoking the ambiguous associations of desire and fear that attend what can be regarded as a historically 'colonial' relationship between Germany and its Eastern neighbours, a relationship that also pertains to

Aschenbach's possessive admiration for Tadzio,[42] but which in both cases is ambiguous, in so far as it is the German protagonist who submits. A Russian (with a French surname from her husband), Chauchat comes from far-off Daghestan beyond the Caucasus, 'einer so wilden, entfernten Gegend' ('such a wild, remote region') (FA5.1, 210), both geographically and in large part culturally cut off from Europe: 'Daghestan, wissen Sie, das liegt ganz östlich über den Kaukasus hinaus' ('Daghestan, you know, that lies far east beyond the Caucasus') (FA5.1, 209). The rendering of the Russian-Slavic as Asian is repeatedly evoked by reference to her slanted ('schräge') and peculiarly coloured eyes, which seem to Castorp not merely similar, but identical, to those of Castorp's childhood love, Pribislav Hippe.

While the Asian-Oriental is the most threatening to Castorp because of its seductive power, there are many manifestations of foreignness in the novel, though these may not be authentically represented.[43] The most severe of these is the cannibalistic sacrifice in the 'Schnee' ('Snow') vision, which has Northern European, rather than classical, connotations, since the child is blonde and the witchlike women curse in a Hamburg dialect.[44] The Southern European is also present in symbolic details: the Spanish ruff of the grandfather's senatorial robes, the Spanish-speaking woman 'Tous-les-deux' who is linguistically isolated, and whose sons both die at the sanatorium, Settembrini from Italy, and Naphta, with his defence of the Spanish Inquisition. But the moral and physical seduction of Hans Castorp, like that of Aschenbach in *Der Tod in Venedig*, is associated by his submission to the allure of the Eastern-Slavic, and here a presumed spiritual alignment with the Asian or Oriental. 'Hier liegt vor allem viel Asien in der Luft' ('here there is above all much Asia in the air') warns Settembrini (FA5.1, 368). Pribislav Hippe, like Aschenbach, is a mixture of Slavic and Germanic heritage. Castorp's seduction by Chauchat is associated with submission to the Asian sense of time and space, the Oriental Weltanschauung as opposed to the European. The implication for Castorp's own native Germanness carried by the Eastern element Chauchat represents is suggested by the fact that her pronunciation in German, not French or Russian, excites him and is described as exotic.

---

[42] Robertson (2000a: 116).

[43] Koppen (1988: 41–42) gives a partial register of nationalities, but does not explain their symbolic function in the novel. Rau's (1994: 89) account is more challenging, arguing that the ubiquity of stereotypical representatives of internationality in Mann's works highlights the problem of Germanness. Although she does not address *Der Zauberberg*, Elizabeth Boa's (2006) point that characters in *Der Tod in Venedig* often fail to conform to national stereotypes is pertinent here as well. See also Elsaghe (1997) and (2000).

[44] Robertson (2006: 58).

The reports by Herr Ferge about the style of life in Russia link Chauchat again both to the Northern and Asian exotic.

> Auch von der dortigen Menschenart, ihrer nördlichen und darum in seinen Augen desto abenteuerlicheren Exotik, ließ er Herrn Ferge erzählen, von dem asiatischen Einschuß ihres Geblütes.
> (And he listened to Herr Ferge tell of the sort of people there, of the northern and thus all the more adventurous exoticism in their eyes, of the shot of Asia in their blood.) (FA5.1, 472)

The exotic, here as the Northern-Asian, is explicitly contrasted to the Western world-view through the pedagogical warnings of Settembrini. The exotic is associated with sloth and entropy, sensuousness, dark femininity, illness, barbarity, and animality. In Settembrini's Eurocentric view, the European and the Asian are polar opposites. The European stands for law, freedom, knowledge, rebellion and criticism, world-transforming activity and progress, while the Eastern represents luxurious sensuality, raw power, superstition, historical immobility, fatigue, and inertia. Castorp's seduction by Chauchat, heightened by his growing affinity for illness and death, suggests that the Alpine setting is dangerously open to infection by the 'asiatische Princip' ('Asian principle') (FA5.1, 240). In reference to the Russians, Settembrini warns Castorp:

> richten Sie sich innerlich nicht nach ihnen, lassen Sie sich von ihren Begriffen nicht infizieren, setzen Sie vielmehr Ihr Wesen, Ihr höheres Wesen gegen das ihre, und halten Sie heilig, was Ihnen, dem Sohn des Westens, des göttlichen Westens,—dem Sohn der Zivilisation, nach Natur und Herkunft heilig ist.
> (do not orient yourself inwardly towards them, do not become infected by their ideas, rather compare your own essence, your higher essence, to theirs, and hold sacred what is by nature and heritage holy to a son of the West, of the divine West, to a son of civilization.) (FA5.1, 368)

As a 'son of civilization', Castorp is in danger of spiritual 'infection'; Settembrini's warning makes explicit the analogies between tubercular contagion and sensual love and the relation of both to the exotic East.

Among other associations, Russian sensibility is aligned with the Asian experience of time and space, which Settembrini views as degenerate. Under its influence Castorp succumbs to what not only Settembrini but also Castorp's Prussian cousin, regard as moral degeneration.

> Diese Freigebigkeit, diese barbarische Großartigkeit im Zeitverbrauch ist asiatischer Stil,—das mag ein Grund sein, weshalb es den Kindern des Ortens an diesem Orte behagt.

(This liberality, this barbaric generosity in the use of time is the Asian style—that may be a reason why the children of the East are compelled by this place.) (FA5.1, 369)

This barbaric relationship to time in the East is here linked to the experience of time at the Berghof and explains the Russians' affinity for the lifestyle of the sanatorium. But this sensibility is also explicitly related to the geographical space of Asian lands:

> Leicht zu denken, daß die Nonchalance dieser Menschen im Verhältnis zur Zeit mit einer wilden Welträumigkeit ihres Landes zusammenhängt. Wo viel Raum ist, da ist viel Zeit. . . . Nehmen Sie unsere großen Städte als Sinnbild, diese Zentren und Brennpunkte der Zivilisation. . . . In demselben Maße, wie der Boden sich dort verteuert, Raumverschwendung zur Unmöglichkeit wird, in demselben Maße . . . wird dort auch die Zeit immer kostbarer.
>
> (It is easy to think that the nonchalance of these people in their relation to time is connected with the savage spaciousness of their land. Wherever there is a lot of space, there is more time. . . . Take, for example, our cities as a symbol, these centres and focal points of civilization. . . . In the same measure, that the ground becomes more precious, wasting space is impossible, in the same measure, so too time becomes more precious.) (FA5.1, 369)

The European continent, with its dense cities, is characterized by the contraction and focus of human energy, which is reflected in the efficient use of time, as Simmel argued in 'Die Großstädte und das Geistesleben' ('The Metropolis and Mental Life') and *Philosophie des Geldes (Philosophy of Money)*. Germans, for example, are characterized as phlegmatic and energetic but also 'hart und kalt' 'hard and cold' (FA5.1, 301). The Asian-Russian continent, with its vast spaces unconquered by civilizing habitation, allows for expansion of time and correlate slackness, dissipation of energy, such as the doctor experiences in *Der Amokläufer* as he festers in the tropical wilderness. When Castorp is first visited by a memory of Pribislav Hippe, his nosebleed reduces him to a state of 'sonderbarer herabgesetzter Lebenstätigkeit' ('peculiarly reduced vivacity') (FA5.1, 183), indicating infection by Asiatic sloth and sensuousness similar to that which also overtakes Aschenbach at the Munich cemetery and again in Venice. Settembrini identifies inactivity as a defining principle of the Asiatic world-view:

> Der Osten verabscheut die Tätigkeit. Laotse lehrte, daß Nichtstun förderlicher sei als jedes Ding zwischen Himmel und Erde.
>
> (The East rejects activity. Laotse teaches that doing nothing is more demanding than anything between heaven and earth.) (FA5.1, 568)

Inactivity is associated not only with reduced vitality but also, for the European, with physical and spiritual death. Because the 'Zauberberg' ('magic mountain') is saturated by Asian influences, Castorp's soul is endangered. Settembrini warns:

> Nur im Tiefland können Sie Europäer sein, das Leiden auf Ihre Art aktiv bekämpfen, den Fortschritt fördern, die Zeit nutzen ... verlieren Sie sich nicht an das Fremde!
>
> (You can be a European only in the flatlands, actively fight suffering in your own way, promoting progress, using time well ... do not lose yourself in a foreign world! (FA5.1, 375)

Through these associations, the space of *Der Zauberberg* is constructed by symbolic and physical contest with exotic forces. The Alpine setting cannot be regarded then as a 'blank space' within which identities are projected and contested.[45] Castorp's particular experience of the surroundings, his enchantment, and the process by which he submits to it, seem to evade a colonialist impulse. For Castorp yields submissively to erotic seduction and physical illness; he proceeds not through masculine self-assertion and determination, but through gradual abandonment of will and 'European' dignity. His most powerful visions (the memory of Hippe, the 'Schnee' vision) are characterized by diminution of vitality and opiumlike intoxication associated by Settembrini with the Oriental. The inertia and stupor of Castorp's eventual collapse are associated with the anonymity of the individual in Asian culture.

The surrounding landscape is also rendered exotic through the overlay of exotic images upon those of the natural surroundings. While Nenno's characterization of the space as 'blank' neglects the power of this exotic construction, Engelberg's equation of the *Zauberberg* with a symbolic East risks reducing the significance of Castorp's deep affinity for it. Engelberg claims that the East is 'transplanted onto the mountain' as an 'alien territory'.[46] But Castorp's vulnerability to exotic influences suggests the presence of the exotic impulses within his own German nature. Thus, the novel is not set in the East, but in the heart of Western Europe; and his most powerful vision in the 'Schnee' chapter refers to the cultural sources of Western civilization.

As in the novellas discussed above, a deep resonance emerges between Castorp's own cultural identity and the exotic influences. This conflict is

---

[45] In focusing on the 'colonialization' of blank cartographical space and the 'colonizing impulse' that in her view links the Alpinist to the expeditioner to foreign lands, Nenno (1996: 305, 314) overlooks some of the features of Castorp's experience of the exotic.

[46] Engelberg (1999: 106).

in part displaced onto the arguments between Settembrini and Naphta, who each represent cultural values that might influence Castorp. But this resonance is also suggested by the evocation of childhood memories. Details from Castorp's own German childhood have prepared for his vulnerability to the exotic: the grandfather's exotic appearance in his portrait, the love for Pribislav, the description of Hamburg as a port city, with traffic from exotic places and the smells and sights of the wares brought back from such, and Castorp's early acquaintance with death. Although both 'mittelmäßig' and 'hochzivilisiert' ('average' and 'highly civilized'), Castorp succumbs to foreign forces that resonate within him. The exposure to the exotic draws up the primitive stirring deep within his own nature. Thus, the exotic rendering of the 'Zauberberg' is highly ambiguous: it is both foreign and, while radically defamiliarizing, resonant of some forgotten aspects of home. Like the suggestion of Castorp's inherited tendency to illness, a latent vulnerability to foreign influence belongs to Castorp's heritage, just as it does to Aschenbach's, from his dark and sensuous Bohemian mother.

This latent tendency is suggested by the intertwining of images from the past and present. Contemplating his desire for Chauchat, Castorp recalls a landscape image of a canoe ride at twilight on a lake in Holstein, which he first recollected while listening to Settembrini's discourse on the opposition of European and Asian world-views. From his canoe Castorp observes, just after sundown, a lingering daylight to the West, whereas turning to the East he can see 'eine... höchst zauberhafte, von feuchten Nebeln durchsponnene Mondnacht' ('a most magical moonlit night, enveloped in moist fog') (FA5.1, 236). Castorp is floating on waters that situate him between Western daylight and an enchanting Eastern night. Castorp recalls the image a second time, where onto it is superimposed an image of Chauchat:

> Dort befand sich... Clawdia Chauchat,—schlaff, wurmstichig und kirgise-
> näugig; und indem Hans Castorp ihrer gedachte... war es ihm wieder, als
> säße er im Kahn auf jenem holsteinischen See und blickte aus der glasigen
> Tageshelle des westlichen Ufers... hinüber in die nebeldurchsponnene
> Mondnacht der östlichen Himmel.
> (There was... Clawdia Chauchat—limp, worm-eaten, and Kirghiz-eyed;
> and when Hans Castorp thought of her... it seemed again that he was sitting
> in the canoe on that lake in Holstein and looked from the glassy daylight of
> the Western shore... over to the moonlight night, enveloped in fog, of the
> Eastern sky.) (FA5.1, 245)

The exotic image of Chauchat recalls an early view of landscape and sky in Castorp's native land, symbolizing now the polarity between Western civilization, with its diminishing light of reason, and the enchanting Eastern moonlight.

Just as Aschenbach's fate is tied to the specific topography of Venice, the setting of *Der Zauberberg* is by no means—as Peter Rau suggests of both places among other settings of internationality and foreignness in Mann's fiction—broadly interchangeable. In Rau's account Mann's settings outside Germany offer generalized spheres of internationality that effect dissolution of national and individual identity.[47] But this dissolution occurs in both texts through specific topographical means. The topography of the Alps is given exotic colouring through description of the weather and seasons, as well as particular elements of the landscape experienced during Castorp's outings, each of which induces or presages a major psychological event. Atmospheric elements—the air, light, and weather—seem to participate in the protagonist's transformation. For the climate is not only good for treating illness, it also brings 'latent' illness to the fore. Perhaps the most estranging and powerful element is the confusion of the seasons, which persistently defy any logical expectations. This motif is familiar from the Munich walk in *Der Tod in Venedig*, where a May afternoon is sultry as if in August. Here this motif is persistently evoked in the narrative. The peculiarity of the climate refuses meteorological order: one finds snow in the middle of the summer, and a sultry sunny day in November. This uncanny reversal of seasons leads one to equate winter and summer, an erasure of oppositions that reflects the Berghof sense of reality, its perverted metaphysics. Just as the cultural oppositions between health and illness, death and life, seem to give way, so to the weather leads to psychological and existential confusion.

Along with the weather, three scenes of outings into the nature surrounding the Berghof suggest the exotic rendering of the Alpine landscape, here through the intertwining of images of nature with those of the Eastern-Asian that so seduces Castorp. The first walk through the landscape provokes memories of Castorp's childhood love Pribislav Hippe, with his exotic Slavic features, and recognition of the latter's connection to Chauchat. While Chauchat had reminded Castorp of something he could not quite conjure up, the intoxicating solitude he experiences while resting from the mountain walk enables the definite and detailed recollection, in particular, of Hippe's Slavic physiognomy. Following this, images of the common Asian-exotic features of the desired figures are intertwined with those of landscape.

[47] Rau (1994: 97).

Somewhat reminiscent of Castorp's initial approach to the sanatorium, the progress of his first outing into nature is serpentine: 'Er stieg noch höher, in Serpentinen' ('He kept climbing higher, along the serpentine path') (FA5.1, 181). He finds himself in a landscape that seems its own world; swallowed by a pine forest, and then, finding his way out again, standing before 'einer intim geschlossenen Landschaft von friedlich-großartiger Bildmäßigkeit' ('an intimately secluded landscape of peaceful magnificent painterliness'). The landscape seems to envelop him; and then he stands before the scenery as if before a painting. Any aesthetic disinterestedness that might be suggested by this painterly description would soon dissipate, for the solitude has an intoxicating effect—'Rauschende Abgeschiedenheit waltete über dem schönen, einsamen Ort' ('A rustle of isolation reigned above this beautiful, remote place') (FA5.1, 182). The effect of his walk in the elevated atmosphere is also physical: a nosebleed overcomes and exhausts him, and he lies on a bench inert, with diminished vitality, a point that is recollected again later. A memory transports him into a previous stage of life, 'die das Urbild eines nach neusten Eindrücken gemodelten Traumes war' ('which was the original image of a dream first modelled after new impressions') (FA5.1, 183). The 'Bildmäßigkeit' of the painterly landscape is now superimposed with the 'Urbild' of Castorp's memory. It is a memory of Pribislav Hippe and his exotic appearance to the German pupils of Castorp's school. Although he is blond (like the child devoured in the 'Schnee' vision), Hippe has an exotic appearance owing to protruding cheekbones and slanted 'Kirgisenaugen' (FA5.1, 187), among other features, resulting from 'einer alten Rassenmischung, einer Versetzung germanischen Blutes mit wendisch-slawischem—oder auch umgekehrt' ('an ancient mixing of races, a mixing of German blood with Slavic-Wendish—or also the other way around') (FA5.1, 184). The colour of his eyes is described in ambiguous, metaphorically laden terms, which link the memory to Castorp's present surroundings in the Alps. Just as the Alpine seasons cannot be distinguished from one another given the strange turns of weather, Hippe's eyes are of a not precisely determinable colour: 'blaugrau oder graublau vom Farbe—es war eine etwas unbestimmte und mehrdeutige Farbe, die Farbe etwa eines fernen Gebirges' ('blue-gray or grey-blue in colour—it was an indeterminate and equivocal colour, something like that of a far mountain') (FA5.1, 184). The description of Chauchat's appearance, 'von nördlicher Exotik und geheimnisreich' ('northernly exotic and mysterious') is similar (FA5.1, 223). Indeed, Castorp identifies her eyes as those of Pribislav (FA5.1, 191). Clawdia's, too, are 'schlechthin zauberhaft geschnittenen Kirgisenaugen, deren Farbe das Graublau oder Blaugrau ferner Berge war' ('absolutely magically shaped Kirghiz-eyes, with the grey-blue or blue-grey colour of faraway mountains') (FA5.1, 223). The description of the exotic colouring of the eyes of both beloveds with distant mountains suggests that Castorp's infatuation on the magic mountain recalls a primal *Fernweh* first evoked in childhood.

The description of the landscape in the 'Schnee' chapter resonates with several suggestions about the Oriental-Asian made elsewhere in the novel. The space is homogenized by the snow, so that an all-reigning whiteness erases distinctions between mountain and sky; the world is blurred, and the view of human habitation in the valley is completely obscured. Like the sea described in 'Strandspaziergang' in the following chapter, the landscape becomes a monotonous void; but here the tone is negative: a 'dunstige Nichts', 'gewaltig nichtssagend' ('misty nothing', 'powerfully reticent'). Castorp is lost 'im Eisig-Leeren' ('in the icy void') (FA5.1, 720). The position of the sun, the Platonic symbol for rational order and the good, is obscured: 'Der Stand der Sonne war kaum zu erkennen, so dicht umnebelt war sie' ('the position of the sun could hardly be determined, it was so thickly wrapped in fog') (FA5.1, 722). Instead of universal forms, the absolute individuality of snowflakes fascinates Castorp, as he examines 'den Myriaden von Zaubersternchen' ('the myriads of magical stars'). Unlike the stars themselves (the movement of which in the Platonic view generate the imperceptible music of the spheres and symbolizes the rational order of the universe), the regularity of these star-shaped crystals of snow is not associated with life but is 'das Geheimnis des Todes selbst' ('the secret of death itself') (FA5.1, 723). Recalling Aschenbach's last vision of Tadzio in the sea, here the blurring of objects, including the sun, into a blank monotony, suggests the vastness of great Asian plains and the Russian steppes, and metaphorically the Oriental relation to space and time vilified by Settembrini.

> Dabei jedoch war gar kein Vergnügen, denn man sah nichts vor Flockentanz, der scheinbar ohne zu fallen in dichtestem Wirbelgedränge allen Raum erfüllte. . . . Es war das Nichts, das weiße, wirbelnde Nichts, worein er blickte, wenn er sich zwang, zu sehen.
>
> (But in this there was no enjoyment in it, for one could see nothing in the dance of snowflakes, which, apparently without falling, filled all of the space in a dense swirling crush. . . . It was nothingness, the white, swirling nothingness into which he gazed, when he forced himself to see.) (FA5.1, 727–728)

Castorp's unchartered progress is a venture into the void, a 'weißliche Transzendenz' ('whitish transcendence') (FA5.1, 721); but it also evokes images of the 'Kirgisenaugen' that will be directly intertwined with place. When Castorp pierces the snow with his ski pole, he sees a blue light emitted from the depths of the hole.

Es war so ein eigentümliches zartes Berg- und Tiefenlicht, grünlich-blau, eisklar und doch schattig, geheimnisvoll anziehend. Es erinnerte ihn an das Licht und die Farbe gewisser Augen, schicksalblickender Schrägaugen, die Herr Settembrini vom humanistischen Standpunkte aus verächtlich als 'Tartarenschlitze' und 'Steppenwolfslichter' bezeichnet hatte,—an früh erschaute und unvermeidlich wiedergefundene, an Hippe's und Clawdia Chauchat's Augen.

(It was such a peculiar tender light of the mountains and from the depths, greenish-blue, clear as ice and yet shadowy, alluringly mysterious. It re-minded him of the light and the colour of certain eyes, slanted eyes that looked into destiny, which Herr Settembrini, from a humanistic standpoint, had described disdainfully as 'Tartar-slits' and 'Steppenwolf-eyes'—it reminded him of eyes he had seen early in life and inevitably found again, of Hippe's and Clawdia Chauchat's eyes.) (FA5.1, 721)

This light of the depths, evocative of the Russian steppes and the Tartar race, is directly opposed in this passage to the humanistic Western sensibility represented by Settembrini. The slant on which Castorp glides for a while ('an der Schräge') recalls this image of slanted-Asian eyes ('Schrägaugen') so often evoked in the novel, as in the passage above (FA5.1, 733, 721). As the snowstorm rages, Castorp is soon overtaken by fear, confronting 'blinde und unwissende Elemente' most terrifying in their monstrous indifference to life. It recalls the description of Daghestan beyond the Caucasus, beyond the topographical boundary that divides Europe from Asia. The snowy landscape, further, is aligned with images of desert ('Dünenlandschaft') and sea ('Seeluft'), further indicating the vulnerability of this space to imaginary exoticization.

es sei wie bei einem Sandsturm in der Wüste, der die Araber veranlasse, sich aufs Gesicht zu werfen und den Burnus über den Kopf zu ziehen.

(it was like in a sandstorm in the desert, where the Arab would throw himself facedown and pull his burnous over his head.) (FA5.1, 731–732)

While this image of an Arab in the desert is culturally and topographically foreign, it does not evoke the intense longing associated with the Asiatic-Russian images, or with the Mediterranean, possibly Greek landscape of Castorp's lush hallucination (FA5.1, 740); it serves, rather, to identify the surrounding space as the exotic per se. In the hallucination Castorp enters into a landscape of sunlight, youth, and beauty, all classical Greek values enchantingly described in Castorp's vision, and since the eighteenth century linked with the spiritual destiny of the German *Geist*. The classical image of Arcadia is attended by the suggestion of the Platonic theory of recollection, 'Ja, das war eigentümlicherweise ein Wiedererkennen' ('Yes, it was, strangely enough, a recollection') (FA5.1, 740). While the narrative treatment of this theory in *Der Tod in Venedig* is largely ironic, implying Aschenbach's misuse of philosophy to justify his predatory paedophilia, here the tone is less a personal indictment of the much younger Castorp, than an exposure of his vulnerabilities. The primal experience is now re-envisioned in the dreamer's soul; this recalls the 'früh erschaute und unvermeidlich wiedergefundene' images of the Slavic-Asian eyes. The dream vision's turn to the nightmarish scene of cannibalistic sacrifice is hideous, and any Platonic resonances are abandoned. That the old women devouring a child speak Hamburg dialect, however, disallows displacement of the violence onto the foreign or exotic. The resulting insight, of which Castorp maintains only a brief command (the dream fades before he reaches the Berghof), suggests a sharp critique, through a foreign image, of Castorp's own civilization:

> Mir träumte vom Stande des Menschen und von seinen höflich-verständigen und ehrerbietigen Gemeinschaft, hinter der im Tempel das gräßliche Blutmahl sich abspielt. Waren sie so höflich und reizend zueinander, die Sonnenleute, im stillen Hinblick auf eben dies Gräßliche?
>
> (I dreamed about the state of man and of man's polite, reasonable, respectful community, as a ghastly bloody feast went on in the temple behind them. Were they so courteous and charming to each other, these people of the sun, in silent regard for just that ghastliness?) (FA5.1, 747)

In view of the grotesque and murderous ritual in the temple, the children of the sun remain undisturbed. This image leads to the suggestion that those forces one would have opposed as opposites—life and death, reason and brutality, the Western principle and the Asian—are in fact intimately related. The 'homo Dei' must stand 'in der Mitte' ('in the middle') (FA5.1, 747). As Freud attempted to show, the primitive lies within. When Castorp awakens from his vision, the weather clears, suggesting a direct correlation between circumstances of landscape and Castorp's inner life.

The description of a third outing allows for a rendering of the Alpine landscape in exotic tones. Castorp's trip to the waterfall includes the company of some exotic figures, including Peeperkorn—the Dutch coffee grower from the East Indies whose tropical disease ('maligne Tropenmitgift') is exacerbated by the unusual climate of the 'Zauberberg' (FA5.1, 929)—along with Peeperkorn's Malay servant, and Chauchat. The landscape itself is exoticized in ways that will be particularly resonant with the figure of Peeperkorn. In order to arrive at the waterfall, they must pass through a forest disfigured by lichen:

> Der Wald war nicht wie andere, er bot einen malerisch eigentümlichen, ja exotischen, doch unheimlichen Anblick. Er strotzte von einer Sorte moosiger

Flechten, war damit behangen, beladen, ganz und gar darin eingewickelt, in langen, mißfarbenen Bärten baumelte das verfilzte Gewirk der Schmarotzerpflanze von seine umsponnenen, gepolsterten Zweigen: man sah fast keine Nadeln, man sah lauter Moosgehänge,—eine schwere, bizarre Entstellung, ein verzauberter und krankhafter Anblick. Dem Walde ging es nicht gut, er krankte an dieser geilen Flechte, sie drohte ihn zu ersticken. (This forest was not like others; it offered a peculiarly painterly, even exotic, uncanny view. It teemed with a sort of mossy lichen, was laden with it, draped, entirely wrapped up in it, in long, miscoloured beards that dangled from branches already cushioned and webbed in it: one could see hardly any needles, one saw a mossy draping, a heavy, bizarre disfiguration, a sickly enchanted scenery. The forest was not well, it was sickly from this rank lichen, which threatened to suffocate it.) (FA5.1, 938)

The description of the forest is suggestive of disease and death, as in the 'Urweltwildnis' and its strange trees in Aschenbach's vision, and the steamy tropics in which the doctor runs amok in Zweig's novella. Yet it is also aesthetically intriguing, as India is to the German tourist on the 'Oceania', offering a painterly ('malerisch') uniqueness, perhaps reminiscent of the gloomy nature scenes of Romantic painters, but also reminiscent of the narrator's aesthetic terminology ('Bildmäßigkeit' and 'Urbild') in describing Castorp's first outing into nature. The lichen's eerie devouring of the forest recalls Settembrini's warnings about the Asian influence—'Asien verschlingt uns'—and his association of the Eastern with an inert submission to disease. In a castigation of Castorp, he argues:

Aber auch Ihr Verhalten zum Leiden sollte ein europäisches Verhalten sein—nicht das des Ostens, der, weil er weich und zur Krankheit geneigt ist, diesen Ort so ausgiebig beschickt. . . . Mitleid und unermeßliche Geduld, das ist seine Art, dem Leiden zu begegnen.

(But your reaction to suffering should also be a European one—not that of the East which, because it is weak and prone to suffering, is so well represented here. . . . Sympathy and endless patience, that is its way of encountering suffering.) (FA5.1, 370)

The trees seem to represent the passivity and even cultivation of illness with which Settembrini associates an Eastern sensibility. The description of the lichen itself, while eerie, is also sexually suggestive, for the adjective 'geil', which also appears in Aschenbach's tropical vision (FA2.1, 504), is used to describe the parasitic growth nearly suffocating the trees; it threatens to take full possession of them. The image of the silently disfigured forest provides a counterpoint to the 'Höllenspektakel' ('hellish spectacle') of the roaring waterfall, the sound of which is violently masculine:

diese Dauerkatastrophe aus Schaum und Geschmetter, deren irres und über-mäßiges Brausen sie betäubte, ihnen Furcht erregte und Gehörstäuschungen verursachte. Man glaubte hinter sich, über sich, von allen Seiten drohende und warnende Rufe zu hören, Posaunen und rohe Männerstimmen.

(this incessant catastrophe of chaotic foam, the intense and insane roar of which deafened them, provoked fear and auditory confusion in them. One believed to hear threatening and warning calls, trumpet calls and raw male voices, from behind, from above, from all sides.) (FA5.1, 939)

The nature here described then evokes disfigurement, disease, and mascu-line sexual threat, anticipating the imminent fate of the exotic figure of Peeperkorn, who carries both Northern European physiognomy and tropical disease, and who will soon commit suicide in response to his own impotence painfully contrasting to revelation Chauchat's sexual affair with Castorp. Images of both the falls and the forest are superimposed onto images of Peeperkorn. Amidst the roar and spray of the falls, Peeperkorn holds an inaudible speech in an absurd figuration as an 'idolhaft' ('idolatory') heathen priest (FA5.1, 941); that the falling water completely obscures his utterances suggests a dehumanizing submission to the natural forces. The description, too, of the forest's disfigurement and near suffocation anticipates Peeperkorn's suicide via poison that leads to suffocation and the swift disfigurement ('Entstellung') of his corpse (FA5.1, 946, 944). At both the waterfall speech and the suicide scene, the Malay servant is standing in attendance, and at the latter he wears a native costume, a fact which evidences the assistance of the servant, 'der wachhabende Exot' ('the exotic vigilant'), in Peeperkorn's suicide. The suicidal implement is likewise exotic, a syringe of ivory among other materials modelled on a cobra's bite and filled with a poison imported from the East Indies where Peeperkorn contracted his disease (FA5.1, 945). Peeperkorn, like the doctor in *Der Amokläufer*, had thus become knowledgeable about exotic substances impervious to Western science. For the German doctor Behrens can guess at the contents of the solution only in the vaguest terms: a 'Kombination von Tierischem und Pflanzli-chem' ('combination of something animal and botanical') (FA5.1, 946). The mention of plant matter cannot but echo the disfigured forest described a few paragraphs earlier, while the animal matter is kin to the Asian servant as he is depicted: 'Die braunen Tieraugen des Malaien überwachten die Szene seitwärts gerollt, so daß sie ihr Weißes zeigten' ('The brown animal eyes of the Malay watched over the scene as he rolled his eyes to the side, so that the whites showed') (FA5.1, 947). This representation of native South-east Asians as animalistic is also character-istic of *Der Amokläufer*, where the colonialist attitude is, however, implic-itly criticized.

In these ways the topography of the exotic in *Der Zauberberg* is mapped onto, if also removed from, European civilization. Castorp does not lose himself in an eastward journey, but yields to exotic seductions that infect him above the centre of his own civilization. Europe's own contradictions, its latent primitive tendencies, its own decadence seems to be brought, like a latent illness, 'zum Ausbruch' ('to eruption'). The final chapter on the First World War can be interpreted as this 'Ausbruch', though it is an ambiguous depiction. The struggle for Castorp's soul and health had concerned the maintenance of oppositions, most basically between life and death. But life and death are interchangeable whenever disease itself is eroticized. They come together in psychoanalysis via Krokowski's lectures in which love (and the promotion of life via sexual reproduction) is identified as illness. In Castorp's perverted analysis of materiality and spirit in the 'Forschung' ('Research') chapter, Castorp looks to pathological biology for an explanation of life as infection. He attempts to find the link between inert matter and organic life, thus closing the gap between life and non-life, or death. The collapse of this opposition signifies nothing less than the endangerment of Western thought, a return to Heraclitean chaos. Mastering contradictions (after the 'Schnee' vision) leads not to a productive dialectic, but to nihilism. The insight that arrives with the apocalyptic vision fails to motivate a change in Castorp's outlook, and his stupor suggests both indifference to and infection by the forces with which he has tarried.

By the novel's end, it seems that life and death are no longer separable for the narrator either. For in the final chapter it is the outbreak of war, its death and destruction, that shocks Castorp out of his Asian-Oriental 'Stumpfsinn'. The presentation is ambiguous, but it recalls Kant's ambivalent acceptance of war as a means to sharpen human capacities, and his depiction of war as sublime.[48] The battlefield scene is ambiguous, with the feverish energy of the soldiers representing life amidst the brutalities of modernized warfare. Castorp's entrance into the war might bring to symbolic consummation the fragile and potentially explosive contest between irreconcilable forces.[49] If Venice and its morally destabilizing infection expose Aschenbach to his own repressed desire, the exotic topography of the 'Zauberberg' provokes an exotic defamiliarization at a hermetic remove from European civilization, which seems to be threatened most by the precariousness of its own repression of what might come 'zum Ausbruch'. The ending of *Der Zauberberg* seems to bring to fruition the dark omen at the beginning of the pre-war novella,

---

[48] Kant, *Kritik der Urteilskraft*, 263 (Ak).   [49] See Gökberk (1999: 68).

the story of which begins 'an einem Frühlingsnachmittag des Jahres 19...das unserem Kontinent monatelang eine so gefahrdrohende Miene zeigte' ('On a Spring afternoon of the year 19...which had shown our continent such a menacing countenance for months') (FA2.1, 501). Evocations of the distant foreign, and its invasion of Castorp's psychic and physical world through sexual penetration and infection, draw out the latent primitive close to the heart of Castorp's own origins. In at least these senses, then, *Der Zauberberg*, like *Der Tod in Venedig*, and *Der Amokläufer*, a sharp critique of the European and German self is expressed through the infectious-erotic rendering of place.

CONCLUSION

In this chapter it has been shown how the construction of exotic spaces through metaphors of sexuality and disease challenges the European sense of self. Autonomy, rationality, and presumed cultural superiority collapse as protagonists yield to destructive seductions by the exotic. Associations with disease and death, but also with powerful sexual allure, render the foreigners and foreign places in these works dangerously provocative. Rational, autonomous, even ordinary bourgeois selves—a celebrated writer, a doctor, a young engineer, all German—seem to be ruptured by, and in some sense become vessels for, mysterious, uncontrollable, and intoxicating forces. In each case these forces are associated with the primitive, with the Asian-Oriental, the Eastern; and in each case they are depicted in the context of contagion.

While the structure and generic characteristics of *Der Zauberberg* differ considerably from the two novellas, the contest presented between the self and the exotic is similarly constructed. The descent to Venice and the exile to colonial India expose the respective protagonists to the infectious influences of environments rendered exotic through narrative description. In Mann's novella, Venice serves as the unguarded port of entry for exotic influences (African winds, Asian pestilence, and Eastern European travellers). In Zweig's novella, the exotic space of the East Indies is appropriated by the European colonist who, radically compromised by it, can neither master nor stave off the forces it unleashes within him. The exotic space of *Der Zauberberg*, in contrast, must be more elaborately constructed through the overlaying of foreign, desirous, and mysterious images onto the Alpine setting. The 'Zauberberg' signifies then not an empirical location, but an imaginative construction seemingly cut off from Europe as if in another world. While this construction requires the massive detail and expansive narrative space that the epic form of the novel affords, it also draws upon the kinds of associations with exotic places that are more historically rooted in the settings of the novellas. In all of these works, the setting is significantly distanced from European everyday life. This distance is, however, partly obscured by the duality of the exotic locales. While in *Der Tod in Venedig* the Lido hotel offers Aschenbach his accustomed class comforts and the illusion of normality, the magical architecture of Venice itself rests on stilts that are slowly sinking into the sea, and the city is infected by cholera. The 'Zauberberg' is reached by passing over water, and seems suspended above the flatlands, while the climate and the Berghof environment encourage tubercular infection. The Amokläufer's story is told to the narrator on a ship in the Naples harbour, from which the doctor also plunges to his death in the sea; in the East Indies he had succumbed to the mental breakdown. The doubling of these settings—Lido/Venice, Alps/sanatorium, ship/East Indies—allows expression of the tensions that pertain to the European conflict with the exotic. They also allow contrasting environments in which different aspects or stages of the protagonist's breakdown are provoked or become visible. The extraordinary nature of these settings for the European is in each case highlighted by the intensity of sexual desire and reckless indifference to, or even longing for, the fatal infections experienced there. Through this sexual desire and the infection bound up with it, otherness is intimately related to the self, as primitive drives are unleashed. The infectious-erotic forces each protagonist to confront or submit to primitive forces within, and exposes boundaries between self and other, between self and uncontrollable space, as fragile, even fictitious. Colonialist associations that may be evoked in these texts, through German protagonists' pursuit of a cultural 'other', are also transgressed by the consequences of such contact.

3

An Intimate Elsewhere

Imagination of Distance and Vastness in Kafka

While Kafka's contemporaries travelled to exotic places, reaping literary profit from the invigorating effects of radical change in place, Kafka, with unremarkable exceptions of some trips to places such as the Bohemian Forest, Italy, Paris, and Switzerland, more or less clung to his writing desk, and all the more so after his literary breakthrough in 1912. Yet travel itself, along with the distant and vast spaces to be examined in this chapter, such as America, China, and Russia, is an important motif in Kafka's writings. Kafka's evocation of these places is, however, far removed from realistic or historical depiction, and not only because Kafka had not travelled to them. As Adorno claims, 'fast jeder offene Hinweis auf Historisches' ('almost every reference to the historical') is avoided in Kafka; and Walter Sokel has argued that Kafka 'equates the call of literature with a hidden, powerful inner world that . . . stands in complete opposition to ordinary life'.[1] Yet this opposition and the difference between the places Kafka evokes and any empirical or historical referent offer rich potential for interpretation.

Adorno's account in 'Aufzeichnungen zu Kafka' presents Kafka's descriptive spaces as an existential void, characterized by 'unabdingbaren Entfremdung' ('unconditional alienation'). Any empirically realistic presentation of space and time is rejected in favour of 'absolut subjektiven Raum' ('absolute subjective space') said to exist only 'im objektlosen Innen' ('in objectless interiority').[2] Kafka's spaces are, accordingly, not worldly spaces at all, but depictions of an alienated subjectivity. In a similar vein, Erich Heller refers to Kafka in terms of modern subjectivity, symbolized as a land surveyor 'without land to survey'.[3] While these characterizations capture the existential resonances of some moments in Kafka's writings, both Adorno and Heller overlook the specific nature of

---

[1] Adorno (1977: 269); Sokel (2002: 69).
[2] Adorno (1977: 275).
[3] Heller (1959: 130).

the distance and difference between the empirical and the real in Kafka; the spaces Kafka describes, in so far as they depart from any real experienced place, may also liberate the writer's imagination from the given world, allowing 'distance' both from its physical realities and from social, cultural, and historical determinations from which Kafka may both depart and borrow. It will be argued in this chapter that Kafka envisages exotic places as a means to imagine escape from the familiar world in favour of imaginative possibility; and while these places may be described in terms of subjective inwardness, they also suggest imaginative exploration of unforeseen possibilities of life, intimacy, and artistic creativity that should not be reduced to alienation or an inner void.

Kafka's spaces have invited a wide range of interpretative characterizations, from the historical and psychological void to reconstructable, historically recognizable territories. In arguing that '[a]lle seine Geschichten spielen in demselben raumlosen Raum' ('all of his stories play within the same spaceless space'), Adorno homogenizes the spaces of Kafka's imagination and so overlooks specific possibilities of liberation that Kafka envisages.[4] In Adorno's account, '[e]in Bann liegt über Kafkas Raum; das in sich verschlossene Subjekt halt den Atem an, als dürfe es nichts anfassen, was nicht ist wie es' ('a spell hangs over Kafka's space—the subject, closed in itself, holds its breath, as if it may touch nothing, that is not as itself is'), and thus Adorno presents Kafka's texts as documents of existential paralysis.[5] Yet the counter-tendency of recent interpretation, informed by post-colonial or cultural studies, neutralizes altogether Kafka's deliberate transgressions of empirical realism. While Adorno risks veering towards the void, recent post-colonialist critics may err in the opposite direction. Their often innovative readings offer much insight into contemporaneous cultural discourses and practices of travel and colonialism; yet in aiming to reconstruct the historical-topographical realities and cultural ideologies that Kafka is said to represent, even when Kafka has taken pains to erase any determinate reference to them, they diminish the central motive of liberation within Kafka's imaginative generation of exotic spaces. A critical review of recent post-colonial interpretations, however, may help to illuminate the idiosyncratic nature of Kafka's 'exotic' spatial imagination, and so will be the focus of the first section of this chapter. The sections following outline the specific spaces of Russia, America, and China in terms of tensions Kafka establishes between the empirical and the imaginary. It will be seen that Kafka's images of vastness and containment, distance and obstruction, in particular, rely

[4] Adorno (1977: 268).   [5] Adorno (1977: 275).

expressly upon the relative erasure or neutralization of recognizable features of place. Through such imagery, Kafka evokes manifestations not, as Adorno would have it, of a paralysed interiority, but of 'elsewhere', where regions of possible experience, and new kinds of intimacy liberated from ordinary life and its constraints, may be (imaginatively) realized.

POST-COLONIALIST INTERPRETATIONS OF TRAVEL AND EXOTIC SPACES IN KAFKA

Following the historical turn in cultural studies and Edward Said's post-colonialist interpretations of literature, a body of recent criticism has treated exotic spaces and travel in Kafka according to a dialectic between the foreign and the *Heimat* typical of colonialist literature—wherein a place imagined as a symbolic cultural origin is discovered or established in a foreign territory—or as a critical reflection upon Orientalist ideology.[6] Travel becomes not merely a vehicle for finding new and exciting literary content but a motivation for re-examining the loss and (potential) reassertion of self through exposure to the exotic. In this context Kafka's evocation of distant places is equated with a kind of symbolic tourism and assessed in terms of colonialism. Weary of travel himself, as John Zilcosky claims, Kafka develops in the place of real travel a 'travelling style' or, as Rolf Goebel similarly argues, becomes a 'textual traveller', refashioning literary, commercial, and journalistic representations of far-off and exotic places.[7] Mark Anderson's readings of Kafka, in which the notion of a 'travelling narrative' or 'travelling text', wherein the 'protagonist has no property, is always on the road, never knows what is about to happen, and never asks why he is there at all', formulates how a central text of Kafka's 'travels', *Der Verschollene*, fundamentally differs from traditional nineteenth-century novels or 'property narratives'. Anderson resituates Kafka's texts within the exchanges of the surrounding material and semiotic culture.[8] These accounts can be appreciated in their correction of a too subjectivist or existentialist approach typified by Adorno's interpretation.

Recent treatments of Kafka's texts in post-colonial or cultural studies may be characterized by two related methodological approaches. First, critics attempt a reconstruction of historical contexts or topographical

---

[6] Anderson (1992), (1989a), (1996); Piper (1996); Peters (2001); Goebel (2002), (1997); Zilcosky (2003).
[7] Goebel (1997: 1); Zilcosky (2003), 12.
[8] Anderson (1989a: 153).

referents for Kafka's often vague or under-determined spaces.[9] For since Said, the eradication or reduction of indigenous features of a place and/or its people is seen to be aligned with symbolic colonialist appropriation; reconstruction of these features would then expose and resist such appropriation. Secondly, critics identify a dialectic operative in Kafka's writings between the familiar and foreign, or between the self and the 'other', typical of colonialist discourse.[10] Through this dialectic, writers are thought to project a sense of home upon an environment represented as foreign, thus justifying through literary description a symbolic appropriation of territory, or to present protagonists that function as symbolic colonialists. Within these frameworks of interpretation, Kafka's texts are identified either as promoting, or as deliberately undermining, colonialism or Orientalism.

While the setting of *In der Strafkolonie* is an obvious subject for postcolonial study, most of Kafka's major works have been subject to such critique. Zilcosky's study of Kafka's travels begins with the early novel fragment Kafka wrote with Max Brod, 'Richard und Samuel', as 'undermining the popular exotic discourse of the *Heimat*' in which German-speaking travellers aim to establish a sense of national 'home' within a foreign, colonized territory.[11] Goebel focuses on 'Beim Bau der Chinesischen Mauer', which offers the most distant and exotic place in all of Kafka's works, precisely because the setting is not, despite China's nineteenth-century tensions with the West, a colonial or former colonial territory of Europe, as are the penal colony and America. The space of Kafka's China is also 'distant' because, while it evokes Orientalist motifs, as Goebel argues, the descriptive space admits little real correspondence to cartographical or authentic cultural space. While Goebel focuses on Kafka's use of Orientalist motifs, the 'China' in this text, like the Russian interior of 'Erinnerungen an die Kaldabahn' ('Memories of the Kalda Railway') is largely composed of reflections on spatial, temporal, and cultural distances and on vastness itself. Although Piper recognizes Kafka's erasure of specific determinations of place, her criticism of *In der Strafkolonie* and other works overlooks the potentially affirmative significance of under-determined spaces in Kafka's writings.[12]

Kafka described his writing as an attempt to arrive 'in das Freie der eigentlichen Beschreibung ... die einem den Fuß vom Erlebnis löst' ('into the freedom of genuine description ... which releases one from experi-

---

[9] See Anderson (1989a) and Goebel (2002,1997).
[10] See Piper (1996); Peters (2001); Zilcosky (2003).
[11] Zilcosky (2003: 39).
[12] Piper (1996: 48).

ence') (KA/T, 87). Successful description for Kafka is not determined by
mimesis of actual places and events; rather it achieves transcendence of the
actual, a movement that can promote the other possibilities of being.
Interpretations of post-colonial and cultural studies may obscure this
transcendence. While Anderson defends Kafka's rejection of mimesis
even as he uncovers the material culture in which he re-contextualizes
Kafka's writing, scholars such as Goebel have explicitly set upon the task of
a 'reconstruction of the referentiality of Kafka's texts'.[13] Zilcosky, too,
draws at least analogous equivalents for real places in order to support a
post-colonial reading. For example, *Das Schloß* is interpreted in colonial
terms on the grounds that it might have been inspired by a German castle
above a Bohemian town, and the land surveyor's profession is aligned with
Europeans' grab for territory in the colonies; on this basis the space of
Das Schloß is compared to descriptions of the colonist in South America
in Schaffstein's novel about a sugar-plantation baron. In respect to *Der
Verschollene*, Brunelda's apartment is held to mirror Kafka's own visits,
with Brod, to brothels in Paris and Milan; these encounters are interpreted
as scenes of exoticizing sexual objectification.

While Anderson's account of Kafka's travelling narrative is presented
within the context of modern perceptual life, with its impressionistic and
cinematic features of instability and mobility, Zilcosky's account situates
even this instability within the dialectic of the familiar and the foreign
rooted in colonialist literature. The narrative technique of 'Richard und
Samuel' is associated with the assault on 'exotic self-location' that 'affirms
the traveler's power over a foreign world'.[14] By reporting a double and
thus partially obscured mode of seeing, further occluded by the means
through which they travel—in one scene a speedy trip around Munich by
car shows the city from below—Kafka and Brod, in post-colonialist
fashion, are said to dismantle what Pratt calls the 'monarch-of-the-all-I-
survey view'.[15] Part of their assault on exoticist literature, according to
Zilcosky, is the very choice of place as a 'calculated' transcendence of
exoticism: Brod and Kafka 'toured decidedly prosaic Central and Western
Europe: Germany, Switzerland, Northern Italy, and Paris', a trajectory
that for Zilcosky is '[d]eliberately monotonous' and therefore partly
deserves its 'subsequent critical neglect'.[16] While Brod and Kafka, in
their prefatory paragraph, do acknowledge that the journey of Richard
and Samuel is not 'exotic'—presumably in comparison to popular travel

[13] Anderson (1989a: 149); Goebel (1997: 65).
[14] Zilcosky (2003: 27).
[15] Pratt (1992: 205).
[16] Zilcosky (2003: 23).

literature—it by no means follows that Central and Western Europe are 'decidedly prosaic' or 'monotonous'. The localities through which they travel are far from prosaic for their contemporaries: Northern Italy is highly mysterious and alluring for Hofmannsthal (*Andreas*) and Musil (*Grigia*). Both Italy and Switzerland are sites of exotic allure and entanglement in Mann (*Der Tod in Venedig, Der Zauberberg*); and so are parts of Germany, since from the perspective of Lübeck, Bavaria is culturally foreign (*Buddenbrooks*). Paris is for Rilke (*Die Aufzeichnungen des Malte Laurids Brigge*) a distressingly foreign place. In all of these works, travel from one point to another within the region of Central and Western Europe initiates radical changes in a character's psychology, self-understanding, or fate. While Zilcosky successfully defends a mobile concept of the exotic— that it can be 'transcended' by being located even within the home—his account nonetheless homogenizes Europe in order to dichotomize the exotic and the prosaic or familiar.[17]

Cross-cultural tensions or territorialist wanderings are important features of some spatial constructions in Kafka's works, yet they operate idiosyncratically, as a means to visualize possibilities of artistic creativity and freedom of the generative imagination from the constraints of mimesis as realistic representation. This may be related to Kafka's philosophical motivations as discussed in recent scholarship. Corngold refers to 'Kafka's idealism' in addressing the writer's aim to raise 'die Welt ins Reine, Wahre, Unveränderliche' ('the world to the pure, the true, the immutable') (KA/T, 838) and to promote its autonomy from social and political experience.[18] The motivation may also be spiritual; Robertson has described Kafka's development of the sense of an ethical task as, at least in part, freeing oneself from the entanglements of empirical and sensuous life.[19] Kafka's aim 'is to confront the world of falsehood . . . by opposing it to a fictional world which, just because it is fictional, rises above the deceits of the physical world and approaches truth'.[20] These motives are compatible with places where the imagination might wander, places that transcend, and by implication criticize, the actual and historical, even while Kafka's spatial evocations also evoke the difficulties of this transcendence. For Kafka's topographical descriptions, precisely in so far as they transcend the historical and empirical referents evoked, could be seen as glimpses of possible worlds; and descriptive space also functions negatively, symbolizing obstruction of such possible, though imagined, realms. Thus, Kafka's spaces are by no means homogeneous: imagery in particular of vastness and distance, 'das Freie' ('the free'), which departs from determined

---

[17] Zilcosky (2003: 24).   [18] Corngold (2004: 203, 202).
[19] Robertson (2002b: 142–149).   [20] Robertson (1985: 218).

experience, may express Kafka's aim to access a higher and permanent reality accessible to the imagination, a spiritual-artistic autonomy; images of containment and spatial restriction (for instance in 'Der Bau') could, then, be seen to signify obstacles, both empirical and psychological, to such aims.

Even where Kafka's imagery of exotic spaces has recognizable referential or analogical content, it is often under-determined. These topographies may be regarded as semiotically 'blank' space, what Anderson helpfully calls an 'antiworld', wherein whatever cultural signs are invoked do not determine its inner development or its deepest significance.[21] But this need not be reduced to Adorno's 'raumlosen Raum'. The distance or vastness Kafka evokes is not blank in an existential sense, but generative of possibilities of experience that are not swallowed up by the vagaries of political and historical life. In such an idealized space, the signs of culture may be absent or effaced, or they may be contradictory, incompatible, or incomplete. The tendency of much recent criticism is, however, to disqualify Kafka's strategies of erasure or cancellation. For instance, in 'Ein altes Blatt', Kafka removed the reference to Peking in favour of an unspecified locale; although the temporal confusion suggested by the title echoes a central problem of 'Beim Bau der Chinesischen Mauer' ('The Building of the Chinese Wall'), the topography is undetermined. This text has been shown to resonate with Flaubert's account of Carthage,[22] yet Goebel's reading restores the Chinese referent in order that the text serve as evidence of Kafka's anti-Orientalism.[23] Similar to Goebel's approach is that of Peters, who presents German colonialism in Africa as the backdrop for Kafka's *In der Strafkolonie (In the Penal Colony).*[24] While Peters convincingly corrects traditional interpretations, which ignore any possible connection to German colonial violence, and exposes this violence as an operative force at the fin de siècle, the irreducible uncertainties of Kafka's colonial landscape (including the unrecognizability of the place and the unspecified ethnicity of the prisoner) are eclipsed in his interpretation of this text. That it was partly inspired by a narrative set in China, Octave Mirbeau's *Le Jardin des supplices* (*The Garden of Suffering*), and also has been linked to Kafka's interest in Dostoevsky's descriptions of Russian penal practices suggests that it is unlikely to have been written with any mimetic fidelity to a specific place or with the aim of uncovering colonialism's inner essence.[25] If read as a critique of violence, this text may be seen more philosophically, as a critique of punishment and its

---

[21] Anderson (1989b: 5).   [22] See Kühne (1997).
[23] Goebel (1997: 99).   [24] Peters (2001).
[25] See Dodd (1983); Robertson (1985: 153).

relationship to law itself or, as Adorno claims, as 'Reaktion auf grenzenlose Macht' ('reaction to boundless power').[26]

Piper, too, criticizes Kafka's 'tendency to erase clear markers of ethnicity' and abstraction from 'geographically or culturally recognizable locales' as a reflection of 'Austro-Hungary's "pre-nationalist nostalgia for empire" and "multinational rhetoric"'.[27] Piper's charge of erasure, first of all, ignores the real, not merely rhetorical, advantages of such a 'multinational' empire, including its tolerance of Jews such as Kafka, who would be disadvantaged by the demise of Austria-Hungary and endangered by the ensuing rise of local nationalisms. More methodologically, Piper's argument presumes a mimetic fidelity as the basis for Kafka's settings: they must be modelled after specific cultural and national places, in order for their identifying features to have been erased. Yet not only does Kafka aim to pry description loose from the experienced world; the inevitable or deliberate cultural references in Kafka's narratives tend to cancel out others in order to prevent such identification. Kafka's spaces, even when culturally recognizable, may evoke a variety of incompatible representations, which leads to a partial erasure even as traces of the recognizable world remain. Where vestiges of varying and incompatible referents remain, the texts might be seen as palimpsests of descriptive space, rather than abstractions of Austro-Hungarian imperialism. At the same time, the variety of cultural clues should not be distilled into a general historical category, for instance of colonialism or imperialism in general. In this vein Peters equates Kafka's unspecific penal colony with 'an actual historical topography'; while the penal colony, Peters admits, cannot be given with any precision a geographical or cultural specificity, it is taken to stand for all colonial spaces and histories, for 'the landscape of colonialism' itself, its 'primal scene'.[28]

In line with Piper, Goebel argues that Kafka's 'narratives of dislocation, migration, and estrangement are really allegories of transcultural hermeneutics'. But the topographical imagination of space in these texts may have a more idiosyncratic significance apart from the problems of political territoriality or 'transnationality and cross-cultural translation'.[29] Whereas this can be seen in the cultural assignments, however vague, in 'Schakale und Araber' ('Jackals and Arabs') and *In der Strafkolonie*, the story 'Beim Bau der Chinesischen Mauer', which records no European presence, evades at least at some level the problem of transnationality, deferring it to the threat, unrealized in the narrative, of invaders from the North. Goebel admits that the 'potential meaning' of 'Beim Bau der Chinesischen

[26] Adorno (1977: 267).   [27] Piper (1996: 48–49).
[28] Peters (2001: 401, 403).   [29] Goebel (2002: 189).

Mauer' is not restricted to this transcultural hermeneutics; but he still defends an identification of an original basis for the work, which can then be reconstructed by the post-colonial theorist: '"Beim Bau der Chinesischen Mauer" undeniably originates from within the ideological horizon of colonialism and Orientalist discourse.' In defending the relevance of this discourse for Kafka's writings, Goebel goes so far as to reinstate Kafka's erased or crossed-out spatial referents (for instance, the China evoked in the earlier version of 'Ein altes Blatt').[30] But Kafka exploits the motif of vastness in China, as he does the Russian interior, for a story concerned more essentially with contemplating the possibilities, through spatial metaphors, of freedom for the imagination.

The post-colonial account of Kafka's topographies also casts Kafka's protagonists, for instance Karl Rossmann in America, as variations on the exploitative tourist, and other characters as their 'native' prey; such interpretation often focuses on sexual subjectivity as a site of some exploitive encounter between the self and the foreigner. The sexual perversion ascribed to these encounters renders the traveller's self-exoticization; the traveller proceeds not in order to find a more authentic self, but to lose himself irrevocably, promoting this loss through sexual pain inflicted or desired. Yet this account requires the establishment of analogies that do not respect the nature of Kafka's settings. America becomes analogous to Paris and Milan in Kafka's own travels with Brod. Where Brod reports on Kafka's not sleeping with prostitutes in the brothels they entered in Paris and Milan, but merely looking at them, Zilcosky finds evidence of Kafka's Flaubertian 'scopophilia' and therefore of sexual perversity, projected onto the young Karl Rossmann in *Der Verschollene*.[31] The protagonists of the work Kafka wrote with Brod on the basis of their actual travels, 'Richard und Samuel', are also interpreted according to the model of the touristic and exoticizing gaze, which is thought to be deliberately undermined. Zilcosky's illuminating account of the descriptive method assigns this to the assault on the imperialist 'structure of exotic self-location' of a monarchical view over a symbolically gained territory.[32] Yet the two explicit aims of 'Richard und Samuel' are interconnected. The aim, mentioned in the 'Vorbemerkung' ('preface') to the work, to see new places with a special regard—'die bereisten Länder... in einer Frische und Bedeutung sehn zu lassen, wie sie oft mit Unrecht nur exotischen Gegenden zugeschrieben werden' ('to let well-travelled countries be seen in the freshness and significance often granted only to exotic realms')—is linked with another: to study the nuances of male friendship, 'Die vielen Nuancen, deren

[30] Goebel (1997: 99).   [31] Zilcosky (2003: 58).
[32] Zilcosky (2003: 27).

Freundschaftsbedingungen zwischen Männern fähig sind, darzustellen' ('to represent the many nuances of which the conditions of friendship between men are capable') (KA/DL, 420). Whereas Zilcosky reads the text and its collaborative method as a challenge to exoticism—'The goal of their book, we could rephrase, is to challenge exoticism precisely by *transcending* it'[33]—the change in place functions more primarily to allow for an unusual intimacy between the characters by placing them 'elsewhere', outside the ordinary conventions, obligations, and constraints of their familiar worlds. Richard and Samuel are brought together by an intimate and communal study of the 'nuances' of their experience, on their natural affinities and tensions as they experience a changing environment, in a space apart from ordinary life.

INTIMACY IN THE SPACES OF 'ELSEWHERE': RUSSIA AND AMERICA

In works that present the constraining nature of familiar everyday spaces, this other space must be more radically projected. Nuances of intimacy emerge between Richard and Samuel during their travel through Switzerland, but male friendship symbolizes a more drastic contrast to home in Kafka's breakthrough text, *Das Urteil* (The Judgment), written in the following year. Here the space of friendship crosses distances that are more striking and enigmatic. Georg Bendemann and his unnamed friend in St Petersburg are, like Richard and Samuel, former schoolmates. They now communicate outside their native sphere, not through common travel, but in the 'nowhere' space of correspondence via letters. The friend is reported to have left their hometown, 'zu Hause unzufrieden' ('discontented at home'), for Russia (KA/DL, 43). Beyond this empirical fact, the text gradually suggests that the friend might represent an imagined, though perhaps unacknowledged, realm of escape for Georg himself.

The correspondence between Georg and his friend comes to represent a fragile and threatened space of refuge from the tensions of family life that lead to Georg's death. Their relationship may have been inspired by Kafka's friendship with the Yiddish actor Yitskhok Löwy, a travelling actor from Eastern Europe of whom Kafka's father was vocally disapproving.[34] Just as the travelling Löwy stirred up Kafka's interest in the Yiddish theatre, the expatriate friend in Russia might be associated with Georg's unexpressed creativity. The first mention of the friend in Russia, never

---

[33] Zilcosky (2003: 24).   [34] See Robertson (2005: 36).

named in the text, is associated with writing ('Brief' and 'Schreibtisch'), with playful daydreaming ('spielerische Langsamkeit'), and with distances imagined (both the 'Ausland' in which the friend lives and the gaze 'aus dem Fenster'):

> Er hatte gerade einen Brief an einen sich im Ausland befindlichen Jugendfreund beendet, verschloß ihn in spielerischer Langsamkeit und sah dann, den Ellbogen auf den Schreibtisch gestützt, aus dem Fenster auf den Fluß, die Brücke und die Anhöhen am anderen Ufer mit ihrem schwachen Grün.
>
> (He had just finished a letter to an old friend from his youth who was now living abroad, folded it up in playful slowness and, with his elbows propped on the desk, gazed out the window at the river, the bridge, and the hills on the far bank with their pale green.) (KA/DL, 43)

The description relates the friend's distance and Georg's own gaze out the window, away from his familial home towards hints of another life, suggested by springlike green that appears on the hills on the other side of the river. But the references to river and bridge also foreshadow Georg's death, as he will drown himself there at his father's command; Georg will not reach that other side.

While Georg's unsuccessful friend is ostensibly a source of worry— 'Was wollte man einem solchen Manne schreiben, der sich offenbar verrannt hatte' ('what could one write to such a man who had so obviously gone astray')—he in fact becomes the problematic point of tension in Georg's own life, as an argument with his father about the friend ensues. What are presented as the friend's failures—his bachelorhood, his isolation in Russia estranged also from the 'Kolonie seiner Landsleute' ('colony of his countrymen'), his failing business, his being out of touch with commerce in his native country—are symbolically ambiguous, for they also represent freedoms from some of the constrictions about which Kafka himself was highly ambivalent. Georg reasons that his friend should not come back, for he would probably not do well upon returning as 'ein für immer Zurückgekehrter' ('one who would always be thought of as having returned') (KA/DL, 44), a situation recalling that of Hofmannsthal's narrator of *Die Briefe des Zurückgekehrten*, who encounters severe difficulty readjusting to life in Central Europe after years abroad, as discussed in Chapter 1. But Georg's opinion about the friend might reveal precisely his symbolic importance, representing an alternative reality; this symbolic alternative may explain Kafka's decision to strike out specific phrases in the text concerning Russia that may have evoked an image of pogrom.[35] Their correspondence provides Georg a contact with a distant realm away

---

[35] See Robertson (1985: 12).

from home and all its interrelated trappings—marriage, domestic life in the family, work and business, civic loyalty or tension—a contact that would be lost if he were to come home. Male friendship, particularly outside the native sphere, is important, then, for affording another perspective on the world; even correspondence with a woman friend, such as Kafka himself carried on intensely at different periods in his life, would not provide such distance, as there looms the possibility of marriage and the re-establishment of home.

In this story Russia stands for a far-off 'elsewhere', made accessible through masculine friendship, however slightly filled out in the story, or in Georg's actual experience; such friendship becomes symbolic of escape. The intimacy established by Georg's communication with his friend in letters has already been threatened by just those aspects of Georg's success he has long feared to report. News of his impending marriage into a prosperous family is especially threatening to their friendship, and his own successful management of his father's business contrasts painfully with the friend's reported failures; both of these facts would establish Georg's rootedness in the familial sphere, precluding adventure and escape. The friend becomes the pivotal theme in the scene of fatal conflict with Georg's father. When Georg's father calls into question the very existence of the friend—'Du hast keinen Freund in Petersburg' ('You have no friend in Petersburg') (KA/DL, 53)—and then, even more problematically, appropriates him by claiming his own correspondence with him, Georg's autonomy collapses.

The conflict between the reserved 'elsewhere' of male friendship and the more antagonistic father–son relation at home may be illuminated by Kafka's 'Brief an den Vater'. In this letter Kafka describes in detail his father's oppressive and imposing presence. Kafka's attempts to escape this presence have been interpreted in post-colonial terms, the letter said to demonstrate 'how his writing is, figuratively, an attempt to grab land from an apparently colonial father'.[36] Taking into account the significance of the 'space' of male intimacy in 'Richard und Samuel' and *Das Urteil*, Kafka's assertions might be interpreted in light of other possibilities offered by a departure from familiar space. Kafka highlights the absence of any comforting, non-threatening masculine intimacy in the father–son relationship: he refers to 'Kälte, Fremdheit, Undankbarkeit. Und zwar wirfst Du es mir so vor, als wäre es meine Schuld' ('coldness, estrangement, ingratitude. And still you accuse me, as if it were my fault!'); and again: 'als Vater warst Du zu stark für mich' ('as a father you were too

---

[36] Zilcosky (2003: 148).

strong for me') (KA/NSII, 144, 146). He recalls having been 'ein ängstliches Kind' ('an anxious child') and refers to himself within the father—son relationship as 'der Sklave' ('the slave') (KA/NSII, 148, 156). Kafka's admission of his own attempts to escape his insensitive and domineering father through literary writing are marked in Zilcosky's reading as a literary counter-colonialism. But they might be projected rather against other possibilities of intimacy, such as Kafka imagined in friendship between men in 'Richard und Samuel', and as he probably experienced with Max Brod, for whom Kafka professes love in his diary (22 May 1912): 'Wenn ich mich liebe, liebe ich ihn noch stärker' ('If I love myself, I love him even more strongly') (KA/T, 421). This relationship seems not to resonate with the homoeroticism that may be attributed to Kafka's descriptions of other men and that characterizes the *Wandervogel* movement for which both he and Brod expressed appreciation, and so it does not fall prey to sexual opposition and potential appropriation that could be regarded in 'colonialist' terms. What joins the motifs of male friendship in 'Richard und Samuel' and *Das Urteil* is their common requirement of an elsewhere, a space away from home and the configurations of familial relationships. This connection can also be seen in Kafka's narrative 'Erinnerungen an die Kaldabahn' (as it has been called, since the fragment in the *Tagebuch* bears no title) and in the relationship Karl Rossman establishes with the stoker in the first chapter of *Der Verschollene*.

Russia figures again as a radical elsewhere wherein an alternative mode of intimacy is possible, in Kafka's narrative 'Erinnerungen an die Kaldabahn'. In this story homosocial intimacy, unambiguously physical, is also evoked within a setting far away from ordinary domestic and civic life, an elsewhere of which Russia's great vastness becomes symbolic. The narrator attends a railroad station in the Russian interior, far from any city, on a railroad line that is not and may never be finished. The narrator's isolation is interrupted by monthly visits from his supervisor. The supervisor's initial hostility on each occasion gives way to songs and confidences shared over schnapps in the evening, and then to physical embraces: 'und schließlich fielen wir gemeinsam auf die Pritsche nieder in einer Umarmung die wir oft zehn Stunden nicht lösten' ('and finally we fell down together on the plank bed in an embrace that we did not release for ten hours'). During this ten-hour embrace, it is suggested, the narrator and his supervisor are 'ganz einig' ('entirely one'): the power dynamic between the supervisor and his subordinate has been suspended, as the narrator suggests with 'fielen wir gemeinsam' ('we fell together') and in reporting its resumption on the following morning: 'Am nächsten Morgen reiste er wieder als mein Vorgesetzter weg' ('The next morning he set off again as my superior') (KA/T, 684–685). While at the outset of the evening the power dynamic is operative, as the narrator is keen to secure his monthly salary and the supervisor toys with withholding it, this gives way to a different kind of intimacy—a physical, presumably sexual communion—that might be possible for them only in this virtual nowhere of the station-house.

Parody or ironic presentations of such intimacy can also be seen in the radically non-domestic, dislocated spaces of *Der Verschollene,* a work to be discussed in more detail in the next section. The first person that Karl Rossmann befriends in America is the ship's stoker, with whom he almost immediately forms a bond of intimate solidarity. The stoker is, like the friend in Russia, a German abroad, away from home, a bachelor without a family, lacking ties to his fellow 'Landsleute' (he is oppressed by his Romanian superior) and having trouble with his job. While *Das Urteil* presents the nowhere space of correspondence between (presumably) Prague and Russia, and the setting of 'Erinnerungen an die Kaldabahn' seems virtually in the middle of nowhere, Karl's friendship with the stoker is made in a dislocated setting, on the ship in the New York harbour before Karl disembarks. Upon meeting him, Karl immediately, and absurdly, identifies with the stoker and imagines following in the stoker's choice of occupation—'Jetzt könnte ich auch Heizer werden' ('Now I could become a stoker too') (KA, v. 12). As a parody of intimacy, Karl is pulled into the stoker's room and pressed onto his bed and prevented from leaving—a pressure similar to that exerted by the maidservant at home who seduced Karl and thus caused his exile. But in contrast to his feeling of confused disgust when he is seduced by Johanna, the stoker soon gives Karl a feeling of comfort. Within the course of a single conversation, Karl feels at ease on the stoker's bed, evidencing a ludicrous discrepancy between the fact that they are strangers (they have not even exchanged names) and Karl's naive loyalties. Feeling himself involved in the stoker's case against his superior, Karl is excited by their solidarity. Resting on the bed, Karl has found refuge in an alternative space of freedom from the anxieties brought by the world outside the stoker's room, including those demands of home from which he has been expelled. Away from his familial guilt, not yet subjected to the trials of life as an immigrant, held back from the dizzying city over which he will never achieve a clear overview, liberated temporarily from his uncertain future, and for a moment immune to the instability of the elements, Karl is as happy here as at any other point in the novel.

> Er hatte fast das Gefühl davon verloren, daß er auf dem unsicheren Boden eines Schiffes, an der Küste eines unbekannten Erdteils war, so heimisch war ihm hier auf dem Bett des Heizers zumute.

(He felt so well, so at home on the stoker's bunk that he had almost lost the feeling that he was on the precarious board of a ship beside the coast of an unknown continent.) (KA, v. 14)

The comparison made here between the spaces of friendship in this first chapter of *Der Verschollene* and *Das Urteil* can be extended to the dissolution of this space. Just as the father's intervention annihilates the space of correspondence between Georg and his friend in Russia, Karl's friendship with the stoker, whose case he aims to present to the ship's captain, ends with the discovery of his relation to his uncle Jakob—a father figure who will, like Karl's parents, also disinherit him. In both works the space of masculine intimacy, whether tragic or comic, serves as an escape from the instabilities and violent or inhumane conflicts that family life is revealed to be. Karl's acquaintance with the brutal Delamarche and the more submissive but equally problematic Robinson—neither of whom are, like the stoker, German—could be read as parodies of masculine friendship, suggesting the exclusion of this kind of humane relationship within the cultural space of the New World.

THE PARODY OF *FERNWEH* AND IMMANENT VASTNESS IN *DER VERSCHOLLENE*

The topography of *Der Verschollene* is constructed of distances and vastness, and the contrast between large, uncontrollable spaces and small, constraining ones. Through this topography, Kafka parodies the motif of *Fernweh* and highlights the setting of America as an imaginative space, rather than as mimetically represented. Since Alfred Wirkner's detailing of the sources for Kafka's representation of America, critics have analysed the incompatibility of the space of *Der Verschollene* with a 'real' America; it has been seen as a composite of representations, drawn not only from Holitscher's *Amerika: heute und morgen* (*America: Today and Tomorrow*) but also Soukup's lectures in Prague—as well as representing both inner and outer reality (Manfred Engel); as a fictional, auto-referential space behind which the real disappears (Dieter Heimböckel); and as a space 'somewhere between realism and fantasy' (Ritchie Robertson).[37] Relevant to this discussion is also the fact that Kafka himself, according to Brod, considered emigration to America, as several of his relatives had done. This at least associates the idea of America with *Fernweh*, a feeling also evoked

---

[37] Wirkner (1976); Robertson (1985: 54); Engel (1996); Heimböckel (2003: 143).

in 'Richard und Samuel'.[38] Yet Karl's chronic lack of orientation and his recurrent spatial containment—within, first, his uncle's abode in the city (of which he sees only his uncle's street), then the suburban house of his uncle's colleagues, then the Hotel Occidental and its elevator, then Brunelda's apartment and her balcony—are remarkable in their sharp contrast to the vastness of America from which he is held back. The parody of *Fernweh* in *Der Verschollene* is then constructed by the tension between vastness and containment that characterizes Karl's experience of the 'American' topography. Just as the space of exile and elsewhere in *Das Urteil* and 'Erinnerungen an die Kaldabahn' allows imagination of other modes of life or of intimate contact in contrast to familial and familiar spaces, the topography of *Der Verschollene* reflects the protagonist's ambiguous status between adolescence and autonomous subjectivity, that is, between dependence and freedom, a situation incompatible with the point of view of a symbolic colonialist or tourist.

Evocations of *Fernweh* in some of Kafka's other narratives will help to illuminate its parody in *Der Verschollene*. Kafka's paragraph-long narrative 'Der Aufbruch' ('The Departure') expresses the uncertainty and urgency of *Fernweh* as an intimate call to an undetermined elsewhere. The call of far-off places is symbolized by the inexplicable sound of a trumpet in the distance. For the narrator, who has ordered his horse from the stable, the departure is itself the destination. This is revealed in a conversation with his servant, who does not hear the call of the trumpet:

In der Ferne hörte ich eine Trompete blasen, ich fragte ihn, was das bedeute. Er wußte nichts und hatte nichts gehört. Beim Tore hielt er mich auf und fragte: 'Wohin reitest Du, Herr?' 'Ich weiß es nicht,' sagte ich, 'nur weg von hier, nur weg von hier. Immerfort weg von hier, nur so kann ich mein Ziel erreichen.' 'Du kennst also dein Ziel,' fragte er. 'Ja,' antwortete ich, 'ich sagte es doch, "Weg-von-hier"; das ist mein Ziel.'

(In the distance I heard the sounding of a trumpet, and I asked him what it means. He knew nothing and had heard nothing. He stopped me at the gate and asked: 'To where are you riding, master?' 'I don't know,' I said, 'away from here, just away from here. Ever forward away from here, only this way can I reach my destination.' 'So you know your destination,' he said. 'Yes,' I answered, 'I said it already, "away from here"—that is my destination.') (KA/NSII, 372–375)

---

[38] Zilcosky (2003: 67). While Zilcosky focuses on the myopic experience of travel in that work, and the study of supposedly prosaic spaces, he overlooks Richard's longing for far distances, his *Fernweh*: 'die Begierde nach weiten Reisen, die ich jetzt habe!' ('the desire for distant journeys that I now have!') writes Richard (Kafka, GW/E, 297).

This passage identifies departure both with distance and with destination. In contrast, 'Das Schweigen der Sirenen' treats the classical figure of *Fernweh*, Odysseus, through a reversal of its allures. Odysseus manages to resist the song through which the sirens lured passing travellers, their song reaching the sailors across the waves and so obstructing their return home. Odysseus with wax in his ears and chained to the mast of his ship evades the call of *Fernweh* their song represents. In Kafka's version of the legend, the sirens then employ silence as a still more powerful weapon. While they appear to be singing, Odysseus feels triumphant at his ability to evade their song, not realizing (since his hearing is blocked) that they are in fact silent. So it is the silence, not the song of *Fernweh*, which Odysseus, gazing into the distance, fails to perceive. Their bodily gestures are completely overlooked by his gaze into the distance:

> Bald aber glitt alles an seinen in die Ferne gerichteten Blicken ab, die Sirenen verschwanden ihm förmlich und gerade als er ihnen am nächsten war, wußte er nichts mehr von ihnen.
>
> (But soon all of this faded from view as he fixed his gaze on the distance, the sirens vanished from his sight and just as he was nearest to them, he knew nothing of them any longer.) (KA/NSII, 41)

Overwhelmed by the reserve of Odysseus, the sirens give up their seduction altogether: 'sie wollten nicht mehr verführen, nur noch den Abglanz vom großen Augenpaar des Odysseus wollten sie solange als möglich erhaschen' ('they no longer wanted to seduce, only to hold as long as possible onto the radiance from Odysseus's great eyes') (KA/NSII, 41). The positions of Odysseus and the sirens are now reversed: the silent sirens are enraptured by Odysseus passing into the distance. But both Odysseus and the narrator of 'Der Aufbruch' can be seen to assert their will in respect to the unknown distance—either to press forth towards it, or to avoid being lured further away from home. If, however, Odysseus's success can be attributed not to his 'Entschlossenheit' ('resolve') (see KA/NSII Apparatband, 206), but, as the text suggests, to his naivety or 'kindische Ahnungslosigkeit' ('childish cluelessness'), in that he does not register the sexuality of the sirens,[39] then he is a figure whose ambiguity is quite similar to that of Karl Rossmann.

In contrast to the departing horseman in 'Der Aufbruch' who is riding towards the 'Ziel' of 'Weg-von-hier' ('goal of away-from-here') and to Odysseus on his journey towards home, Karl Rossmann has no 'Ziel'. Both his departure and his arrival are governed by a collapse of an immature will. In this respect, Karl's experience might be seen as an

---

[39] Robertson (2002b: 143).

innovative parody of *Fernweh*. Not only Karl's perspectival disorientation, but his naivety, entirely overlooked in the post-colonialist interpretation of Karl as a visual exploiter of the native land-as-bodyscape, make him unfit as a traveller. The defining features of *Fernweh*—longing for a far-off and usually exotic place, and for the necessary distance from home this entails—are reversed in Karl's experience. He does not long to go off to the unknown, to arrive 'an der Küste eines unbekannten Erdteils' ('on the coast of an unknown part of the earth') (KA, v. 14). Karl's parents expelled him from home for a strikingly passive, unenjoyed, and fumbling sexual 'transgression' with a thirty-five-year-old maidservant Johanna, nearly twenty years older than Karl, who conceives a child by him. While the narrator of 'Der Aufbruch' is in a position of command with respect to his servant, Karl submits despite his horror and displeasure to the family servant's maternal-sexual advances. Upon arrival in America, Karl then is detained in the ship; he is disoriented, has forgotten his umbrella, and worries about his suitcase as he crawls into the bed of the first friend (the stoker) he makes upon arrival. He is adopted by his uncle on the ship, only to be disinherited again a few weeks later, just as his parents also disinherit his child by the servant—for Karl is sent away not only to avoid scandal but explicitly 'zur Vermeidung der Alimentenzahlung' ('in avoidance of alimony') (KA, v. 40). Karl then suffers the 'Ferne' in an unusual, inverted way: in not getting very far into the city, in having no money for further passage, and, for most of the novel, held back from America's spatial vastness and ostensibly limitless freedom of which it is symbolic.

Spatial imagery in *Der Verschollene* presents this tension between containment and vastness, a tension that mirrors Karl's ambiguity as an adolescent exile. Johanna's seduction of Karl is presented through contrasting, even contradictory spatial metaphors that highlight Karl's inexperience and sexual bewilderment. It also foreshadows (though told in hindsight) Karl's deportation to far-off and vast America, where he will be subjected to one form after another of containment and expulsion.

> Einmal sagte sie 'Karl' und führte ihn . . . in ihr Zimmerchen, das sie zusperrte . . . und . . . entkleidete sie in Wirklichkeit ihn und legte ihn in ihr Bett, als wolle sie ihn . . . streicheln und pflegen bis zum Ende der Welt.
>
> (Once she said 'Karl' and led him to her little room, which she locked . . . and really undressed him and laid him on her bed, as if she wanted to stroke and pamper him to the ends of the earth.) (KA, v. 42)

The small space in which Karl is locked is ironically disproportionate to the consequences of his seduction there: Karl is indeed caressed 'bis zum Ende der Welt', as the seduction leads to his forced emigration to a distant land, the European discovery of which forced a reassessment of the 'ends' of the earth. That this expulsion into the distance follows from what happens in a small, locked room (indicated by the diminutive 'Zimmerchen') both expresses the parody of *Fernweh* in the novel and highlights Karl's helplessness, just as Karl's smallness and subordination are highlighted in contrast to the massive Hotel Occidental in which he finds work, with its thirty lifts, five or seven floors, and over five thousand guests. Analogous to his topographical displacement is the precariousness of adolescence, as Karl is situated between childhood, from which his first sexual experience has permanently expelled him (since he has now fathered Johanna's child), and adulthood, for which he is inadequately prepared.

Two passages from Karl's experience at his uncle's house serve as images of immanent vastness, and both render Karl small in comparison. Karl's recitation to his uncle of an American poem about a fire, and Karl's experience of taking a bath in his uncle's house, both present striking images where vastness is ambiguously 'contained'. An oft-noted aspect of Karl's attempts at assimilation in America is his study of English, which the narrator presents as his foremost task during his stay at his uncle's house. In the course of learning English, Karl recites to his uncle in the evening. The poem Karl recites is not named, but is referred to as an American poem about a fire. While the fire image is ostensibly disconnected from anything Karl will experience, it is striking in respect to its spatiality, as the threat of fire is precisely to grow illimitably beyond control, enveloping and destroying through its own growth. Kafka may have been inspired here by Holitscher's imagery of fire in *Amerika: Heute und morgen*. Holitscher describes apartment houses with their fire escapes zigzagging down them, and 'gut heizbare Häuser, die aber in 5 Minuten bis auf den Keller niedergebrannt sind, wenn ein Funken aus dem Ofen auf den Teppich hinüberspringt' ('houses easily heated but which are burned down to the cellar in five minutes if a spark from the oven hits the rug'). The relationship between the minute ('ein Funken') and a projected immensity is striking, as Holitscher's progression of images mimics fire's threat of spreading beyond control: 'Brennt erst eins von diesen Häusern, so ist bei wehendem Wind bald die ganze Straße weg' ('If one of these houses burns, soon the whole street is gone when the wind picks up').[40] Holitscher's further references to the plurals 'Straßen' ('streets'), 'Städten' ('cities'), and then to 'Verwüstung' ('devastation') evoke increasing spatial expansion. But there is another possible source of the fire image, the disastrous blaze in New York City on March 25,

---

[40] Holitscher (1912: 424).

1911.[41] Kafka may have taken at least a humane interest in reports that more than 140 garment workers, mostly immigrant women and girls, died in the Triangle Shirtwaist Company factory; the doors of the factory had been locked by the company bosses to keep track of the women, despite their strike in the previous year in which they unsuccessfully fought for fire escapes, unlocked doors, and other safety precautions. Most of the workers jumped out of the high windows in order to avoid a more painful death by fire. The absence in Kafka's text of such gruesome real-world referents is itself noteworthy. Kafka could have described the poem as depicting a real fire; but the resonances of the fire image support only the possibility that the American poem could refer to an uncontained and destructive blaze. As a negative image of vastness (as suggested in Holitscher's 'Verwüstung' with its root 'Wüste'), fire also evokes the sublime, the experience of nature's immensity and power associated with America's vastness; and it can be entrancing. Indeed Karl's recitation of the poem 'machten diesen [Onkel] tiefernst vor Zufriedenheit' ('sobered him deeply in contentedness') (KA, v. 62). Yet as the subject of a poem, fire becomes an ambiguous image, a fire 'contained' by the limited textual and temporal 'space' of a poem brief enough to memorize and recite. This is not unlike the scale of some of Kafka's miniature prose texts, such as the tiny 'Wunsch, Indianer zu werden' ('Wish to become an Indian'), in which the vast American landscape seems to be glimpsed just as the features of the rider-narrator and his horse disappear. The poem, marked rhythmically by the uncle's hand movements, is in meter and is thus also formally constrained.

> Sie standen damals beide an einem Fenster in Karls Zimmer, der Onkel sah hinaus, wo alle Helligkeit des Himmels schon vergangen war, und schlug im Mitgefühl der Verse langsam und gleichmäßig in die Hände, während Karl aufrecht neben ihm stand und mit starren Augen das schwierige Gedicht sich entrang.
>
> (They both stood then at the window of Karl's room, the uncle staring out where all the sky's luminosity was already gone, and tapped his hands together, slowly and regularly, in time with the verses, while Karl stood straight next to him and, with a fixed stare, delivered up the difficult poem.) (KA, v. 62)

As Karl recites the poem, staring vacantly in concentration, his uncle gazes out the window at the sky's vastness, linked to the fire image through the waning light, in that 'alle Helligkeit des Himmels schon vergangen war' ('All the sky's luminosity was already gone') (KA, v. 62). The uncle's view from Karl's window, in a house on a street in Manhattan, is described only

---

in reference to the sky; the description effaces the usually obstructing other buildings that prevent Karl himself from gaining an overview of his surroundings. The image of Karl in his uncle's bathtub also invokes an intriguingly ambiguous space, a symbol of immanent vastness. The scale is distorted, as the spray of the shower is as large as the whole tub: 'Über die ganze Wanne der Länge und Breite nach spannte sich das Sieb der Dusche' ('the spray of the shower spanned over the whole length and breadth of the bathtub') (KA, v. 63). This discrepancy highlights the imaginary nature of the American spaces, and perhaps also the childlike aspects of Kafka's imagination buried, as Adorno puts it, 'in verschollener Frühe des Menschen' ('in the vanished dawn of humanity'). Adorno continues, 'Der so blicken will, muß sich ins Kind verwandeln und vieles vergessen' ('Whoever wants to look in that way has to transform himself into a child and forget much').[42] Karl childishly delights in a bathtub whose size dwarfs anything known at home, imagining the envy of his classmates: 'welcher Mitschüler zu Hause...besaß etwas Derartiges und gar noch allein für sich' ('which classmates back home possessed something like this, much less for him alone'). The bathtub is wide enough for him to stretch out both his legs and arms, thus encompassing his bodily space and rendering Karl relatively small:

> und da lag nun Karl ausgestreckt, in dieser Wanne konnte er die Arme ausbreiten, und ließ die Ströme des lauen, heißen, wieder lauen und endlich eisigen Wassers nach Belieben teilweise oder über die ganze Fläche hin auf sich herab.
>
> (And there Karl lay now stretched out, as he could extend his arms in this tub, and let the stream of tepid, hot, again tepid and finally icy water flow down over him as he washed part by part or over the whole surface of his body at once.) (KA, v. 63)

The indications of vastness—'der Länge und Breite nach', 'spannte sich', 'ausbreiten', 'die ganze Fläche'—not only contrast with the contained, albeit generous, space of the bathtub. They are also followed by a description of the individual drops of water, a detail that shrinks the scale of attention to miniature:

> Wie in dem noch ein wenig fortlaufenden Genusse des Schlafes lag er da und fing besonders gern mit geschlossenen Augenlidern die letzten, einzeln fallenden Tropfen auf, die sich öffneten und über das Gesicht hinflossen.

---

[42] Adorno (1977: 266).

(Like in the last warm enjoyment of sleep, he lay there and with especial pleasure caught the last single falling drops with his closed eyelids, drops that as they broke flowed over his face.) (KA, v. 63–64)

With his eyes closed as in a dream, Karl seems to enjoy the stereotypical vastness of 'American' space in a large bathtub, where the individuality of the drops of water can still be registered.

This play on containment and vastness symbolically mirrors the tension between dependency and freedom. The parody of *Fernweh* in *Der Verschollene* is expressed in part through Karl's adolescent assumption of a relation to parental figures, needed to help him negotiate the wide and unfamiliar spaces of America. While first the stoker, and then Uncle Jakob, serve as temporary father figures to Karl, other characters become repositories for 'scattered parental attributes', a technique on Kafka's part that may be borrowed from Dickens. While Mark Spilka, in his account, focuses on Jakob and his colleagues Pollunder and Green, he also shows how Brunelda's apartment in the chapter 'Ein Asyl' ('An Asylum') becomes a household resembling a dysfunctional family, a convincing enough rendering even if Spilka's assignment of models from Kafka's own family seems strained.[43] Brunelda and Delamarche are substitute parents, upon whom Karl, like Robinson, is wholly dependent. Clearly distinguished from Robinson with his sexual longings, Karl defers to the authority of Delamarche and Brunelda as would an adolescent servant, even as he imagines negotiating with them. Karl's sexual innocence throughout the novel—his naive position vis-à-vis the stoker (lying on his bed), Johanna (pressed into sexual relations), and Brunelda (as her personal attendant pushing her in the wheelchair in the fragment 'Ausreise Bruneldas' ['Brunelda's Departure'])—is ambiguous because of his indeterminate identity between dependant, expelled father, and adolescent runaway, roles none of which Karl has assumed willingly. In the second fragmentary chapter this ambiguity is expressed in physical terms: Karl is referred to by the policeman as 'Kleiner' ('little one') but is clearly physically much more robust than the older medical student who helps him carry Brunelda down the stairs; the latter is 'viel schwächer als Karl... wie sich bei dieser Gelegenheit herausstellte' ('much weaker than Karl... which stood out on this occasion') (KA, v. 381).

This ambiguity is unregistered in Max Brod's interpretation, which oversimplifies Karl's childishness; but it is equally overlooked in postcolonial readings, which ignore the ambiguities surrounding Karl's youth, reflected in his experience of space as much as in his relation to others.

---

[43] Spilka (1963: 156, 160–163).

In Brod's presentation of the novel, Karl is unequivocally a child. In his preface to the first edition, Brod describes the situation of Karl as 'die Hilflosigkeit eines unerfahrenen Kindes mitten in dem von Leben tobenden "Amerika"' ('the helplessness of an inexperienced child in an "America" raging with life') (Kafka, GW/A, 377). Yet in the post-colonial reading Karl's youth is unrecognized, effacing what Brod calls Karl's 'kindliche Unschuld und rührend naive Reinheit' ('childish innocence and touching naïve purity'), in order that Karl can represent the objectifying gaze of the (adult male) modern traveller, an incompetent or perhaps impotent Flaubert (Kafka, GW/A 358). Yet Brod, too, seems to miss the humour of moments wherein the fifteen- or sixteen-year-old Karl is cast as childish—for he is a well-developed adolescent. This makes Karl a target for parody that plays on his ambiguous status between boyhood and manhood. While a significant aspect of male adolescence ought to be sexual awakening and perhaps preoccupation, this no way characterizes Karl's experiences despite the very reason for his expulsion to America. Kafka parodies this ambiguity in the figure of Karl, who, like a child, seems to experience no sexual desire, but, like a man, has fathered a child himself.

In the spaces of *Der Verschollene*, images of vastness, often contrasted to containment or to the minute, serve to augment the play between freedom and obstruction that resonates with Karl's own ambiguous status. Karl's experience in the small space of Mr. Pollunder's car, gazing at his waistcoat and watch-chain, not only illustrates a perceptual myopia but also, like the scene in Johanna's 'Zimmerchen' ('little room'), meaningfully contrasts the contained space with the immeasurable (streets, traffic, masses of people), and so presents Karl as focused on the immediate, shying from the more uncontrolled or uncertain elements beyond it. Again Karl is here physically pressed to the body of another person, suggesting both constraint and shelter. While his lived space is narrowed both by the car and by this contact with Herr Pollunder, who holds Karl's hand and 'erzählte' ('narrated to him') as if to a child, the perceptual space outside the car is composed through metaphorical depth (the 'fremdes Element' ['foreign element'] of the traffic), mass (the demonstrators), and endless trajectories (the streetcar's tracks).

> Sie saßen eng beieinander, und Herr Pollunder hielt Karls Hand in der seinen, während er erzählte.... Obwohl er am Abend noch niemals durch die New Yorker Straßen gefahren war, und über Trottoir und Fahrbahn, alle Augenblicke die Richtung wechselnd, wie in einem Wirbelwind der Lärm jagte, nicht wie von Menschen verursacht, sondern wie ein fremdes Element, kümmerte sich Karl, während er Herrn Pollunders Worte genau aufzunehmen suchte, um nichts anderes als Herrn Pollunders dunkle Weste, über die quer eine dunkle Kette ruhig hing.

(They sat close together, and Herr Pollunder held Karl's hand in his own while he talked. . . . Although he had never been driven through the streets of New York in the evening, and pavements and roadways changed direction every moment like in a whirlwind and roared with noise that was not really human-made but like some strange element, Karl paid attention to nothing as he tried to catch Herr Pollunder's every word, except Herr Pollunder's dark vest, across which a gold chain hung calmly.) (KA, v. 73–74)

The imagery of the proximal and minute in Karl's staring at the waistcoat and watch-chain contrasts to the 'fremdes Element' of the traffic, and in the following passage, to the wide streets, masses of people, including metalworkers on strike with their voices raised in common protest, and seemingly endless tracks of the tram.

Durchquerte dann das Automobil, aus dunkleren, dumpf hallenden Gassen kommend, eine dieser, ganz Plätzen gleichenden, großen Straßen, dann erschienen nach beiden Seiten hin in Perspektiven, denen niemand bis zum Ende folgen konnte, die Trottoirs angefüllt mit einer in winzigen Schritten sich bewegenden Masse, deren Gesang einheitlicher war als der einer einzigen Menschenstimme.
(When the automobile, emerging from dark, dully echoing lanes, crossed one of those great avenues as wide as whole squares, there opened out on both sides an endless perspective of pavements filled with a moving mass of people moving forward in tiny steps, whose song was more unified than even a single human voice.) (KA, v. 74)

This description offers images of expanse in which the 'winzige[n] Schritte[n]' ('tiny steps') of the mass of people—like the waistcoat and chain—serve as a marker of scale. But it also reflects the way space is perceived by Karl as he is transported from the shelter of one father figure to another.

Karl's relief imagining his arrival 'in einem beleuchteten, von Mauern umgebenen, von Hunden bewachten Landhause' ('in a well-lit country house surrounded by walls and guarded by dogs') highlights one psychological implication of the play between vastness or endless distance and containment. While the limitlessness of vastness provokes uncertainty, not least about future, containment promises rest and shelter, though perhaps also claustrophobia and constraint (KA, v. 75). Karl's anticipation of the walled and guarded suburban country house, and his difficulty in leaving it, also anticipates Kafka's story 'Der Bau' (1923–1924), the plot of which details a creature's obsessive meditations on the fortification of his underground structure and whether it is safe to leave it. For Karl the psychological comfort of containment is soon troubled by ambiguous indications, both that the country house harbours incongruent vastness, and that he might not be permitted to leave. The view from the outside the house, which is lit only from below, renders not only a myopic perspective, but one that diminishes the viewing subject: 'konnte man gar nicht bemessen, wie weit es in die Höhe reichte' ('one could not even estimate how far it rose upwards') (KA, v. 76). Karl gets lost in 'dem großen Haus, den endlosen Gängen, der Kapelle, den leeren Zimmern, dem Dunkel überall' ('in the big house, in the endless passages, the chapel, the empty rooms, the darkness everywhere') (KA, v. 105). The house and its locality thus present a highly ambiguous space, both contained and vast, both protective and threateningly confining. When Karl feels most confined—alles beengte ihn hier' ('everything confined him here') (KA, v. 108)—he feels drawn back towards his uncle's abode from which, however, he will be expelled before ever arriving. The distance imagined between the country house and his uncle's is more impressive than even Karl's desire to return. The feeling of being confined in the house ('beengte') is juxtaposed to the way out, which seems to beckon through a metaphorical voice ('Stimme') resonant with the sirens' song in which voices also lure one away:

> der Weg zum Onkel durch die Glastüre, über die Treppe, durch die Allee, über die Landstraßen, durch die Vorstädte zur großen Verkehrstraße, einmündend in des Onkels Haus, erschien ihm als etwas streng Zusammengehöriges, das leer, glatt, und für ihn vorbereitet dalag und mit einer starken Stimme ihm verlangte.
>
> (the way to his uncle through the glass doors, over the steps, through the alley, over the country roads, through the suburbs to the large avenue of traffic leading to the uncle's house, seem to him as something that all strictly belonged together, that lay there ready before him empty and smooth and compelled him with a strong voice.) (KA, v. 108)

Before Karl manages to free himself, he plays a tune on the piano for Klara, which further suggests progress towards the *Ferne*, as the end of the melody leads in fact to another. While he plays, Karl feels 'in sich ein Leid entstehen, das, über das Ende des Liedes hinaus, ein anderes Ende suchte und es nicht finden konnte' ('a sorrow emerging which, beyond the end of the song, sought another end and could not find it'). Although Karl's piano playing does come to an end, he is unable to feel a sense of arrival, and he comes close to weeping: '"Ich kann ja nichts," sagte Karl nach Schluß des Liedes und sah Klara mit Tränen in den Augen an' ('"But I can do nothing," said Karl after the end of the song and looked at Klara with tears in his eyes') (KA, v. 119).

The sense of endlessness resonates from many spatial images in the work. Running from the police in Brunelda's suburb, Karl foolishly avoids cross-streets even though one of these would better throw off his pursuer;

he sticks to the main street and concentrates on its vanishing point in the distance:

> [E]r wollte sich, solange es nur ging, an diese weithin übersichtliche Straße halten, die erst tief unten in eine Brücke auslief, die, kaum begonnen, in Wasser- und Sonnendunst verschwand.
>
> (He wanted, as long as it was possible, to keep to this main street, which could be observed in each direction, since it did not terminate until far below in a bridge that, hardly begun, vanished in a haze of mist and sunshine.) (KA, v. 284)

Interior spaces, like Pollunder's house, also afford glimpses of perceived or seeming endlessness, which casts Karl in the position of helplessness. The ascent to Brunelda's apartment affords a similar perception: 'die Treppe war noch nicht einmal zu Ende, sondern führte im Halbdunkel weiter, ohne daß irgend etwas auf ihren baldigen Abschluß hinzudeuten schien' ('the stairs were not yet at an end, but rather led farther in half darkness, without any indication that they would terminate soon') (KA, v. 289). When Karl finally leaves Pollunder's house, 'erstaunt im Freien' ('astonished in the open air'), he has nowhere to go; he thus chooses a direction at whim 'und machte sich auf den Weg' ('and set out on his way') (KA, v. 127). Karl's eventual destination of 'Das Naturtheater von Oklahama' ('The Nature Theatre of Oklahama') (as it was spelled by Holitscher) is also discussed with Fanny in a shared reverence for its almost mystical immensity. This almost endless theatre becomes Karl's last goal, of course unreached within the finished text.

DISTANCE AND VASTNESS: THE UNDETERMINED SPACES OF KAFKA'S CHINA AND RUSSIA

A central text in Kafka's construction of exotic places is the story 'Beim Bau der Chinesischen Mauer', in which vastness and distance also play an important symbolic role. Among other exotic motifs in Kafka's story set in China is the anecdote in which emperors' wives are said to lasciviously devour their husbands' blood while lying on silk cushions. This anecdote in Kafka's story manifests several important parallels to the sadistic treatment of the condemned man by the officer in *In der Strafkolonie*. While Paul Peters identifies the subject of *In der Strafkolonie* as the inhumane practices by German colonists in Africa, and as colonialist space in general—'the colonial and Kafka's "texts" are one', he writes—the story has been linked to penal practices in (non-colonial) China, and admits striking similarities to 'Beim Bau der Chinesischen Mauer'.[44] In both texts, personal and imperial violence—violence of an individual against the body of another but under the auspices of imperial authority—is described. In both cases this takes place outside Europe and its social mores, in an exotic place: the colonized island, in *In der Strafkolonie*, and ancient China in 'Beim Bau der Chinesischen Mauer'. In both cases this violence has overtones of sadism or sexual gratification for the one who inflicts it. Historical discontinuities, too, govern both of the texts. Like the infliction of bloody torture in the punishments advocated by the old colonial rule in the penal colony, ancient imperial bloodletting described in China belongs to the past in contrast to present imperial rule. In the penal colony, the new commandant advocates an ostensibly more humane punishment, which threatens to wipe out the practices of the old authority.[45] The officer suffers from the extinction of the old penal practices and is apparently their last victim.

Yet the historical exigency in China is reversed: while the departed emperors among whom the violence takes place are revered, the new authorities in China are not even recognized by the populace: 'Es [das Volk] weiß nicht welcher Kaiser regiert' ('The people know not which emperor reigns') (KA/NSI, 352). The present, not the past, is endangered, and the ineffectuality of the present seems to be guaranteed by the spatial vastness of the country; for by the time people hear of a far-off revolution, it is considered long over and an old wound healed: 'So bereit ist man bei uns, die Gegenwart auszulöschen' ('Here one is ready to extinguish the present') (KA/NSI Apparatband, 299). In this reversal of historical progress, Kafka may reproduce here Orientalist images of Asia as immune to cultural change or modern enlightenment (as represented in Settembrini's condemnation of 'das asiatische Prinzip' ('the Asian principle') in Mann's *Der Zauberberg*, discussed in the previous chapter); but this immunity is also an immunity to colonization by imagined 'invaders' from the North, against whom the Great Wall is being built. A further reversal of the power dynamics of the penal colony is characteristic in Kafka's China: the old emperors in China, not their powerless subjects, are victims of sexual sadism.

> Die kaiserlichen Frauen, überfüttert in den seidenen Kissen, von schlauen Höflingen der edelen Sitte entfremdet, anschwellend in Herrschsucht, auffahrend in Gier, ausgebreitet in Wollust, verüben ihre Untaten immer

---

[44] Peters (2001: 419).
[45] This 'progress' is also parodied (for the condemned are stuffed with sugar candies that make them vomit and gagged with ladies' handkerchiefs provided by the commandant's female attendants).

wieder von Neuem; je mehr Zeit schon vergangen ist, desto schrecklicher
leuchten alle Farben und mit lautem Wehgeschrei erfährt einmal das Dorf,
wie eine Kaiserin vor Jahrtausenden in langen Zügen ihres Mannes Blut
trank.

(These imperial wives, overly pampered on their silk pillows, alienated
from noble customs by conniving courtiers, swelling with ambition, raging
with greed, uncontrollable in their lust, practice their misdeeds ever anew;
the more time passes the more horrific flow the colours of their deeds, and
with a loud cry of suffering the village finds out how an empress thousands of
years ago drank her husband's blood in long gulps.) (KA/NSI, 353)

While there may be indications of the power dynamics between the native
and the colonizer in *In der Strafkolonie*,[46] the sexual sadism attributed to
the ancient empire in China escapes the logic of self and other. Chinese
empresses drink the blood of their own husbands and emperors, their
closest allies in nationality, class, and legal-familial affiliation. The sexual
sadism is thus not a master–slave dialectic, but perhaps a narcissistic
cannibalism on the part of the old regime; this violence correlates to the
imperial status as self-referential vector of authority, national identity, law,
and spiritual orientation that fails to reach beyond itself to the villages, as
well as to the far frontiers. In the 'Untaten' the difference between
feminine and masculine, too, is nearly erased: the masculine 'Herrsch-
sucht' of the women does not obliterate the femininity of their sexual
desire, as they are also depicted 'überfüttert in den seidenen Kissen'. The
sadistic sexuality of this legend does not involve the domination of the
foreign, or the *Heimat* and *Fremde*, of colonialist discourse. Kafka's
presentation of China here is outside the sexual *Verkehr* central to recent
cultural studies readings: the sexuality does not travel beyond the imperial
interior; the travel (of legends and rumour and time itself) proceeds
ineffectually across the irreducible vastness. The vastness, it is suggested,
is unvanquishable by cultural determination. The overwhelming power of
space to swallow up not only imperial power, but the effects of its violence,
suggests that the most important topographical theme of 'Beim Bau der
Chinesischen Mauer' is not the erotic space of the central authority, but
the vastness that neutralizes its relevance.

The vastness of China functions in this story not merely as an Orientalist cliché, but as a spatial neutralization of cultural and political author-

[46] Peters (2001: 410–411) casts the prisoner as native African, 'firmly beyond the pale of
all contemporary codes of the "European"', though Kafka gives no racial identification to
his characters. Some of the adjectives applied to the prisoner, which count for evidence of
the African as perceived by the colonialist oppressor, for instance, 'hündisch', are found in
many other contexts in his writings, not least his protagonist in *Forschungen eines Hundes*
(*Investigations of a Dog*).

ity that would radiate across the vast territory. This neutralization may be related to the topographical meaning of the miniature story 'Von den Gleichnissen' ('On Parables'), for its very theme is undetermined space, or space that cannot be located on a map, within a recognizable cultural or topographical space. Like Keats's sonnet 'On the Sonnet', which describes the sonnet itself as a space (a human body) that must be constrained (bound) through metre and controlled through rhyme, 'Von den Gleichnissen' is textually self-reflexive, suggesting a commentary on the poetic 'space' of the parable. But in contrast to the sonnet, which, as Keats emphasizes, requires containment, the parable concerns an open, or undetermined, spatial referent. Kafka's brief text presents the problem of under- or undetermined spaces, resistant to mimetic representation. The wisdom of parables ('Gleichnis') refers to no actual place, but to a place always beyond the world at hand.

> Wenn der Weise sagt: 'Gehe hinüber', so meint er nicht, daß man auf die andere Straßenseite hinüber gehn solle . . . sondern er meint irgendein sagenhaftes Drüben, etwas was wir nicht kennen, was auch von ihm nicht näher zu bezeichnen ist und was uns also hier gar nichts helfen kann.
>
> (When the wise one says: go over there, he does not mean that someone should cross to the other side of the street . . . rather, he means some legendary 'over there', something of which we know nothing, which cannot be indicated more precisely, and which therefore cannot help us here at all.)
> (KA/NSII, 531–532)

This 'sagenhaftes Drüben', a place 'das wir nicht kennen', is an 'elsewhere' within the imagination, which 'hier' cannot be of help at all. The tension between determined cultural space and this vague, undetermined elsewhere structures the topography of Kafka's most exotic story, aspects of which cannot be registered in post-colonialist attempts to reconstruct a determinate spatial reference. The elsewhere is a deterritorialization (to adapt Deleuze's term specific to language) of the spatial imagination.

Yet 'Beim Bau der Chinesischen Mauer' is central to Rolf Goebel's reconstruction of cultural reference in Kafka's writing. Goebel shows how Kafka, in texts evoking China, assembles a vision of the Chinese land and culture from fin-de-siècle Orientalist discourse and readings, yet effaces the real topographical and cultural China on which they are based. Goebel aims then to 'reverse the self-decontextualization' of Kafka's works, to undo texts' own effacement of referents of place. Just as post-colonialist readings present Kafka's texts as alternatively undoing or promoting European colonialism of exotic spaces, Goebel's criticism aims to counter Kafka's unspecific spaces by reconstructing their 'referentiality', in order to show how Kafka deliberately undermines Eurocentric representations of the 'Oriental'.[47] In Goebel's account, Kafka subverts Orientalist discourse precisely by treating with ironic distance the pastiche of views of China he inherits. Kafka is then an unwitting post-colonial critic: his images of China are constructed 'in order to critique the Western project of representing the Orient'. On this view, Kafka's work 'performs a self-reflective critique of Orientalism's ideological positions'. While Goebel claims that China fascinates Kafka 'as a cultural text of surfaces, indecipherable signifiers, and appearance without tangible essences or ultimate truths', the topographical imagery of 'Beim Bau der Chinesischen Mauer' does not correspond to this depiction of an unreadable cultural text. The 'signifiers' in question are not merely indecipherable, like the script written by the apparatus in *In der Strafkolonie*, but are neutralized by space. The anecdote of imperial violence and the imperial message that cannot reach its destination during the emperor's lifetime are both neutralized by the distances that render them ineffectual; and the project of the Great Wall is itself rendered forever incomplete by virtue of the vast space and the laboriously described distances. The violence, imperial edict, and border building, which reflect imperial power, are all compromised by space, thus freeing the inhabitants from absolutist determinations. While Goebel details how Kafka 'self-reflexively suspend[s] the mimetic reflection of the actual China', his reading neglects the significance of this suspension in order to reconstruct the presumed mimetic origin of Kafka's depiction.[48]

'Beim Bau der Chinesischen Mauer' is an essential text for understanding Kafka's 'travels' because it evokes a space both recognizably foreign and under-determined. The China as described by the narrator is a topography that is identifiable in cultural and historical terms, and a space in which such significations are explicitly neutralized. The unfinished and seemingly perpetually built wall neutralizes the dialectic of *Heimat* and *Fremde* even while it fails to secure the space from foreign invaders. The motif of exotic but under-determined spatial distance emerges then as an analogy for imaginative freedom and whatever threatens it. The narrative absorption in spatial dimensions and orientations reveals a relationship between space—particularly distance and unconquered vastness—and the imagination.

Kafka's Russian topographical motifs similarly rely upon evocations of distance, vastness, and under-determined space, and may help to indicate further the significance of the under-determination of space in 'Beim Bau der Chinesischen Mauer'. The imagined escape afforded Georg

---

[47] Goebel (1997: 65).   [48] Goebel (1997: 2, 8).

Bendemann by the friend in St. Petersburg in *Das Urteil* relies upon the distance and vastness that Russia calls to mind. In reference to Dostoevsky Kafka evokes the 'unendliche Anziehungskraft Rußlands' ('endless appeal of Russia'), evocative both of freedom and desolation (KA/T, 727). These associations of Russian topography are explicit in the narrative 'Erinnerungen an die Kaldabahn', wherein the only named city is a place to which the narrator never arrives, as the train tracks leading to Kalda are left unfinished, ending somewhere in the Russian interior. Here Kafka presents the vastness of Russia as a terrain in which distance predominates over human effort and the cultural life that directs it. The unspecificity of the vague Russian landscape is reflected not only in the aborted project of finishing the tracks but also in the narrator's withholding of details concerning the project itself and his role in it. The narrator recalls his position working for a small railway 'im Innern Rußlands' ('in the Russian interior'). He is evasive about why he had sought out a very remote place to settle: '[a]us verschiedenen Gründen, die nicht hierher gehören' ('due to various reasons that are irrelevant here'). The purpose for the building of the railway is also withheld, the narrator referring only to 'irgendwelchen wirtschaftlichen Absichten' ('some sort of commercial aims'). With funds for finishing the line to Kalda lacking, the railway stops five days' journey by cart from its destination. The narrator settles into the one-room station of a small settlement 'geradezu in einer Einöde' ('exactly in the middle of nowhere') (KA/T, 549); this space, and the surrounding flat countryside, becomes a world of its own, most describable by its not seeming to be situated anywhere in particular but in a nearly uninhabited terrain. As he reflects on this remoteness and the loneliness it brings, the narrator emphasizes the vastness of the surrounding space. While the station serves as a point of orientation for the narrator, the arbitrariness of its location is striking, as it does not offer a point of connection among the surrounding villages.

> Ein regelmäßiger Verkehr war es natürlich nicht. Von den fünf Dörfern, die für mich in Betracht kamen, war jedes einige Stunden sowohl von der Station, als auch von den andern Dörfern entfernt. Allzuweit mich von der Station zu entfernen durfte ich nicht wagen, wenn ich nicht meinen Posten verlieren wollte.
>
> (There was, of course, no regular traffic. Of the five villages I could even consider, each was several hours from the station, as well as from each other. I was not permitted to venture too far from the station, if I did not want to lose my post.) (KA/T, 551)

Yet the narrator's own activities maintaining the line further emphasize his experience of space and distance. Required to clean the tracks for a kilometre in either direction from the station, he extends his scope and proceeds four more kilometres along the track, highlighting the distance from the station.

> Ich hielt mich aber nicht an diese Bestimmung und ging oft viel weiter, so weit, daß ich gerade noch die Station sehen konnte. Bei klarem Wetter war das noch bei etwa 5 km Entfernung möglich, das Land war ja ganz flach. War ich dann soweit, daß die Hütte in der Ferne mir schon vor den Augen fast nur flimmerte, sah ich manchmal infolge der Augentäuschung viele schwarze Punkte sich zur Hütte hin bewegen.
>
> (I did not, however, stick to this, and often went much farther, so far that I could just still see the station. In clear weather, that was possible for about 5 kilometres, since the land was so flat. Sometimes when I had reached such a distance that the little cabin in the distance was but a flicker, I saw as a result of this visual distortion many black spots move towards it.) (KA/T, 686)

The main topographical feature is the flatness of the land, which allows him to view objects very far in the distance, so that they seem unreal. Distance, it can be suggested, supports unreality, a sense of uncertainty about one's grasp on the world suggested by 'Augentäuschung'.

The desolation of the land brings to mind Siberia. While the narrator attempts to go hunting to secure provisions for the winter, he realizes that there is no wildlife to be hunted but bears and wolves; this desolation, along with the rats he confronts in the station house, suggests the isolation Kafka may have imagined reading Dostoevsky's account of his Siberian imprisonment (KA/T, 528). The possibility of starving also echoes Kafka's preoccupation with Napoleon's foray into Russia and the disastrous retreat.[49] But here these associations are more symbolic than cartographical. That the narrator has been misled about the indigenous game is due to the indeterminateness of this space:

> Die Leute hatten mich nicht falsch unterrichtet, die wildreiche Gegend bestand, nur war sie drei Tagereisen entfernt,—ich hatte nicht bedacht, daß die Ortsangaben in diesen über hunderte km hin unbewohnten Ländern notwendiger Weise unsicher sein müssen.
>
> (The people had not instructed me wrongly, it is just that the area rich with wildlife is three days' travel away—I had not considered that the specification of place in those lands, unpopulated for a hundred kilometres, would necessarily have to be uncertain.) (KA/T, 689)

As in the vast space of China, in the Russian interior, national and cultural events remain distant and incomprehensible. The station-keeper receives

---

[49] For a discussion of Kafka's fascination with Napoleon, see Robertson (1985: 132–133).

news only from old newspapers tossed once in a while from the train windows. One character from a serialized novel, a revenging commander, becomes a figure in his dreams, recalling the ambiguous relationship with his superior, to whose insulting inspections and precarious moods he is subject until the evening when schnapps and physical embraces render them 'ganz einig'. While the isolation of the station offers a space for their intimacy, this is dissolved each time the station-master boards the train again. The refuge within the vastness provides an 'elsewhere' apart from ordinary administrative and commercial life, and the social or sexual solidarity that is developed in the station-house is not sustainable over distance. This vastness is also ambiguous with respect to the narrator's livelihood; because of the distance to be crossed, the train project, albeit unfinished, provides a job for the narrator; but the isolation also brings about the narrator's illness. The narrator must walk two hours to fetch water from a stream and to bathe, and catches a potentially fatal chill:

> Es begann mit einem starken Husten. Etwa zwei Stunden landeinwärts von der Station entfernt, war ein kleiner Bach, aus dem ich in einem Faß auf einem Schubkarren meinen Wasservorrat zu holen pflegte. Ich badete dort auch öfters und dieser Husten war die Folge dessen.
>
> (It began with a strong cough. Some two hours into the country from the station was a small stream, from which I filled a barrel in a wheelbarrow with my water supply. I bathed there often and this cough was the result of that.)
> (KA/T, 693)

The locals call his illness 'Wolfshusten' or wolf's cough, an image that evokes wildness and the savage effects of isolation in the vast interior of Russia. But this isolation is also freedom from whatever unspecified circumstances, the 'verschiedenen Gründen, die nicht hierher gehören', which drove the narrator to seek out a very remote place.

The descriptive space in 'Beim Bau der Chinesischen Mauer' also profits from the play on distance and vastness as undetermined by functional civic and social life. A brief review of the spatial descriptions in this text can help to highlight its narrator's obsessive preoccupation with imagining and calculating the vast space of China. The narrative begins with an account of spatial coordinates; seven initial sentences concern spatial dimensions: north, south, east and west; spatial measurements; or gaps in the wall where it is as yet incomplete. These are followed by considerations of the spatial aspects of the construction: jointure of parts; again reference to northern invaders and the problem of discontinuity of the defensive construction; the vulnerability of the incomplete parts of the wall; and the spatial perspective given by the overview of the higher officials, as opposed to the immediate point of view of the lowest workers. The narrator then describes the preparations and training required of the population to undertake the project of building a wall around 'ganzen China' ('the whole of China'), and there is a reflection of this project in miniature, when the narrator recounts 'wie wir als kleine Kinder...im Gärtchen unseres Lehrers standen, aus Kieselsteinen eine Art Mauer bauen mußten' ('how as small children...standing in the little garden of our teacher, we had to build a kind of wall out of pebbles') (KA/NSI, 340). Towards the end of this pages-long paragraph, there is a shift in spatial terms from the horizontal project of the building of a wall to the vertical hierarchy of the various participants, from overseers to the lowest worker: 'oberste Prüfung der untersten Schule'; 'die oberste Höhe der ihnen zugänglichen Ausbildung'; 'Bauführer...untersten Ranges'; 'die oberen Führer' ('the highest examination of the lowest school'; 'the highest level of education accessible to them'; 'building foreman...of the lowest rank'; 'the superior leader'). Some of these vertical positions intersect with horizontal materiality of the wall itself or with metaphorical extension: 'die mittleren Führer sahen von dem vielseitigen Wachsen des Baues genug' ('the middle leaders saw enough of the multidimensional development of the wall construction'); and the narrator refers to 'die untern, geistig weit über ihrer äußerlich kleinen Aufgabe stehenden Männer' ('the underlings, men who stood spiritually far above their apparently small assignments'). Further in this paragraph are mentioned regions ('Gebirgsgegend', 'Quartieren'), and measured distances ('hunderte Meilen', 'fünfhundert Meter', 'tausend Meter'), as well as topographical demarcations—forests, mountains, the depths of the land. Despite this survey of the land, the final image of the paragraph is 'das unendliche China' ('boundless China') itself, a space which, for all the effort expended narratively on the survey and described in the building of the wall, defies both circumscription and containment (KA/NSI, 340–342).

The depiction of China's vastness in fact undermines the laboriously considered plans for building a wall around the whole country to protect it from invasion. For 'das unendliche China' is a space that cannot be mapped, as it is an imaginary space that defies totality: 'So groß ist unser Land, kein Märchen reicht an seine Größe, kaum der Himmel umspannt es' ('Our land is so vast that no fairy tale can contain it, the sky hardly covers it'). The narrator's reference to the imperial centre—'Peking ist nur ein Punkt, und das kaiserliche Schloß nur ein Pünktchen' ('Peking is just a dot, and the castle only a tiny dot') (KA/NSI, 350)—introduces both the political and temporal-historical aspects of the story, and provides a point of reference, a focal point from which significant space could be imagined to extend. Yet this centre is diminished culturally to the point of irrelevance for the inhabitants living at great distances from it.

The political weakness and historical immobility of the imperial authorities—revealed as decadent by the anecdote of their sadistic bloodletting—are important points of tension for imagining freedom within that vastness. Losing connection with the present emperor but not with the 'Kaiser als solcher' of ages past, the people of the region experience the triumph of vastness over determination, of imaginative possibility over determinate actuality, and thus, in Aristotle's terms, of the poetic over the historical. While the emperor of old was 'groß durch alle Stockwerke der Welt', the emperor of the present lies only in a bed that is thought by the populace to be 'nur schmal und kurz' ('only slight and short'). The vertical image of 'Stockwerke' ('stories') is replaced by a horizontal one, suggesting a collapse of hierarchy and a diminution of authority. The present emperor is 'tausende Meilen im Süden' ('a thousand miles to the South')—almost in another country, bordering 'doch schon fast ans tibetanische Hochland' ('in fact almost on the Tibetan highlands') (KA/NSI, 350). Distance here signifies diminution of power, but a corresponding empowerment of those from whom the emperor is distant; they adhere, therefore, to a spirituality respecting emperors of ages past who, however, no longer hold power over the present.

The inset narrative, 'Eine kaiserliche Botschaft', within this story links the descriptive space of 'Beim Bau der Chinesischen Mauer' explicitly to the imagination and calls to mind the 'irgendein sagenhaftes Drüben' ('some kind of legendary over there') of Kafka's parable. The anecdote concerns the problem of distance ('in die fernste ferne geflüchteten Schatten' ['shadows fled to the most distant distance']) and obstacle, as the messenger must travel through the palace, descending ever again more steps, through another palace, through more courtyards, and so on, and will not arrive at his destination before the emperor is dead. While this passage reflects the ineffectuality of an imperial regime, it is also spatially evocative, as longing for passage into the distance is suggested to the reader: 'Öffnete sich freies Feld, wie würde er fliegen und bald hörtest Du das herrliche Schlagen seiner Fäuste an Deiner Tür' ('If an open field gave free passage, how he would fly, and soon you would hear the magnificent sounding of his fist on your door'). The address in the second person explicitly evokes daydreaming or imagining, and suggests one basis of interpretation for the story as a whole: 'Du aber sitzt an Deinem Fenster und erträumst sie Dir, wenn der Abend kommt' ('But you sit at your window and dream it when evening falls') (GW/B, 79; KA/DL, 281, 282). Like the window out of which Georg Bendemann gazes in *Das*

Urteil, the window here offers a view not only to the outside, but off into the distance, which, as imagined, need respect no limits.

While Goebel neglects this imaginative aspect of 'Eine kaiserliche Botschaft', the representation of imperial China as essentially ahistorical, beset by a cycle of ineffective revolutions, may very well be an aspect of Kafka's inheritance of European and even specifically German Orientalist views of China. While Goebel's account of this inheritance is compelling, in the story itself the political regime seems to offer above all a means by which to evoke the unconquerable vastness of space, for which the Chinese topography is ideally symbolic. A similar motif concerning historical change or lack of change and revolutions is described also in the 1920 fragment 'Unser Städtchen liegt nicht etwa an der Grenze' ('Our little town does not lie on the frontier'), which, like 'Ein altes Blatt', suggests but does not refer to China; thus this work offers a culturally indeterminate space. Certain features recall the description of the distance to the frontiers and the crowded capital of Peking in 'Beim Bau der Chinesischen Mauer'. But here the cultural topography is blank: there are only the capital, the small cities and large ones, the frontier, and the distances between them:

> Unser Städtchen liegt nicht etwa an der Grenze, bei weitem nicht, zur Grenze ist es noch so weit, daß vielleicht noch niemand aus dem Städtchen dort gewesen ist, wüste Hochländer sind zu durchqueren, aber auch weite fruchtbare Länder. Man wird müde wenn man sich nur einen Teil des Weges vorstellt und mehr als einen Teil kann man sich gar nicht vorstellen.
>
> (Our little town does not lie on the frontier, not even close to the frontier, it is still so far that perhaps no one in our town has even been there, there are desolate highlands to cross but also vast fertile plains. Just imagining a part of the road makes one tired, and one can imagine no more than a part.) (KA/NSII, 261)

The frontier's unreachable distance provides both a vanishing point and, like Kant's relegation of the regulative ideals (for instance, the idea of God) to a 'focus imaginarius', a point by which the distance and the destination can be 'measured' at all. Not only desolate highlands but also the fruitful plains have to be crossed. The passage evokes not primarily a physical crossing—since there is no subject for the passive 'wüste Hochländer sind zu durchqueren' ('desolate highlands to be crossed')—but rather an imaginative one. The difficulty of imagining the distance serves to reflect the imagination of the narrator (and reader) as active generator of such vast spaces and brings to mind Kant's notion of the dynamically sublime. The vastness of space is further evoked by indications of difficult communication, which also allows the narrator to report a difficult and alienated relation to authority. For even further from the narrator's town than the frontier is the capital: 'Aber doch noch weiter als bis zur Grenze ist . . . also noch viel weiter als bis zur Grenze ist es von unserem Städtchen zur Hauptstadt' ('But still further than to the frontier . . . what from our town is even further than to the frontier is the distance to the capital') (KA/NSII, 261–262). The area of the disputed border is, though distant, communicatively closer to the narrator's home: 'Während wir von den Grenzkriegen hie und da doch Nachrichten bekommen, erfahren wir aus der Hauptstadt fast nichts' ('While we receive now and then news about border wars, we experience nothing of that in the capital') (KA/NSII, 262).

In both texts, then, references to (ineffective) revolutionary unrest are rendered in terms of spatial distance.[50] The distance of Peking from the local villages is described as both spiritual and geographical: 'Peking selbst ist den Leuten im Dorf viel fremder als das jenseitige Leben' ('Peking itself is, to the villagers, much more foreign than the life hereafter') (KA/NSI, 354). The cultural and geographical alienation from Peking—and thus from the centre of law, authority, and nationality—on the part of the villagers extends to metaphysical scepticism about the capital's very existence:

> Sollte es wirklich ein Dorf geben, wo Haus an Haus steht, bedeckend Felder, weiter als der Blick von unserem Hügel reicht und zwischen diesen Häusern stünden bei Tag und bei Nacht Menschen Kopf an Kopf?
>
> (Is there really such a town where houses stand one after another side by side, covering the fields, farther than what can be seen from our hills, and between these houses so many people packed in day and night?) (KA/NSI, 354)

The image of the imperial centre—and of any densely populated city and its central governance—is replaced by an ethereal image lacking density, centre, and exact location:

> Leichter als solche Stadt sich vorstellen ist es, zu glauben Peking und sein Kaiser wären eines, etwa eine Wolke, ruhig unter der Sonne sich wandelnd im Laufe der Zeiten.
>
> (Easier than imagining such a city would be believing that Peking and our emperor were one, something like a cloud, calmly wandering beneath the sun with the passage of time.) (KA/NSI, 354)

---

[50] In a sentence crossed out of 'Beim Bau der Chinesischen Mauer', and so relegated to the *Apparatband*, it is reported that 'In einer benachbarten, aber immerhin sehr weit entfernten Provinz war ein Aufstand ausgebrochen' ('In a neighboring, but in any case very distant province, a rebellion had broken out') (KA/NSI Apparatband, 298).

This reported questioning of the reality of the imperial centre ought to lead the reader to question the reality of the 'China' the narrator ostensibly evokes. The real China is usurped by the vastness that it symbolizes, as Kafka situates Chinese motifs within an explicitly under-determined topography. In this passage, the supplanting image of a wandering cloud is not only expressive of political discontent; it liberates the people's imagination. Rather than being dominated by authority from the nation's centre, those who hold this view enjoy 'ein gewissermaßen freies, unbeherrschtes Leben' that affords even 'Sittenreinheit', or moral purity (KA/NSI, 354).

In 'Beim Bau der Chinesischen Mauer' the vastness of China is evoked in other ways, for instance, numerically, by reference to the ten thousand villages of the narrator's province and the five hundred provinces of China, between which seem to be implied vast distances. While measurement in kilometres and days' travel is also a feature of 'Erinnerungen an die Kaldabahn', here vastness is suggested by quantities difficult to conjure by the human imagination, but easily conceived by reason, as Kant described the mathematically sublime. The impossibility of conjuring in any visual image five million villages (to which Kafka's China would be home if all of the provinces were populated in even distribution) is, however, only an expression of another kind of sublimity, more akin to what Kant called the dynamical sublime, which resists quantification and indeed measurement—the vastness marked only by distant (and so indeterminate) frontiers, by the distance of the imperial centre, and by the far-off but pressing threat of invasion, all of which must be imaginatively generated rather than rationally conceived.

The imagination of the inhabitants of this 'China' is evoked further by the narrator. While the narrator claims caution with respect to generalizing the attitude of the Chinese people, his own observations or readings are nevertheless credited with providing opportunity 'durch die Seelen fast aller Provinzen zu reisen' ('to travel through the souls of nearly all the provinces') (KA/NSI, 355), and he proceeds to make just such a generalization about the people's attitudes. The institution of the empire has failed to reach 'bis an die fernsten Grenzen des Reiches' ('to the farthest frontier of the realm'). While the narrator ostensibly criticizes the authorities, his immediate turn to the 'Vorstellungs- oder Glaubenskraft beim Volke' ('the people's power of imagination or belief') is telling. The imaginative capacities of the people have been too weak to transport the empire symbolically from distant Peking to their own hearts. But in fact this weakness has preserved their very freedom from domination and is called 'geradezu der Boden, auf dem wir leben' ('the very ground on which we live') (KA/NSI, 356). The refusal of the narrator to go further into the

question of the essence of this weakness—'darum will ich in der Unter-
suchung . . . nicht weiter gehen' ('because of that I do not want to go on in
the investigation') is the positive image of the inability of the imperial
institution to dominate the far reaches of the province. Thus, both in
reference to the reader ('Du') and to the imperial subjects, the vastness of
China and the distances within it afford an indeterminacy that is explicitly
linked to the freedom of imagination.

Goebel defends his practice of reconstruction of determinate referents
in these texts in terms of Kafka's 'conceal[ment]' or 'suppression of
discursive cultural contexts'.[51] This characterization of Kafka's writing
and editing process is not neutral. It presumes the primacy of potential
cultural referents over the text's own descriptive space. The terminology of
concealment or suppression invokes a moral or political authority for the
critic who rescues cultural content. And it presumes mimetic description,
even if textually based or parasitic on other discourses, as the fundamental
origin of the work, which need be only uncovered or made legible by the
critic. It obscures what Corngold has called Kafka's 'leap into higher and
more incalculable zones', which may be accomplished in Kafka's writing
when it departs from the realm of the experienced.[52] The priority of
restoring the cultural referent is projected over and against Kafka's own
method of writing and the imaginative freedom upon which, as has been
shown here, it explicitly reflects. This interpretative approach, while
helpfully illuminating Kafka's cultural context, assumes a double standard
with respect to the autonomy of the text: authorial intention does not
determine the meaning of the text, and yet this meaning—evoked in the
notion of the text's true 'origin'—can be determined by the cultural
discourses in so far as they are, at least in principle, recoverable by the
critic. To his credit, Goebel acknowledges that this approach is a 'reading
against Kafka's intention'.[53] Yet Kafka's intention as a writer—in so far as
that can be ascertained—is not the only element of his work that is
overridden or dismissed in this reconstruction. Since they are aligned
with a network of cultural signs embedded in contemporaneous or inherited discourse, the originality and descriptive idiosyncrasy of Kafka's
topographies is no longer recognizable. Descriptive imagery can be regarded only as reproductions, plays upon, combinations, distortions, or
erasures of signs and discourses already available within the cultural world
at large.

[51] Goebel (1997: 99).
[52] Corngold (2004: 112).
[53] Goebel (1997: 99).

CONCLUSION

While Kafka's exotic spaces are distinct in essential ways from any real empirical places, they need not be, as Adorno argues, 'geschlossen logisch durch und durch und des Sinnes bar' ('logically closed through and through and devoid of any sense').[54] If they are, as Heller's reference to Kafka suggests, geographical symbols for the turn inward, for disoriented and groundless self-reflection, they also promote liberation that does not preclude potential content for the imagination and directives for living. Yet it has been shown in this chapter that the most exotic of Kafka's spaces are incompatible with empirically liveable or politically identifiable spaces. The evocation of topographies in Kafka's writings are not symbolic equivalents for a grab for land, nor do they establish a second, more original home for the tourist or colonialist in a foreign place. Instead, they extricate the imagination from the determinations of empirical actualization and familiar constraints.

In this chapter Kafka's exotic topographies of travel, vastness, and distance have been shown to offer alternative possibilities for conceiving spatial experience; faraway and vast places in particular help to negotiate between the social and cultural determinations of the self and the possibilities that lie beyond them. Kafka has offered an alternative perception of the world through the non-oppositional intimacy of friendship, principally expressed in 'Richard und Samuel' and *Das Urteil* and treated in 'Erinnerungen an die Kaldabahn'; a parody of *Fernweh*, principally in *Der Verschollene*, with its portrait of Karl as an ambiguously adolescent exile; and a projection of imaginative freedom through spatial vastness, prominent in 'Beim Bau der Chinesischen Mauer'. These topographies, in various ways, express the difficulties of achieving imaginative freedom within the entanglements and spaces of the actual world; they reflect Kafka's aim, cited at the outset of this chapter, to raise the world to a higher, purer, truer reality.

Kafka's exotic imagery of 'elsewhere' (in 'Eine kaiserliche Botschaft' and 'Die Abweisung') seems to remain immanent to the imagination; such imagery cannot be understood solely according to the dialectic between the familiar and the foreign. In his journals Kafka imagines his own existence in terms of isolation in an indeterminate place. The description of his isolation not only from family but 'von der ganzen Welt' ('from the whole world') evokes the imagery of a Russian winter:

---

[54] Adorno (1977: 268).

Ein Bild meiner Existenz in dieser Hinsicht gibt eine nutzlose, mit Schnee und Reif überdeckte, schief in den Erdboden leicht eingebohrte Stange auf einem bis in die Tiefe aufgewühlten Feld am Rande einer großen Ebene in einer dunklen Winternacht.

(In this respect an image of my existence offers a pole stuck lightly and lopsided in the earth, covered in snow and hoarfrost, in a field turned up to the depth on the edge of a great plain on a dark winter night.) (KA/T, 705)

This cold and dark existence at the edge of nowhere is not an image of any lived or livable topography. But this isolation portrays an 'elsewhere' apart from the constraints of the familiar sphere, where the imagination may become productive, and where other possibilities of communication may emerge. This 'elsewhere' is antithetical both to existentialist reductions and post-colonialist accounts of Kafka's writings. Where post-colonialist critics would see only a 'territorial claim' even in Kafka's most severe image of a longing for elsewhere, that of a refuge on the moon from all that oppresses him, this refuge could not be found in any earthly topography that could be politically identified.[55]

There is a potentially positive implication for this symbolic and imaginative isolation, which can be approached through Kafka's spiritual sensibilities and his persistent longing for freedom from familiar and familial constraints. Robertson describes Kafka's ethical task in part as a struggle against the world, reflecting Kafka's investment in a division between a higher realm of the infinite or 'das Unzerstörbare' and the worldly realm. That Kafka is also concerned with the inevitable division between the self-conscious, reflecting observer of reality and one who lives, as Flaubert put it, 'dans le vrai', suggests at least the possibility of a life from which the higher reality does not remain remote.[56] Corngold also addresses, in reference to Kafka's late aphorisms, Kafka's 'higher mimesis—the rhythmic dawning and vanishing of a constellation of the mind'. Yet the topographical imagery in the texts discussed here does not linger in vanishing, in the 'frenzy of deconstruction' Corngold attributes to the aphorisms,[57] but rather evokes an elsewhere between creation and dissipation that is indebted to its distance from the experienced world. The references to specific places mark the topographies discussed here as exotic; yet they cannot be located in an empirical geography.

While this chapter has presented spaces of and for the liberated imagination, in the following chapter the evocation of exotic spaces reveals

---

55 Zilcosky (2003: 149).
56 Robertson (1985: 202); (2002b: 142).
57 Corngold (2004: 140–141).

deeper strata of the inner life. For some of Kafka's contemporaries, the break from empirical reality—through dreams, aesthetic projections, and mystical awareness—allows exploration of the psyche's primal depths. In Benn, Musil, and Kubin, the exploration of such depths through the motives of exotic space exposes primitive elements of human experience repressed by modern rationality.

4

Inner Depths

*Exotic Topographies of Primal Consciousness
in Benn, Musil, and Kubin*

The previous chapters have shown that the evocation of exotic spaces, whether experienced, metaphorically exoticized, or wholly imagined, has served to highlight and challenge the boundaries of the modern self, and to imagine both dangerous and liberating alternatives to the familiar constitution of the modern world. The motifs of the self's need for epiphany, its vulnerability to breakdown in the transgression of boundaries, and its imaginative longing for elsewhere (highlighted, respectively, in Chapters 1, 2, and 3) converge in works, to be discussed in this penultimate chapter, that turn explicitly inward, to the exotic rendering of the inner life. It will be shown here how reflections on the aesthetic imagination, mystical-erotic reverie, and the interior experiences of dreams in works by Gottfried Benn, Robert Musil, and Alfred Kubin employ exotic topographical imagery, both to undermine the Enlightenment model of a rationally unified self and to explore primal elements of the psyche that may offer a renewal of human life and creativity. These primal elements are expressed by the often-intertwining motifs of the primitive, mysticism, and animality, reflecting the fin-de-siècle influence of Nietzsche (along with Schopenhauer) and the sometimes competing developments of cultural anthropology, psychoanalysis, and neuroscience. In Musil's *Drei Frauen (Three Women)* (1924), Benn's *Gehirne (Brains)* (1916) and related works, and in Kubin's novel *Die andere Seite (The Other Side)* (1909), the cave, the recesses of the brain, and a dream-world founded in the interior of China, respectively, serve as analogies for the opaque depths of the inner life pervaded by primal forces. In all of these works, exotic topographies (whether African or Asian, Mediterranean, sea, jungle or desert terrain) are evoked both in contrast to ordinary life in modern Europe and as analogies for aspects of the human psyche—available in aesthetic, mystical, and dream experiences—excluded from its dominant forms of experience.

This chapter begins by briefly tracing the Western representation of the self as interior space and metaphoric depth, and, in modernism, its pervasion by exotic forces. The influence of Nietzsche is then established as a common source for the stylistically divergent authors discussed in this chapter, in their respective critiques of rational subjectivity and of the dominance of scientific thought, and in their affirmations of the body as the organic substrate of the vital self.[1] The chapter then proceeds to outline three related modes of exploring the topography of primal consciousness in the writings of Benn, Musil, and Kubin: the aesthetic projections of southern or eastern exotic landscapes, mysticism, and the evocation of dreams. It will be shown that all of these writers contend with the modern self as split between a spiritually impoverished rationality and the depths of more primitive animality that emerge when its inner fragmentations are exposed. By exploring this danger, the texts by Benn, Musil, and Kubin propose new ways of living and develop a new aesthetic out of the fragmentation and decay.

THE INNER TOPOGRAPHY OF THE SELF AND ITS EXOTICIZATION

The spatial representation of the self as an inner 'topography' has developed in Western thought in three significant ways. First, the mind or self has been represented as an 'inner' space as opposed to the space of the external world. Secondly, the self's inner space has been imagined as having expanse and depth, suggesting inaccessibility or opacity to self-reflection. Finally, in modernism, this opaque inner topography has been rendered exotic, through metaphors of jungle, desert, tropical, or other primitive, uncivilized landscapes, associating these 'depths' with primal forces underlying consciousness and usurping its autonomy. The notion of a rational, autonomous self is further undermined by the influence of nineteenth- and early twentieth-century developments in psychology, cultural anthropology, and neurophysiology.

Self-contemplation has been expressed through spatial imagery since Augustine, for whom truth is found in the soul. Augustine's *Confessions* provides not only a religious autobiography but also a diary of the self vacillating between external influences and inner sources of truth. Augustine solves the puzzle of time, for example, by turning away from the

---

[1] Nietzsche's influence on modern German literature is well established in the scholarship; see, for example, accounts relevant to the authors in this thesis in Martens (1971); Reichert (1975); Pasley (ed.) (1978); May (1988); Keith (2000).

Aristotelian model, based on the external observation of movement and change, to the internal processes of the mind's own recollection, attention, and anticipation.[2] In Augustine's metaphysics, as Charles Taylor has shown, the self is expressed 'not just occasionally and peripherally, but centrally and essentially in terms of inner/outer' dimensions; thus Augustine establishes in Western thought 'the inwardness of radical reflexivity'.[3] This division between inner and outer realms is maintained throughout Descartes's *Meditations*, in which certainty can be established by first disregarding the external world known by the senses, and then by founding 'first philosophy' on the clear and distinct, that is, innate, ideas of the mind. In the realm of aesthetics, Hegel charts the distance between classical Greek and modern art in terms of the development of interiority.[4]

In post-Cartesian depictions, however, this interiority becomes both vaster and deeper, and so more opaque to self-reflection. While for Descartes self-reflection was transparent, in so far as dreams and hallucinations could be banished from the cogito, Romantic art, as T. S. Eliot writes, comes to 'represent the depths of feeling into which we cannot peer'.[5] Erich Heller has described the aesthetic 'journey into the interior' initiated by Shakespeare's Hamlet, for whom the importance of the outer world diminished as he turned to the 'infinite space' of his obsessive imagination. In Heller's account this journey is undertaken through the 'inscape' of Romantic reflection, and then by Baudelaire and the Symbolist poets, culminating in Rilke.[6] In Proust, too, the self is described as an expansive interior space accessible through memory: 'j'entends la rumeur des distances traversées' ('I hear the echo of great spaces traversed').[7] This expansiveness can also be expressed through the metaphor of 'depth', which emphasizes the self's inexhaustibility. While Augustine and Descartes orient Western thought towards inwardness, it is with the idea 'of articulating our inner nature [that] we see the grounds for construing this

---

[2] See Augustine, *Confessions*, Book XI.

[3] Taylor (1989: 129, 141).

[4] Hegel (1955: 117).

[5] Eliot (1932: 148). While, as Taylor (1989: 548) shows, the notion of inner depths as 'a domain which we can never fully exhaust' rarely appears before Romanticism, it does appear in Montaigne's *Essais*: 'C'est une espineuse entreprise, et plus qu'il ne semble, de suyvre une alleure si vagabonde que celle de nostre esprit; de penetrer les profondeurs opaques de ses replis internes' ('It is a thorny undertaking, and more so than it seems, to follow a movement as wandering as that of our mind, to penetrate the opaque depths of its innermost folds') (1978: 378).

[6] Heller (1959: 129). In its extreme forms this interiority severs ties with external reality such that 'the only real world is the world of human inwardness', a condition Heller regards as culminating in Rilke's *Duineser Elegien*, 98. Taylor(1989: 489) also refers to Rilke's elegies in this context.

[7] Proust (1954: 67).

inner domain as having *depth*, that is, a domain which reaches farther than we can ever articulate, which still stretches beyond our furthest point of clear expression'.[8] Charles Taylor summarizes this characterization of the modern subject:

> The modern ... subject really has, unlike the denizens of any earlier culture, 'inner depths'. ... The sense of depth in inner space is bound up with the sense that we can move into it and bring things to the fore. This we do when we articulate. The inescapable feeling of depth comes from the realization that whatever we bring up, there is always more down there. Depth lies in there being always, inescapably, something beyond our articulative power.[9]

This inaccessibility to articulative power is due, however, not only to inexhaustibility but also to the modern recognition of the limits of rational self-reflection and the discovery of motivations that lie in more primal and mysterious forces than the rational will. For Schopenhauer, the intellect represents an illusory individuation; it is a mere partial reflection of a cosmic will that obscures the true nature of reality, a 'veil of Maya', as it is described through terms borrowed from Indian mysticism. Nietzsche praises, in *Die Geburt der Tragödie*, the Dionysian forces of nature opposed to individuated consciousness,[10] and elsewhere attributes human action not to conscious motivations, but to drives and affects that lie beneath the surface.[11] Freud, of course, develops this configuration of surface and depths as the operations of which we are not aware. In *Das Unbehagen in der Kultur*, he challenges the idea of any immediate connection between self and world, and thus of the notion that the 'ozeanische Gefühl' described by Rolland is an intuition that joins the human being directly with his environment. In attempting to explain this feeling, Freud distinguishes between the 'surface' of the self and its recesses:

> Normalerweise ist uns nichts gesicherter als das Gefühl unseres Selbst, unseres eigenen Ichs. Dies Ich erscheint uns selbständig, einheitlich, gegen alles andere gut abgesetzt. Daß dieser Anschein ein Trug ist, daß das Ich sich vielmehr nach innen ohne scharfe Grenze in ein unbewußt seelisches Wesen fortsetzt, das wir als Es bezeichnen, dem es gleichsam als Fassade dient, das

---

[8] Taylor (1989: 389).
[9] Taylor (1989: 390).
[10] Land (1991: 250) helpfully lists the associations of the Dionysian as 'a delirious collective affirmation of insurgent alterity (nature, impulse, oracular insight, woman, barbarism, Asia)'.
[11] Land (1991: 249) views Nietzsche's notion of the Dionysian as an adaptation of Schopenhauer's notion of will. A convincing summary of their differences, however, is offered in Janaway (1991: especially 129–130).

hat uns erst die psychoanalytische Forschung gelehrt. . . . Aber nach außen wenigstens scheint das Ich klare und scharfe Grenzlinien zu behaupten. (Normally nothing is more secure to us than the feeling of our self, our own ego. This ego appears to us as autonomous, unified, strictly demarcated from everything else. That this appearance is deceptive, that the ego rather continues inward, without sharp boundaries, into an unconscious mental being that we call the id, and for which it serves as a façade, this was first revealed to us by psychoanalytic research. . . . But externally at least the ego seems to assert clear and distinct boundary lines.) (WA, ii. 368–369)

Only in the state of love, or in pathological states, does the boundary between ego and object threaten to melt away. Freud's researches, in any case, have established the metaphoric depth of the psyche and the notion that the boundaries of the ego are not constant.

The opacity and inaccessibility of the inner 'depths' of the modern self emphasized by Taylor and Heller are exoticized in the first decades of the twentieth century: Freud focuses on primitive relations within the psyche (discussed in more detail in the next chapter),[12] and the inner life described by modern writers is often explicitly characterized by exoticism. To plumb the depths of the soul is to voyage through exotic and rationally unsurveyable landscapes, such as suggested by the title metaphor of Joseph Conrad's *Heart of Darkness* (1902). In the *Gehirne* stories and related texts, Benn projects imagery of the Mediterranean, Africa, and the tropics just as he contemplates the collapse of the modern self's identity and rational integrity and its dependence on the organic substance of the brain. Kubin's dream-world, set in China, evokes an inaccessible 'other' realm dominated by dream, Asian mysticism, and a voraciously aesthetic will. And Musil's Homo dies in a cave in the state of erotic disorientation provoked by the exoticized peasant Grigia, a scene exploring the potential of mystical union, one version of that state Musil (GW, viii. 1145, 1141) named 'den "anderen Zustand"' ('the "other condition"') and associated with primitive consciousness as studied by the anthropologist Lévy-Bruhl. In these texts, protagonists do not merely travel to and describe, or imaginatively inhabit exotic spaces; imagery of these spaces is integrated into the very experience of breakdown, the release of primitive forces, and the imagined possibilities for aesthetic or existential renewal.

This exoticism breaks down the long-reigning theoretical separation of the soul or psyche from the animal organism and reflects not only the fin-de-siècle interest in exotic cultures but also advances in philosophy, psychology, and neuroscience that challenge the notion of a unified self.

---

[12] See R. Berman (1998: 152, 169).

Nietzsche and Schopenhauer profoundly influence modernist writers in their search for alternatives to the fragmentation, aesthetic impoverishment, and alienation of modern culture. The correlative turn towards the psychic interior, however, does not arrive at a tranquil refuge from the chaos of modern life, but offers instead an access to deeper sources of vitality that had been left unexpressed or even repressed by modern European culture; these sources may be fragmenting or irrational forces that do not respect the autonomy or unity attributed to the subject by Kant. Schopenhauer insisted on the essential animality of the human self: self-consciousness is conditioned 'durch das Gehirn und seine Funktion' ('through the brain and its function') (SW, ii. 358–359); and he proposed, against Kant, a zoological account of the intellect as arising 'aus dem Organismus' ('from the organism') (SW, ii. 358). Schopenhauer viewed Kant's notion of the transcendental unity of apperception (which allows for the sense of subjectivity or attribution of all representations to 'I') in organic terms, as the 'Brennpunkt der gesamten Gehirntätigkeit' ('focus of the whole activity of the brain') (SW, ii. 359).[13] Nietzsche posits instinct or drives rooted in physiology, and not rationality and its subordinate will, as the origin of thought and action. The self, for Nietzsche, is to be reborn through giving up the fiction of individual identity and tapping its repressed animality; the unselfconscious immediacy of animals is praised in *Also sprach Zarathustra* in hope for humankind's rebirth into a new creative culture.[14]

With psychoanalysis, human motivation is attributed to an erotically and violently charged unconscious. The erotic and aggressive drives are seen to underlie both the human psyche and its civilization. Musil acknowledges sexuality, love, and other heightened states of sensuous awareness as points of access to another 'Geisteszustand' ('spiritual state') that acknowledges 'das Dastehn einer andern Welt' ('the presence of another world') alongside, but in the shadows of, the world as we ordinarily perceive it through rational and practical orientation (GW, viii. 1144). Finally, nineteenth- and early twentieth-century medical research undermines the traditional notion of an autonomous soul or mind by locating the source of motor function, sensation, and language in specific areas of the brain, by implication grounding human will not in the soul

---

[13] See Janaway (1991: 120–123) for an account of Schopenhauer's critique of Kant with respect to the animal organism.
[14] See Reed (1978: especially 173, 177), for a discussion of animality in Nietzsche. Although not focusing on animality as such, a critical account of Nietzsche's biological and physiological metaphors is given more recently in Moore (2002).

but in the material organism.[15] A map of the brain was developed in 1906 by Korbinian Brodman, with regions differentiated by cellular structure.[16] Benn's early prose work 'Unter der Großhirnrinde. Briefe vom Meer' ('Under the Cerebral Cortex: Letters from the Sea') (1911) explores the disturbing implications of brain research, as a doctor imagines experiments on a live human brain similar to those performed on animals at the time,[17] and in response despises *Naturforscher* and longs for regression to a primitive state and 'eine Negation des Intellekts' ('a negation of the intellect') (Benn, SW, vii/1. 359, 356). For modern writers aware of these developments, the evocation of exotic topographies serves the dual task of responding both to a 'disenchanted' European culture (as described in the first chapter) and to the exploration of the challenged modern self.[18] Images of inaccessible interior spaces—Kubin's dream-world set in the interior of China, recesses of the brain imagined by Benn's Rönne, the cave where Musil's Homo meets his death—are all associated with an experience of the mystical and primitive, with a vitality preceding and exceeding scientific rationality; and their descriptions are interwoven with 'südlich', tropical, African, or Asian imagery. With these developments, the self's inner landscape, in German modernism, comes to be expressed in exotic terms.

THE INFLUENCE OF NIETZSCHE ON THE EXOTIC RENDERING OF PRIMAL CONSCIOUSNESS

Through dreamlike, rapturous, or hallucinatory evocations of exotic places in works by Benn, Musil, and Kubin, the stability of self and world is compromised, giving way to emerging consciousness of deeper and more original strata of the human psyche. These writers trace the inner topography through the aesthetic imagination, mystical reverie, or dream; these serve as regressions to primal states, and all of these writers enlist exotic imagery as means of both inducing and expressing such states. While their writings follow the 'Pfeile der Sehnsucht nach dem anderen Ufer' ('arrow

[15] See Breidbach's history of nineteenth-century brain research (1997) and Schonlau's summary of the same (2005: 52–59).

[16] Oeser (2002: 224 f.).

[17] Oeser (2002: 173). See Schonlau's (2005: 60–61) discussion of Benn's relation to this research.

[18] Musil was himself involved in scientific research and psychology; see Luft (1980: 78–88), and his more recent account (2003: chapter 3), which emphasizes the relation of Musil's scientific background to his investment in 'non-ratioid' inwardness. Gottfried Benn (along with Hofmannsthal) was aware of specific developments in neuroscience and medical research, of which Schonlau (2005: 57–62) provides a recent account.

of longing for another shore') with which Nietzsche characterized a new
possible humanity, they also reveal the darker aspects of regression, as
provoking the fragmenting and dangerous forces of primal consciousness
prominently addressed in Nietzsche's thought (KG, vi/1. 11).

   In the Rönne narratives of Benn's *Gehirne* (1916) and related texts such
as 'Diesterweg' (1917), the Rönne drama 'Ithaka' (1914) and 'Unter der
Großhirnrinde' (1911), also featuring a medical researcher,[19] and in the
novellas of Musil's *Drei Frauen* (1924), and in Kubin's novel *Die andere
Seite* (1909), primitive, hallucinatory, mystical, or dreamlike states are
juxtaposed to the clarity of rational consciousness. Despite their significant
stylistic differences, and variations in their views of the scientific intellect,
all of these writers promote Nietzsche's affirmation of the sub-rational
forces of instinct and sensuality, dream, the earthy and the animalistic, and
Nietzsche's view that these forces evade ordinary conceptual language and
cannot be expressed by a self-certain rational consciousness. While
Nietzsche's influence is widespread throughout modernism, in the
works discussed here Nietzsche's ideas are formative, and these authors
all acknowledge Nietzsche as a major source for their creative thought.
Musil read Nietzsche studiously, consistently naming Nietzsche among
'entscheidende geistige Einflüsse' ('decisive spiritual influences').[20]
Nietzschean concepts appear in Benn's early prose; and, in his later
lectures on Nietzsche, Benn admits a lifelong relationship to the thinker
to whom he credits the inauguration of aesthetic modernism.[21] Kubin
writes in his autobiography that in his formative years he read everything
of Nietzsche he could find.[22] Musil's interest in reconciling such

[19] The unnamed protagonist of *Unter der Großhirnrinde. Briefe vom Meer* anticipates
Rönne in several respects: he is a medical researcher, has become exhausted through medical
work (in this case experiments), and finds reprieve in southern-exotic places, though
through actual travel, rather than only imagining them. The 1917 story features the doctor
who renames himself 'Diesterweg'.
[20] Musil, letter to Josef Nadler, 1 December 1924, *Briefe 1901–1942*, 368. He mentions Nietzsche again in 1938, in the same context of recalling major influences (B, 837).
Nietzsche appears at least twelve other times in the collected letters from 1901 to 1942. His
notations in the *Tagebücher* on Nietzsche—sometimes direct transcriptions from his readings—are copious (well over a hundred references) and include notations on Nietzsche's
critique of modernity (T, 29, 32). In 1908 Musil credits Nietzsche with having introduced
'hundert neue Möglichkeiten', which, if realized, would accomplish a millennium of
cultural progress (T, 50).
[21] Benn, *Nietzsche nach 50 Jahren* (SW, v. 198–208). This lecture and the complexity of
Benn's relationship to Nietzsche over several decades have been outlined by Keith (2000:
116f.). Benn's criticisms of Nietzsche in the lecture of the 1940s are not reflected in the
adaptations of the 'Dionysian' in the early prose discussed here.
[22] Of Nietzsche, Kubin writes: 'Er ist wirklich—*unser* Christus!' ('He is really—*our*
Christ!') (AL, 52). On Nietzsche's influence on Kubin, see Rhein (1989: 40–44);
Neuhäuser (1998: 22–24).

oppositions as mathematics and mysticism, precise thinking and soulful feeling can be related to the Apollonian–Dionysian structure Musil found in Nietzsche's account of tragedy,[23] and this same structure has been related to the principal tensions and characters in Kubin's novel.[24] The Dionysian motif is explicitly affirmed by Benn's characters. In the wake of Nietzsche, Lévy-Bruhl's anthropological studies, mentioned by Musil in his essay 'Ansätze zu neuer Ästhetik' ('Toward a New Aesthetic') (1925), contribute to the broader cultural interest in the 'primitive' provoked by Nietzsche and may also shed light on the contemporary imagination of primitive states of consciousness described figuratively by Nietzsche through the motives of Dionysus and Zarathustra. While Lévy-Bruhl has been criticized for his characterization of 'primitive' mentality as wholly different from that of a practically and scientifically oriented society,[25] these writers evoke primitive consciousness as a desirable (if also, for the European, perilous) mode of experience—what Lévy-Bruhl described as a participatory relation to the world[26]—that is accessible to the European psyche in states of regression.

These psychic topographies evoked in modernism correspond to the modern imagination of 'primitive' cultures, so admired by the letter-writer of Hofmannsthal's *Briefe des Zurückgekehrten* discussed in Chapter 1. 'Primitive' cultures, usually outside or on the margins of Europe, may be regarded as inferior, as 'mystics, in tune with nature, part of its harmonies',[27] they may also be admired as more original, purer, and more vital than the modern European self, which is worn out by reflection and alienated from a world it regards in positivistic or other scientific terms. The European subject cannot look to its familiar, modern surroundings for access to a more original experience; this can be provoked by imagining other, exotic realms within the psychic interior, which take on more significance in the fragmentation of the rational self. Despite Nietzsche's rejection of the traditional Western notion of an individuated self or soul, the association of the exotic with metaphoric depths and inward contemplation is made in Nietzsche's recognition that Christian inwardness, at least, has made modern humanity more interesting, in his praise (however ambivalent) of the Asian and Oriental, and in his characterization of Southern Europe in those terms. In Southern Europe 'findest du … einen Menschen für sich, der das Meer, das Abenteuer, und den Orient kennt' ('you find a human being for himself, who knows the sea, adventure, the Orient') (KG, v/2. 212). Like Hofmannsthal's later

---

[23] Grill (2007: 335).   [24] Rhein (1989: 40).
[25] Robertson (1991: 23–25).   [26] Lévy-Bruhl (1926).
[27] Torgovnick (1990: 8).

praise of the integrity of less 'civilized' peoples, Nietzsche recognizes in
Asian comportment an admirable lack of duplicity; while the European
character, as Hofmannsthal's *Zurückgekehrter* similarly claims, suffers
from contradiction between words and deeds, 'der Orientale ist sich treu
im täglichen Leben' ('the Oriental is true to himself in everyday life')
(KG, vii/2. 52). While Nietzsche does not advocate a Buddhist (or
Schopenhauerian) negation of the will, he lauds in Greek tragedy a
'synthesis of Indian passivity and Roman assertiveness',[28] praises Buddhism as 'hundertmal realistischer als das Christentum' ('a hundred times
more realistic than Christianity') (KG, vi/3. 184) and as self-liberating
(KG, v/1. 83), and refers to Buddhist contemplation as the key to overcoming European *Ressentiment* (KG, vi/3. 271).[29] '[W]ie ferne', he writes,
'ist Europa noch von dieser Stufe der Cultur!' ('How far Europe still is
from this level of culture') (KG, v/1. 83). This view clearly does not fit
within the 'primitivist discourse' and its 'rhythms of control, domination,
and exploitation' thematized by Torgovnick in her critique of primitivism,
however valuable for its exposure of its political implications.[30]

In *Also sprach Zarathustra*, the new humanity Nietzsche promotes is
evoked through topographical imagery: as a bridge over an abyss, as an
arrow of longing for another shore, as a sea that must absorb the impure
rivers (of modern consciousness), as storm and sky (KG, vi/1. 9–10). This
topography is exoticized as Nietzsche praises a more primitive way of
being that is associated with 'morgenländische Luft' ('oriental air') and
with deserts, oases, and Africa (KG, vi/1. 376). This southern and eastern
aesthetics is embodied in the Persian figure of Zarathustra. Ernst Bertram,
whose book *Nietzsche: Versuch einer Mythologie* is cited by Benn (SW, v.
199) as the most important study of the thinker, presented Zarathustra as
the figure that completes the Orientalization of Nietzsche's thought:

> Zarathustra ist der Versuch Nietzsches, der Alexander des Deutschtums zu
> werden: durch Eroberung des östlichen Gedankens Europa . . . zu retten.
> Es träumte ihm . . . von solchem Alexanderzuge in den alten Osten jene
> selbe Weisheit für Deutschland heimzubringen.[31]
>
> (Zarathustra is Nietzsche's attempt to become the Alexander of the
> Germans: to save Europe by conquering Eastern thought. He dreams . . . of

[28] Young (1992: 47).
[29] On Nietzsche's relation to Buddhism, see Mistry (1981); Parkes (1996: 356–377); on
Nietzsche and Hinduism, see Smith (2004).
[30] Torgovnick (1990: 127–128).
[31] Bertram (1965: 385–386). While his study was first published in 1918, this quotation is from the chapter 'Alexander (der östliche Nietzsche)' ('Alexander (the Eastern
Nietzsche)') appearing in the second edition of 1919.

such movements of Alexander in the old East, to bring home the same wisdom for Germany.)

While Bertram's characterization invites post-colonialist criticism—in so far as Europe is to profit from the appropriative 'domination' of Eastern thought—Nietzsche was in fact highly critical of Europeans and their violent domination of the colonies: 'Wie der Europäer Colonien gegründet hat, beweist seine Raubtier-Natur' ('The way Europeans founded colonies proves their predatory nature').[32] His admiration for the East, in other words, is not merely appropriative, but sympathetic. 'Die asiatischen Menschen' ('The Asians'), he writes, 'sind hundertmal großartiger, als die europäischen' ('are a hundred times more magnificent than the Europeans') (KG, vii/2. 52).

In addition to Zarathustra, Dionysus is associated with the Eastern occult and represents 'the last instance of the occident being radically permeable to the outside'.[33] The evocation of exotic and primitive alternatives to modern rational consciousness by German writers owes much not only to these Asiatic figures but also to Nietzsche's revaluation of the body, his critique of the autonomy and identity of the self, and his promotion of aesthetic creativity and perspectivism. Most of these features of Nietzsche's thought are, in turn, indebted to the Asian-inspired philosophy of Schopenhauer.[34]

The human body, as a vessel of animalistic drives and our most immediate relation to nature, is considered by Nietzsche and Schopenhauer as the vital substrate of the thinking and reflecting self. For Schopenhauer, our inner sensations of the body and of embodied action are the most direct experiences we have of the cosmic will. In *Die Welt als Wille und Vorstellung* (*The World as Will and Representation*), insight into the real nature of the material world is held to be possible through embodied experience, 'weil mein Leib das einzige Objekt ist, von dem ich nicht bloß die *eine* Seite, die der Vorstellung, kenne, sondern auch die zweite, welche *Wille* heißt' ('because my body is the single object of which I know only one side, that of representation, but also the second, which is called *will*') (Schopenhauer, SW, i. 190). As embodied beings, we are 'das Ding an sich' ('the thing in itself'); and thus we have an inner access to the 'inneren

---

[32] For a competing interpretation of this passage, see Holub (1998: 43). Holub implicates Nietzsche in the colonialist activity of his brother-in-law and sister, and regards Nietzsche's philosophy as tainted by colonialism. While giving a compelling account, Holub overlooks the strikingly positive affirmations of non-Europeans such as those as cited here.

[33] Land (1991: 250).

[34] On Nietzsche's relation to Schopenhauer, see Janaway (1991); Land (1991); Young (1992: 5–24, 39); Nussbaum (1999).

Wesen der Dinge' ('inner essence of things') (SW, i. 253).[35] Nietzsche argues for the primacy of the body over reason, elevating pleasure and pain, ecstasy, dream, instinct, health, and physical vitality by associating them with the essence of creative humanity. In *Die Geburt der Tragödie*, the Dionysian principle of fusion with nature, in tension with Apollonian form, is considered in terms of bodily experiences; Nietzsche praises the orgiastic sexuality, intoxication, and physical suffering and pleasure involved in the cult worship of Dionysus. Throughout *Jenseits von Gut und Böse*, the will to truth is considered in terms of a physiological *Trieb*. The chapter 'Von den Verächtern des Leibes' ('On Disdain for the Body') in *Also sprach Zarathustra* argues for the flesh, rather than the rational *Geist*, as the powerful source of the self:

> 'Ich' sagst du und bist stolz auf dies Wort. Aber das Größere ist—woran du nicht glauben willst—dein Leib und seine große Vernunft: die sagt nicht Ich, aber tut Ich. . . . Hinter deinen Gedanken und Gefühlen . . . steht ein mächtiger Gebieter, ein unbekannter Weiser—der heißt Selbst. In deinem Leibe wohnt er, dein Leib ist er.
>
> (You say 'I' and are proud of this word. But your body—which you do not want to believe—with its great reason is the much greater: it does not say 'I,' but does 'I' . . . Behind your thoughts and feelings . . . is a powerful master, an unknown wise man—It lives in your body, it is your body.) (KG, vi/1. 35)

Nietzsche's promotion of the body and its inner physiological forces is reflected in Benn, Musil, and Kubin in varying ways: in the breakdown of scientific analysis of the body in favour of more primitive bodily experience, in the heightened importance of sensuality and sexuality, and in the metamorphosis, procreation, and destruction of organic life in fantastical dream imagery, respectively.[36] Nietzsche's persistent use of medical imagery is most directly reflected in Benn, himself a doctor, for whom medical science expresses the crisis of modern humanity.[37]

Benn, Musil, and Kubin are linked in their affirmation of the Dionysian aspect of reality admired by Nietzsche. The title of Benn's collection of novellas *Gehirne* (along with the earlier 'Unter der Großhirnrinde') refers both to the physical organ and to the modern scientific reduction of

---

[35] See Janaway's account of the body as inner access to will (1989: 342–357) and (1994: 28, 32–33, 35–37) and Nussbaum (1999: 345–348).

[36] Nietzsche incorporated current developments in physiology in his view of the organism. See Moore (2002: 39–40).

[37] 'Der Philosoph als Arzt der Cultur' ('The Philosopher as Physician of Culture') was the title of a treatise Nietzsche attempted in 1873. See Pasley's discussion of medical imagery in Nietzsche (1978: 127). A more recent account of Nietzsche as 'cultural physician' is offered in Ahern (1995). This metaphor is also used in Nietzsche, *Die fröhliche Wissenschaft* (KG, v/2. 17).

human thought to calculable physical operations. The protagonist Dr. Werff Rönne is peculiarly exhausted by having dissected thousands of corpses; his scientific tendencies of analysis turn against him. For Rönne the human body is an object of clinical study; but his awareness that the body, in particular the brain, is the substance underlying his own experience leads to self-dissociation. Rönne finds relief in sensual, Dionysian images of exotic landscapes, and in sexual fusion with a woman whom he regards as an exotic landscape in his imagination. In the drama 'Ithaka' Rönne explicitly calls on the need for a 'Dionysian' alternative to the impoverished view of the self promoted by empirical science. The Dionysian sensuality of the body awakened through an exotic setting is also central to Musil's 'Grigia', the first novella of the collection *Drei Frauen*. The culture of German-speaking peasants in South Tyrol is characterized by its 'southern' air, the intimacy of its people with nature and animals, by their physical labour, and by their unrestrained sexual and emotional expressiveness. After Homo, enchanted by the isolated world of the mountain landscape, experiences a moment of earthly transcendence, he feels released from his former life, and soon becomes the lover of an earthy peasant woman. The thrill of freedom from his northern social and intellectual structures induces a state of consciousness—in which 'der andere Zustand' is anticipated—in which sensations are more vivid and savoured; but it is haunted by an implicit longing for death, as the ultimate regression to a primal unity with nature. In Kubin the tension between the Apollonian and the Dionysian is embodied in Patera, whose 'regelmäßige Schönheit... glich eher einem griechischen Gott als einem lebenden Menschen. Über den Zügen lag ein tiefer Schmerz' ('perfectly regular beauty... resembles more a Greek god than a living person. A deep pain marks his features'). Patera's beauty and the grotesque physical metamorphosis his dreams provoke ('Das Mienenspiel wechselte chamäleonartig— ununterbrochen—tausend—nein hunderttausendfach' ['The play of gesture changed like a chameleon—incessant—in a thousand—no, in a hundred thousand ways']) render his body a scene of conflict for the primal drives of formation and destruction in nature (AS, 110). His visage takes on not only innumerable human faces but also those of animals, thus mingling the Apollonian dream principle with the fusions of Dionysian animality. The artist becomes mediator between the Apollonian and the Dionysian, also embodied in the conflict between Herkules Bell and Patera.[38] If, as Nietzsche suggests, modern rationality is the inheritance of the Socratic theoretical intellect—and thus as the Apollonian principle

---

[38] Rhein (1989: 40–44) discusses the essential conflicts and characters of the novel in terms of the Apollonian and Dionysian principles.

of thought robbed of its Dionysian counterpart—the advocacy of another, more inward aspect of reality can be characterized as a resurgence of the Dionysian. What links these quite different writers is, then, their turn to this neglected side of reality buried in the primal consciousness, expressed in strikingly similar motifs. Kubin affirms 'die andere Seite' ('the other side'), Musil 'den andern Zustand' ('the other condition'), and Benn 'das andere Leben' ('the other life').[39] This passage to the other region of a primal, inward state of being is expressed in Benn's post-Nietzschean conviction that 'Alles Transzendente ist tierisch' ('everything transcendent is animalistic') (SW, iii. 391). Musil claims, 'Der Mensch ist eben nicht nur Intellekt, sondern auch Wille, Gefühl, Unbewußtheit und oft nur Tatsächlichkeit wie das Wandern der Wolken am Himmel' ('The human being is after all not only intellect, but rather will, feeling, unconsciousness and often only as actual as the wandering of the clouds in the sky') (GW, viii. 1057).

Nietzsche's attack on humanistic-philosophical models of the self, in particular on Descartes's theory of autonomous consciousness, for which the body is only a physical shell and conduit of sensation, is also echoed in these works (KG, vi/2. 11, 23–24). A loss of autonomy and individuated identity is correlated with the intensification of bodily and sensuous experience. In his sensual enchantment, Musil's Homo is subject to a kind of dissolution, in which, as the narrator describes,

> diese fremden Lebenserscheinungen Besitz von dem ergreifen, was herrenlos geworden ist. Sie gaben ihm aber kein neues, von Glück ehrgeizig und erdfest gewordenes Ich, sondern sie siedelten nur so in zusammenhanglos schönen Flecken im Luftriß seines Körpers.
>
> (These foreign appearances of life took possession of that which had become without master. Yet they did not give him a new 'I', animated by happiness and grounded, but rather only settled in unrelated, beautiful spots in the cavities of his body.) (Musil, GW, vi. 248)

The usurpation of the continuous self by fragmentary sensuous impressions is suggested by the 'zusammenhanglos schönen Flecken'. Similar moments of reflection are expressed in Benn's novellas, as Rönne becomes aware of his breakdown: 'Wo bin ich hingekommen? Wo bin ich? Ein kleines Flattern, ein Verwehn' ('Where have I arrived? Where am I? A little flutter, a blowing away') (Benn, SW, iii. 31). The question of his location points to the uncertainty of the self with respect to surroundings he no

---

[39] Musil's notion of the 'other condition' is described in 'Ansätze zu neuer Ästhetik' (1925) (GW, viii. 1144–1145). Benn's notion of 'the other life' appears in a 1917 Rönne story (in which the protagonist renames himself 'Diesterweg') (SW, iii. 72). Kubin's notion of the 'other side' serves, of course, as the title of his novel.

longer dominates. In 'Unter der Großhirnrinde', the self is reduced to 'Eine Messe von Empfindungen' ('a mass of sensation'). Followed by two further sentence fragments ('Eine Perlenschnur von Sukzessionen räumlich-zeitlicher Geschehnisse. Ein Jahrmarkt von Vorstellungen') ('A strand of pearls made of the succession of spatio-temporal events. A fair of representations'), this description is composed of predicates. Lacking both subjects of identification and verbs that could be attributed to a subject, it exposes the passive and fragmentary nature of modern human experience (Benn, SW, vii/1. 361). Kubin's narrator in *Die andere Seite*, too, is astonished by the loss of autonomy of the inhabitants of the dream state, who not only live but perceive according to the transformations of Patera's dreams. In an epiphanic moment the narrator himself comes to recognize the illusion of individuated selfhood, 'daß mein Ich aus unzähligen "Ichs" zusammengesetzt war, von denen immer eines hinter dem andern auf der Lauer stand.... auf einer höheren Stufe der Erkenntnis gab es den Menschen überhaupt nicht' ('that my "I" was composed of countless "I's", where one is always behind the next lying in wait... at a higher level of intellection, there was no person at all') (AS, 137). This bears the stamp less of Schopenhauer's notion of an underlying will than of Nietzsche's hypothesis that the subject is a multiplicity.[40] Through this epiphany, as well as the narrator's gradual realization that Patera appears in many guises and that he and Bell are two aspects of the same being, Kubin illustrates Nietzsche's critique of the individuated self as a fiction. The turn to the 'inner' exotic landscape of the dream reveals fragmentation, and the self is recognized as 'a multiplicity of impulses or drives'.[41]

The radical nature of Nietzsche's critique of the self opens up new possibilities not only for depicting protagonists or characters but also for form, language, and narration. For Benn's generation, Nietzsche was 'das Erdbeben der Epoche' ('the earthquake of the epoch'), and Benn (SW, v. 199) credits Nietzsche with showing the way to modern forms of expression. Nietzsche's proposal for the liberation of language from convention is related to his critique of subjectivity and is powerfully enacted in the narrative form and imagery of Benn's prose in *Gehirne*. The rational ego as the ostensible centre of the self is more essentially determined by other forces, the acceptance of which might break down the conceptual structure holding together self and world. Benn's Rönne experiences this as self-dissolution: 'Es war ein Strömen in ihm, nun ein laues Entweichen. Und nun verwirrte sich das Gefüge, es entsank fleischlich sein Ich' ('It was a current in him, now a tepid escaping. And now the structure became

[40] See Nietzsche's criticism of Schopenhauer's 'ich will' in KG, vi/2. 23, 25–26.
[41] Janaway (1991: 134–135).

confused, his "I" receded carnally') (SW, iii. 56). The narrative structure in *Gehirne* alternates, often ambiguously, among objective narration, quoted monologue, and interior subjective narration. In so far as it is able to present consciousness as a stream of fragmented perspectives, this structure follows Nietzsche's critique of the rational subject. Perhaps it is not that I think, Nietzsche argues against Descartes in *Jenseits von Gut und Böse*, but rather 'es denkt' ('it thinks'); and even this formulation, according to Nietzsche, preserves too much grammar of subject and predicate: even this 'es' ('it') must be conceived as the process itself, a process of thinking that is not conducted by an epistemological centre, but is merely a flow of physiological forces (KG, vi/2. 25). The self's loss of centre is a major theme in 'Ithaka', written two years before the Rönne stories, but featuring the same character at the pathological institute from which, in 'Gehirne', he had taken leave two months earlier. Rönne challenges his anatomy professor's faith in science and in humanistic values. Rather than the professor's 'northern' numbness of meaningless analytical intellection, Rönne and his young colleagues demand an explicitly 'southern' return to primal forces of nature, which they associate with exotic places.

In *Gehirne*, however, Rönne's response to this de-individuation is neither an insistence on the re-establishment of a continuous personal identity nor a flight to the far-off landscape of real 'südlichen Ländern' ('southern lands') as in 'Unter der Großhirnrinde', but rather an aesthetic project. While the narrator of the 1911 story describes his change in physical place, Rönne of *Gehirne* internalizes the exotic topography and begins to write; the narrative can often be related to his empirical perceptions, but these are transformed by an exotic imagination. Images of an exotic and 'southern' landscape become independent ciphers that do not refer to any real perceptions and do not require logical arrangement of a rationally oriented, individuated subject. The activity of consciousness itself is given as a stream of creative impulses that may be expressed in exotic imagery:

> es flutet der volle Lebensstrom. Gegen tropische und subtropische Striche, Salzminen und Lotosflüsse, Berberkarawanen, ja gegen den Antipoden selbst steht der Schiffsbauch gerichtet... Europa, Asien, Afrika... Noch stand es schweigend, schon geschah ihm die *Olive*.
>
> (The full stream of life is flooding. The ship's prow is directed towards tropical and subtropical points, salt mines, and lotus rivers, Berber caravans, indeed towards the antipode itself... Europe, Asia, Africa... Still it stands silent, already the *Olive* happened to him.) (Benn, SW, iii. 59–60)

In this passage the impersonal 'es flutet', the tropical images of nature in lotus and olive, the evocation of travel by ship and caravan are only loosely associated images that do not evoke empirical space but rather convey an exotic atmosphere, whether Africa, Florence, the South Seas, or the Mediterranean—for all of these locations are evoked in the course of the novellas. Even as projections of Rönne's imagination, these images are at least in part independent of his will, and so are experienced passively ('geschah ihm die *Olive*' ['the *Olive* happened to him']), emerging in a current of forces in which his consciousness seems to be swept up.[42] The evocation of the Bacchanalian and of Venice shortly after this passage both echoes Nietzsche and connects this narrative to Aschenbach's Dionysian dream in *Der Tod in Venedig*, discussed in Chapter 2. But while Mann's depiction of Venice projects Aschenbach's visions onto a still stable reference of the real-world city, Benn's exotic places are wholly projections of Rönne's imagination, reflecting the turn to the inner topography of primal consciousness in contrast to empirical space.

The discovery of primal consciousness is reflected not only in the motifs or settings of these works but more deeply in the narrative structures they develop and in their narrative maintenance or breakdown of a coherently experienced world. These formal elements echo Nietzsche's revaluation of the self, language, and reality, including his promotion of 'das Perspekti-vistische' ('the perspectivistic') (KG, vi/2. 4). Nietzsche, against the meta-physics of the will underlying Schopenhauer's philosophy, rejects the notion of a world in itself, a single truth, a determinable reality; rather, any perspective is but one reflection of the manifold and ever-changing nature of reality. The consequences of this view can be seen in the mimetic ambiguities of Benn's narrative, as well as in Kubin's treatment of the *Traumreich* as a compelling vision of reality's 'other side' that is radically unstable, formed of illusions not wholly distinguishable from reality. In Musil's works, the rejection of the notion that the world is absolutely knowable by scientific means, and of the diametrical opposition of good and evil, is illustrated through the mystical power of the landscape and the incomprehensibility and uncontrollability of the forces that drive events in human lives.[43] In 'Grigia' the landscape that is described as *märchenhaft*

---

[42] Benn comments on this passage in 'Schöpferische Konfessionen' ('Creative Confes-sions') (1919), emphasizing the passivity of Rönne's perception (SW, iii. 108).

[43] In 'the other condition', as Musil describes it, 'gut und böse fallen einfach weg . . . und an Stelle aller dieser Beziehungen tritt ein geheimnisvoll schwellendes und ebbendes Zusammenfließen unseres Wesens mit dem der Dinge und anderen Menschen' ('good and evil simply fall away . . . and at the place of all of these relations comes a secretive swelling and ebbing flowing together of our being with that of things other humans beings') (GW, viii. 1144). On this aspect of Musil's ethics, see Luft (1980: 100–121) and (2003: 109); and McBride (2006).

holds a real power over the enchanted visitor,[44] and in 'Die Portugiesin' the shadowy powers of forces beyond reason are reflected through interaction with the medieval surroundings. Nietzsche's perspectivist rejection of a world in itself frees linguistic depiction from the necessity to distinguish between appearance and reality, between subjective and objective aspects of experience, which still underlines Schopenhauer's thought. For Schopenhauer, aesthetic experience allows the human subject to approach, however fleetingly, the timeless reality of the thing in itself, mediated 'durch einen Leib' ('through a body') (SW, i. 253).[45] For Nietzsche, the notion of a 'Ding an sich' is an intellectual construct obscuring the primal becoming of nature, where illusion and reality cannot be separated.

'DAS ANDERE LEBEN': AESTHETICS OF THE SOUTHERN/EASTERN EXOTIC AND PRIMAL CONSCIOUSNESS

Nietzsche's affirmation of more primal states of being is expressed, among other ways, through imagery of southern and eastern exotic landscapes. In *Also sprach Zarathustra*, a 'gute helle morgenländische Luft' is praised as 'am fernsten vom wolkigen feuchten schwermütigen Alt-Europa' ('farthest from cloudy damp melancholic old Europe'); the imagery that predominates is of the desert and its cloudless 'blaues Himmelreich' ('blue heavenly realm') (KG, vi/1. 376). The song of the wanderer composed 'unter Töchtern der Wüste' ('among daughters of the desert') includes exclamations such as 'Afrikanisch feierlich!' ('African festive!') and references to dates, other 'Südfrüchte' ('southern fruits') the sphinx, and palm trees (KG, vi/1. 376, 105). In *Die Geburt der Tragödie*, Nietzsche points to the prehistory of the Greek tragic chorus 'in Kleinasien, bis hin zu Babylon und den orgiastischen Sakäen' ('in Asia Minor, from there to Babylon and the orgiastic sects'), and imagines the chariot of Dionysus drawn by panthers and tigers, surrounded by 'Raubtiere der Felsen und der Wüste' ('predators of the cliffs and of the desert') (KG, iii/1. 25). The contrast of exotic southern or eastern places with modern Europe serves to indicate the inability of modern rational consciousness to grasp and accept the reality of existence and its deeper forces.

The inspiration Nietzsche finds in the southern and eastern exotic is echoed in Benn, Musil, and Kubin. What Benn calls 'das Problem des

---

[44] In the *Tagebücher* Musil describes the situation depicted in 'Grigia' as 'an der Grenze von Märchen' ('bordering on fairy tale') (T, 343).
[45] On this aspect of Schopenhauer, see Hamlyn (1980: 110); Foster (1999: 214, 228).

südlichen Worts' ('the problem of the *southern word*') is central to his early prose (SW, iii. 108); southern images induce a primitive state of being, in correlation to the breakdown of the rational order of the world and of ordinary perception. While Kubin's language remains relatively conventional in describing fantastic transformations of organic life in dreams (discussed in the last section of this chapter), and Musil's use of the southern exotic can be best understood in the context of mysticism (discussed in the next section), Benn's syntax and narrative structure reflect most directly the disruptions of 'southern' exoticism and so will be the main focus of this section. Against the isolation of intellectual consciousness, Benn responds 'mit der südlichen Zermalmung... in ligurische Komplexe bis zur Überhöhung oder bis zum Verlöschen im Außersich des Rausches oder des Vergehens' ('with the southern crush... in Ligurian complexes to the sublimation or the extinguishment in ecstasy of intoxication or of dissolution') (SW, iii. 109). This experience of ecstasis, though conditioned by breakdown, evolves by the later story of *Gehirne*, 'Der Geburtstag' ('The Birthday'), into epiphany, in the promise of aesthetic renewal.

The development of the southern aesthetic admits several aspects, which, while they may be thematically distinguished from one another, are interwoven in the texts themselves. First, the critique of northern rationality is established through contrast to 'southern' imagery, which provokes the collapse of the rational self. Secondly, this collapse is enacted through specific literary means, including the bombardment of the senses through exotic imagery, the displacement of empirical space by such imagery, the repetition and construction of image-complexes, and the breakdown of narrative structure and syntax. Thirdly, this collapse of self engenders more primal modes of feeling and perception, culminating in experiences of sexual ecstasis or consummation. Breakdown and ecstasis lead, finally, to a reconstruction of an aesthetic perspective, also expressed through the projection of southern exotic imagery. To correct earlier interpretations, it will be argued that Benn's evocation of a southern consciousness neither aims at mere 'collapse' of the self, nor projects a utopian paradise or *Wunschraum* as its imagined destination 'im Erlebnis des Rausches' ('in the experience of intoxication').[46] Rather, the counterpart to dissolution is the reconstruction of an aesthetic, a correlation that bears some comparison with the abstract primitivism of modern painting. It must also be said that Benn's use of exotic imagery, though problematic, does not fit the pattern of Orientalism outlined by Said and post-colonialist

---

[46] Ritchie (1972: 47); Reif (1975: 59).

theory, as described in previous chapters of this study. Like Nietzsche's evocation of the exotic, Benn's texts, as well as those of Musil and Kubin, suggest neither symbolic appropriation of exotic places, nor projection of a mysteriousness that is to be decoded through the epistemological triumph of the Western subject over the 'Oriental'. Benn's use of exotic imagery is meant to critique the very foundations of Western rationality and to promote a new aesthetic reconstructed in the wake of its collapse.

The essential dilemma in Benn's texts is expressed through the contrast of exotic southern imagery with northern rational consciousness. The narratives in *Gehirne* are set in Northern Europe, which provides the symbolic contrast for the imagined projection of exotic landscapes, which relieve the protagonist of his overstrained intellectualism. A similar contrast between northern sensibility and southern exoticism appears in both Musil's 'Grigia' and in 'Die Portugiesin' ('The Portuguese Woman'), two of the stories of *Drei Frauen* (*Three Women*), while the third, 'Tonka', invokes the impenetrability of the Slavic (Czech) character of the title figure, with which the scientifically minded narrator has a fateful erotic relationship.[47] The transition between two worlds in 'Grigia' is evoked upon Homo's arrival in the Italian mountains: 'In den Straßen war eine Luft, aus Schnee und Süden gemischt' ('There was an air in the streets mixed from snow and the South') (Musil, GW, vi. 235). But the 'Süden' is amplified by primitivist African and Asian imagery: the smell of the hay in which Homo has sexual relations with Grigia is like the drinks of Africans, 'die aus dem Teig von Früchten und menschlichem Speichel entstehn' ('composed from the dough of fruits and human saliva') (GW, vi. 249) and the women are compared to Africans and Japanese (GW, vi. 239). The tension of 'Die Portugiesin' results from a similar opposition between the 'northern' mentality of Herr von Ketten—whose ancestors 'waren aus dem Norden gekommen und hatten vor der Schwelle des Südens halt gemacht' ('had come from the North and stopped at the threshold of the South')—and the southern mysteriousness of his Portuguese wife. But the von Kettens, who also use the Italian 'delle Catene' when it is advantageous, are poised to negotiate with the foreignness of a 'southern' world and bring their brides home 'von weit her' ('from far away') (GW, vi. 253). The protagonist himself resolves this tension only by his near collapse and reawakening through the vigorous physical experience of climbing a steep cliff under the family castle. For Benn and Musil, Northern European culture is too one-sided, sterile, overly intellectual, and calculating, whereas the 'southern' is characterized by

---

[47] See Robertson (2000a).

primitive vitality, sensuousness, and mystery. In Kubin's *Die andere Seite*, too, Patera's dream-life is linked to the indigenous religion of a peculiar race of native inhabitants in the interior of China. The total isolation from modern Europe allows Patera's realm to be constituted by the mysterious forces of dreams, which culminates in an apocalyptic mingling of exotic life forms.

In Benn's works, northern consciousness is not merely contrasted with southern imagery, but is radically challenged, to the point of collapse. Rönne's breakdown is initially presented by an objective narrator, who reports that the previous two years spent at a pathology institute have disturbed the doctor—'es waren ungefähr zweitausend Leichen ohne Besinnen durch seine Hände gegangen' ('about two thousand cadavers had passed through his hands unreflectedly'). But this disturbance is more radical than the narrator initially admits: 'das hatte ihn in einer merkwür- digen und ungeklärten Weise erschöpft' ('this had exhausted him in a peculiar and opaque way') (Benn, SW, iii. 39). Not only the doctor himself, but the values that underlie his education, profession, and even personal identity, have been exhausted by his experiences treating diseased bodies and dissecting corpses. Reflecting Benn's own experiences as a doctor at a venereal clinic in wartime Brussels, Rönne's breakdown will reveal not only an individual crisis but a crisis of modern Northern European culture. Expressing this crisis, the narration becomes increas- ingly unstable, oscillating between objective communication and halluci- natory evocations of southern imagery that point to the primitive depths of the inner life. The perception of primal inner 'depths' correlates to Rönne's loss of faith in his former outlook on the world, an outlook that had been governed by science; this loss is also suffered by the narrator of 'Unter der Großhirnrinde' and by Rönne in 'Ithaka'. While Musil seeks a middle zone between the too sharply polarized realms of artistic and scientific thought,[48] Benn is more radically critical. Scientific terminology will be evoked in later stories as Rönne attempts to stabilize a chaotic perception of the world, but at the outset of *Gehirne* any residual faith in his science has already been broken, in a scepticism described explicitly by Rönne and his colleagues in 'Ithaka'. In *Gehirne* this break with science is only confirmed by Rönne's recognition of the dishonesty of its attending institutions, as dying patients at the clinic are discharged under the pretence that they are cured.

Exotic southern imagery expresses Rönne's breakdown and loss of orientation. In the first of the stories, 'Gehirne', the setting and situation

[48] As Musil argues in 'Anmerkung zu einer Metaphysik' (GW, ii. 651).

remain recognizable until the final climax; it takes place at the mountain sanatorium in Northern Germany where Rönne has taken up a position as a substitute for the vacationing director. The opening sentence describes Rönne between locations, as he is travelling northward by train. This prepares the reader for the 'movement' throughout the stories between empirical reality and the projections of Rönne's disoriented imagination, projections that increasingly evoke the exotic South. In this first story there are only three references to exotic localities—'eine fremde Stadt' ('a foreign city'), Florence, and 'Trümmer[n] des Südens' ('the ruin of the South'); but even at the outset the narrator hints at imaginative inhabitation of exotic places. That Rönne 'sah in die Fahrt' ('looked into the journey') describes a vision already transfixed upon an imagined projection, in contrast to present perceptions, which he cannot stabilize. The vineyards and poppy fields he sees from the train window evoke intoxication and the Dionysian. In this vein of heightened perception, Rönne views the sky and houses: 'ein Blau flutet durch den Himmel, feucht und aufgeweht von Ufern; an Rosen ist jedes Haus gelehnt, und manches ganz versunken' ('a blue floated through the sky, moist and blown up by shores; every house leans on roses, some of them entirely lost in them') (Benn, SW, iii. 29). The image of houses 'versunken' in roses suggests impending collapse into dreams or primitive states of mind. 'Versunken' is repeated in a reflection on Rönne's feeling of having lost the past to obscurity:

> Ich will mir ein Buch kaufen und einen Stift; ich will mir jetzt möglichst vieles aufschreiben, damit nicht alles so herunterfließt. So viele Jahre lebte ich, und alles ist versunken.
>
> (I want to buy myself a notebook and a pen. I want now to write down as much as possible, so that everything doesn't just evaporate. I lived so many years, and everything is lost.) (SW, iii. 29)

Rönne is no longer certain whether his experiences had always dissipated as they do now. He suffers from the lack of personal continuity and a collapse of purpose in thought and action, all of which will, however, induce primal modes of perception. Attending to a broken finger, Rönne 'horchte in die Tiefe, wie in dem Augenblick, wo der Schmerz einsetzte, eine fernere Stimme sich vernehmen ließe' ('listened to the depths, just like in the moment when pain begins, a farther off voice can be perceived') (SW, iii. 30). Rönne imagines the pain of his patient all too deeply, as a voice from a more primordial past that minimizes the significance of the individual.

Rönne's collapse is that of the unified individual self so challenged by Nietzsche and Schopenhauer, and this leads to disorientation in his surroundings. Whereas Rönne claims in 'Ithaka' that he has lost the centre, this loss is expressed in further spatial terms in 'Gehirne':

> Es schwächt mich etwas von oben. Ich habe keinen Halt mehr hinter den Augen. Der Raum wogt so endlos; einst floß er doch auf eine Stelle. Zerfallen ist Rinde, die mich trug.
> (Something weakens me from above. Behind my eyes here is no refuge. Space surges off endlessly on all sides—once it must have flowed together at one place. The cortex that held me up has crumbled.) (SW, iii. 32)

More than just a point of orientation, what is lost is a feeling of personal structure, of self-differentiating form ('Rinde'). Ordinary consciousness no longer operates to order the surrounding space, and so the horizons and limits cannot be secured. Like Musil's Homo, Rönne begins to feel in this collapse that he belongs to a wider organic world, and he experiences a heightened sensory perception, the dream-state of an ancient mode of consciousness. For Musil's Homo the break with his old life, his family, and cultural ties in the North, yields a similar sense of connection to a southern landscape:

> Dennoch stand es fest, daß er nicht umkehrte, und seltsamerweise war mit seiner Aufregung ein Bild der rings um den Wald blühenden Wiesen verbunden . . . zwischen Anemonen, Vergißmeinnicht, Orchideen.
> (But it was certain that he would not turn back and strangely in his excitement he was joined with an image of the fields blooming all around the forest . . . between anemones, forget-me-nots, orchids.) (Musil, GW, vi. 240)

Homo's connection to the landscape involves the perceptual imagination: Homo's 'Aufregung' is connected to 'ein Bild' of the meadows in bloom. The distinction between image and reality, truth and illusion, have been blurred. Similarly, Rönne feels himself taken into the organic world through images. As Rönne rests on his balcony, having locked himself in his room unable to carry out his duties, he experiences an animalistic hallucination: 'Außer ein paar Vögeln war er das höchste Tier. So trug ihn die Erde leise durch den Äther und ohne Erschüttern an allen Sternen vorbei' ('Aside from a few birds he was the highest animal. So the earth carried him lightly through the ether and past all the stars without any shock') (Benn, SW, iii. 33–34). Expression of his final breakdown in exotic imagery projects, as an alternative to the modern Northern European world of the medical institute, a constellation of images of the South, the ancient, and the animalistic. These images together cannot constitute an empirical destination that would serve as a *Wunschraum,* for they express not a utopian destination, but a disoriented imaginative projection.[49]

The initial collapse of self that Rönne experienced is not merely described, but enacted through literary means. These include the exaggerated role of exotic imagery that displaces empirical spatial orientation, the construction and repetition of image-complexes, and the fragmentation of syntax and narrative structure. A comparison of Benn's earlier Rönne prose with *Gehirne* shows increasing fragmentation and disorientation. In 'Unter der Großhirnrinde' ('Under the Cerebral Cortex'), the narrator suffers from having conducted scientific experiments on the brain, admitting in response 'eine Sehnsucht... nach Flucht und Ferne und südlichen Ländern' ('a longing... for escape and distance and southern lands') (SW, vii/1. 355). This story is told in the first person, in language still rooted in a continuous self. The narrator's change in place (he is writing 'vom Meer', 'from the sea') has been deliberately undertaken and so reflects an autonomous decision and an awareness of the radical difference between the familiar surroundings he has left behind and the island landscape he now explores. Unlike the already disturbed Rönne of *Gehirne*, but much like Rönne in his 'Ithaka' appearance, the narrator is able to contrast modern humanity, and its imagined future, to a longed-for primitive state:

> Es ist so schön zu denken, daß wir mal im Laube gewohnt und uns in Erdlöchern gewärmt haben. Und daß wir mal geschlafen haben, wo man grade stand und müde war, vielleicht an einer Baumwurzel wie die Iltisse. Ich denke manchmal, es wird die Zeit kommen, da schlafen die Menschen nicht mehr. Denn das ist doch das Letzte aus der anderen, der stummen getriebenen Welt: ... ein Überzug über die Großhirnrinde, ein Zurückgebrachtwerden an die niederen Zentren ... an alles das, was nicht zum Bewußtsein gesteigert werden kann.
>
> (It is so lovely to think that we once lived among the foliage and warmed ourselves in caves. And that we once slept just where we stood and became tired, perhaps at the root of a tree like the Iltisse. I sometimes think the time will come that human beings will not sleep at all anymore. For that is the last remnant of the other, the mutely driven world ... a coating on the cerebral cortex, a being brought back to lower centres ... to all that which cannot be elevated to consciousness.) (SW, vii/1. 356)

But in *Gehirne*, where Rönne is more profoundly disturbed, this longing for a past state of primal existence cannot be reported on self-reflectively; it is expressed, instead, through a constellation of repeated 'southern' images

---

[49] In contrast to Reif's (1975: 60–61) characterization and that of Ritchie (1972: 45).

(including blue, orchids, violets, anemone and poppies, ruins and marble, blood, palms, sea, islands, storm, desert, and references to Africa, the Mediterranean, and Asia), which suggest a primal connection between the depths of human consciousness and animal and vegetative life. Depth is suggested, for instance, in the sentences: 'Rönne lauschte. Tieferes mußte es noch geben' ('Rönne listened. There must be something deeper') (SW, iii. 60). Exotic images that initially express only Rönne's detachment from his immediate circumstances, from which he never empirically departs, come to dominate and transform his experience of reality.

In the climax of the narrative, when the director has had to return to relieve Rönne of his duties, Rönne speaks irrationally about his path to an exotic elsewhere, but there is no coherent image of a potentially inhabitable space:

> Aber nun geben Sie mir bitte den Weg frei, ich schwinge wieder—ich war so müde—auf Flügeln geht dieser Gang—mit meinem blauen Anemonensch-wert—in Mittagsturz des Lichts—in Trümmern des Südens—in zerfallen-dem Gewölk—Zerstäubungen der Stirne—Entschweifungen der Schläfe.
>
> (But now please let me through. I am taking flight again—I was so tired— this stride goes by wings—with my sword of blue anemones—in the midday fall of sunlight—in the ruins of the South—in the crumbling clouds—skulls disintegrating into dust and the collapsing of their temples.) (SW, iii. 34)

The syntax here is fragmented, leaving a logically unconnected series of phrases. The images are not merely metaphors, but indications of an emerging aspect of consciousness.[50] These images work not merely to transport meaning from one context or image to another, but to act as independent manifestations of the creative consciousness. By the third dash in the above-cited passage, there are no verbs that might link the imagery to time and action; images become indications of complete moments of feeling that cannot be seen merely as a mimesis of ordinary life or of nature. The unusual composite nouns of 'Anemonenschwert' and 'Mittagsturz des Lichtes' in the above-cited passage combine harsh or violent dynamic images (Schwert, Sturz) with positive and elemental natural imagery of flowers and light. The turning to dust of the 'Stirn' evokes both the decomposition of the brain and the return to an elemental substrate. This ambiguity makes such images regressive and also highly modern, comparable to Paul Gauguin's paintings of Tahitian natives and

---

[50] Metaphors, as Rönne views them in 'Der Geburtstag', are merely 'eine Fluchtversuch, eine Art Vision und ein Mangel an Treue' ('an attempt to escape, a kind of vision and a lack of truth') (SW, iii. 1).

Max Pechstein's of Palau, the latter of which is the subject and title of one of Benn's most striking exotic poems.

Southern exotic imagery, then, displaces real spatial orientation. 'Die Eroberung' ('The Conquest') takes place in an unnamed city that has been conquered by a foreign power.[51] As a hated associate of the occupying forces, Rönne longs to 'conquer' it by being accepted: 'Liebe Stadt, laß Dich doch besetzen! Beheimate mich!' ('Lovely city, let yourself be possessed! Make me at home!') (SW, iii. 35). This longing to conquer and possess characterizes the masculine consciousness that will, however, yield to more 'feminine' images of the exotic. Unable to dominate his immediate surroundings, Rönne projects Mediterranean images in which the adjectival images of 'südlich' and 'blau' reappear. To the conquered city he declares:

> Du bist so südlich; Deine Kirche betet in den Abend, ihr Stein ist weiß, der Himmel blau. Du irrst so an das Ufer der Ferne. Du wirst Dich erbarmen, schon umschweifst Du mich.
>
> (You are so southern; your church prays in the evening, its stone is white, the sky blue. You err so on the shore of distance. You will pity yourself, already you evade me.) (SW, iii. 35–36)

It is not that Rönne himself longs to travel to a faraway place; in 'Die Reise' ('The Journey') he is not even able to undertake a planned trip to Antwerp. Rather, to Rönne the term 'südlich' ('southern') connotes an access to communal consciousness, closed off to him both because of his foreign status as an occupier and because he inhabits a modern rationalized world. Rönne intermittently reverts to a 'northern' severely analytical way of regarding his surroundings: he muses on the solidity of numbers in counting and recounting the cow's legs and the sheep on a picture hung in a café, instead of being able to relate to the patrons; in a barber shop watching a man's hair being powdered, he thinks about the refraction and the 'Brechungskoeffizienten' ('refraction coefficient') of light; in a slaughterhouse he considers the technology of the modern sanitation system. Yet this absurdly arbitrary application of analytical thinking fails to provide Rönne with a stable sense of reality.[52] Clarity is won when Rönne reflects critically upon the rational mode of consciousness, recognizing that this has ceased to operate with any continuity in his own experience:

---

[51] Benn's own experience at the time of writing the Rönne novellas was of Brussels under German occupation; in 'Die Eroberung', red and yellow flags hang on the houses and jackets of the native population. Yet the city is not named, perhaps to preserve the ambiguity of the title, which refers not only to a military occupation but also to an attempt, by the protagonist, to dominate his perceptions of his surroundings.

[52] In contrast to Dierick (1987: 91–92), who views Rönne as gaining clarity through scientific thought.

Man muß nur an alles, was man sieht, etwas anzuknüpfen vermögen, es mit
früheren Erfahrungen in Einklang bringen und es unter allgemeine Gesicht-
spunkte stellen, das ist die Wirkungsweise der Vernunft, dessen entsinne ich
mich.

(From everything one sees one has only to be able to go further, to bring it
in harmony with earlier experiences and place it under general aspects, that
is, the functional means of reason which I recall.) (SW, iii. 38)

In contrast to the harmony of rationally generalized and contextualized
experience are Rönne's 'southern' exotic impressions, which, however, do
not yield to rational reflection; rather, they provoke waves of imagistic and
phonic associations. The violets in a girl's basket provoke a string of images:

blau wie Stücke der Nacht, mit Orchideenbündeln, weichen Zusammen-
flusses aus hellblau und orange.... Die Orchidee, lachte er selbstgefällig, die
Blüte des heißen Afrika.
(Blue like fragments of night, with bunches of orchids, soft confluence of
pale blue and orange.... The orchids, he laughed amusing himself, the
blossoms of hot Africa!) (SW, iii. 38–39)

'Blüte' here denotes blossoms, but the phonic association with 'Blut' can
be heard, and this would add to the resonances of 'heißen', which qualifies
the image of Africa. In 'Unter der Großhirnrinde' ('Under the Cerebral
Cortex') too, the narrator links blood and flowers with the sea: 'Und aus
der Ferne, überall vernehmbar, immer das blaue Lied... wie eine Lache
aus Kornblumenblut: das Meer' ('and from the distance, perceptible
everywhere, always the blue song... like a pool of cornflower blood: the
sea') (SW, vii/1. 362–363). But there the image is presented metaphorically, evoking, but not yet invoking, as in *Gehirne*, a direct experience. In
that 'Lache' denotes not only 'pool' but 'laugh', the landscape image is
humanized. The coupling of blood, flower, and exotic landscape within a
human context appears again at a key moment in Rönne's process of
'Eroberung'. During a night walk in which he visits a forest that seems to
be glowing blue, and a local dance hall, Rönne 'perceives' the life pulsing
near the surface of a pregnant woman's belly 'über einer Landschaft aus
Blut, über Schwellungen aus tierischen Geweben' ('above a landscape of
blood, above swellings of animal tissue') (SW, iii. 40). This provokes his
exotic submission; the following morning he finds himself in the gardens:
'Ich wollte eine Stadt erobern, nun streicht ein Palmenblatt über mich hin'
('I wanted to conquer a city, now a palm leaf caresses me') (SW, iii. 41).
The collapse of self and its displacement by exotic southern imagery
culminates in erotic experience, which in Rönne's transformation is inseparable from the creative projections of a new aesthetic. This culmination is
reached in 'Der Geburtstag', in which Rönne has turned thirty and suffers

an existential crisis, '[e]in Drängen nach dem Sinn des Daseins' ('an urge to find the meaning of existence') (SW, iii. 50). He considers his origins, recalling the contrast between northern immobility and liberating southern movement:

> Aus der norddeutschen Ebene stammte er. In südlichen Ländern natürlich war der Sand leicht und lose; ein Wind konnte—das war nachgewiesen—Körner um die ganze Erde tragen; hier war das Staubkorn, groß und schwer.
> (He originated from the north German plains. In southern lands, the sand, of course, was light and loose; a wind could—this was proven—carry seeds around the whole earth; here the kernels of dust were large and heavy.)
> (SW, iii. 50)

'Northern' thinking has left Rönne with a lack of belief in the world: 'über allem schwebte ein leises zweifelndes Als ob: als ob Ihr wirklich wäret Raum und Sterne' ('A quiet doubting "as if" hung over everything: as if you really were space and stars') (SW, iii. 50). In response Rönne reflects on the aesthetic generation of his imagery, thus striving to articulate an aesthetic vision; but this striving is coupled with the intensification of erotic desire. As he walks out of town towards the hospital, he contemplates the seemingly swaying path, with its growth of violets; and the crocuses provoke associations with Greek and Roman culture, saffron fields by the Mediterranean. Rönne considers the Greek and Arabic terms, and enjoys 'so ausgiebig zu assoziieren' ('to associate so generously') (SW, iii. 52). In the hospital, his imagination seizes on the 'Veilchenblut' ('violet blood') of a woman's vein, drawing on the association with the violets he has just seen on the path and again linking *Blüte* with *Blut*. It is now clear that blood and blossoms symbolize feminine sexuality, no longer observed through the eyes of a doctor, but experienced as mysterious otherness to rational thought. This association also made in Musil's 'Grigia', as Homo, in a mystical epiphany, associates his wife's genitalia with 'eine zart scharlachfarbene Blume' ('a tender, scarlet-coloured flower') that exists 'in keines anderen Mannes Welt, nur in seiner' ('in no other man's world, only in his') (GW, vi. 240).[53] For Rönne the female body now serves not merely as a vessel of primal nature, but as a surface on which to project his aesthetic imagination. Thus, Rönne transforms

---

[53] While this metaphor echoes Novalis, Musil's source for this metaphor is Adolphe Retté, *Paradox über die Liebe* (1905), from which Musil transcribes in his *Tagebücher*: 'Da warf sie sich . . . quer über das Bett hin, um so ihre heimliche Blume noch besser anzubieten. . . . Und ich besaß sie so, daß bloß unsere Geschlechter sich berührten und ineinander drangen . . . und wir konnten das Blut sehen' ('Here she threw herself . . . across the bed, in order to better offer up her secret flower. . . . And I possessed her so, that only our sexual parts caressed each other and penetrated each other . . . and we could see blood' (T, 106). See Eibl (1978: 108).

empirical detail of the patient on the examining table into graphic images
of a 'primitive' and exotic sexuality:

> Sie haben die Narben zwischen den Schenkeln, ein Araberbey; große Wun-
> den müssen es gewesen sein, gerissen von den lasterhaften Lippen Afrikas.
> (You have scars between the thighs, an Arab lord, it must have been large
> wounds, torn from the wicked lips of Africa.) (SW, iii. 53)

The nihilism of this passage echoes Benn's collection *Morgue*, wherein in
one undoubtedly racist poem the speaker imagines a violent sexual act
between two corpses, a European woman and an African man. That
Rönne (like Benn) is a doctor treating urban prostitutes may be a factor
in his inhumane objectification of them. Since the prostitutes live at the
margins of society, and service sexual drives isolated from social context,
they are all the more easily associated with the sexual licentiousness
problematically attributed to natives of 'exotic' lands and the violence of
their domination. The racist implications are undeniable, in these and in
other images used by Benn.[54] Yet it is, again, the breakdown of the European
culture, rather than the appropriation of the African, that is his focus.

The erotic culmination Rönne imagines is expressed through topographical imagery loaded with sensuous detail:

> Einen Augenblick streifte es ihn am Haupt: eine Lockerung, ein leises
> Klirren der Zersprengung, und in sein Auge fuhr ein Bild: klares Land,
> schwingend in Bläue und Glut und zerklüftet von den Rosen, in der Ferne
> eine Säule, umwuchert am Fuß; darin er und die Frau, tierisch und verloren,
> still vergießend Säfte und Hauch.
> (For a moment it touched his head: a slackening, a soft clanking of
> breakage, and an image came into his eye: clear land, oscillating in blue, a
> glow jagged by the roses grown rampant around a column in the distance.)
> (SW, iii. 71)

The cipher-images of blue, roses, glow, and columns, the last suggesting
ruins of ancient culture, recall the 'Trümmer[n] des Südens' at the end of
'Gehirne'. These motives are here coupled with an explicitly erotic image
of physical and animalistic sexuality, evoking both the vitality of sensual
pleasure and the Dionysian dissolution of individuality; thus, Rönne and
the woman are described as 'tierisch und verloren' ('animalistic and lost').
The explicit physiology of the phrase 'in sein Auge fuhr ein Bild' suggests a
paradoxical role for the imagination: at once passive and productive.

---

[54] On the category of race in Benn and for a critical account of his problematic
acceptance of a 'biological foundation' for history, see Roche (1991: 61).

Rönne's aesthetic realization arrives together with his sexual awakening. The result of this sexual-aesthetic complex is his creation—on the basis of a prostitute he sees in the corridor—of Edmée. The encounter is imagined as 'sauber und ursprünglich' ('clean and original') (SW, iii. 54). Rönne creates the vision of an ideal in his fantasy; on the basis of this prostitute he imagines 'eine Reinheit ohne Ende und um die Lider eine Anemone' ('a purity without end and around the lids an anemone')—an image that connects this lover to evocations of the exotic South in previous stories. His further description of the woman with European features—'blond, und Lust und Skepsis aus ernüchterten Gehirnen' ('blonde, and desire and scepticism of a disillusioned brain')—differentiates Rönne from a Gauguin or a Flaubert, longing to flee from civilization into the arms of an exotic native (SW, iii. 54). The European features of the lover—like the blue eyes of the indigenous inhabitants of Kubin's *Traumreich*—highlight the creation of an aesthetic realm rather than a colonialist fantasy. For Rönne this aesthetic realm is inspired by the elemental quality of the southern, but is engendered by the collapse of his own civilization. It is as this autochthonous creation that he freely associates his 'Edmée' with an Egyptian landscape.

> War das Ägypten? War das Afrika um einen Frauenleib, Golf und Liane um der Schultern Flut? Er suchte hin und her. War etwas zurückgeblieben? War Hinzufügbares vorhanden? Hatte er es erschaffen: Glut, Wehmut und Traum?
>
> (Was that Egypt? Was that Africa around a woman's body, gulf and liana flooding around the shoulder? He searched here and there. Was there something left behind? Was there something close that could be integrated? Had he created it: glow, agony, and dream?) (SW, iii. 55)

The culmination of this passive-productive creativity is erotic. In the garden Rönne experiences sexual consummation as 'Vermischung', and in the depiction there is no longer a clear distinction between aesthetic imagery and reality, subject and object. Forms and differentiations dissolve:

> Im Garten wurde Vermischung.... Eine Blüte, die trieb, hielt inne und stand im Blauen, Angel der Welt. Kronen lösten sich weich, Kelche sanken ein, der Park ging unter Blute des Entformten. Edmée breitete sich hin. Ihre Schultern glätteten sich, zwei warme Teiche. Nun schloß die Hand, langsam, um einen Schaft, die Reife in ihre Fülle, bräunlich abgemäht an den Fingern, unter großen Garben verklärter Lust—:
> Und nun verwirrte sich das Gefüge, es entsank fleischlich sein Ich—:
> (There was mixing in the garden ... A blossom, which was sprouting, held back and stood in blue, angel of the world. Crowns softly came loose,

chalices sunk in, the park subsided in the flowering of the deformed. Edmée spread herself. Her shoulders shined, two warm pools. Now the hand closed, slowly, around a shaft, ripe in its fullness, on the fingers under great sheaves of transfigured desire ... and now the structure became confused, his 'I' dissipated carnally.) (SW, iii. 56)

This loss of ego, this dissolution of self into the sensations and imagery of the flesh, is similarly evoked in 'Grigia', where the landscape seems to work against his individuation, and Homo is drawn into a sexual liaison that offers a feeling of fusion with nature: 'Noch einmal rann Grigia wie weich trockene Erde durch ihn' ('Yet again Grigia ran through him like soft dry earth') (Musil, GW, vi. 251). Just as Rönne's sexual experiences take place in the park, Homo's sexual liaisons with Grigia take place in very earthy settings: 'Man brauchte sich nur zu erinnern, daß man hier unter Wilden lebte, so entstand schon ein Rausch in der Hitze des engen, von gärendem Heu hochgefüllten Raums' ('One only had to remember that one lived among savages here, so an intoxication arose in the heat of the narrow room filled with baking hay') (GW, vi. 249). But the setting for Rönne is transformed by images of other places. A flurry of topographical references underlines the ecstasis of the sexual experience: Egypt is evoked and then supplanted by Florence, and then 'Europa, Asien, Afrika' are evoked together in one breath, surrounded by fragmentary expressions including the typical images of blue, forests, roses, the 'bacchantisch' ('bacchanalian') city of Venice, poppy, flutes, the Nile, blood, and dream (Benn, SW, iii. 60). The primitive consciousness Rönne seeks is expressed not in an image of a utopian paradise in which he might complete himself, but rather as a Dionysian realm of self-dissolution: 'das Schweigen unantastbaren Landes, rötlichen, toten, den Göttern geweiht. Dahin ging, das fühlte er tief, nun für immer sein Weg' ('the silence of an inaccessible country, reddish, dead, dedicated to the gods. Now he went there forever—this he felt deeply'). Two flutes Rönne hears in the distance converge, 'schlagen hoch zu einem Traum' ('strike to the heights of a dream') (SW, iii. 61).

In the wake of Rönne's initial collapse, this sexual ecstasis initiates the aesthetic reconstruction of a perspective on reality grounded not in reason but rather in the imagination. While the reality known to the northern-minded doctor has dissolved away, aesthetic form has become more deliberate and explicit. It is as if, as Benn writes in reference to Nietzsche, 'die ästhetische Deutung sei bereits unsere jetzige Natur geworden' ('the aesthetic interpretation has already become our current nature') (SW, iv. 403). While Rönne's use of exotic imagery earlier has tones of escapism, gradually it becomes evident that Rönne aims not merely to escape reality but to transform it, in part by creating a new syntax in which images are no longer subordinated to the traditional flow of plot, narrative depiction, and the grammar of subject and predicate. Thus, his experience of language is not, like the writer of Hofmannsthal's 'Ein Brief' (the 'Chandos' letter), merely one of breakdown; the crisis becomes aesthetically productive.[55]

Thus, while in 'Grigia' the fusion with a primitive atmosphere induces his submission to death, for Rönne (and for Kubin's narrator and Ketten in 'Die Portugiesin') it provokes a creative or existential revival. Although at first Rönne begins to write merely to stabilize his painfully chaotic perception of reality, this becomes a painful transformation into an aesthetically creative consciousness. Nietzsche established the relation between pain and creativity:

> Schaffen—das ist die große Erlösung vom Leiden, und des Lebens leicht-werden. Aber daß der Schaffende sei, dazu selber tut Leid Not und viel Verwandlung.
>
> (Creation—that is the great release from suffering, and of life becoming bearable. But that the creator is, that itself causes pain, deprivation, and much transformation.) (KG, vi/1. 106)

For Nietzsche, becoming a creator requires 'viel bitteres Sterben' ('much bitter dying') (KG, vi/1. 107). Rönne's collapse and creative renewal of self, like Patera's apocalyptic transformations in Kubin's *Die andere Seite*, and Ketten's illness and recovery in 'Die Portugiesin', might be thought of as a kind of death and creative rebirth. In 'Tonka', too, it is through suffering and death—albeit of his lover—that Musil's protagonist finds the inspiration to continue his work.

In Kubin's novel *Die andere Seite*, the breakdown of a rationally ordered world similarly allows for a potential new configuration of sense experience and thought. In the section on 'Die Klärung der Erkenntnis' ('The illumination of cognition'), Kubin's narrator attempts to intensify his perception of objects in abstraction from their practical and scientific associations with other things. He uses abstract formulations to describe light, sounds, and even self-awareness: 'Ich entsinne mich jenes Morgens, da ich mir wie das Zentrum eines elementaren Zahlensystems vorkam. Ich fühlte mich abstrakt, als schwankender Gleichgewichtspunkt von Kräften' ('I recall one morning, when I seemed to be the centre of an elementary system of numbers. I felt abstract, as an oscillating point of balance of forces') (AS, 136). Like Rönne, the narrator's senses are sharpened so as to see qualities rather than conceptual generalities. Those conceptual generalities give way to 'neuartige Empfindun-gen' ('new sensations') (AS, 136). For the narrator sheer existence becomes

---

[55] See Schonlau (2005), who compares the crisis of language in Hofmannsthal's 'Ein Brief' and Benn's 'Unter der Großhirnrinde'.

palpable in things, and seems to reach him from infinity. This new mode of seeing correlates not only to the narrator's deeper understanding of the dream-world, but to revolutions in his own artistic productivity. In this respect, both Benn and Kubin may be associated with contemporaneous movements in modern art. Kubin's narrative reconstitutes the world according to dream 'logic', a reconstitution that is, like Kubin's own drawings and paintings, more surreal and fantastical; just as the Surrealists drew from dream imagery, the *Traumreich* is an 'eingebildete Welt... aus dem Nichts' ('world imagined... from out of nothing') (AS, 137). Rönne's reconstitution of the world through images is closer to modern Cubist and to primitive art as well, the connection between them having been established by Benn's acquaintance in Brussels, Carl Einstein, who was in turn influenced by Wilhelm Worringer's theory of modern and primitive abstraction as expressing a psychological *Raumscheu* (anxiety about space).[56] Einstein's account emphasizes not only simplicity of primitive forms in modern abstraction but also the reduction of three-dimensional reality to the two-dimensional surface of an artwork; by abandoning representation of three-dimensional perspective, which must be seen from a localized point of view, it eschews any reference to what Worringer called the 'Einfühlung' ('empathy') of the individual viewer. Like African sculpture, which is structured to be effective from a variety of receptive positions, Cubist painting combines many perspectives on the same object. This reconfiguration necessarily leaves out mimetic representation of dimensionality and detail. Rönne's perception is a kind of abstraction:

> Aus dem Einstrom der Dinge, dem Rauschen der Klänge, dem Fluten des Lichts die stille Ebene herzustellen, die er bedeutete.
> Es war eine fremde Gegend, durch die er ging.
> (He intended to position the still surface from out of the confluence of things, the ecstasy of sounds, the fluttering light.
> It was a foreign region that he walked through.) (SW, iii. 46)

The 'fremde Gegend' refers less to the suburbs through which Rönne wanders, than to the space of perceptual abstraction in his imagination, 'die stille Ebene'. It is a world both received and reconstructed by an aesthetically charged imagination.

Yet while the world as Rönne experiences it through exotic imagery is vital and essential, it is, like Kubin's *Traumreich*, also subject to constant transformation. Both authors' descriptions recall Nietzsche's Heraclitean

---

[56] See Williams (1983), for a discussion of Einstein's influence on Benn. See also, more recently, Williams (2005: especially 89–93 and 98–103).

view of reality as a continual flux, which in tragedy is expressed through Dionysian excess. In *Die andere Seite* this is expressed in the tumultuous interchange of natural forms in Kubin's dream-world as it approaches *Untergang*. But while Kubin's transformations play with the mimesis of reality, fantastically and grotesquely rearranging and merging still recognizable entities, Benn's images are associative and formal, isolating a single object, or merging indeterminate atmospheric elements (night, colours, stones, sea, south). The establishment or 'event' of form is constantly threatened by loss of form, as when it begins to rain during his walk:

> Zwischen die Straßen rinnt Nacht, über die weißen Steine blaut es, es verdichtet sich die Entrückung; die Sträucher schmelzen, welches Vergehn!—
> Nun fiel ein Regen und löste die Form.
> (The night flows through the streets, it blues on the white stones, the rapture condenses—the shrubs are melting—what dissolution! Now a rain falls and the form dissolves.) (SW, iii. 48)

The syntax in this passage is striking: Benn's omission of articles ('rinnt Nacht') allows for de-substantiation, and his typical transformation of the adjective 'blue' to a verb ('blaut es') enlarges its power beyond its attribution to a specific object.[57] The dash after the penultimate sentence suggests the absoluteness of the thought without respect to any larger complex; and the mimetic ambiguity of the last sentence at once returns the thought to Rönne's location in real time and space—since it is raining and thus objects appear blurry—and refers to the process of abstraction from this same reality. A later reference to the river, probably seen in the rain, evokes formal creation and dissolution of nature, which in Kubin's novel is magnified to apocalyptic proportions as it rains and the river overflows and floods the city. While this creation and dissolution is of the world itself as experienced in Kubin's realm of dreams, and so of the unconscious dream-life, in Benn the real referent of this creation and dissolution is put into question. Through the linked images of play, fever, and senselessness, it is linked to the irrational activity of wakeful consciousness, 'ein Wurf von Formen, ein Spiel in Fiebern' ('a tumult of forms, a feverish play') (SW, iii. 49).

Rönne's descriptions of women are now more akin to abstract primitivism, echoing Picasso's breakthrough painting of prostitutes, 'Les Demoiselles d'Avignon' of 1907, inspired by African masks, and primitivist paintings by German Expressionists of prostitutes and cabaret singers

---

[57] See the accounts by Requadt (1962a, 1962b) and Overath (1987) on the symbolic value of blue in Benn and German modernism more generally.

(discussed in more detail in Chapter 5).[58] Without losing its reference to
sexual animality, the prostitute's body, which Rönne at first regards from
the point of view of a clinician, is reduced to primitive forms:

> Eine kannte ich, die war an einem Tag von Männern einem Viertelhundert
> der Rausch gewesen, die Schauer und der Sommer, um den sie blühten.
> Sie stellte die Form, und es geschah das Wirkliche. Ich will Formen suchen
> und mich hinterlassen; Wirklichkeiten eine Hügelkette, o von Dingen ein
> Gelände.
>
> (I recognized one, who in one day had been the rapture of a quarter-
> hundred men, the shudder and the summer around which they blossom. She
> posed the form, and the real happened. I want to seek form and leave myself
> behind; to realities a chain of hills, oh a landscape of things.) (SW, iii. 45–46)

In this passage, the clinical quantification of the woman's sexual partners,
in a peculiar, dehumanizing syntax, gives way to images conjuring physical
sensations and processes—'Rausch, Schauer, Sommer, blühten'. A shift in
perspective is thus initiated immediately from Rönne as doctor and
relatively disinterested observer, who recognizes the woman, to voyeur
and sensual participant. The succession of abstract nouns which follows—
'Form, das Wirkliche, Formen, Wirklichkeiten, Dingen,' and 'Gelände',
the last of which suggests both contour and topography—sketches a
further impulse towards aesthetic productivity, one not only perceptually
sensuous but reaching the elemental substrate of reality. This movement
from analytical to sensual to elemental consciousness leads to the paradox
of self-dissolution and creation, the height of which is the achievement of a
new reality, 'das Wirkliche'. The phrase 'Ich will . . . mich hinterlassen' is
densely ambiguous, for the will to leave self behind is aimed at both sexual
ecstasis and sexual reproduction. In this intertwining of sexual and aesthetic creativity, the height of self-exertion is self-overcoming. Nietzsche
describes such self-forgetting in his account of the creative-erotic Dionysian *Trieb*: 'bei dem gewaltigen, die ganze Natur lustvoll durchdringenden
Nahen des Frühlings erwachen jene dionysischen Regungen, in deren
Steigerung das Subjektive zu völliger Selbstvergessenheit hinschwindet'
('in the violent approach of spring, which lustfully penetrates the whole of
nature, these Dionysian impulses awaken, in the intensification of which
the subjective disappears in total self-forgetfulness') (KG, iii/1. 25). In
'Diesterweg' Rönne has even forgotten his name. But this self-loss in
Gehirne is the condition for aesthetic renewal, and it offers a way to
experience what Benn's narrator, in 'Diesterweg', calls 'das andere

---

[58] While this painting has been criticized for its colonialist appropriation of African
imagery, Leighton (1990) gives an anti-colonialist interpretation of Picasso's painting.

Leben' (SW, iii. 72). The phrase 'O von Dingen ein Gelände' in the above-cited passage consummates the aesthetic telos: by merging with the woman in this intensely articulated erotic ecstasis, the elemental substrate of material existence seems to be opened up: of things, a landscape may emerge, here from the aesthetically creative and sexually procreative use of her feminine form.

In *Gehirne* self-dissolution is followed by aesthetic renewal. In 'Die Insel' Rönne is employed as a doctor for an island prison; exploring the landscape and the humble fishing village in his free time occasions flights of fantasy in which he imposes imagery of an exotic landscape upon the perceived surroundings.

> Also, eine Insel und etwas südliches Meer. Es sind nicht da, aber es könnte da sein: Zimtwälder. . . . Ja, das war eine Insel, die in einem Meer vor Indien lag.
> (So, an island and some southern sea. They don't exist, but they could: Cinnamon forests . . . yes, that was an island that lay in a sea near India.)
> (SW, iii. 63)

Rönne's imagination transforms the island he inhabits into an island in the South Seas, an image gradually projected as an autonomous world. And though the empirical surroundings are not wholly suppressed—'Und durch die Insel schritt er, zwischen Roggen und Wein, abgeschlossen und still umgrenzt' ('And he stepped through the island, between rye and vineyards, closed up and quietly bordered on all sides')—Rönne is aware of his imaginative power: 'Sein Urteil ist Begehren, der Satzbau Stellung nehmend' ('His judgment is desire, the syntax taking position') (SW, iii. 64). The equation of judgment and desire, and the reference to grammatical 'Satzbau', highlight Rönne's awareness of his own creative imagination. He not only uses language in a new way but also reflects upon this innovation.

Like Kubin's narrator in the chapter 'Die Klärung der Erkenntnis', Rönne deliberately sets himself the task of an alternative perception of reality divorced from rational concepts. Yet while Kubin's narrator is inspired by Asian consciousness, Rönne's concern is the collapse of his own 'northern' conceptual thinking: 'Die Begriffe, schien ihm, sanken herab' (SW, iii. 64). Rönne reflects on the impotence of concepts to grasp the essential quality of particular things, gradually abandoning the drive towards conceptual generalization of objects, just as Kubin's narrator attempts a mental passivity in the reception of things. While Kubin's narrator must struggle for a non-conceptual mode of perception, Rönne is now able to compare the sea as he would have formerly understood it, 'ein allgemeinster Ausdruck', with the vital intensity of the singular experience, imagining the masses of water, the sting of the lips and the scent of storm and the wildlife, the sensuously given, elemental totality: 'alles Ruhelose' ('all chaos'). This, he finds, can be intuited but not scientifically analysed. The rationally constructed world gives way to one sensuously associative, 'südlich', here African and Mediterranean: 'Auch daß er hin und her die Augen aufschlug: in helle Himmel, über Wüsten, am Nil, und an den Myrtenlagunen die Geigenvölker' ('But that he opened his eyes here and there: the bright sky, in deserts, on the Nile, and on the myrtle lagoons, the violin people') (SW, iii. 65).

Having transgressed rational thought, the subject heeds 'den dunklen Sturm, der aus dem Leibe brach' ('The dark storm that irrupted from the body'). Instead of the man of science and his 'Hypothese von Realität', Rönne promotes the 'schöpferische[n] Mensch' whose thought is based on intuition (SW, iii. 70). Rönne's admission is followed by a regressive feeling of sleep—a state associated with primitive humans in 'Unter der Großhirnrinde'—and, as in other endings, an observation of a garden landscape, the features of which are said to glow 'grenzenlos und für immer' ('boundlessly and forever') evoking ahistorical and perpetual nature (SW, iii. 71). But this limitlessness and perpetuity is not an indication of the transcendent in any religious sense; it remains earthly and sensual and firmly rooted in Rönne's aesthetic-erotic imagination.

'DER ANDERE ZUSTAND': MYSTICISM AND PRIMAL STATES OF CONSCIOUSNESS

While Benn promotes the aesthetic reconstruction of reality in the wake of rationality's collapse, and so brings forth 'das andere Leben' buried deep in the human psyche through exotic imagery, Musil criticizes the polarization of intellect and feeling in modern experience. Musil rejects the reductive abstractions of modern life, in terms similar to those used by Hofmannsthal in *Die Briefe des Zurückgekehrten*. In Musil's view, our experience of the world has become restricted to those aspects recognized in the 'normale[n] Zustand' of purposive practical activity, 'das Messen, Rechnen, Spüren, das positive, kausale, mechanische Denken' ('measuring, calculating, sensing, positive, causal, mechanical thinking'); this suppresses other, more intense and indeterminate modes of experience, which Musil imagines as more fully lived in primitive stages of humanity (GW, viii. 1143). According to Musil, modern life has lost access to a truer, more participatory relation to the world based on feeling, intuition, and empathetic fusion, a relation which, however, is the basis for sexual love, religious feeling, ecstasy, and art. This other relation to the world emerges in mystical experiences, albeit fleeting ones, accounts of which Musil had found in eclectic sources, such as Martin Buber's anthology *Ekstatische Konfessionen* (1909), and in Novalis, whose work the protagonist of 'Tonka' is reading.[59] This relation is described by Musil as 'der andere Zustand', a notion often associated with *Der Mann ohne Eigenschaften*, but also relevant to the novellas of *Drei Frauen*.[60] While this notion was outlined in detail in 'Ansätze zu neuer Ästhetik', it had preoccupied Musil considerably earlier[61] and reflects Musil's lasting interest in the primitive states of consciousness indicated in Nietzsche's descriptions of the Dionysian and analysed anthropologically by Lévy-Bruhl.[62] In 'Grigia' and 'Die Portugiesin', the mystical state of consciousness is evoked through topographical motifs, leading however, to different possible outcomes: to self-dissolution and death, suggesting that its primitive intensity is not without risk to the self, and to self-overcoming and rebirth.[63] Both of the stories deal with erotic relationships, but while the protagonist of 'Die Portugiesin' overcomes his estrangement from his wife and returns to life invigorated, the protagonist of 'Grigia' feels connected to two women (the title character and his wife) in contrasting ways and sinks into death. Both of these possibilities are described in the mystical experiences in Kubin's *Die andere Seite*, but there the dream-realm ultimately yields to apocalyptic collapse.

The topographical motifs through which Musil evokes mystical experiences will be the main focus of this section. First, in the stories discussed here, the topographical isolation of Musil's settings—both are set in South Tyrol, where Musil was stationed during the war—situates an internal conflict for the characters. The settings rely on the contrast between the northern and southern so central in Benn's writings; like Benn, Musil highlights this contrast through exoticizing imagery. The settings are

[59] See Goltschnigg (1974).
[60] Robertson (1991) has shown the results of Musil's engagement with the primitive in 'Die Portugiesin' and *Der Mann ohne Eigenschaften (The Man Without Qualities)*. Luft (1980) argues that the novella is for Musil the most effective form for the presentation of the other condition and of a new relation to the world (179) and interprets *Drei Frauen* accordingly (180–183). Grill's study of mysticism in Musil (2007), like much scholarship on the other condition, is exclusively focused on *Der Mann ohne Eigenschaften*.
[61] A reference to the other condition appears in Musil's *Tagebücher*, Heft 11, which is dated '2. April 1905–1908 oder später, ca. 1918/19' (T, 191).
[62] Grill (2007: 335), associates the Apollonian and Dionysian with Musil's conceptual pairs; for Luft (1980: 193) the normal and other conditions are 'roughly equivalent' to the Apollonian and Dionysian. On Musil's interest in primitivism, see Robertson (1991) and Grill (2007: 338–340, 342–343).
[63] Given Homo's demise, Reif (1971: 76) argues for the 'anti-exotistisch' nature of 'Grigia', comparable to that of *Der Tod in Venedig*; yet in the light of 'Die Portugiesin' Homo's fate can be seen as but one possible outcome of the exotic-ecstatic experience.

contrasted to the normal state of life in modern Europe through a character's movement between North and South, and through historical anachronism. The primitivism of these isolated regions may be, as in the case of 'Grigia', also emphasized through some communication with other 'uncivilized' realms. Secondly, the landscape in these stories is exoticized through primitive imagery and through association with exoticized women, both of which provoke transformations in the inner lives of the protagonists through their experiences of epiphany and ecstasis.[64] Thirdly, Musil invokes mystical symbolism, in which objects in the surroundings, often animals, take on mysterious significance and are identified with a relation to the beyond. These mystical evocations, finally, culminate in ecstatic experiences of death or self-overcoming, in direct conflict with the primitive landscape: Homo dies in a cave, suggesting submission to the darker forces of existence brought out through primitive experience, and Ketten climbs a massive rock face in an intense physical struggle, in order to overcome a nearly fatal illness contracted through an infectious insect bite.

'Grigia' and 'Die Portugiesin' are both set in isolated, primitive worlds. Grigia's culture is isolated from the wider world both geographically and linguistically, and allows Homo to become completely cut off from his former life. The von Ketten castle is both geographically and structurally isolated in South Tyrol, within a border region between German and Italian languages. Beneath its walls runs a wild river that blocks out all noise, including, significantly, the church bells, and it is bordered by a forest that is described in magical terms, with reference to unicorns and dragons. While the medieval setting of 'Die Portugiesin' sets it apart from Musil's other stories, the setting of 'Grigia' is also anachronistic: it appears to Homo as 'ein vorweltliches Pfahldorf' ('a prehistoric village on posts'), and the inhabitants' mode of speech, dress, and manners 'wiesen sie weit in die Jahrhunderte der Altvordern zurück' ('throw them back to the centuries of their ancestors') (GW, vi. 238). But much of the tension in 'Grigia' is due to the contrast between this anachronistic isolation and the decadence of modern Northern Europe; the latter is represented by those who, like Homo, come to the region to take part in a gold-mining project resurrected by Mozart Amadeo Hoffingott. Their 'Goldgräberleben' ('life of gold prospecting') both brings adventure and exposes their decadence, symbolized by the 'Fleischvergiftung' ('meat poisoning') they contract by eating somewhat rotten meat during their evening's drinking, gambling, and listening to recordings of popular songs. Their modern decadence

---

[64] Musil writes in the *Tägebucher*: 'Extase ist der Anfang der völligen Entdeckung unseres Wesens' ('Ecstasy is the beginning of the full discovery of our essence') (T, 135).

seems amplified in this isolated natural setting, as the men in their makeshift casino under the stars imagine 'ein astraler Geruch von Puder, Gaze, ein Nebel von fernem Varieté und europäischer Sexualität' ('an astral smell of powder, gauze, a fog of distant varieté and European sexuality') (GW, vi. 244). In this context of European decadence, they are reduced to speaking 'eine Tiersprache' ('an animal language') (GW, vi. 243).[65]

Exchange between this 'primitive' region of Europe and the 'Gold-gräberleben' of America figures in 'Grigia' twice, further exoticizing the region and symbolizing adventurism and unstable personal identity. The effect of the references to America is to compound the exoticism of the Italian mining region by its association with another foreign place, like-wise uncivilized but also decadently modern, and an uncontrollable com-petitor with Europe. The gold-mining expedition of Hoffingott (whose ironic name couples the weight of the great composer with a sense of abandonment to fate) is supported by American means and thus is afforded 'großen Stil' ('great style') (GW, vi. 235). Its failure, which coincides with Homo's death in the mine, reveals both the hopeless nature of the enterprise, and the vulnerability of Europeans to misadventure. Local miners also migrate to America; when they return they bring back money, diseases from the brothels, and 'die Ungläubigkeit, aber nicht den scharfen Geist der Zivilisation' ('the atheism, but not the sharp spirit of civilization') (GW, vi. 238). One miner returning from America swindles the locals by taking on the identities in turn of several local miners whom he had met there. Narratively this anecdote foreshadows and subjectively legitimizes Homo's own self-estrangement and infidelity. But the anec-dote also draws attention to the instability of personal identity in a 'primitive' culture; for before he is eventually arrested, the local women, despite their reservations, tolerate the imposter longer, and enjoy him more, than they ought to do: 'So waren diese Weiber' ('So were these women') (GW, vi. 238). This instability of personal identity in an exotic, isolated setting is also a major motif of *Die andere Seite,* in which Kubin also makes use of an American influence. Patera's physical form changes according to his dreams, but he also takes on new identities, appearing as a street sweeper, an old woman, a border patrolman. Herkules Bell, Patera's American rival who attempts to overthrow Patera's anachronistic domina-tion of the *Traumreich,* is eventually revealed to be one with Patera himself, to be the other, destructive pole of Patera's own *Doppelwesen.*

---

[65] Nietzsche's critique of modern decadence is referred to in detail in Musil's *Tagebücher* (T, 27).

'Die Portugiesin', too, relies upon the evocation of mystical forces that are closely related to the geographical and cultural spaces the protagonist and his wife inhabit. The location of the Ketten *Schloß* on the borderline between Northern and Southern European worlds is highly significant, for it sets up the expectation of uncertainty about the relation between them. The uneasy relation of northern and southern influences correlates to the opposing tendencies of the masculine, warfaring, and unsentimental Kettens—whose strength is said to emerge not from their bodies but rather 'aus Augen und Stirnen' ('from the eyes and forehead')—and the 'geheimnisvoll' ('mysterious') beauty of the protagonist's exotic Portuguese wife (GW, vi. 253, 254). But it is the isolation of the setting that infuses this conflict with a sense of mystery. The setting is described in the novella's second paragraph:

> Seitlich des großen, über den Brenner nach Italien führenden Wegs, zwischen Brixen und Trient, lag auf einer fast freistehenden lotrechten Wand ihre Burg; fünfhundert Fuß unter ihr tollte ein wilder kleiner Fluß so laut, daß man eine Kirchenglocke im selben Raum nicht gehört hätte, sobald man den Kopf aus dem Fenster bog. Kein Schall der Welt drang von außen in das Schloß der Catene, durch diese davorhängende Matte wilden Lärms hindurch; aber das gegen das Toben sich stemmende Auge fuhr ohne Hindernis durch diesen Widerstand und taumelte überrascht in die tiefe Rundheit des Ausblicks.
>
> (Alongside the great road across the Brenner pass to Italy, between Brixen and Trent, was their castle on an almost sheer, free-standing crag; five hundred feet below coursed a savage little river so loudly that one would not have heard the church bells in the same room, as soon as one had leaned his head out of the window. No sound from the world could reach into the delle Catene castle, through this curtain of wild noise; but through all the deafening noise the gaze could pass unimpeded and plunged suddenly into the deep encircling panorama.) (GW, vi. 253)

The wildly rushing river beneath the fortification cuts off any other sound from the outside world as if by a curtain. The contrast between this deafening noise and the open view is strikingly emphasized by the lack of 'Hindernis' and the 'Widerstand' of sound overcome by the depth of vision the view offers. The location of the *Schloß* and its striking external surroundings are described, but the interior is indicated here only indirectly, as one imagines the view of the landscape from a window.

Through their isolation from a wider world, these settings can be used to magnify symbolic contrasts. Along with the contrast between northern and southern cultures, Musil contrasts exterior life and interiority, symbolized through open and interior spaces. In 'Grigia', Homo experiences freedom, enchantment, and epiphany in the open landscape and submission to death in a dark cave. In 'Die Portugiesin', Ketten's psychological situation is expressed through a persistent contrast of inner and outer spaces. After bringing his wife from afar, Ketten remains home only on two brief occasions—each hardly a day—in the course of an eleven-year campaign against the Bishop of Trent, where Ketten often sleeps in open encampment. The narrative avoidance of interior description of the castle corresponds to Ketten's fear of the inner life, which his mysterious wife embodies. The reader is told of his fear 'länger zuhause zu bleiben, wie sich ein Müder nicht setzen darf' ('to remain at home any longer, the way a tired person dare not sit down') (GW, vi. 257). Ketten experiences tender intimacy with his wife as 'unheimlich' ('uncanny'), and despite her bearing him two sons she remains to him 'fremd wie der Mond' ('foreign as the moon') (GW, vi. 259). This interior will play a symbolic role again when, after climbing the rock face and thus overcoming both his illness and his rival, Ketten crawls into a bedroom window and hears the river roaring below. It is only after this feat that the love between Ketten and his wife is restored.

The settings are not only isolated, but exoticized through imagery and through their association with the 'otherness' of an erotically desired woman. Like Benn's depiction of women in *Gehirne*, Musil associates a feminine object of erotic love with the incalculable or uncivilized, with animals or animality, and with mysterious forces penetrating the human world from beyond it. All of the male protagonists, including that of 'Tonka', the third story of the collection, take a foreign lover or wife whose native language is not entirely comprehensible to them. Grigia becomes aligned with Homo's illusion of metaphysical transcendence, while rooted in an uncivilized nature and representing its freedoms. Homo's sexual attraction to Grigia is based on her foreignness and wildness, her difference from his orderly bourgeois life; her strange way of speaking is likened to 'Zauberworte' ('magic words') and Homo nicknames her after her cow (her real name is Lena Maria Lenzi) because that sounds 'so paradiesisch sinnlos' ('so paradisically nonsensical') (GW, vi. 245). In 'Grigia', the women of the region are described in primitive exotic terms: they are compared to Japanese, Africans, and animals. The women are provocative in their sexual expressiveness, but equally so in their way of sitting, walking, spitting in the manner of men, and of carrying huge bundles of hay on their backs. Their primitive way of being is alluring to the visitors as liberation from the repressive manners of bourgeois society; for Homo they provoke a raw awareness of physical existence. The beautiful Portuguese wife of Herr von Ketten is also exotic, not least because of her southern appearance and manner. She is rumoured to have devilish powers. Ketten comes home to find her reading an illuminated book 'mit geheimnisvollen Zeichnungen' ('with mysterious drawings') likened to 'Zauberei' ('magic') (GW, vi. 259). She communicates intuitively with animals and remains spiritually impenetrable to her husband who, after eleven years away fighting, must struggle against illness and spiritual stasis to regain her love.

The exotic qualities attributed to the women in these stories are reflected in the surrounding landscapes. The second description of the *Schloß* invokes the Portuguese wife's point of view as she sees it from the distance for the first time. This time the wildness attributed in the first description to the river seems to describe the setting as a whole. To the Portuguese wife, the place appears both alienatingly ugly—it is said to exceed description—and wondrously mystical.

> Wild stieg das Schloß auf. Da und dort saßen an der Felsbrust verkümmerte Bäumchen wie einzelne Haare. Die Waldberge stürzten so auf und nieder, daß man diese Häßlichkeit einem, der nur die Meereswellen kannte, gar nicht hätte zu beschreiben vermögen. Voll kaltgewordener Würze war die Luft, und alles war so, als ritte man in einen großen zerborstenen Topf hinein, der eine fremde grüne Farbe enthielt. Aber in den Wäldern gab es den Hirsch, Bären, das Wildschwein, den Wolf und vielleicht das Einhorn. Weiter hinten hausten Steinböcke und Adler. Unergründete Schluchten boten den Drachen Aufenthalt. Wochenweit und –tief war der Wald, durch den nur die Wildfährten führten, und oben, wo das Gebirge ihm aufsaß, begann das Reich der Geister. Dämonen hausten dort mit dem Sturm und den Wolken. . . . es war eine Welt, die eigentlich keine Welt war.
>
> (The castle rose up savagely. Here and there stunted trees emerged from the rock-face like single hairs. The wooded mountains rose and fell so abruptly that one could not even describe its ugliness to one who knew only the waves of the sea. The air, which had grown cold, was herbaceous, and everything was as if one rode into a huge burst cauldron that contained some strange green colour. But in the woods there was the stag, bear, wild boar, the wolf, and perhaps the unicorn. Further beyond there were ibex and eagles. Unplumbed gorges offered harbour for dragons. The forest was weeks' travel wide and deep, where only wildlife ventured, and above, where the cliffs towered above him, began the realm of spirits. Demons lurked there with the storm and the clouds . . . it was a world, that was not actually a world at all.) (GW, vi. 255)

This world that seems unworldly is not only striking for its 'Häßlichkeit' but for its evocation of magical creatures and powers, in the latter aspect echoing Goethe's poem 'Kennst du das Land' ('Do You Know the Land').[66] This

---

[66] The last stanza of Goethe's poem transforms 'das Land, wo die Zitronen blühn' ('the land, where the lemon trees blossom') into a more disconcerting landscape of disorienting fog, caves, and dragons.

description invokes an irrational perception in medieval imagery, a perception for which imaginary beings such as unicorns, dragons, spirits, and demons cannot be dismissed as illusory products of fantasy. For the non-rational mind, the inclusion of these beings as potential inhabitants of the natural surroundings owes not merely to an active imagination; their inclusion is due rather to something, to quote to Lévy-Bruhl's description of primitive mysticism, 'more like direct apprehension or intuition'. The primitive mentality does not infer the existence of supernatural beings from the given data of perception, but rather perceives them along with what is given: 'At the very moment when he perceives what is present to the senses, the primitive represents to himself the mystic force which is manifesting itself thus.'[67] Later in the story, the wolf's 'schweigende Wildheit' ('silent savagery') evokes for the wife the presence of her husband, and the cat whose demise stands in for that of Ketten, is equated with the presence of God (GW, vi. 260, 270). This recalls Lévy-Bruhl's observation that for the primitive consciousness 'all that which appears unusual, fortuitous, extraordinary, striking, or unforeseen is interpreted as a manifestation of occult powers'.[68]

The exotic landscape of 'Grigia' transforms Homo, as a feeling of communion with nature alienates him from his former attachments. The paradoxical nature of this detachment is that of sublimation: in an ecstatic experience in the meadow Homo feels united with his beloved in the beyond; as in Novalis, such a projection makes possible an earthly departure from his commitments.[69] This situation reflects Musil's own experiences in 1915, while he was stationed in Southern Tyrol, with Magdalena Maria Lenzi on whom Grigia is based.[70] The paradox of transcendent union with and earthly detachment from his wife makes possible his infidelity with Grigia; she herself is mentioned for the first time only in the second half of the novella, after much more detailed description of the landscape. Like that of 'Die Portugiesin,' the landscape of 'Grigia' has mystical resonances, where boundaries between the earthly and the transcendent are blurred: 'man konnte kaum unterscheiden, was noch goldgelbe Ferne des gesegneten Tieflands war und wo schon die unsicheren Wolkenböden des Himmels begonnen hatten' ('one could hardly differentiate the golden yellow distance of the blessed plain from where the sky's uncertain ground of clouds had begun') (GW, vi. 236). This confusion of ground and horizon parallels psychological and meta-

---

[67] Lévy-Bruhl (1966: 60).
[68] Lévy-Bruhl (1966: 98).
[69] A note in Musil's *Tagebücher* suggests the solution of this paradox: 'Indem er [seine Frau] ekstatisch liebt, kann er den niedrigen Lüsten Freiheit geben' ('Because he loves [her] ecstatically, he can give free reign to baser desires') (T, 307).
[70] Corino (2003: 528–529).

physical confusions, as when Homo's sexual experiences with Grigia seem
to bind him to an eternal fidelity to his wife: Grigia, his peasant lover,
becomes for Homo 'nur der Teil einer Sendung... die ihn mit seiner
Geliebten in Ewigkeit weiter verknüpfte' ('only a part of a mission...
which further connected him to his beloved in eternity') (GW, vi. 247).
Homo's susceptibility to such confusion is evident upon his arrival in the
region. He resides not in a guesthouse but with a local acquaintance of
Hoffingott:

> Homo wohnte nicht im Gasthof, sondern, er wußte eigentlich nicht warum,
> bei einem italienischen Bekannten Hoffingotts. Es gab da drei Dinge, die
> ihm auffielen. Betten von einer unsagbar kühlen Weichheit in schöner
> Mahagonischale. Eine Tapete mit einem unsagbar wirren, geschmacklosen,
> aber durchaus unvollendbaren und fremden Muster. Und ein Schaukelstuhl
> aus Rohr; wenn man sich in diesem wiegt und die Tapete anschaut, wird der
> ganze Mensch zu einem auf- und niederwallenden Gewirr von Ranken, die
> binnen zweier Sekunden aus dem Nichts zu ihrer vollen Größe anwachsen
> und sich wieder in sich zurückziehen.
>
> (Homo did not stay in the inn, rather, he did not really know why, with
> the Italian acquaintance of Hoffingott. There were three things that struck
> him there. Beds of unspeakably cool softness in lovely mahogany.
> A wallpaper with an unspeakably confusing, tasteless, but strange and
> incompletable pattern. And a cane rocking chair; if one rocked in this
> chair and looked at the wallpaper, his whole person seemed to become a
> rising and falling tangle of tendrils, that in the interstice between two seconds
> would emerge out of nothing and grow to their full size and then disappear
> into themselves again.) (GW, vi. 235)

The foreignness of these domestic surroundings is managed by Homo
through a mental note-taking of details. Yet the narrator already signals
Homo's willingness to submit to the allure of foreignness. The details that
Homo notices all evoke psychological submission to uncertainty, confusion, and even self-dissolution. The repetition of 'unsagbar' ('unspeak-
able') suggests that the nuances of Homo's feelings are savoured rather
than reduced to language, and the beds with their cool softness implicitly
evoke submission to sleep, dreams, erotic sensuality, or the permanent rest
of death. The wallpaper, while not elegant, fascinates Homo by its foreign
and 'unvollendbaren' pattern; and while rocking in the chair the viewer is
confused by the pattern, as if he himself is a 'Gewirr von Ranken,' welling
up and returning to an abyss of nothingness. This complex of images
identifies the human both with natural, plant-like forms and with the
chaotic illusion of rudimentary creation and dissolution, motifs that echo
Nietzsche's Heraclitean view of nature, for which reality is a constant state
of change.

But it is in the surrounding natural landscape, and the primitive state of consciousness it has induced in Homo, that perceptual confusion yields to a mystical connection with a sense of the beyond. Homo intuits manifestations of other-worldly meaning, which seem to liberate him from his ordinary identity and his attachments to the transient world. Like Benn's Rönne, Homo becomes especially receptive to colour and shapes of natural phenomena:

> Weiß und violet, grün und braun standen die Wiesen. Er war kein Gespenst. Ein Märchenwald von alten Lärchenstämmen, zartgrün behaarten, stand auf smaragdener Schräge. Unter dem Moos mochten violette und weiße Kristalle leben. Der Bach fiel einmal mitten im Wald über einen Stein so, daß er aussah wie ein großer silberner Steckkamm.
> (The meadows were white and violet, green and brown. It was no phantom. A fairy-tale forest of old larches with the tender green hair of new leaves covered the emerald slope. Violet and white crystals could be living under the moss. The stream in the middle of the wood fell over a stone in such a way that it looked like a great silver comb.) (GW, vi. 240)

This bejewelled 'Märchenwald' itself seems to harbour earthly signs of a transcendent reality. For Homo, who loves his wife but has already become distanced from her, these signs are read as confirmations of his marital love, of an eternal, religious fidelity and reunification in a life after death. But their very appearance in the earthly realm seems, paradoxically, to liberate Homo from these very bonds. The narrator turns directly from the above-cited description of the landscape to Homo's breaking off of communication with his wife. Rather than responding to her letters, he attends to the natural landscape and its religious signs:

> Er beantwortete nicht mehr die Briefe seiner Frau. Zwischen den Geheimnissen dieser Natur war das Zusammengehören eines davon.
> (He no longer answered his wife's letters. Their belonging together was one more secret among the secrets of this nature.) (GW, vi. 240)

Homo's fidelity becomes sublimated as mystical experience: 'Das kam ihm in diesem Augenblick so wundervoll unsinnig und unpraktisch vor, wie es nur eine tiefe Religion sein kann' ('It seemed to him in this moment so wonderfully senseless and impractical, as only a deep religion can be') (GW, vi. 240). This 'tiefe Religion' is integrated into Homo's enchanted perception of the landscape. Only in the middle of this contemplation of landscape does Homo come to realize that he has separated himself from his wife and allowed himself to be driven 'von seiner eigenen Strömung' ('by his own current') (GW, vi. 240). The word 'Strömung,' with its associations of both fluidity and natural movement, suggests dissolution of rational identity. Homo sinks to the forest floor and extends his arms as never before in his life, and experiences an ecstatic self-dissociation, as if he had been taken out of his own arms. He feels the hand, voice, body of his beloved—as if reunited in another world—and yet feels bound to the landscape: 'Dennoch stand es fest, daß er nicht umkehrte, und seltsamerweise war mit seiner Aufregung ein Bild der rings um den Wald blühenden Wiesen verbunden' ('Yet it was certain that he would not return, and strangely there was bound with his excitement a picture of the meadows blooming all around the forest') (GW, vi. 240). This connection with nature is nothing less than a mystical experience, for the surrounding landscape is felt as a manifestation of the very beyond in which reunification beyond death would be experienced. In this mystical communion, Homo does not so much abandon as transcend his earthly loyalties:

> Er erkannte die persönliche Vorsehung, welche sein Leben in diese Einsamkeit gelenkt hatte, und fühlte wie einen gar nicht mehr irdischen Schatz, sondern wie eine für ihn bestimmte Zauberwelt den Boden mit Gold und Edelsteinen unter seinen Füßen.
> Von diesem Tag an war er von einer Bindung befreit.
> (He recognized the personal providence that had guided his life towards this solitude and felt the ground under his feet, with its gold and precious stones, like a treasure that was no longer of this earth, rather as an enchanted world made just for him. From this day on he was free from bonds.) (GW, vi. 241)

Thus, Homo feels paradoxically liberated, because the exotic landscape itself seems to confirm his entrance into an eternal world, a 'Zauberwelt' beyond death; this in turn liberates Homo from fear of death, from 'Bindung an das Lebendigseinwollen, dem Grauen vor dem Tode' (GW, vi. 241). His epiphany is experienced as liberation, but dissolution of the self is threatened.

In the context of an isolated and exoticized setting, objects in the protagonists' surroundings take on symbolic meaning. In both stories animals come to signify the presence of the divine. After Homo's experience of ecstasis, he begins to see everywhere signs of a secret transcendent power at work. The dogs that have been assembled to deter theft gather in groups and seem to be praying: 'ihre gleichförmig langsam mahlenden Mäuler schienen zu beten. Man durchschnitt ihren Kreis wie den einer dämmrigen erhabenen Existenz' ('their uniform mouths seemed to be praying as they slowly chewed. One intersected their circle as if a sublime twilight existence'). Horses, too, seem to be arranged in the field 'nach einem geheim verabredeten ästhetischen Gesetz' ('according to some secretly prearranged aesthetic principle'). When Homo walks past them in the early morning, the horses look on, 'und man fühlte in dem wesenlosen Frühmorgenlicht sich als einen Gedanken in einem sehr langsamen Denken' ('and one felt in the ghostly early morning light as one thought in a very slow thinking') (GW, vi. 242). Homo's impression of the horses confounds activity and passivity, thinking and being thought, the human and the animal. This confusion of humanity and animality also contributes to the magical atmosphere of 'Die Portugiesin', where alternately the wolf and the cat are uncannily intertwined in the fate and marriage of the protagonists. She adopts a wolf, which her husband later orders killed, and she is especially fond of a cat that not only acts as if it were human but seems other-worldly, as if adorned with a halo. According to Lévy-Bruhl, the 'primitive' consciousness sees 'mystic forces always and everywhere present,' and while Homo slips in certain moments into this mode of seeing, it is part of the natural perspective of the medieval protagonists of 'Die Portugiesin'.[71]

The experience of the primitive and mystical, which Musil associated with the other condition, culminates in a dangerous provocation of ecstatic self-overcoming. Both Homo and Ketten are endangered by primitive forces in their surroundings and by their own inability to master the exotic alterity of a desired woman. For both the protagonists the surroundings harbour threatening elements, as Homo is trapped within the mountain, and Ketten is infected by a fly just as he is returning to his wife after many years away at war. The infection indicates Ketten's vulnerability to the presence of danger in nature and, symbolically, in erotic love; the danger is overcome only by extreme physical exertion, which mobilizes, in response, primitive forces from within. In both stories, exoticized nature is not only alluring and entrancing, but also poisonous, threatening, and elusive. Homo's experiences are haunted by overtones of death; he observes the slow death of a fly in the canteen, and is certain, while lying on the forest floor, that he will soon die. Yet Homo overlooks, in his sexual liberties with Grigia, the possibility of her husband's vengeance; when he eventually realizes that they are the subject of gossip, even this is exoticized, as he remembers 'einer sonderbaren Bäurin, die einen Schädel wie eine Aztekin hatte,' ('a strange woman farmer whose bony face was like an Aztec's') who had observed him with Grigia (GW, vi. 250). While Ketten sinks into a state of extreme passivity in his illness, but is able to summon his strength in order to oppose both his own death and the Portuguese rival, Homo does not take pains to avoid his fate; in the context of his mystical transformation, death even become alluring as an affirmation of the beyond. This coupling of love and death echoes Nietzsche, whose Zarathustra declares: 'Lieben und Unter-

[71] Lévy-Bruhl (1926: 97).

gehn: das reimt sich seit Ewigkeiten. Wille zur Liebe: das ist, willig auch sein zum Tode' ('love and demise: that rhymes since eternity. Will to love: that is, willingness too to death') (KG, vi/1. 153). In the novella's climax, when Homo and Grigia have been trapped in a mineshaft, the narrative tone is deliberately ambiguous. Grigia has escaped, but Homo remains:

> Grigia hatte feine Glieder, aber auch er, mit großer Gewalt, müßte sich da vielleicht durchzwängen können. Es war ein Ausweg. Aber er war in diesem Augenblick vielleicht schon zu schwach, um ins Leben zurückzukehren, wollte nicht oder war ohnmächtig geworden.
>
> (Grigia had slight bones, but even he, with greater force, must be able perhaps to force through there. It was a way out. But he was in this moment perhaps too weak to turn back to living, or did not want to, or had become unconscious.) (GW, vi. 252)

The twice-employed 'vielleicht' ('perhaps') conveys the ambivalence of Homo's consciousness at an impasse between life and death, desire and resignation. The fluid tempo of the comparison between Grigia's lithe slippage through the opening and Homo's potentially more forceful escape, a rhythm resumed two sentences later in the list of reasons Homo might not attempt it, is sharply contrasted to the terse and, in comparison, reductive syntax of the middle sentence: 'Es war ein Ausweg.' It is as if the dream-like state of Homo's consciousness is interrupted by a moment of clear recognition, only to lapse again into fateful, dream-like submission.

The setting of Homo's demise, in a cave-like mine shaft, symbolizes a radical regression to a primitive state of pre-rational consciousness buried in the inner life. Its darkness and inaccessibility, as well as its dangerousness, correlate to the uncertainty and instability of the other condition. The setting is not only suggestive of the maternal womb;[72] the cave is also Plato's metaphor for the soul unenlightened by reason and caught up in the semblances of sensuous experience and ungoverned desires. In Nietzsche, a cave serves as Zarathustra's primitive refuge, where he dwells with animals. A cave is also the scene of Patera's final transformation and death in *Die andere Seite*, where the natives exercise their ancient spirituality in the dark temple. Entering the shaft, Grigia and Homo 'tasteten nun mit großer Vorsicht in ein immer enger werdendes Dunkel hinein' ('felt their way now very carefully into a darkness that became ever narrower'). The narrowing darkness evokes at once the physical pleasure they seek, the departure from civilization, and the death that awaits them. Homo does not feel the need to light a match. In this passage the light of

---

[72] Reif (1975: 76).

day and of fire is contrasted to the dark coolness of earth on which they lie, and which becomes a metaphor for Grigia's sexuality:

> Der Boden unter ihren Füßen machte einen guten trockenen Eindruck, sie legten sich nieder, ohne daß Homo das Zivilisationsbedürfnis empfunden hätte, ihn mit dem Licht eines Streichholzes zu untersuchen.
>
> (The ground under his feet seemed quite dry enough, they lay themselves down, without Homo having felt the civilized need to look around with the help of a lit match.) (GW, vi. 251)

The husband appears in the light of the entrance, and then disappears again as he levers a great boulder before it, trapping them; but even this fateful event is described as a perception, emphasizing Homo's subjectivity. Homo looks to the entrance and registers 'das Bild ihres Mannes,' underscoring the dream-like aspect of his submission to death. Homo's recognition that he is going to die entrapped there is also 'traumhaft' ('dreamy') and his submission is compared to a long sleep, recalling the soft beds that Homo had noticed upon his arrival (GW, vi. 252). Grigia and Homo, in their state of nearing death, are compared to the sea at twilight, where only small islands of wakefulness remain.

The sleepiness of Homo's submission to death is echoed in Ketten's extreme illness. The febrile illness from a fly's infectious bite forces him into a state of near paralysis, ironically compelling the rest and inactivity that he had so long avoided. Illness brings on a dream-like fatigue and stupor, and then of brooding contemplation and self-estrangement:

> Er schlief viel und war auch mit offenen Augen abwesend; wenn aber sein Bewußtsein zurückkehrte, so war doch dieser willenlose, kindlich warme und ohnmächtige Körper nicht seiner, und diese von einem Hauch erregte schwache Seele seine auch nicht. . . . er war mit einem Teil seines Wesens vorangestorben und hatte sich aufgelöst.
>
> (He slept much and was absent when his eyes were open; but when his consciousness returned, it seemed this faint, childishly warm and will-less body was not his, and this weak soul disturbed by a breath was not his either. . . . part of his being had gone ahead, already died and had dissolved.) (GW, vi. 262)

This withdrawnness, after so many years of absence during which he embodied a heroic ideal, has also alienated Ketten from his wife, who in turn is distracted by the attentions of a Portuguese suitor: 'In den Nebeln der Krankheit, die ihn umfangen hielten, erschien ihm die Gestalt seiner Frau weicher, als es hätte sein müssen' ('In the fog of illness that had enveloped him, the figure of his wife seemed tenderer than it must') (GW, vi. 265). But when he finally breaks the fever and recovers his force of life by the ostensibly impossible act of scaling the rock wall, Ketten is transformed. He is not only brought back to a state of health and vitality, but is able to communicate once again intuitively with this wife. The description of Ketten's climbing of the rock face by moonlight fuses imagery of the physical setting and Ketten's inner experience, suggesting the inward effect of his action:

> Der Mond zeichnete mit Schattenpunkten die kleinen Vertiefungen, in welche Finger und Zehen hineingreifen konnten. Plötzlich brach ein Stein unter seinem Fuß weg; der Ruck schoß in die Sehnen, dann ins Herz. Ketten horchte; es schien ohne Ende zu dauern, bevor der Stein ins Wasser schlug.
> (The moon showed with spots of shadow the small crevices in which one could grasp with fingers and toes. Suddenly a stone fell away under his foot; the shock ran through his sinews, then to his heart. Ketten strained to listen; it seemed to go on without end before the stone hit the water.) (GW, vi. 269)

Not unlike a Nietzschean 'Übermensch'—a notion which Musil associates with 'das ethisch = äesthetische Selbst' ('the ethical self = aesthetic self') (T, 155)—Ketten transcends his weakness and infection through a dangerous exertion of will. Ketten's climb is a 'Kampf mit dem Tod' ('struggle against death') that allows 'Kraft und Gesundheit in die Glieder zu fließen' ('strength and health to flow into the limbs') (GW, vi. 269). In his transformation, the forces of vitality that draw Ketten out of his malaise and into action are balanced with the psychic interiority his wife's enigmatic presence has represented. The final scene takes place inside the castle, after Ketten has climbed through a window. He discovers that his rival has left in the night but finds his wife in her own bed. In the bedroom he opens the curtain, behind which the roar of the wild river below is audible:

> Er zog den schweren Vorhang vom Fenster zurück, und der Vorhang des Brausens stieg auf, hinter dem alle Catene geboren wurden und starben.
> (At the window he pulled aside the heavy curtain, and the curtain of noise rose up behind which all Catene had been born and died.) (GW, vi. 269–270)

The repetition of 'Vorhang' ('curtain') suggests the parallel between the interior of the castle and the natural river that surrounds it. The evocation of birth and death does not oppose them as opposites, but suggests the natural cycles that pertain to human lives. In this final scene, Ketten is also referred to by the Italian name 'Catene', suggestive of a regained affinity to the foreign wife and to the 'southern' sensibility with which she is associated. She speaks of the cat and identifies the cat with God, as if its appearance and demise had somehow miraculously brought Ketten back to himself and to her. The narrative claim that 'sie wußten, kein Laut davon drang aus diesen Mauern hinaus' ('but they knew that no sound could penetrate beyond these walls') not only defuses her sacrilege, but affirms Ketten's arrival in an inner life that is, between husband and wife, privately communicable through a common perception of mystical forces (GW, vi. 270). With this conclusion, 'Die Portugiesin' offers an affirmation of mystical experience that counters the image of demise in 'Grigia'. The mystical ecstasis may lead to disastrous enchantment, but may also provoke new ways of being and communicating that emerge from an awakened inner life.

'DIE ANDERE SEITE': DREAM-TOPOGRAPHY AND PRIMAL STATES OF CONSCIOUSNESS

The breakdown of rationality and the affirmation of mystical elements of reality are closely associated with the mode of consciousness experienced in dreams. Benn's Rönne and Musil's protagonists all experience sleepiness and a dimming of awareness, which signify transition from a rationally oriented perception of the world to an aesthetic or mystical one, in which abstract ideas, perceptions, and hallucinations are interwoven. Benn's critique of the Cartesian model of consciousness is confirmed in part by Rönne's incapacity to differentiate reality from illusion, and Musil Homo's submission to death is rendered in a dream-like lethargy. Ketten's transformation, too, occurs through an illness that forces an extended dream-like state of semi-consciousness. The affirmation of dream-reality is part of Nietzsche's implicit rejection of rational philosophy in *Die Geburt der Tragödie*, and the inner world of dreams serves as the shadowy 'other side' of waking reality in Kubin's *Die andere Seite*.

Dreams in Kubin's novel serve as both metaphor and substance of the inner landscape of primal consciousness.[73] It will be shown in this section how Kubin's evocation of dream-topography relies, first, on the exotic and isolated setting of the novel and its contrast with modern European reality. The basic structure of the dream-world, secondly, reflects the tension between the Apollonian and Dionysian forces as described by Nietzsche. Thirdly, the protagonist's gradual submission to the dream-logic induces primitive modes of perception that contribute to the de-individuation of the self. While Nietzsche is able to describe this perception and deindividuation, in the novel the transition from waking consciousness to dream-perception must be enacted, fourthly, by specific literary means. As in

---

[73] On the history of the *Traum* as metaphor as the context of Kubin's novel, see Geyer (1995: 104–111). See also Robertson's (2001) account of dream-theories in the nineteenth century.

Benn's *Gehirne*, this transition, then, leads to the development of a new aesthetic, less akin to expressionism than to surrealism, but the radical instability of its modes of perception and expression correlates, finally, to the eventual collapse of the dream-world. This collapse, like Homo's demise in the cave, highlights the fragility of the 'other' side of reality, and of our access to the primal depths of human consciousness.

The establishment of a dream-world relies on its isolation from modern Europe and its association with exotic surroundings, by which Kubin had been fascinated:

'Das Meer, Italien, der Orient, Dinge, die ich in Wirklichkeit nie gesehen habe, prägten sich mir... ein, ein unvergänglicher, idealer Wert' ('the sea, Italy, the Orient, things, which I have not seen in reality, imprinted themselves upon me... an immutable, ideal value'), he writes (AL, 14–15). The Traumreich is set in an isolated region of interior China, which symbolizes its inaccessibility to modern Western consciousness. Patera himself is exoticized in that he is not only likened to 'einem Götterbildnis der antiken Welt', but is also worshipped by the ancient blue-eyed Asian tribe, appearing as 'ein Engel aus einer buddhistischen Legende' ('an angel from a Buddhist legend') (AS, 232). These associations with different exotic divinities suggest the connection between a primal substrate of ancient European consciousness and Asian spirituality, a connection also established by Nietzsche in his oriental descriptions of Dionysus. The history of the Traumreich's establishment also bears traces of an exotic *Märchen*. Patera had left school to join a band of gypsies; he then became a sailor, found his way to China, and by saving the life of a wealthy, childless Chinese woman, becomes heir to her and her husband's immense fortune. Hunting for a rare Persian tiger 'in dem weitläufigen Tien-schan oder Himmelsgebirge, welches zu dem chinesischen Zentralasien gehört' ('in the vast Tien-Shan, or the Mountains of Heaven, which lie in Chinese central Asia'). Patera is injured and looked after by a healer from a strange blue-eyed race of natives (AS, 19). This indigenous tribe lives isolated from the surrounding Mongolians and practises a mysterious religion; it maintains an ostensibly marginal existence in the Traumreich Patera founds, inhabiting the village across the river from the capital Perle.

The empirical isolation and exotic location of the setting allow for metaphysical transformations of reality as it is perceived by the modern European. It gradually becomes evident that this isolation and distance are not merely geographical, for Patera's Traumreich lies on 'the other side' of a world ordered by Western rationality. Ordinary laws governing time, space, and causality are suspended in favour of an alternative order that shares some features of the mysticism evoked by Musil. The Traumreich, although also empirical, is constituted by 'Stimmung'; its substance is given form not by physical laws, but by the force of imaginative desire. As Patera's messenger explains to the narrator at the novel's outset:

> Unsere Leute erleben nur Stimmungen, besser noch, *sie leben nur in Stimmungen*; alles äußere Sein, das sie sich durch möglichst ineinandergreifende Zusammenarbeit nach Wunsch gestalten, gibt gewissermaßen nur den Rohstoff.
>
> (Our people experience only moods or, better still, they live only in moods; all external being which they through the most possible communal effort form according to their wishes, provides to a certain extent only the raw materials.) (AS, 12–13)

External being becomes merely the raw material for the formation of a world that is atmospheric rather than substantial, and in which events evade rational explanation. The dream exposes the waking world as only one manifestation of its possible appearances, recalling Nietzsche's affirmation of Schopenhauer's intuition 'daß auch unter dieser Wirklichkeit, in der wir leben und sind, eine zweite ganz andre verborgen liege, daß also auch sie ein Schein sei' ('that also under this reality in which we live and are, a second entirely other one may lay buried, which may also be an appearance') (KG, iii/1. 22). The Traumleute not only validate the world of dreams but favour it over waking life: 'Doch glaubt der Träumer an nichts als an den Traum' ('Indeed the dreamer believes in nothing but his dream') (AS, 13).

The isolation of the Traumreich is not only geographical but also structural and cultural. A wall is erected to seal off the region, and it is aggressively guarded. All implements of modern civilization are forbidden, for Patera rejects 'alles Fortschrittliche, namentlich auf wissenschaftlichem Gebiete' ('all progress, particularly in the scientific domain') allowing for the nostalgic reestablishment of a pre-modern way of life. The city itself is composed of old European buildings imported by Patera. The realm is entirely protected against modernization, as a 'Freistätte für die mit der modernen Kultur Unzufriedenen' ('an asylum for those discontent with modern culture') (AS, 11). The narrator's initial feeling of familiarity is revealed to be illusory: all that has been imported from Europe takes on the quality of artifice and illusion, for it is torn out of the context of a European sense of reality. The arrival of the American Herkules Bell and his efforts at modernizing the Traumreich suggest the opposing pole of the subconscious forces at work: he struggles against Patera's anachronism, towards the future that is dominated by technology, economic development, and scientific progress. The struggle between past and future, nostalgia and change, primitivism and modernity, tears the dream-world apart; but even its collapse exposes its primal motivating energies: the forces of creation and dissolution, being and becoming.

These forces, and the structure of the Traumreich itself, can be understood through Nietzsche's description of the motivating principles of
artistic creation, which include the Apollonian instinct towards the creation of forms in dream-imagery, and the form-dissolving Dionysian
instinct.[74] Nietzsche's affirmation of both instincts in *Die Geburt der
Tragödie* is linked to his rejection of modern rationalist philosophy. In
Descartes's *Meditations*, where the imagination is rejected in favour of
rational cognition, dream-illusions pose an initial threat to the clarity of a
rational ego and are linked to hallucinations and madness. Yet the demand
for clarity, initiated by Socrates and inherited by rationalism, can be
regarded from Nietzsche's standpoint as the isolation of the Apollonian
instinct from its Dionysian counterpart. In Nietzsche's perspectivism,
Descartes presents merely an illusion of order and rational clarity, which
precludes a deeper, if also more frightening, grasp of the radical instability
of underlying nature and the multiplicity of the self. But dreams are also a
source of artistic inspiration, because they seem to uncover pre-rational
states of consciousness. While Benn's Rönne invokes the Dionysian
Rausch, Kubin invokes, first of all, the Apollonian drive of artistic creation
through the *Traum*. This creative drive is expressed through the formation
of images, which occurs in every human consciousness in its generation
of dreams, but becomes expressive in the aesthetic imagination. Kubin's
narrator recognizes the power of the imagination in its very creation of the
dream-reality. Qualities, for example, are no longer regarded as perceptual
attributes of individual objects, but as productions of the imagination
(which, in the German term, connotates a power or capacity):

> Immer mehr fühlte ich das gemeinsame Band in allem. Farben, Töne und
> Geschmacksempfindungen waren für mich austauschbar. Und da wußte ich
> es:—Die Welt ist Einbildungskraft, *Einbildung—Kraft*.
> (More and more, I felt the common bond in everything. Colours, tones,
> and sensations of taste were interchangeable for me. And then I knew: the
> world is imagination, the power of image.) (AS, 136)

While for Nietzsche 'de[r] schöne Schein der Traumwelten' ('the beautiful
appearance of the dream-world') is the Apollonian basis of art, in Kubin's
novel the *Traumwelt* eclipses all waking reality (KG, iii/1. 22). The
tension with the Dionysian dissolution of form is central, revealing the
transient nature of Patera's dreams and leading to the destruction of the
Traumreich itself; but the dream-world's initial formation relies on the
mode of consciousness Nietzsche associates with the Greek god Apollo.
Patera, with his 'schöngelockte Kopf antiken Zuschnittes' ('classically

[74] See Rhein (1989: 40–44).

shaped head of beautiful curls') is an Apollo-like figure, promoted to divine status by virtue of his dreams (AS, 9). For Nietzsche dreams are that mode of consciousness 'in deren Erzeugung jeder Mensch voller Künstler ist' ('in whose cultivation every human being is an artist'). If the dream is 'die Voraussetzung aller bildenden Kunst, ja auch... einer wichtigen Hälfte der Poesie' ('the presupposition of all plastic art, indeed even... an important half of poetry'), it is the very basis and form of Patera's creation (KG, iii/1. 22).

In Nietzsche's account of tragedy the Apollonian is the principle of individuating form, and in tragedy it is coupled with the Dionysian principle associated with dissolution, intoxication, sexual fusion, chaos, and suffering. The tension between them expresses the creative and destructive forces of nature itself, for which the artist's imagination is only a conduit. Kubin's *Traumreich* expresses this tension through the dreamer's will to create forms out of the abyss of nothingness: 'Dem Nichts mußten sie ihre eingebildete Welt abringen, und von dieser eingebildeten Welt aus das Nichts erobern' ('They had to wrest their imagined world from out of nothingness and conquer nothingness from this imagined world') (AS, 137). Although it is associated with Patera's creative consciousness, his being is dispersed among all the forms of creation:

> Patera war überall, ich sah ihn im Auge des Freundes wie des Feindes, in Tieren, Pflanzen und Steinen. Seine Einbildungskraft pochte in allem, was da war: Der Herzschlag des Traumlandes.
>
> (Patera was everywhere; I saw him in the eye of a friend as of an enemy, in animals, plants, and stones. His imagination pulsated in everything that existed: the heartbeat of the dream-land.) (AS, 137)

The dream-logic that dominates the Traumreich determines not only its atmosphere but the fantastical events that take place there.[75] These follow a strange and inexplicable pattern according to the movements of Patera's dreams. Invisible forces seem to be at work in everyday events, and the narrator's attempts to understand their source remain mystified. This mystification is linked to the gradual loss of individual identity. The contrast between the events in the dream-world and the narrator's expectations of ordinary reality gradually fades, to the point where the narrator is completely entranced. This acceptance of the dream-world by the original *Traumleute* and the narrator is contrasted to the modern Europe from which the realm is cut off and aligned with the 'primitive'

---

[75] The relation of this dream-logic to fantasy literature is discussed in the collection by Freund, Lachinger, Ruthner, eds. (1999).

ancient consciousness of the indigenous tribe. According to Lévy-Bruhl, dreams play a significant role in 'primitive' views of reality, and their difference from the order of waking reality does not disqualify them:

> What is seen in dreams is, theoretically, true. To minds which have but slight perception of the law of contradiction, and which the presence of the same thing in various places at one and the same time does not perturb in the least, what reason is there for doubting these data more than any others? Once having admitted the idea which primitive mentality forms of sleep and of dreams, since nothing seems more natural to him than the communication between the seen and the unseen worlds, why should he mistrust what he sees in dreams any more than what he sees with his eyes wide open?[76]

Lévy-Bruhl's analysis centres on the attitude about dreams among peoples of various indigenous non-Western cultures, for whom events in dreams are not dismissed as unreal, but responded to as omens or interventions of mystical forces. Kubin's references to the 'Asian', in contrast, do not present an accurate picture of the world-view of specific, actually existing peoples, but refer loosely to some features of the Buddhist religion and other 'Oriental' motifs to create a fictional spirituality. Yet Kubin's rendering does seem to correspond to the general discoveries of 'primitive' ethnology; for what can be generalized from Lévy-Bruhl's analysis is true of the *Traumreich*: the 'primitive' sense of reality is not less, but in fact more, complex than that of a modern European, for invisible forces, which may appear in dreams, compound the data available to consciousness. The distinction between waking perceptions (what Husserl would call 'natural' perception) and those of dream or hallucination is not relevant as a criterion for truth. If the emotional effect is powerful enough, appearances in dreams are accepted and cannot be invalidated by contrary evidence from waking experience. Nietzsche also affirms the 'truth' of dreams. In those dreamers who can continue a dream's 'Causalität' over several nights, Nietzsche finds:

> Tatsachen, welche deutlich Zeugnis dafür abgeben, daß unser innerstes Wesen, der gemeinsame Untergrund von uns allen, mit tiefer Lust und freudiger Notwendigkeit den Traum an sich erfährt.
>
> (facts that give clear evidence that our innermost being, the common subterrain of us all, experiences the dream with deep desire and joyful necessity.) (KG, iii/1. 23)

There is, Nietzsche claims, in dreams a necessity that expresses a deeper truth, and this deeper truth resides within the human consciousness, in

---

[76] Lévy-Bruhl (1966: 101).

its deepest strata.[77] For Nietzsche what we dream belongs 'so gut zum Gesammt-Haushalt unsrer Seele, wie irgend etwas 'wirklich' Erlebtes' ('as much to the total household of our soul, as something experienced in "reality"') (KG, vi/2. 116). For this reason the ancient Greeks associated dreams with the sun god; but the illumination of the deepest truths can occur only in the inner world and its images:

> Diese freudige Notwendigkeit der Traumerfahrung ist gleichfalls von den Griechen in ihrem Apollo ausgedrückt worden: Apollo, als der Gott aller bildnerischen Kräfte, ist zugleich der wahrsagende Gott. Er, der seiner Wurzel nach die 'Scheinende', die Lichtgottheit ist, beherrscht auch den schönen Schein der inneren Phantasie-Welt. Die höhere Wahrheit, die Vollkommenheit dieser Zustände im Gegensatz zu der lückenhaft verständlichen Tageswirklichkeit, sodann das tiefe Bewußtsein von der in Schlaf und Traum heilenden und helfenden Natur ist zugleich das symbolische Analogon der wahrsagenden Fähigkeit und überhaupt der Künste, durch die das Leben möglich und lebenswert gemacht wird.

> (This joyful necessity of the dream-experience is equally expressed by the Greeks in their Apollo: Apollo, as god of all plastic arts, is at the same time the prophetic god. Apollo, who according to his origin is the one who appears shining, the divinity of light, reigns also over the beautiful appearances of the inner world of fantasy. The higher truth, the perfection of these states in contrast to the only partially graspable reality of daytime, the deep consciousness of healing and helping nature in sleep and dream, is also the symbolic analogue of prophetic capacity and of art as such, which make life possible and worth living.) (KG, iii/1. 23–24)

For Nietzsche the beautiful Apollonian images of art make bearable an apprehension of the painful, Dionysian chaos at the heart of reality.

But this apprehension reveals not only the illusory nature of ordinary reality but of the individual's own identity. In the epilogue, the narrator is still entranced by the power of dreams. While he has survived the destruction of the Traumreich, its effects linger, as his own nostalgic dreams threaten to overwhelm his consciousness. He recognizes a primitive form of existence that is residual in the modern consciousness in its mode of dreaming:

> Ich verlor in ihnen meine Identität, sie griffen oft in historische Perioden zurück. Fast jede Nacht brachte mir entlegene Begebenheiten, und ich bin der Meinung, daß diese Traumbilder aufs engste verkettet waren mit Erlebnissen meiner Ahnen, deren seelische Erschütterungen sich vielleicht organisch geprägt und vererbt haben. Noch tiefere Traumschichten öffneten sich mir im Aufgehen in Tierexistenzen, ja im bloßen bewußten Hindämmern in

---

[77] On Nietzsche's later, more sceptical view of dreams, see Robertson (2001: 34).

Urelementen. Die Träume waren Abgründe, denen ich mich willenlos preisgegeben sah. (I lost my identity in them, they often reverted to historical periods. Almost every night I experienced anachronistic events, and I am of the opinion that these dream images were closely connected with the experiences of my ancestors, whose soulful convulsions were perhaps organically imprinted and passed on. Still deeper strata of dreams opened up to me in the animal existences, indeed in the bare conscious extinguishment in the primal elements. The dreams were abysses, to which I saw myself helplessly given over.) (AS, 250)

In the dream as rendered by Kubin, individual identity is dissolved. Consciousness is not anchored in a self-certain 'I', but is merely the conduit for experiences inherited from ancient ancestors, for forces of animal existence and elemental nature. For the modern consciousness, it seems, the dream expresses both the Apollonian instinct towards the formation of images and the access to a buried Dionysian instinct for dissolution. This mingling of form and dissolution is expressed earlier in the text not only through Patera's transformations, but through the mingling and intertwining of life-forms, grotesquely creating 'vorweltlich, monströse Geschöpfe' ('prehistorical, monstrous creations') in the Traumreich's decline (AS, 184).

The transition from waking life to dream-consciousness, and thus from the outer to the inner world, is reflected at two levels in the novel, through the psychological development of the protagonist and in the specific literary means by which this is enacted for the reader. The psychological transition is made gradually in Kubin's novel through the figure of the narrator-protagonist, who is invited to the thriving *Traumreich* established by Patera. The narrator is visited by a messenger bearing Patera's invitation, and several factors help to convince the narrator. Not the description of the *Traumreich* alone, but Patera's portrait is most persuasive for the narrator who, as a visual artist, is receptive to the power of images and may be able to intuit the significance of the dream-life. Patera's image immediately reminds the narrator of their common childhood, suggesting also that the appeal of the dream-life is connected to remembrance of childhood consciousness (AS, 14–15). Moreover, the narrator has suffered from *Fernweh*, since a planned trip to Egypt and India had to be cancelled for lack of funds (AS, 24); the narrator can now satisfy his longing to visit exotic places. While he is initially disappointed at the unexotic scenery, as they travel further east, he finds it increasingly alluring:

Eine langgestreckte Häusermasse, Minarets, Kirchen—Samarkand! Samarkand!— Buntglitzernd spiegelte sich die Sonne in den blau- und grünglasierten Ziegeln, und beim Näherkommen nahm die Farbigkeit immer noch zu.

(A long extension of houses, minarets, churches—Samarkand! Samarkand!—colourfully sparkling, the sun reflected in the blue- and green-glazed tiles, and as we came nearer the colours increased in intensity.) (AS, 36)

The narrator's resistance, however, to exoticizing the scenery in tourist fashion—dismissing as 'Tausendundeinenacht-Szenen' ('A Thousand and One Night Scenes') views of Oriental cities he sees along the way—is important in establishing his initially objective, sober point of view from which the strangeness of the Traumreich can be gradually registered (AS, 37). Upon arriving in its capital Perle, the narrator is disappointed that everything seems so familiar. He will soon realize that the Traumreich is in fact quite different, not least by virtue of its monotonously grey weather:

aber der Himmel, der sich darüber spannte, war ewig trübe; *nie* schien die Sonne, *nie* waren bei Nacht der Mond oder Sterne sichtbar. Ewig gleichmäßig hingen die Wolken bis tief zur Erde herab. Sie ballten sich wohl bei Stürmen, aber das blaue Firmament war uns allen verschlossen.

(but the sky that spanned above was always overcast; the sun *never* shone, the stars at night or the moon were *never* visible. The clouds hung, always the same, down to the earth. Though in storms they condensed, the blue firmament remained hidden from us all.) (AS, 51)

The permanent lack of sunlight symbolizes the absence of rational order, and the clouds and fog correlate to its mystification and hiddenness. As the Traumreich nears destruction, day and night become indistinguishable.

The narrator's arrival in the Traumreich only gradually provokes changes in his sense of reality, and this change is reflected in literary form. In comparison to the syntactic fragmentation of Benn's prose, and the subtly entrancing narrative tone and rhythm of Musil's, Kubin's narrative style remains for much of the novel deceptively realistic. The descriptions of places and events remain straightforward, and the language neither departs from ordinary syntax, nor develops a narrative tone that would correspond to the confusions of a dream-state. Gradually this realism is worn away in correlation to the increasing uncanniness that accompanies the narrator's psychological transformation into a dream-state. He reports such details as the uncontrollability of perceptions, particularly certain noises and smells, the strange grey-green colour of the vegetation, and the seductive allure of the ticking of the clock-tower, with its monstrously large clock, the observation of which is the object of a cultic devotion. The narrator and his ill wife are subject to increasing anxiety and despair, having mysteriously run out of money and realized that they are trapped there. When the narrator's distrust grows, ominous forces seem to converge against him. Trying to reach Patera's palace in the middle of the night, the narrator stumbles into a shady part of town and is chased by a threatening mob; he uncannily glimpses his nightgown days later in the street, torn by dogs. As in Kafka, the narrator's feeling of persecution comes to be expressed in real persecutions; while all his attempts to reach Patera in his palace fail, the narrator sees him in the guise of a worker lighting the streetlamps.[78] A doctor's advice to take his wife to the countryside leads to a disturbing trip through a gloomy landscape, in which the electrified air of an iron mountain fatally exacerbates her illness. The narrator finally reaches Patera in a nearly abandoned palace and finds him in a state of intermittent sleep, where his expression and figure change rapidly from one form to the next. Realism is gradually usurped by the surreal. As a visual artist the narrator is able to articulate the tone of his impressions in aesthetic terms that evoke surrealism:

> Aus der allgemeinen Dämmerung, die alles verwischte und riesenhaft vergrößerte, sprangen unnatürlich körperliche Details: Ein Pfosten, ein Ladenschild, ein Gatter.
> (In the general fog that blurred and monstrously magnified everything, unnatural physical details jumped out: a post, a store sign, an iron fence.)
> (AS, 96)

The isolation of details and the magnification of images become gradually more disturbing: the viper-like eyes of a woman beggar, a blind and starving horse in a subterranean labyrinth under the mill, and Patera's face changing into animal forms, are among the ominous signs of chaos festering within the illusory order. The disintegration of order is reflected in the invasion of the Traumreich by animals, suggesting both apocalyptic pestilence and primitive regression of the psyche.[79] The possibility that even this dream-world is but a reflection of yet another, deeper and more chaotic reality is suggested by the appearance of mystical signs amid increasing chaos:

> Ich nahm wieder meine abendlichen Spaziergänge am Flußufer auf. Da hatten die Wellen unzählige Muscheln, Korallen, Schnecken, Fischgräten, und –schuppen ans Ufer geschwemmt. Überrascht war ich, häufig Überreste zu finden, welcher der Meeresfauna angehören. Wie von mystischen Zeichen übersät schien das Ufer. Ich war überzeugt, daß die Blauäugigen diese symbolische Sprache verstehen würden. Sicher waren hier Geheimnisse; auch die Flügel der oft prächtigen Insekten, Nachtfalter, Käfer, zeigten

---

[78] Kafka's relation to Kubin is discussed in Neuhäuser (1998).
[79] On the significance of animals in the Traumreich, see Lippuner (1977: 106–113). The apocalyptic dimension of the novel is studied in Gerhards (1999: 47–59).

Flecken, die vergessene Buchstaben sein mußten. Mir fehlte der Schlüssel dazu.

(I resumed my evening walks on the riverbank. There the waves had brought up countless shells, corals, snails, fish skeletons and scales. I was surprised to find remnants that belonged to sea fauna. The bank seemed saturated with mysterious symbols. I was convinced that the blue-eyed ones would understand this symbolic language. There were certainly secrets here; also the wings of splendid insects, nocturnal moths, beetles, bore marks which must have been the letters of a forgotten alphabet. I lacked the key to them.) (AS, 183)

The blue-eyed Asians are again aligned with a secret spirituality that may be at work in the dream-world, but the precise nature of their involvement is never revealed in the novel. With the death of his wife and his last ties to an outside world severed, the narrator is increasingly unable to distinguish reality from dream.

The narrator's submission to the dream-world, however, provokes a fury of artistic creativity. As in Benn's *Gehirne*, the breakdown of the rational view of reality provokes the development of a new aesthetic grounded in the tension between imagery and linguistic form. The narrator of Kubin's novel thus experiences inspiration in the midst of the chaos of an irrational dream-world:

Es überfiel mich ein Arbeitsdelirium; im nächsten halben Jahre produzierte ich unter dem Drucke des Schmerzes meine besten Sachen. Ich betäubte mich im Schaffen.

(I was overtaken by a delirious drive to work; in the next half-year I produced my best things under the pressure of pain. Through creating, I numbed myself.) (AS, 128)

Not only through his drawings for the illustrated magazine, but in other independent works, the narrator develops a new aesthetic:

Hier versuchte ich unmittelbar neue Formgebilde nach geheimen mir bewußt gewordenen Rhythmen zu schaffen; sie ringelten, knäuelten sich und platzten gegeneinander. Ich ging noch weiter. Ich verzichtete auf alles bis auf den Strich und entwickelte in diesen Monaten ein seltsames Liniensystem.

(Here I attempted to create directly new forms based on rhythms that had mysteriously come to me; they writhed, coiled, burst against one another. I went still further. I rejected everything but line and developed in these months a strange linear system.) (AS, 128–129)

This development resembles Rönne's invention of a new syntax to express his fragmentary projections of an exotic world. But whereas Rönne's imagination pushes language towards the expressions of abstract painting, the drawings of Kubin's narrator push imagery towards language: this 'fragmentarischer Stil' ('fragmentary style') is 'mehr geschrieben wie gezeichnet' ('more written than drawn'). The narrator names his new method 'Psychographik' (AS, 129). The relation to language of Kubin's narrator reflects Kubin's own artistic development; while he was principally a painter and graphic artist, the novel itself initiates the transformation of his own visual surrealist aesthetic into literary form.

The promotion of new aesthetic energy draws on the Dionysian instability that is revealed to operate beneath the apparent order. The dissolution of that order unleashes primitive creative energies, which are reflected in the literary form itself, as the destruction of the Traumreich provokes the most imaginative descriptions of the novel, its often grotesque mingling of forms in dissolution of their individuation. While Kafka's most grotesque metamorphoses are distinguished from dream, since 'Es war kein Traum' ('It was no dream') as the narrator instructs the reader in 'Die Verwandlung' (KA/DL, 115), Kubin's novel affirms the dream as a means to trace the primitive landscape within the inner life of consciousness. But it also reveals the radical instability of the 'other side' of reason, and the precariousness of our access to it.

CONCLUSION

In contrast to the exotic evocations of Hofmannsthal and Dauthendey discussed in Chapter 1, the *Fernweh* expressed in the exotic imagery of Benn, Musil, and Kubin serves an interior purpose, rather than a projection of some real places to which the author might travel. The protagonists' breakdowns differ, too, from those in the works by Mann and Zweig discussed in Chapter 2, which expose the fragility of the self's boundaries through contact with alluring or infectious foreign influences. The major contest is not between the self's boundaries and an external otherness, but rather between the rational, civilized aspect of the psyche and the 'primitive' wilderness buried beneath it. Kafka's exotic spaces, considered in Chapter 3, do point in the direction of interior places. While other writings such as *Die Verwandlung* and *Ein Bericht für eine Akademie* directly evoke the primitive substrate of human existence, the distances and vastness associated with exotic spaces such as China, Russia, and America correlate to the potentiality of the liberated imagination, and what obstructs such liberation. For Benn, Musil, and Kubin, exotic landscapes are integrated into both depictions of rational breakdown and the alternative inwardness of aesthetic creativity, mystical enchantment, and the life of dreams.

The authors discussed in this chapter do not merely describe lived, metaphorically embellished, or wholly imagined exotic places, but integrate imagery of exotic realms into their accounts of the self's breakdown and/or renewal. Exotic topographical motifs express the exploration of primal aspects of consciousness felt to be buried in the inner depths of modern humanity and reflect the criticisms of modern consciousness presented in Hofmannsthal's *Die Briefe des Zurückgekehrten*. Despite significant stylistic and ideological differences among these writers, they manifest a common understanding of the alterity within, suggested by strikingly similar motifs: 'das andere Leben', 'der andere Zustand', 'die andere Seite'. Promoting Nietzsche's insights, expressed through exotic imagery, of a more vital life accessible to artistic consciousness, physiological experience, and dreams, all of these writers project exotic topographies as a means of access to a new aesthetic or new ways of living and being, even while registering the potential dangers of a loss of rationality.

While their imagery of exotic places and peoples invites criticism of racist or racially insensitive presentations, this imagery functions nevertheless neither as symbolic appropriation of territory nor to evoke a distant *Wunschraum*, but rather as invocation of another, neglected side of the modern European self. As one scholar has written of Musil's 'other condition', these invocations refer 'not to another world but to a lost relation to this one, and, concomitantly, to a recovery of a suppressed half of the self'.[80] For Musil, Benn, and Kubin, this recovery is made necessary by the extreme one-sidedness of modern experience, which neglects more vital sources of life and feeling, a view that these writers share with Hofmannsthal, with an account of whom this study began. Musil suggests:

> Die Welt, in der wir leben und gewöhnlich mitagieren, diese Welt autorisierter Verstandes- und Seelenzustände, ist nur der Notersatz für eine andre, zu der die wahre Beziehung abhanden gekommen ist.
> (The world in which we live and with which we usually interact, this world of authorized states of understanding and soul, is only the necessary substitute for another, to which the true relation has been lost.) (GW, viii. 1054)

For Musil, along with Benn and Kubin, this other world is to be found not externally distant realms, but within.

The present study began, then, with depictions of far-away and exotic places to which an author had travelled, and followed in subsequent chapters the increasingly metaphorical and imaginative evocation of exotic spaces that served in this chapter as a depiction of the inner life and its

<hr>

[80] Luft (1980: 179).

primitive 'depths'. In the works examined in the next and final chapter, the localization of the ordinary familiar world of modern Europe and its contrast to an exotic elsewhere is inverted, such that the 'primitive' exotic converges with the heart of modernity itself, the metropolitan city, symbolizing its underlying vital and destructive impulses.

5

Primitive Modernity and the Urban Jungle in Brecht

The mobility of the concept of the exotic and the ambivalence with which it has been evoked are reflected in contradictory depictions of the modern city. Throughout this study, it has been established that the bureaucratization and intellectualization of modern Europe, as described by Hofmannsthal, Weber, and Simmel, has led to a disenchantment to which the exotic, in writers from Hofmannsthal to Musil, has served as a radical contrast. In the previous chapter, literary works were examined in which evocations of the primitive suggested a primal, more vital stratum of the modern self. Still other features of modernity, which are exclusive to the metropolis and studied extensively by Simmel—urbanization in particular—may be critically rendered through the exotic motive. In modern works, the city itself may be exoticized as a 'primitive' realm, a symbolic convergence of the spaces of external urban experience and the inner psyche. While this may be seen as a 'kind of orientalism that folds in on itself, where the Self views itself through the exoticized lens normally reserved for the Other',[1] the implication to be addressed in this chapter on the city is the implicit critique of Western modernity in such depictions by blurring or inverting the terms of this opposition.

The 'primitive' analysed here expresses, often in hyperbolic form, those aspects of experience that tend to be minimized in or excluded from Western 'rationalization' and 'intellectualization' in Weber's sense (discussed in the first chapter). The 'primitive' may be associated with instinct, intense physical experience, aggression and sexuality, the 'older' olfactory and auditory senses, extreme emotion, and an intuitive grasp of reality's underlying core. In the context of literary and aesthetic expressionism, Rhys Williams defines the primitive as a 'grasp of what is essentially human [that] will involve the peeling away of the bourgeois accretions of an over-civilized, over-cerebral existence in a European

---

[1] Corne (2006: 95).

society that has lost touch with humanity's essence'.[2] In this account, the articulations of the 'primitive' do not necessarily suggest the reduction to a less complex or less human state of being. If, as Marianna Torgovnick claims in her study of primitivism, the 'basic grammar and vocabulary of . . . primitivist discourse' is one in which 'primitive' others would 'exist at the "lowest cultural levels [whereas] we occupy the highest,"' this may be called into question by evoking the metropolitan or urban centre of modern life as itself a 'primitive' space.[3]

In literature, the modern city may be exoticized and primitivized by depictions of fragmentation of perception, intense emotional and sexual struggle, and by use of metaphors comparing the city to a jungle or a swamp. In such depictions, the artifices of civilization are presented as threatened by breakdown and ruin. Fractured sensations, animalistic lust, fear, or aggression, and confusion between imagination and objective reality, threaten the ostensibly rational order of urban life and may lead to the unveiling of a more essential substrate. The example to be studied here is Bertolt Brecht's rendering of Chicago in *Im Dickicht der Städte* (1921–1927), which may shed critical light on modernity through its primitivizing characterizations of the city. Brecht's drama, in line with Expressionist depictions,[4] relies explicitly on an exotic motive, presenting the fracturing of the individual and his social foundations in urban spaces. Brecht's method is to explore the primitive through social antagonism, in which aggression (along with sexuality) paradoxically isolates the individual and overcomes the isolating nature of urban life. What is important for this study is that in his drama, as in some Expressionist fiction and poetry, the city and the human psyche symbolically converge. Before turning to his dramatic work, Brecht's exoticizations should be understood in the context of the city as a central motif in modernism more broadly—in literary and aesthetic renderings, and in theoretical accounts.

[2] Williams (2005: 92).
[3] Torgovnick (1990: 8).
[4] The problematic nature of the term 'Expressionist' seems to preface every serious discussion of the subject; varying accounts of its origins are given in Elger (2002: 7–9) and Wolf (2004: 6–7). See also Muschg (1963: 11–23); Furness (1973: 3–12, 16); and Best (1974: 17–19). On the Expressionist elements of Brecht's drama *Im Dickicht der Städte*, see Walker (1998: 120–124). Despite Brecht's distance from the movement, Muschg argues that one can understand Brecht only in the light of his inheritance of Expressionism, and that one can understand Expressionism only by seeing that it lives on in Brecht. Muschg (1963: 335). Willet (1984: 74, 76), in contrast, argues that to speak of Brecht as an Expressionist 'was, and is, to court instant contradiction', but nevertheless shows close ties between Brecht and that movement considered in a broad sense, particularly in the early version of *Im Dickicht der Städte*.

THE CITY AND ITS EXOTICIZATION
IN MODERNISM

The city is unquestionably a central topos of modernism, for which Baudelaire's *Tableaux parisiens* in the 1861 version of *Les Fleurs du mal* often serve as an initiating point of reference.[5] The depictions of Joyce's Dublin in *Ulysses*, Döblin's Berlin in *Berlin Alexanderplatz*, and John dos Passos's New York in *Manhattan Transfer* offer further presentations of the city as not merely a setting but also as a motif interwoven in the psychology and fate of central characters.[6] If, as Benjamin argued, Baudelaire's *flâneur* anticipates the desolation of the inhabitant of the modern metropolis, by the twentieth century the urban metropolis may be observed from a perspective of agitation, nervousness, and alienating anonymity.[7] The rapid industrialization and urbanization of Europe may be seen as the context for this development. By the First World War, Berlin had become the largest industrial city in Continental Europe.[8] Paris, with commercial arcades built already in the 1820s and 1830s, had been modernized throughout the mid-century, and at the Universal Exposition of 1900 the first Paris Métro was in operation.[9] The momentum of modern urban life, the spatio-temporal, technical, communicative, and personal relations idiosyncratic to the city, and the challenges these pose to individual integrity and autonomy, demand innovation in literary and artistic depiction. The transformation of modern perceptual experience 'renders traditional modes of representation inadequate'.[10]

Modernist innovation may take the form of exoticization, as it does in some Cubist and German Expressionist paintings. Picasso's rendering of prostitutes in the 1907 painting 'Les Demoiselles d'Avignon' and other depictions of marginalized city inhabitants with faces resembling African masks, may challenge modern European cultural hierarchies by projecting

---

[5] See Benjamin, GS, v. 45–59; see also Harvey (2003).

[6] Harding's (2003) account takes up the city in modernism in English-language literature, with a particular focus on Joyce. See also Walker (1998) and McLaughlin (2000). In the German context, see Meekseper and Schraut (eds.) (1983) and Huyssen and Bathrick (eds.) (1989: part II).

[7] Benjamin GS/V, 54. See Radkau (1998: 61–66) and Cowan (2008: 21–24).

[8] In Germany, the percentage of the population working in agricultural or forest *Wirtschaft* dropped from 75 percent in 1800 to less than 23 percent in 1925. Industrialization was particularly strong between 1870 and 1910. By 1910 over half the population lived in *Großstädten* exceeding 100,000 inhabitants. Pleister (1982: 8–10).

[9] See Harvey (2003).

[10] Haxthausen (1991: 67).

'primitive' features associated with its colonies.[11] Influenced by developments in Paris, as well as aesthetic treatises by African or other non-Western art by Carl Einstein and Wilhelm Worringer, similarly exoticizing motives can be seen in early twentieth-century painters' depictions of metropolitan cities like Berlin. Street scenes by Ernst Ludwig Kirchner (for instance, 'Five Women on the Street', 1913, and 'Two Women on the Street', 1914), and 'Großstadt' ('Metropolis') paintings by George Grosz (1916–1917), and Otto Dix (1928) present the city in primitivist ways. Angular distortions of bodies and vegetation, garish colour, jazz musicians, feathers and furs may be featured, and the depiction of human figures in particular suggests a break with traditional social mores. Ludwig Meidner's apocalyptic depictions of Berlin as in 'Die brennende Stadt' (1912, 1913) bear some features of 'primitive' abstraction,[12] despite his criticism, shared by Max Beckmann, of German painters' mimicry of objects on view in ethnographical museums and their turn to a foreign, anachronistic source of inspiration.[13] Kirchner's women in the street scenes aforementioned may be seen as 'predatory figures with their mask-like faces and jagged Africanized forms'. Along with the zoological garden, the café, the streetcar, and commercial spectacle as subjects, the cabaret and the circus are exploited by Expressionist painters as modern manifestations of tribal ritual, such that the 'paradox of their primitivism … goes hand in hand with their modernity'.[14]

Worringer theorized the paradoxical coupling of primitivism and modernism in his account of modern abstraction in *Abstraktion und Einfühlung* (first published in 1908). In Worringer's view the geometric distortions and other features of modern painting manifest a 'Raumscheu' or 'Platzangst' in the modern world analogous to so-called primitive cultures' fear of natural threats (and more generally of surrounding space) expressed in their art forms.[15] The advance made by this thesis, however problematic in its 'neo-orientalist characterization of non-Western peoples'[16] is the refusal to dismiss 'primitive' art as simplistic and as less technically competent than European styles, a view also

[11] Leighton (1990: especially 610, 626) regards Picasso's painting as a critical response to European modernity and colonialism. Gikandi (2003) presents a more negative account of Picasso's appropriation of the mask motif from African art and of Picasso's relation to its origins.

[12] On the city as Expressionist subject, see Lloyd (1991: 85–101) and Elger (2002: 203–233); on Kirchner's paintings of Berlin, see Haxthausen (1991) and, more recently, Lloyd and Moeller (eds.) (2003); on Meidner's apocalyptic rendering of Berlin, see Wolf (2004: 72–73); on the city as subject in Max Beckmann, see O'Brien-Twohig (1984: 91–109).

[13] See Lloyd (1991: 85–86).   [14] Lloyd (1991: 85).

[15] Worringer (1959: 20–21).   [16] Corne (2006: 97).

expressed in Einstein's appreciation for African art.[17] While Worringer does not detail the reasons for modern perception of space as threatening, his source can be located in Simmel's account of the metropolis, with which Worringer had become familiar in Simmel's lectures in Berlin. On his own account, it was a chance meeting with Simmel at the Trocadéro Museum in Paris, the same collection of non-Western art that influenced Picasso, which inspired Worringer's thesis.[18] Such collections by European nations have been rightly criticized as colonialist exploitation,[19] but reactions to these objects by modern writers and artists include new estimations of the 'primitive' that may in significant ways counter the cultural and aesthetic hierarchies attending colonial politics.

As in visual art, literary exoticization can convey the city as a Hobbesian state of nature rather than as the height of civilization, or challenge the presumption that the incalculable forces of animal vitality and instinct are localized elsewhere, far outside the urban centres of Western culture. Upton Sinclair's novel *The Jungle* (1906) is set not in colonial India, like Rudyard Kipling's similarly titled *The Jungle Book* (1894), but in Chicago, and while Kipling's text can be read as a deliberately colonialist narrative,[20] Sinclair meant to expose the brutalities of industrial capitalism through the jungle motive. Both works were influential for Brecht's drama *Im Dickicht der Städte (In the Jungle of Cities)*. The exoticizations in Benn's *Gehirne* are of Brussels under German occupation, and his poem 'Untergrundbahn' ('Subway') compares the underground city train to a foreign woman 'aus den Wäldern' ('from the forest'), proceeding through the darkness with 'Meer-Blut' ('sea-blood'). Provocative descriptions of atmosphere, such as 'Götter-Zwielicht' ('twilight of the gods') suggest Nietzsche's exoticizing influence, discussed in the previous chapter. Heym's depiction in 'Der Irre' is of a madman, compared to various jungle animals, rampaging through an urban department store, after having murdered several passers-by on his way through the *Vorstadt*. In such city poems as 'Der Gott der Stadt', in which the masses worship a wrathful pagan god and the smoke from the factories is blue 'wie Duft von Weihrauch' ('like smoke from incense'), Heym usurps the image of the city as a centre of enlightened culture. The target of such depictions is not

---

[17] See Michel's (1998: especially 149–150) nuanced account of Einstein and African art. See Williams (2005: 91); (1983: 249).

[18] See Gluck (2000: 164) and Corne (2006: 96). Worringer discusses this in the preface to the 1948 edition of his book.

[19] Clifford (1990), for example, calls for a critical history of collecting in the context of colonialism.

[20] On Kipling's novel as a colonial space, see McBratney (2002) and Nyman (2008). See Said (1979/2003: 226–227).

any particular city, but the modern city as such.[21] While some of these evocations of the exotic may replicate colonialist metaphors, they nevertheless function outside the symbolism of territorial and imperialist claim, offering a critique of the pretensions of modern civilization by effacing any categorical opposition between the familiar modern world and its exotic 'others'.

The drama to be addressed in this chapter, Brecht's *Im Dickicht der Städte*, uses the jungle as its primary metaphor. Although set in Chicago, like Sinclair's novel, it is widely recognized that Brecht's drama reflects his own perceptions of urban distress in Berlin.[22] Sinclair's depiction of the impoverishment and corruption of an immigrant family whose breadwinner works in a brutal meat-processing plant is transformed by Brecht into a psychological and philosophical combat. Brecht's drama follows a young man who gets involved in a shady lumber business as part of a brutal 'metaphysical' power struggle. In Brecht's work, the city is naturalized as a jungle of aggressive exploitation and cruelty, leading to demoralization and violent death. The parallel metaphor of a boxing match enables Brecht to cast the jungle motif as a distinctly modern struggle.

Brecht's metaphoric rendering of the city can be understood better in the light of Simmel's analysis of the modern city in 'Die Großstädte und das Geistesleben' ('The Metropolis and Mental Life') (1903) and *Philosophie des Geldes (Philosophy of Money)* (1900). In these works, Simmel highlights the dynamics of hyperbolic movement, sensory overstimulation, and accelerated change in urban life, and its results for the individual personality. The experience of the city diminishes what Simmel calls the 'subjective culture' of the individual, reducing the particularity and self-reference of inner life at the expense of increasingly abstract or calculative external exchanges. In a milieu so varied and complex as the metropolis, external relations are most efficiently organized by reducing the personal aspects of existence to stable and uniform coordinates. With mass transportation, personal movement demands punctuality; money brings precision, calculability, and exactness into exchanges; contracts eliminate ambiguity; and communication technology eliminates contingency and particularity in favour of uniform transference of information. Imprecision, ambiguity, inexactness, particularity, unpredictability, and contingency are all features of the 'inner' emotional and psychic life of the individual, which are diminished or extinguished in the external relationships of modern urban commerce. The metropolitan mentality emerges in response: Simmel identifies the blasé attitude, the calculative mentality,

<hr>

[21] Perels (1985: 71).
[22] Seliger (1974: 37); Parmalee (1981: 13–14); Weber (1996: 130–132).

the intellectualization of life, and the reserve and latent antipathy towards others as defence mechanisms against the levelling experience. But it is also the nervousness, the strivings towards eccentricity and stylistic unique-ness, the affectations of egocentrism, which reveal the pressure on the individual, as attempts to achieve unique individuality without adequate spiritual resources. If Baudelaire's *flâneur* could relish the experience of the city at a leisurely pace, Simmel's analysis a half century later argues that the hectic nervousness of urban life contributes to the levelling of the individual.

> Die psychologische Grundlage, auf der der Typus großstädtischer Indivi-dualitäten sich erhebt, ist die *Steigerung des Nervenlebens*, die aus dem raschen und ununterbrochenen Wechsel äußerer und innere Eindrücke hervorgeht.
>
> (The basic psychological situation out of which the typology of the metropolitan individuality arises is the *intensification of the nervous life*, which proceeds from the hurried and incessant change of external and internal impressions.) (GA7, 116, emphasis in original)

While this nervosity of the individual can be highlighted through explor-ing modern perceptual life, the social element involved is seen through experiences of alienation or aggression. In Rilke's novel *Die Aufzeichnun-gen des Malte Laurids Brigge (The Notebooks of Malte Laurids Brigge)*, for instance, the overwhelming negative stimulation of the city and its spiri-tual and social impoverishment provokes the title character's nervous breakdown, as well as his 'primitively' magnified perceptions, but in Rilke's text these remain largely a matter for the isolated individual who records his experiences in his notebooks. The metropolitan mentality enlisted in the exoticizations by Brecht, in contrast, is principally one of aggression. Aggression (including an aggressive sexual commerce) is the means by which Schlink and Garga attempt to assert their individuality against one another, for the presentation of which the dialogue and physical enactment of the dramatic genre is ideally suited. In Simmel's estimation, the spiritual struggle is analogous to the primitive struggle for physical survival, and here primitivism and urbanity converge. Urban life is 'die letzterreichte Umgestaltung des Kampfes mit der Natur, den der primitive Mensch um seine *leibliche* Existenz zu führen hat' ('the latest manifestation of the struggle with nature, which primitive man had to lead for his *physical* existence') (GA7, 116). Simmel's metropolis, it has been argued, 'is already modeled on some prior vision of the primitive wild'.[23] Both Brecht and Simmel, to put it one way, inscribe the jungle on the

---

[23] Corne (2006: 100).

textual city, a palimpsestic exoticizing that may uncover a wildness already buried therein. This circumstance is illustrated no more directly in literature than in Brecht's drama.

Simmel recognizes destructiveness and conflict as inherent to modernity itself, an aspect of his thought oriented by the *Lebensphilosophie* he drew from Schopenhauer and Nietzsche. In his lecture 'Der Konflikt der modernen Kultur' ('The Conflict of Modern Culture') (1918), Simmel sees modernity as a particular configuration of the creative and destructive energies of life. According to Simmel, life exhibits 'seine ruhelose Rhythmik' ('its ceaseless rhythm') in the restless and unceasing creation, development, transformation, and destruction of cultural forms of its expression (GA16, 181). But modernity in particular is dominated by the sense that possible forms have been exhausted; life is now seen in a chronic conflict.

> Jetzt erleben wir diese neue Phase des alten Kampfes, der nicht mehr Kampf der heute vom Leben gefüllten Form gegen die alte, leblos gewordene ist, sondern Kampf des Lebens gegen die Form überhaupt, gegen das Prinzip der Form.
>
> (Now we live through this new phase of an old struggle, which is no longer the struggle of the vivacious form of today against the old, lifeless one, but rather a struggle of life against form as such, against the principle of form.)
> (GA16, 182–183)

Thus, the basic impulse behind contemporary culture is a negative one; conflict is the basic theme of modernity. The relationship between Expressionism, primitivism, and the city can be understood in the light of Simmel's view of the destruction of form inherent to modernity. Expressionism (he cites van Gogh among other painters) is, for Simmel, the quintessential art of modernity, breaking through previous forms to express the inner 'Bewegung' ('movement') of the artist. The rejection of the traditional mimetic tasks of representing the world of objects or the realistic perception of objects, that is, the tendency towards abstraction and distortion, is interpreted in terms of life's liberation from already existing forms. Abstraction is the struggle of life itself; the Expressionistic work breaks through the traditional European conventions of art to become an immediate condensation of the inner life. At the same time the inner life is, according to Simmel's own analysis, endangered by the hyperbolic nature of modern perception. The turn to abstract and even 'primitive' forms may be seen as an alternative mode of creativity in which the essence of life may break through.

The creative and destructive principles of *Leben* in Simmel's philosophy of modern culture and in his account of the city are reassigned to the individual human psyche in Freud's *Das Unbehagen in der Kultur (Civilization and Its Discontents)* (1930), which may serve to further contextualize Brecht's primitivization of the city. While Simmel explains the chronic conflict of culture in terms of the diffuse force of 'life' itself, Freud locates them in the primitive drives of the individual subconscious, 'der Todes- oder Destruktionstrieb' ('death or destruction drive') and *eros* (WA, ii. 405). In seeking a spatial metaphor that will help to imagine the persistence of these drives throughout the whole life of the psyche, Freud chooses the image of a city. Freud's image is a complex 'chronotope', to use Bakhtin's notion,[24] for Freud presents Rome as a modern city with an ancient history, all stages of which are imaginatively preserved. The individual psyche and culture at large manifest an analogous development, with the exception that all moments of the development from primitive to more developed stages are maintained within the life of the mind. 'Auf dem seelischem Gebiet ... ist die Erhaltung des Primitiven neben dem daraus entstandenen Ungewandelten so häufig, daß es sich erübrigt, es durch Beispiele zu beweisen' ('In the region of the soul ... the primitive is preserved so often next to the later transformations which came from it, that it is unnecessary to demonstrate this with examples') (WA, ii. 370). Freud attempts to imagine Rome as if all of its various stages of development could coexist in a single space. After describing the history of the 'eternal city' from its founding on the Palatine, Freud remarks on the state of Rome today as both modern and ancient, and asks:

> was ein Besucher, den wir mit den vollkommensten historischen und topo-graphischen Kenntnissen ausgestattet denken, im heutigen Rom von diesen frühen Stadien noch vorfinden mag.... Von Gebäuden, die einst diese alten Rahmen ausgefüllt haben, findet er nichts oder geringe Reste, den sie bestehen nicht mehr.... Was jetzt diese Stellen einnimmt, sind Ruinen, aber nicht ihrer selbst, sondern ihrere Erneuerungen aus späteren Zeiten nach Bränden und Zerstörungen. Es bedarf kaum noch einer besonderen Erwähnung, daß alle diese Überreste des alten Roms als Einsprengungen in das Gewirre einer Großstadt aus den letzten Jahrhunderten seit der Renaissance erscheinen. Manches Alte ist gewiß noch im Boden der Stadt oder unter ihren modernen Bauwerken begraben.
>
> (what could a visitor, whom we imagine as equipped with the most complete historical and topographical knowledge, still be able to find from these early stages in today's Rome.... He would find nothing or only slight remnants of the buildings which once filled out these old frames, for they are standing no longer.... What occupy these spaces are ruins, but not the ruins

---

[24] The 'chronotope' is a term for the time-space constituted by a literary work, as described by Bakhtin (1981: 84). On Freud's metaphor in the context of the city and modernism, see Harding (2003: 1–4).

of the buildings themselves, rather of their renovation from later times after fires and destructions. It hardly needs to be mentioned especially that all of these remnants of old Rome appear as leaps into the tangle of a metropolis from the last centuries since the Renaissance. There are certainly some ancient things buried in the ground of the city or under its modern edifices.) (WA, ii. 371)

Freud abandons the metaphor because of the difficulty of such spatial representation, but his ambivalence may also be understood in the light of his critique of contemporaneous primitivism. Freud attributes 'das ozeanische Gefühl' ('the oceanic feeling') described by Rolland not to a primitive religious instinct, but rather to early ego experiences before differentiation between ego and world (for instance, in the mother's womb and nursing at the breast) and to erotic love, wherein this state of primary narcissism may be revisited. Nevertheless, Freud does recognize the possible subsistence of this feeling within the psyche, despite the fact that later stages of development will have displaced it. While Freud abandons his attempt to imagine the modern city and its coexisting ancient and intermediate forms, he argues that we can imagine coexisting drives or tendencies of culture that bespeak both earlier stages and later developments. In addressing potential objections to his image of the city as analogy for the psyche, Freud writes:

> Zu einem Einwand sollten wir noch Stellung nehmen. Er fragt uns, warum wir gerade die Vergangenheit einer Stadt ausgewählt haben, um sie mit der seelischen Vergangenheit zu vergleichen. Die Annahme der Erhaltung alles Vergangenen gilt auch für das Seelenleben nur unter der Bedingung, daß das Organ der Psyche intakt geblieben ist, daß sein Gewebe nicht durch Trauma oder Entzündung gelitten hat. Zerstörende Einwirkungen, die man diesen Krankheitsursachen gleichstellen könnte, werden aber in der Geschichte keiner Stadt vermißt, auch wenn sie eine minder bewegte Vergangenheit gehabt hat als Rom, auch wenn sie, wie London, kaum je von einem Feind heimgesucht wurde. Die friedlichste Entwicklung einer Stadt schließt Demolierungen und Ersetzungen von Bauwerken ein.
>
> (We must still take a position against a certain objection. It asks us, why exactly we have chosen the past of a city as comparison for the past of the soul. The acceptance of the preservation of everything past holds also for the life of the soul only under the condition that the organ of the psyche has remained intact, that its tissues have not suffered through trauma or inflammation. But destructive effects that one could compare with these causes of illness are missing in the history of no city, even if it has had a less tumultuous past than Rome, even if it, like London, had hardly been visited upon by an enemy. The most peaceful development of a city includes demolitions and replacements of construction.) (WA, ii. 372)

In the conclusion of his work, Freud connects the inevitable destruction within a city, its inner ruins, to the modern age itself. The tendency towards destruction of existing forms, as in Simmel's account of modernity, precedes and potentially outweighs the valence of new ones. While Freud rejects any longing for a return to a more primal state as an escapist illusion, he explains the discontent with modernity in terms of, among other factors, the European discovery of primitive peoples through geographical exploration (WA, ii. 384). Just as Simmel describes the struggle for existence in the modern city in primitive terms, Freud acknowledges, albeit in a critical vein, 'primitive' residues persisting within the structures of modern culture, for which Europeans might yearn in the wake of such discoveries. There is, then, a special relationship between the modern state of the psyche/city and the underlying primitive culture, however fragmentarily subsisting. Benjamin, in describing Baudelaire's Paris, claims that modernity and the primal are linked: 'Aber immer zitiert gerade die modern die Urgeschichte' ('But the modern always cites precisely the primal history') (GS, v. 55).

URBAN AGGRESSION, PRIMITIVISM, AND RACISM IN BRECHT'S *IM DICKICHT DER STÄDTE*

Brecht conceived *Im Dickicht der Städte* in 1920–1921 (it was first entitled simply *Das Dickicht*) and worked on it throughout the 1920s.[25] Inspired by his experience moving to Berlin in 1920, Brecht's drama presents Chicago, 'die kalte Stadt' ('the cold city') from the perspective of an outsider facing poverty and social alienation. Like Rilke's Malte in *Die Aufzeichnungen des Malte Laurids Brigge*, Brecht's protagonist George Garga is uprooted, having arrived in the city from a rural setting, and experiences urban life as hostile and precarious. In Brecht's drama, the noise of traffic and the sounds of human cries penetrate the surrounding atmosphere. This leads Garga's imagination elsewhere; he refers to modern French poetry (quoting Rimbaud and Verlaine) and longs both for a former home and an escape far away from the metropolis: 'Ich bitte um Virginiens Tabakfelder und um ein Billet nach den Inseln' ('I want

---

[25] On the transformations of Brecht's work from the early notes to the 1927 version, see Seliger (1974: 28–50); Parmalee (1981: 40–45); and Weber (1996: 125–127). Brecht's first completed manuscript was finished in 1922; a shortened version of the play was staged in 1923; and a second staging was given in 1924; Brecht revised the work for publication in 1927 as *Im Dickicht der Städte*. In the Berliner und Frankfurter Ausgabe of Brecht's works the 1923 and 1927 are given in the first volume, *Stücke I*. On the genesis of *Im Dickicht der Städte*, see W, i. 584–596.

Virginia's tobacco fields and a ticket to the islands') (W, i. 446). While Rilke's Malte finds escape from Venice in travel (to Venice, Russia, and Southern France), literature, and art, Garga is until the final scene isolated in Chicago, reading travel books and envisioning Tahiti as an imagined escape. Garga suffers the city experience as a collapse of boundaries between the inner life (and its imagination of elsewhere) and the impositions of the urban reality. Brecht relies on the direct metaphor of his title, which is further elaborated through the racial, tribal, and animalistic characterization of Garga's antagonists and their bitter 'Affenkomödie' ('ape comedy') (W, i. 445).

Im Dickicht der Städte opens in the library where Garga works, with Schlink antagonizing Garga by demanding to buy his opinions concerning books. Garga's attempt to preserve at least his own thoughts from monetary exchange illustrates Simmel's thesis of the reduction of the individual's 'subjective culture' to the calculative logic of urban life both symbolized and facilitated by money. Unlike the *Bibliothèque Nationale* where Malte can escape the pressures of poverty, Maynes's lending library is already a commercial enterprise (patrons pay five cents per book per week) and is Garga's place of employment. Schlink's antagonism gets Garga fired, undermines Garga's relationship with his girlfriend Jane (in an early version Jane is murdered), reduces Jane and his sister Marie to prostitution, and he usurps Garga's position within the Garga family by becoming their boarder. The characters become locked in the position of struggle, eventually expressed through a three-week homoerotic affair. Garga, in turn, ruins the lumber business that Schlink had vouchsafed to him, and incites a mob to lynch him, from which Schlink escapes only by committing suicide. The outcome demonstrates, in Freud's terms, the triumph of the *Todes- oder Destruktionstrieb* over the tendencies of *eros*, in the context of the city as jungle.

At the outset of the struggle Garga attempts to maintain the dignity of his inner life—he is a reader and refuses to sell his opinions—but faces the direct challenge of an opponent who thrives on fighting for its own sake, a motif inspired by Jensen's novel (in German translation), *Das Rad*, which Brecht had read in 1920.[26] In this early work, Brecht does not merely presume the 'negation of any inwardness and everything 'inner', but rather presents such negation as a stake in the struggle between Garga and his opponent.[27] The struggle takes the form of tearing down boundaries between self and other, each character eventually usurping the other's psychological, social, and economic foundations. Garga's acute confronta-

---

[26] See Seliger (1974: 28 and 254 n 50) and Weber (1996: 127).
[27] Vaßen (1998: 78).

tion with the unprovoked antagonist from Southeast Asia (Schlink is Malay, from Yokahama) gives a specific, 'exotic', face to the hostility of the city. While Rilke's Malte descends into nervous breakdown, Garga takes up his struggle outwardly, with increasing aggressiveness and coldness, gradually taking on the characteristics of his antagonist. The lumberyard on fire may finally symbolize Garga's externalized aggression, with whatever emotional coolness the arson is incited.

In Brecht's drama, the city as jungle serves, then, as an image of dystopia.[28] Underlying the most modern city are primitive impulses expressed through social injustice and oppression and reactions to them. In his notes, Brecht compares the city to the jungle landscapes of an English colony, with its colonialists and victims. On 11 September 1921, Brecht describes his project:

> Als ich mir überlegte, was Kipling für die Nation machte, die die Welt 'zivilisiert', kam mich zu der epochalen Entdeckung, daß eigentlich noch kein Mensch die große Stadt als Dschungel beschrieben hat. Wo sind ihre Helden, ihre Kolonisatoren, ihre Opfer? Die Feindseligkeit der großen Stadt, ihre bösartige, steinere Konsistenz, ihre babylonische Sprachverwirrung, kurz: ihre Poesie ist noch nicht geschaffen.
>
> (When I considered, what Kipling did for the nation that 'civilized' the world, I came to the epochal discovery, that actually no one had ever described the metropolitan city as a jungle. Where are its heroes, its colonialists, its victims? The animosity of the big city, its cruel, stony consistency, its Babylonian confusion of languages, in short: its poetry has not yet been created.) (W, xxvi, 236)

Brecht had, in fact, read Sinclair's *The Jungle* in German translation (*Der Sumpf*) the previous year, recommending it to readers of his review of a staging of Schiller's *Don Carlos*. Yet Kipling's *The Jungle Book*—set largely in the jungle where the Indian boy Mowgli grows up among, and speaks the language of, animals—suggests the tropical elaboration that Brecht superimposed on an imagined Chicago. Like Worringer's coupling of the modern with the 'primitive' in his psychological comparison of artistic forms, Brecht depicts life in modern Chicago as evoking primitive and ancient impulses, as if it were a struggle among animals in the jungle. At the same time, the quotation marks around 'zivilisiert' and recognition of the 'Opfer' of the British indicate Brecht's critical view of colonialism and exploitation. Although explicitly without motive, the fight is incited by Schlink, essentially a victim of racist oppression, in order to attempt to

---

[28] Walker (1998: 119–120).

overcome, through 'primitive' means, the extreme isolation of urban life and its brutal hierarchies.

While Brecht equates Chicago and Berlin in his notes and letters, he describes his choice of setting as a foreign city. An American city, as opposed to a German one, renders the actions 'ganz und gar fremd, d h [*sic*] eben *auffällig*' ('entirely foreign, that is to say, precisely conspicuous') for his audience (GW, xvii. 971–972). In addition to the effect of *Entfremdung*, the foreignness of Chicago for the German audience assists the metaphorical transformation of city into jungle. While the atmosphere of Chicago could describe 'die der modernen Großstadt an und für sich' ('that of the modern metropolis in and for itself'),[29] an early critic postulated that the American space also allowed for the expression of a 'new' primitivism, of a vitality not available in Europe in the years just after the First World War. In a review of the play in 1924, Herbert Ihering writes:

> Krieg und Revolution trafen auf eine Menschheit, die durch Zivilisation so mechanisiert war, daß sie elementare Ereignisse nicht mehr elementar empfinden konnte. Das Drama konnte nicht wieder einsetzen, wo es abgebrochen war. Es konnte den Amerikanismus nicht leugnen, nicht weglöschen. Notwendig war es aber, ihn... als neuen, primitiven Anfang zu empfinden. Die letzte technische Präzision des Zeitalters konnte nur dann künstlerisch zeugungsfähig werden, wenn es gelang, sie als Barberei zu erleben.[30]
> (War and revolution struck a humanity that was so mechanized through civilization, that it could no longer feel in an elementary way elemental events. Theatre could not take up again where it had broken off. It could not deny Americanism nor extinguish it. But it was necessary to experience it as a new, primitive beginning. The latest technical precision of the age could only become an artistic tool, if it would succeed in experiencing it as barbarity.)

The very modernity of the American metropolis can express a form of barbarity, equivalent to a new primitivism not possible in the exhausted European context. In the early version, the opening scene symbolically evokes an exotic landscape:

> *Braun. Nasse Tabakblätter. Seifengrünes Schiebfenster... Niedrig. Viel Papier.... Schlink in langer, fleckig gelber Sutane.*
> (Brown. Wet tobacco leaves. Soap-green windows.... Low ceilings. Lots of paper.... Schlink in a long, spotted yellow sutane.) (W, i. 346)

The colours brown and green, the wet tobacco leaves, and the opacity of the windows suggest the growth and humidity of tropical climates, perhaps even the atmosphere of a 'Treibhaus', while the yellow evokes the

---

[29] Seliger (1974: 39).   [30] Ihering (1959: 57–60).

Oriental.[31] Ihering, impressed by the innovative rendering of the modern
as primitive in Brecht's play, was disappointed at the elimination of this
jungle-like atmosphere from the 1927 publication. According to Ihering,
Brecht transferred 'das 'Dickicht' aus dem tropischen Klima der ersten,
atmosphärischen Fassungen in die kühlere Luft des sachlichen Kampfes'
('the 'jungle' from a tropical climate of the first, atmospheric version to the
cooler air of material struggle').[32]

Yet, in all versions Garga's experience of the city as jungle is contrasted
to his simpler and more temperate origins. Garga's family is said to come
from Virginia, 'aus den Savannen in das Dickicht der großen Stadt' ('from
the prairies into the jungle of the big city') or 'aus dem flachen Land'
('from the plains'), and suffers poverty and degradation in a brutally
intemperate Chicago (W, i. 438, 440). The Garga family members
often recall their rural origins. The longing for these origins is directly
contrasted to description of the city, as in this statement by Garga's sister
Marie:

> Jetzt erwacht Chicago mit dem Geschrei der Milchhändler und dem lauten
> Rollen der Fleischkarren und den Zeitungen und der frischen Morgenluft.
> Fortgehen wäre eine gute Sache.... Jetzt geht zum Beispiel ein kühler Wind
> in der Savanne, wo wir früher waren, ich bin sicher.
>
> (Chicago is waking up with the cry of the milkman and the loud rolling of
> the meat carts and the newspapers and the fresh morning air. It would be
> good to go away.... Now, for example, a cool wind is blowing in the prairies,
> where we were before, I am sure.) (W, i. 463)

The contrast between Chicago and Tahiti, however, further complicates
the exoticization of the setting, transcending the simple opposition between the rural life and the city. In the opening scene at Maynes's lending
library, Garga recommends a travel book (by Captain James Cook) that
he has been reading (W, i. 439). Garga's longing to travel to Tahiti
is revealed, and Schlink exploits this longing in his attempt to buy
Garga's opinions. In reference to Garga's wish, Schlink describes a primitive ideal:

> Das ist das einfache Leben. An dem Kap Hay kommen noch Stürme vor,
> weiter südlich sind die Tabakinseln, grüne raschelnde Felder. Man lebt wie
> eine Eidechse.
>
> (That is the simple life. On Cape Hay there are storms, farther south are
> the tobacco islands, green rustling fields. One lives like a lizard.) (W, i. 441)

---

[31] See Winnacker (1993: 61, 62).   [32] Ihering (1959: 274).

Like Virginia, the potential escape to Tahiti is held out throughout the drama as a contrasting ideal against which the brutality of urban life, and particularly its reduction of the individual to economic exchange, can be exposed. The 'Tabakinseln' resonates with descriptions of Virginia, yet Chicago threatens to trap its inhabitants as if they were lost in a jungle or swamp. Thus, it is Chicago, not the rural Virginia or Tahiti, that constitutes the truly 'primitive' space. Despite that both Virginia and Tahiti are hot climates like that of Chicago in August, the Chicago summer is described by Garga in contrasting terms, sometimes as the cold city, playing on the metonym 'the windy city', and also as jungle-like heat. The heat in Chicago 'geht durch den Leib wie ein Blitzzug' ('rips through the body like lightning') (W, i. 443). The sweltering heat and the noise of traffic dominate the morning atmosphere in which the drama opens: 'Vierundneunzig Grad im Schatten. Lärm von der Milwaukeebrücke. Der Verkehr. Ein Vormittag. Wie Immer' ('Ninety-four degrees in the shade. Noise from the Milwaukee Bridge. Traffic. A morning. Like every other') (W, i. 441). This complaint about the heat, however, follows soon after Garga's description of Chicago's cold: 'Schläft zu dritt neben einem geplazten Ausgußrohr.... Die Fenster sind geschlosssen, da Chicago kalt ist' ('Sleep three in a bed next to a burst drainpipe.... The windows are closed, because Chicago is cold') (W, i. 440). The coldness of Chicago, often referred to by Brecht in his notes, is both metaphorical and literal, representing the inhumanity of human relationships, as well as the brutality of the exposure to the elements—and so is the heat of the 'asphalt jungle', which provokes both territorial and erotic aggression. Thus, the jungle metaphor is rendered in contradicting terms, allowing it to function as an image of severe disquiet, of broken continuity between past and future, between origins and ideals. The asphalt jungle is a realm between an unreachable past and a fantasized future.[33] Indeed Garga takes up the fight with Schlink under the hopes of finding a means to realize his dream of escaping to Tahiti. This longing for Tahiti is maintained throughout the conflict: the 'Baboon' says of Schlink, who is looking for Garga: 'Er visitiert die Gesichter der Abreisenden, denen es in Chicago zu grausam zugeht' ('He is looking into the faces of all of the people leaving, for whom Chicago is too cruel'). Jane responds, 'Ostwind geht. Die Tahitischiffe lichten die Anker' ('There is an East wind. The ships for Tahiti are weighing anchor') (W, i. 463).

There are, then, two visions of the exotic in Brecht's text: the pristine ideal of Tahiti and the primitive aggression of the city-jungle. While

---

[33] See Perels (1985: 78).

Tahiti is the ideal exotic, perhaps as depicted by Gauguin, Chicago is its negative mirror. References to Tahiti as a distant utopia are countered by the negative exoticization of Chicago itself as a jungle, established by the symbolic scenery (in the early version) and then by the characters antagonizing Garga. Their association suggests tribalism and, as immigrants from various places in Asia, the uprootedness of an urban population. Schlink is Malay, his associate Skinny is Chinese, and other associates have nicknames of animals: the 'Baboon' (der Pavian) and the 'Worm' (der Wurm), who owns a Chinese hotel where several scenes take place. Garga recommends Rimbaud, whose *Une Saison en enfer (A Season in Hell)* he quotes several times in the drama, with its references to desert, Africa, and other exotic and racial tropes, and refers to Goethe's *West-östlicher Divan (West-Eastern Divan)*. Garga's speeches are peppered with striking fragments of animal and sexual metaphors. In the Chinese Hotel, Garga remarks:

> Die dünnen Kleider wie schillernde Schlängenhäute klatschen wie vom immerwährender Nässe durchregnet an die immer erregten Glieder. . . . Ich habe mich in das Weichbild der Stadt geflüchtet, wo in glühenden Dornbüschen weiß die Frauen kauern mit ihren schiefsitzenden orangen Mäulern.
> (The thick dresses like iridescent snakeskins are drenched through with constant rain on their ever-excited limbs. . . . I have fled into the outskirts of the city, where in glowing thornbushes the women crouch white with their crooked orange mouths.) (W, i. 468)

The animalistic description of human beings pertains to Garga too: 'Man hat mich harpuniert' ('Someone has harpooned me') (W, i. 447). Garga himself understands the city as a jungle in which conflicts are experienced in modes of the hunt and other threats in the natural wild. To the ensuing conflict between Schlink and Garga, the 'Baboon' responds, 'Es ist Sumpf' ('It is a swamp'). Garga replies, 'Die Störche leben vom Sumpf' ('Storks live from the swamp'). When Garga's sister is being sold as 'nacktes Fleisch' ('naked flesh'), he responds, 'Das ist der Sumpf, der dich verschlucht' ('It is the swamp that is swallowing you up') (W, i. 449, 452).

While the jungle metaphor provides the context for the dramatic action, *Im Dickicht der Städte* also illustrates the predominance of instinct over reason as the determining factor in human interactions. Compatible then with Freud's thesis on the conflicting drives underlying civilization, Brecht depicts the struggle between Schlink and Garga as unmotivated by any rational grounds. The conflict between Brecht's antagonists is without motive:

Schlink:	Sie nehmen den Kampf auf?
Garga:	Ja! Natürlich unverbindlich.
Schlink:	Und ohne nach dem Grund zu fragen?
Garga:	Ohne nach dem Grund zu fragen.
(Schlink:	Then you are taking on the fight?
Garga:	Yes! Of course, without obligation.
Schlink:	And without asking for the reason?
Garga:	Without asking for the reason.) (W, i. 448)

By isolating two characters in their groundless conflict, Brecht's drama enacts a destruction of traditional plot and suggests the chaotic nature of human sociality. What takes the place of reason—or of conflict for which reasons could be given—is a pact based on sheer instinct, the aggressive drive that Brecht expresses, among other means, through depiction of bodily interaction. 'Reason and the meaningful narratives that it creates are destroyed and what remains is the bare reality of social and physical conflict', as one scholar puts it.[34] The exploitation of the body, in labour and prostitution, and suffering cold, discomfort, and hunger, provide both the conditions of possibility for, and the stakes within, such conflict. The irrational nature of the struggle leads to the destruction of all ideal bonds—between family members and citizens—such that the interpenetration of bodies, in violence or in the final sexual affair between Garga and Schlink, is the remaining mode of connection between individuals. Garga says to Schlink: 'Sie machen einen metaphysischen Kampf und hinterlassen eine Fleischerbank' ('You stage a metaphysical fight and leave behind a slaughterhouse') (W, i. 467).

The meaningless struggle cannot be explained only by the competition and greed characteristic of capitalism. Schlink hands over his lumber business to Garga, who immediately ruins it, and after Schlink builds it up again during Garga's time in prison, Garga incites its arson. Garga does profit, but never makes it to Tahiti, instead retreating, in wake of Schlink's suicide, to New York. Exploitation in this drama is both the context for the hostility of the city and a particular means to express an instinctual antagonism, and thus cannot be explained solely as an anticipation of Brecht's later Marxism. The chaotic nature of the struggle, that is to say, its grounding only in 'Kampfeslust' ('lust for fighting') seems to express rather 'the disorderly nature of human history' and the attempt to overcome the isolation it conditions.[35] The homoeroticism of the relation between Garga and Schlink can be seen as part of this chaotic violence and a response to it. Their sexual relations do not yield the positive, bonding

---

[34] Oesmann (2001: 259).   [35] Oesmann (2001: 258).

effects of eros, but serve as a means for further mutual degradation. While Garga, in Schlink's bedroom, refers to himself in Rimbaudian fashion as a Bräutchen, and later a Witwe, other metaphors are that of violent-phallic penetration (W, i. 464). Of Garga, der Wurm says: 'Die Harpune sitzt fester, als wir glaubten. . . . Jetzt liegt er drinnen in Schlinks Zimmer und leckt seine Wunden' ('The harpoon is deeper than we thought. . . . Now he is there in Schlink's room and is licking his wounds') (W, i. 463). Both the fight and the erotic contact between Garga and Schlink are understood as attempts to overcome human divisions, instituted through rationality and language, by reduction to primitive impulses. The transformation of what Freud called 'Kultur' is necessary to overcome its isolating 'Unbehagen' ('discontent'). Nearing the moment of death, Schlink characterizes the situation thus:

> Ich habe die Tiere beobachtet. Die Liebe, Wärme aus Körpernähe, ist unsere einzige Gnade in der Finsternis! Aber die Vereinigungen der Organe ist die einzige, sie überbrückt nicht die Entzweiung der Sprache. . . . Ja, so groß ist die Vereinzelung, daß es nicht einmal einen Kampf gibt. Der Wald! Von hier kommt die Menschheit. Haarig, mit Affengebissen, gute Tiere, die zu leben wußten. Alles war so leicht. Sie zerfleischten sich einfach.
>
> (I have observed animals. Love, warmth in bodily contact, is our only mercy in the darkness! But it is a union of the organs only, it does not bridge the divisions made by language. . . . Yes, so great is our isolation, that there is not even a fight. The forest! That is where humanity comes from. Hairy, with apes' jaws, good animals that knew how to live. Everything was so easy. They simply ripped each other to shreds.) (W, i. 491)

A regression to the fighting and eros is meant to overcome human isolation. That Brecht deliberately stylizes this opposition in racial terms may have been inspired by his reading not only of Kipling (in the 1923 version Brecht borrows the name 'Moti Gui' for one of Schlink's associates) but of Döblin's novel set in China, *Die drei Sprüngen des Wang-lun* (*The Three Leaps of Wang-lun*), which Brecht admired, along with Rimbaud's poetry.[36] However critical Brecht is of social injustice and racism in the drama,[37] it cannot be denied that he employs racist characterizations to exoticize the struggle between Garga and Schlink. The association of Schlink with the colour yellow and as a 'Gelbhäutiger' ('yellow-skinned') is a typical Orientalizing trope examined by Said (W, i. 454).[38] In the first scene Schlink, as Malay, is called 'ein phlegmatischer Kuli'. In coming to live with Garga's family, Schlink accepts their racism as a matter of fact: 'Meine hand wird Sie nicht berühren. Ich weiß,

[36] Brecht, GW, 13, 10. See Seliger (1974: 34–35).
[37] Parmalee (1981: 48); Oesmann (2001: 268–270).
[38] See Said (1979/2003: 119).

daß ich gelbe Haut dran habe' ('My hand will never touch you. I know that I have yellow skin') (W, i. 460). Unless it is to be interpreted ironically, he has also internalized negative stereotypes, when he says, 'Auch bin ich mir seit Jahren des Geruchs meiner Rasse bewußt' ('And I have been aware for years of the smell of my race') (W, i. 462). The Orientalist assumptions at work in Brecht's characterization are also suggested by the insidious passivity and masochism of Schlink's attack against Garga. As Said puts it, the Oriental is imagined by the Westerner as living 'in a state of Oriental despotism and sensuality, imbued with a feeling of Oriental fatalism'.[39] Yet, the gradual exchange of positions between the white American Garga (described as 'English' in Brecht's notes) and his Asian opponent—as well as their homoerotic affair—may be interpreted as a critique of these same associations. Marie, too, falls in love with Schlink and is unrequited. The racist images in Rimbaud's poetry quoted by Garga—'Ich bin ein Tier, ein Neger' ('I am a beast, a black')—are problematic and ripe for criticism,[40] but in Brecht's use may also be considered, in the context of the gradual transformation of the characters, as a critique of racial categories as such (W, i. 445).

Through these evocations of race and racism, Brecht highlights the primitive physical survival of the struggle within the city. The primacy of instinct—the fight for fighting's sake—seems to undermine racial divisions even as they are exploited as factors in the conflict itself. Astrid Oesmann has shown how Brecht examines 'different genealogies of skin', using the difference between Garga's 'white' skin and Schlink's 'yellow' skin as a stake in their struggle. The racial opposition is inverted as the characters become interchangeable.[41] Despite the gradual rendering of each of the characters with the other's characteristics, and their mutual 'penetration' of each other's skin, this difference is ultimately exploited by Garga as he incites a lynch mob against Schlink. The indictment of the modern 'jungle' as one of racist violence is perhaps even more poignant because the homoerotic affair immediately precedes Schlink's violent end. Brecht's criticism of racial and social injustice in the story may be expressed in the fact that it is ultimately Schlink who, ostensibly losing the fight, has maintained the purity of a fighting spirit and its supreme endurance, despite significant racial and social disadvantages. Schlink has, moreover, risen above the seduction of money and property in favour of human contact and communion, however painfully achieved. Having

[39] Said (1979/2003: 102).
[40] Cf. Ross (1988: 81–88, esp. 82), on racism and exoticism in Rimbaud and his literary context.
[41] Oesmann (2001: 267).

lost his individuality in the fight, Garga's retreat to New York underlines his failure to escape the city-jungle and to realize his freedom in Tahiti, the exotic of his imagination.

CONCLUSION

Brecht celebrates the fight as a 'metaphysical' response to the conditions of the urban jungle, highlighting the failure of erotic and familial love to effect an equivalent transformation of the individual. In the conclusion of *Das Unbehagen in der Kultur*, Freud addresses the fate of a culture in which the aggressive and self-destructive drive ('Aggressions- und Selbst-vernichtungstrieb') fails to be mastered by eros. What Simmel relegated to life's own destruction of 'form' within the modern age is rendered as a vision of extreme violence between human beings. Freud writes:

> In diesem Bezug verdient vielleicht gerade die gegenwärtige Zeit ein beson-deres Interesse. Die Menschen haben es jetzt in der Beherrschung der Naturkräfte so weit gebracht, daß sie es mit deren Hilfe leicht haben, einander bis auf den letzten Mann auszurotten.
>
> (In this respect, perhaps exactly the contemporary time deserves a special interest. Human beings have now brought their mastery of nature's powers so far, that they can with their help easily annihilate one another to the last man.) (WA, ii. 424)

Writing between two world wars, Freud's address to violence suggests a severe critique of modern culture. Despite his rejection of any 'primitivist' alternative, his account challenges any supposition of the superiority of Western culture. Civilization is precarious, based on the 'Kampf zwischen Eros und Todestrieb' ('struggle between eros and the death-drive') which—and here Freud's view converges with Simmel's *Lebensphilosophie*—reveals nothing less than 'das Geheimnis des organischen Lebens überhaupt' ('the secret of organic life as such') (WA, ii. 419).

The evocation of the primitive in the context of the metropolitan city may be seen as a challenge to the presumed superiority of modern Western civilization, even as these evocations contribute to its literary achieve-ments. Brecht's rendering of Chicago as a brutal jungle of exploitation and aggression illustrates both negatively and positively 'primitive' aspects of human experience. This does not help in any direct transformation of the 'generalized notion of the primitive' assigned to non-Western cultures and their peoples.[42] However, what Torgovnick refers to as the 'grammar'

---

[42] Torgovnick (1990: 22).

of primitivism, in which the primitive 'Other' is hierarchically subordinated to the 'Western sense of self', may collapse with this revelation.

If the modern city may be experienced in primitive ways, and reveals a primitive substrate that usurps its rational order, then the distinction between urban Western culture and the imagined primitive other becomes untenable. The incitement of arson and mob violence, as well as homoerotic penetration, in this representation of Chicago, transpose onto modern urban spaces the psychic drives, the 'libidinal, irrational, violent, dangerous' forces projected in Orientalist imagery onto non-Western 'primitives'.[43] The submission of Garga to irrational drives serves to depict the modern Western self as the truly primitive, as precarious and unstable. These depictions of the city subject Western modernity precisely to what Said, referring to 'the primitive community to which we belong natally', called 'interpretive contest'.[44]

[43] Torgovnick (1990: 8).   [44] Said (1979/2003: 332).

Conclusion

The exploration and imagination of exotic spaces, whether described on the basis of empirical observation, or partly or wholly imaginary, allows authors not only to expand the topography of the modern literary imagination but also to examine and contest the modern understanding of the European self and the familiar world which it ordinarily inhabits. The exotic topographies in the works studied in this book are not experienced primarily as opportunities for affirmation of the European subject and its familiar world, and they often undermine such a possibility. The observation, imagination, or appreciation of exotic foreign topographies in nearly all of these works, by Hofmannsthal, Hesse, Dauthendey, Mann, Zweig, Kafka, Musil, Benn, Kubin, and Brecht, provokes critical self-reflection about modern European forms of consciousness. The theoretical context for this critical self-reflection has been worked out here through some of the major thinkers of German modernism and modernity, including Simmel, Weber, Nietzsche, Schopenhauer, Worringer, and Freud. What is yielded by these works is, taken as a whole, an awareness of radically different, often more vital, possibilities for understanding and for living life, and sometimes recognition of the potential dangers of breakdown for the familiar world, and recognition of its precariousness.

The implications of this study extend beyond the particular meanings of exotic space. An examination of exotic space shows the subjective and cultural nature of any space as it is experienced or imagined, as well as the dependence of the self on its ordinary surroundings. Departure from the ordinary familiar world, and confrontation with the foreign, bring about new possibilities of experience that may take the form of epiphany, disorientation, collapse, liberation, intimacy, mystical transcendence, and aesthetic renewal. Surrounding or experienced spaces are not reducible to their measurable and objective coordinates; the human subject does not inhabit space as a neutral observer, but rather endows it with meaning and is, conversely, given its own parameters and orientation by spatial boundaries maintained or breached. Such boundaries are both cultural and subjective, and therefore vulnerable to reconfiguration or dissolution. While the depictions of the exotic studied here are by no means free from prejudice, stereotype, error, or colonialist implications, their strategies of imaginative, metaphorical, and palimpsestic depiction of the 'exotic', and, taken together, their exposure of the mobility of that concept, render visible the subjective and cultural-social nature of place and space. Such exposure of imaginative configuration and reconfiguration of space is required for, and presupposed by, any critical account of 'imaginative geography'. That is to say, any critique of geographical, national, or ethnic demarcations of space, as contingent rather than natural, political rather than neutral, metaphorically constituted and symbolically endowed rather than only empirical and objective, presupposes the work of the imagination of and about spaces and places. The imagination of emplacement and displacement, brilliantly isolated in Kafka, is engaged as a central element of all the works discussed in this book. Taken together in this light, they testify to the power and relevance of imagination, of cultural memory and expectation, of history, emotion, and the aesthetic sensibility in our experience of the world as a shifting symbolic topography.

Reflection on the modern European subject, on the limitations engendered by its forms of consciousness, on its tendency towards one-sided reliance on rationality, quantification, bureaucratic organization, and its familial, political, and social structures, emerges best by invoking a distance, by moving beyond the familiar world. More radical than the travel in a typical *Bildungsroman*, in which the protagonist is to come 'into his own' by experiencing what is other, the *Fernweh* evident in modern German literature signals a desire for a more significant and even compromising departure. It has been established in this book that exotic spaces and places need not be desired in order to conquer the outer world. Although they may reveal underlying, often-unreflected investment in cultural domination, depictions of such spaces and places may also be experienced in other ways that would resist or undermine such domination. Such depictions, as in Hofmannsthal's works discussed in Chapter 1, need not necessarily express imperialist desires, but may allow other modes of being to emerge through movement, change, and distance. This emergence allows for critical and imaginative reflection on the experience of being a 'self', as defined in the Introduction and elaborated upon in several chapters of this book, and of being in a familiar world.

At the same time, what is often projected as 'other' to the modern European consciousness may be revealed as belonging to the repressed aspects of the modern psyche. The exploration of the exotic in modern German literature, it has been established in this book, moves from outward observation in the direction of the inner life, in each case challenging the boundaries between the outer and the inner, the familiar and the exotic worlds. The first chapter showed, first of all, external observation of writers travelling to exotic locales and writing about their experiences there. Yet while such writers as Hofmannsthal, Dauthendey, and Hesse all observed foreign places (from Africa to Asia) first-hand, in each case the outward direction of observation turns inward to show the limits of the familiar world. The protagonists or narrators may become disoriented in and dependent upon the foreign environment in ways that undermine their autonomy. And the division between the self and the foreign is obscured or effaced through the experience of epiphany. Dauthendey is the one among these authors who attempts to imagine the foreign world through foreign eyes, and while this is inevitably problematic (limited, as it is, by the author's European origins and the baggage of cultural stereotypes), it also allows the reader to attempt to imagine non-Western, non-modern modes of experience, an attempt which is, however ethically risky, surely the first step of many in over-coming ethnocentrism. The texts by Mann and Zweig all present a modern European protagonist in an exotic (Venetian or Asian) locale, or in one, like the Swiss Alps, exoticized by projections of the cultural imagination. While erotic allure seems to draw the protagonists out of themselves towards an exotic object of desire, the infection linked to the exotic surroundings or natural forces ruptures the division between self and other from the outside, indicating at the very least a loss of control over the boundaries between self and other. Kafka's descriptions of exotic topographies (marked as America, China, and Russia) transcend the empirical referent, presenting spaces of contest or liberation for the imagination, where other forms of being, of intimacy and creativity, are imagined. While Kafka's spaces, discussed in the third chapter, enable an imagination of the inner life, the works of Benn, Musil, and Kubin, studied in the fourth chapter, move further and deeper into this interior domain. In all of their works, the rational self is broken down to reveal, through aesthetic projections, mystical experiences, and dreams, the pri-mal depths of the modern psyche. While this may replicate 'primitivist' metaphors, the exotic is no longer projected outside the familiar world of the self, but in its repressed depths; and exotic topographies become means of imagining aspects of the self, including its physiology, dreams, erotic and subconscious life, beyond the reach of rational self-reflection. In primitivist depictions of the modern metropolis, studied in the previous chapter, the outward and inward assignments of the exotic converge. Features and forces traditionally and problematically associated with 'primitive' peoples are located, not in an elsewhere far from Europe or America, but in its urban centres. In Brecht's drama, alongside works of Expressionist painters and writers, the depiction of the city serves to illuminate the fragility and precariousness of the modern subject in its

exposure to the experience of urban life. At the same time, this depiction
of the metropolis sheds a critical light on the central material achievement
and prototypical space of modernity.

In the 1994 afterword to *Orientalism*, Said addressed some of the
criticisms of his and other post-colonial theories that expose the depiction
of non-Western cultures and places as politically charged fabrications of
the European (and American) imagination. Said here reflects on the
construction of identity as a polarization between self and other. He
writes:

> The construction of identity ... involves the construction of opposites and
> 'others' whose actuality is always subject to the continuous interpretation
> and re-interpretation of their differences from 'us'. Far from a static thing
> then, identity of self or of 'other' is a much worked-over historical, social,
> intellectual, and political process. . . . What makes [this] difficult to accept is
> that most people resist the underlying notion: that human identity is not
> only not natural and stable, but constructed, and occasionally even invented
> outright.

The hostility to his theory, Said argues, is that it undermines the 'naive
belief in the certain positivity and unchanging historicity of a culture, a
self, a national identity'.[1] Said's work, and post-colonial critics in general,
have contributed immeasurably to exposing the constructed nature of the
identities of 'others'. *Orientalism*'s main charge, as discussed in the
Introduction and mentioned throughout this study, is that the imagination of non-Western others by European writers has contributed to their
exploitation, at the very least by complicit affirmation of the European
perspective. By speaking for and identifying 'others', the European sense
of self and of its own superiority is bolstered. Yet Orientalist critique of
representations of others has worked principally on that pole of this
opposition: how and that the other is defined or identified, and has
done little to interrogate its own assumptions about the apparently dominating 'self' in question. The imaginative engagement with what is
foreign, mysterious, alluring, or frightening, such as the exotic has been
defined in this book, may contest the other pole, the 'us' of the writer and
reader's Eurocentric world from whom the other is perceived as different.
While often beginning with traditional positions of the European or
German self and of the exotic 'other' to which it is exposed (for instance,
Hofmannsthal's Andreas arrives in Venice during his *Bildungsreise*; Hesse
is a tourist in India; Zweig's *Amokläufer* is a colonial doctor in the Dutch
East Indies), the works studied here largely unravel or undermine the

---

[1] Said (1979/1994: 332).

identity of the self in its presumed autonomy, psychological or moral integrity, and professional or cultural neutrality. The exposure to the 'foreign', even imaginatively, does not only work to project and fix an identity for the other; it may also transform the imagined identity of the protagonist, narrator, or implied reader.

This study has served to demonstrate the ways in which modern German literature has enacted various modes of contest for the accepted or traditional sense of self, identity, and culture. Thus, it corrects merely utopian interpretations of exotic spaces in these texts, as well unilaterally critical accounts or dismissals of any evocation of the exotic or primitive as inherently Orientalist. While such interpretations contribute valuable criticism of the material and political contexts of exotic spaces evoked in these texts, it has been shown that they may overlook complex possibilities for critical cultural, existential, and aesthetic self-reflection, for non-appropriative appreciation of what is foreign, or for liberation of the modern imagination. Nearly all of the authors discussed in this study (certainly Hofmannsthal, Hesse, Dauthendey, Musil, Benn, Kubin, Rilke, and Brecht) evoke exotic spaces as a means to critically examine the modern European or Western way of life from the perspective of radically other possibilities of thinking and being. They suggest that exposure to the exotic affords cultural and spiritual renewal, imaginative freedom, and aesthetic creativity precisely because it challenges the dominant forms of Western thinking. For Kafka, too, exotic topographies, particularly those characterized by vastness and interior distances, allow the conception of a critical 'elsewhere' where the imagination can escape the seeming ubiquity of power. Where other authors (Mann and Zweig, in particular) warn more explicitly about the dangers of transgressing the boundary between the familiar and the exotic 'other', they also suggest the illusory nature of cultural attitudes that would keep the exotic other at a safe distance. More radically, they expose the precariousness and even illusoriness of boundaries between the familiar and the foreign, since such boundaries are vulnerable to rupture from without (infection) and from within (erotic desire), and where these converge, from both directions at once.

The unilateral indictment of any evocation of the 'exotic' by European writers may be resisted, then, in favour of a more differentiated and nuanced approach such as that advanced here. This approach addresses within literary texts the mobility and contestation of the very conceptual oppositions fixed upon in such indictments: us and them, self and other, familiar and foreign, ordinary and exotic, Western and Eastern, occidental and Oriental, rational and irrational, scientific and mystical, civilized and natural, tame and barbaric, predictable and unpredictable, and so forth. Even works that are in some ways problematic may be innovative or revolutionary in others. For instance, Brecht's *Im Dickicht der Städte* examined in Chapter 5 reproduces Orientalist stereotypes, even in offensive ways, but the text also invites critical reflection on racial divisions, oppression, and violence. Still more problematic, Benn's evocations of the exotic in *Gehirne*, while relying on problematic and racist imagery of the non-European, nevertheless challenges in a radical way the supposed superiority of Western rationality and of its scientific objectification of humanity, as shown in Chapter 4.

In the wake of the now well-established critique of exploitive and imperialist literary representations of exotic 'others', the status of the exotic, and of self and the foreign, may be examined from a differentiating perspective that registers not only the social and political conditions of literary and cultural production but also, as has been emphasized here, the contradictions and paradoxes immanent to the literary work itself. This requires attention not only to the psychological, political, and cultural event of the work but also to the work's formal qualities, intertextual references, strategies and frameworks of spatial depiction, mobility of focus, narrative stability or instability, contradictory imagery, metaphors, departure from or maintenance of descriptive mimesis and ordinary syntax, ambiguities, its relations to traditional forms and innovations beyond them, and its epistemological assumptions and usurpations. It requires taking seriously the potential liberation from the real afforded by the literary and aesthetic imagination. Far from the mere reproduction or representation of the material and cultural conditions of its genesis, the fictional and the poetic creation may generate other ideas about living and being, other configurations of and perspectives on reality, other registrations of the 'other' than afforded by the political realities of its time or of our own.

Descriptions of the exotic in these works sometimes do fall prey to cultural stereotyping, racially insensitive or racist imagery, and some (though not all) of the authors examined in this book fail to note the disastrous effects of European presence in colonized places. These cases must be critically examined and exposed. Yet these texts also present important explorations of the relationship between self and world, self and other, that cannot be reduced to symbolic colonialism, to an exercise or critique of Orientalism, to a political depiction of the self's existential paralysis, or to the problematic projection of utopian paradise. The possibility of a humane relationship to what is perceived as exotic requires exploration and (re-)negotiation of the boundaries between self and other, even if that comes with risk for both. The imagination itself must be engaged, not only identified as complicit, and though any representation of the other may be implicated in 'urgent social contests', this does not

exhaust their meaning for the underlying human questions that may
motivate them.[2] These include the possibilities of the human imagination
in transforming the world at hand, transcending the given circumstances
of things, include the projection of the possible onto and over the 'actual'
by means of language, and the capacity to shed critical light on assumptions about the very status and form of spaces and places we inhabit.

This study has been framed by the particular focus on the problem of
modern self within the exposure to the exotic and has had to respect some
limitations of scope. Since consideration of some relevant authors and
themes has had to be left aside, it might be mentioned in conclusion what
further avenues for research may be opened up. Expansion of this project
may, first of all, take into account other writers whose exoticizing narratives or poetics further illustrate the contest between the European self-
understanding and the imagination of exotic places or others. For example, without repeating the existing surveys of such texts, Alfred Döblin's
novel *Die drei Sprünge des Wang-lun* (1915), set in eighteenth-century
China, may be mentioned, and similarly the impact of Russia (and his
imagination of the East) on Rilke's poetry and his understanding of the
West. Further, the relationship between Orientalizing exoticism and
cultural identity in German-Jewish writers may be analysed in the works
of Else Lasker-Schüler (for instance in *Die Nächte Tino Bagdads* and *Der
Prinz von Theben*), Franz Werfel (*Die vierzig Tage des Musa Dagh*), and
Friedrich Wolf (*Mohammed: Ein Oratorium*). For all of these writers, the
depiction of exotic places or peoples enabled some exploration of otherness and marginality with which they may have identified, and this would
be only more complicated by the crisis that developed for Jewish writers by
the 1930s. It would be worthwhile to consider how the early Romantic
and Idealist conceptions of the exotic in the previous century (in Hegel,
Novalis, Schlegel, and Hölderlin, for instance) are both echoed and
radically transformed in these texts.

Further research may, too, consider the impact of historical events and
cultural transformations on the imagination of exotic places, and pose new
questions regarding the cultural conceptions of place and space. The
specific impact of the First World War within Europe, not to mention
the attending shifts in colonial and national relations, may be seen to
transform modernist writers' and artists' portrayals of the 'exotic' and of
otherness in general. The description and diagnosis of modernism itself,
too, may be examined in the light of its unravelling juxtaposition with the
exotic. Analysis may focus on the relation between the desire for otherness

[2] Said (1979/1994: 332).

of place and atmosphere adapted from Romantic *Fernweh*, and modernism's self-conscious critical reflection. Finally, the both ethical and existential question may be asked concerning the impact the erasure of the sense of the exotic or of a radical 'elsewhere' for the literary imagination, and for cultural self-understanding in an increasingly global world. If exoticization is complicit in fortifying assumptions about the otherness of seemingly radically different places and peoples, are these places and peoples better understood or more genially approached without the connotations of mystery and inaccessibility that attend the notion of the 'exotic'? To what extent does de-exoticization, in other words, promote a more accurate or generous understanding of cultural others, and to what extent may it diminish real differences, and force an ungenial homogeneity, in the facilitation of assimilation or in the name of efficiency?

Finally, apart from the literary and cultural questions, we can ask about the ecological implications of the original idea, discussed throughout this book, that our experience of place and space is imaginatively endowed. What results from the de-exoticization, in the wake of modernist literature and art, of places thought once to belong to a radical 'elsewhere'? The imagination of natural places and spaces has been subject to radical change; the very idea of an 'elsewhere' in contemporary global culture may be somewhat antiquated or even nostalgic. Contrary to Hesse's assumption (discussed in Chapter 1) that the forests of Asia (and we could add other 'exotic' natural spaces) could never be conquered by technical human efforts, radical and rapid development threatens their very disappearance. It may be that the sense, germane to many indigenous cultures deemed 'exotic' to the modern European writer, that specific natural places may be resistant to total human comprehension, was part of the balance between human activity and ecological integrity. The de-exoticization, or loss of symbolic otherness, of natural places, may be related to their destruction.

Bibliography

*Bibliographical Note: Primary sources cited more than once will be cited in the
text according to the abbreviations below, followed by the volume number, in
the case of collected works. Other sources will be cited in footnotes by author's
name and the year of publication.*

I. PRIMARY SOURCES, FOLLOWED BY ABBREVIATIONS IN BRACKETS

Adorno, Theodor, 'Aufzeichnungen zu Kafka', *Gesammelte Schriften*, 10.1
(Frankfurt am Main: Suhrkamp, 1977). [GS]

Benjamin, Walter, *Gesammelte Schriften*, Unter Mitwirkung von Theodor Adorno
und Gershom Scholem, ed. Rolf Tiedemann and Hermann Schweppenhäuser
(Frankfurt am Main: Suhrkamp, 1989). [GS]

Benn, Gottfried, *Sämtliche Werke. Stuttgarter Ausgabe*, ed. Gerhard Schuster
(Stuttgart: Klett Verlag, 1989). [SW]

Brecht, Bertolt, *Gesammelte Werke. Werkausgabe Edition Suhrkamp*, 20 vols.
(Frankfurt am Main: Suhrkamp, 1967). [GW]

Brecht, Bertolt, *Werke. Berliner und Frankfurter Ausgabe*, ed. Werner Hecht, Jan
Knopf, Werner Mittenzwei, and Klaus-Detlef Müller (Berlin and Weimar:
Aufbau-Verlag; Frankfurt am Main: Suhrkamp, 1989). [W]

Dauthendey, Max, *Geschichten aus den vier Winden* (Munich: Albert Langen,
1921). [GVW]

Dauthendey, Max, *Lingam. Zwölf asiatische Novellen* (Munich: Albert Langen,
1923). [L]

Dauthendey, Max, *Gesammelte Werke* (Munich: Albert Langen, 1925). [GW]

Dauthendey, Max, *Sieben Meere nahmen mich auf*, ed. Hermann Gerstner
(Munich: Albert Langen/Georg Müller, 1957). [SM]

Freud, Sigmund, *Werkausgabe in zwei Bänden*, ed. Anna Freud and Ilse Grubrich-
Smitis (Frankfurt am Main: Fischer Taschenbuch, 2006). [WA]

Hesse, Hermann, *Sämtliche Werke*, ed. Volker Michels (Frankfurt am Main:
Suhrkamp, 2003). [SW]

Hofmannsthal, Hugo von, *Gesammelte Werke in Einzelausgaben. Aufzeichnungen*,
ed. Herbert Steiner (Frankfurt am Main: Fischer, 1959). [GWE/A]

Hofmannsthal, Hugo von, and Schnitzler, Arthur, *Briefwechsel*, ed. Therese Nickl
and Heinrich Schnitzler (Frankfurt am Main: Fischer, 1964).

Hofmannsthal, Hugo von, *Gesammelte Werke in zehn Einzelbänden*, ed. Bernd
Schoeller (Frankfurt am Main: Fischer, 1979). [GW]

Hofmannsthal, Hugo von, *Sämtliche Werke. Kritische Ausgabe* (Frankfurt am
Main: Fischer, 1982–). [SW]

Hölderlin, Friedrich, *Werke und Briefe*, ed. Friedrich Beissner and Jochen Schmidt (Frankfurt am Main: Insel Verlag, 1969). [WB]

Kafka, Franz, *Gesammelte Werke*, ed. Max Brod (Frankfurt am Main/New York: Fischer/Schocken, 1946). [GW]

Kafka, Franz, *Kritische Ausgabe*, ed. Jürgen Born, Gerhard Neumann, Malcolm Pasley, and Jost Schillemeit (Frankfurt am Main/New York: Fischer/Schocken, 1983–). [KA/T = *Tagebücher*; KA/DL = *Drucke zu Lebzeiten*; NS/I and NS/II = *Nachgelassene Schriften und Fragmente I* and *II*].

Kubin, Alfred, *Aus meiner Werkstatt. Gesammelte Prosa mit 71 Abbildunggen*, ed. Ulrich Riemerschmidt (Munich: Nymphenburger Verlagshandlung, 1973). [AW]

Kubin, Alfred, *Aus meinem Leben. Gesammelte Prosa mit 73 Zeichnungen*, ed. Ulrich Riemerschmidt (Munich: DTV, 1974). [AL]

Kubin, Alfred, *Die andere Seite. Ein phantastischer Roman* (Reinbek bei Hamburg: Rowohlt, 1998). [AS]

Mann, Thomas, *Gesammelte Werke in zwölf Bänden* (Frankfurt am Main: Fischer, 1974). [GW]

Mann, Thomas, *Der Tod in Venedig: Text, Materialien, Kommentar*, ed. T. J. Reed (Munich: Hanser, 1983).

Mann, Thomas, *Große kommentierte Frankfurter Ausgabe* (Frankfurt am Main: Fischer, 2001–). [FA]

Montaigne, Michel de, *Les Essais de Michel de Montaigne*, ed. Pierre Villey (Paris: Presses Universitaires de France, 1978).

Musil, Robert, *Gesammelte Werke in neuen Bänden*, ed. Adolf Frisé (Reinbek bei Hamburg: Rowohlt, 1978/1981). [GW]

Musil, Robert, *Briefe 1901–1942*, ed. Adolf Frisé (Reinbek bei Hamburg: Rowohlt, 1981). [B]

Musil, Robert, *Tagebücher*, ed. Adolf Frisé (Reinbek bei Hamburg: Rowohlt, 1983). [T]

Nietzsche, Friedrich, *Werke. Kritische Gesamtausgabe*, ed. Giorgio Colli and Mazzino Montinari (Berlin: de Gruyter, 1968). [KG]

Proust, Marcel, *A la recherche du temps perdu*, vol. i (Paris: Gallimard, 1954).

Rilke, Rainer Maria, *Briefe. Erster Band 1897 bis 1914*, ed. Rilke-Archiv with Ruth Sieber-Rilke (Wiesbaden: Insel-Verlag, 1950). [B/I]

Rilke, Rainer Maria, *Kommentierte Ausgabe in Vier Bänden*, ed. Manfred Engel (Frankfurt am Main und Leipzig: Insel, 1996). [KA]

Schopenhauer, Arthur, *Sämtliche Werke*, ed. Wolfgang Frhr. von Löhneysen (Frankfurt am Main: Suhrkamp, 1986). [SW]

Simmel, Georg, *Gesamtausgabe Band 7. Aufsätzte und Abhandlungen 1901–1908, I*, ed. Rüdiger Dramme, Angela Rammstedt and Otthein Rammstedt (Frankfurt am Main: Suhrkamp 1993). [GA7]

Simmel, Georg, *Gesamtausgabe Band 8. Aufsätze und Abhandlungen 1901–1908, II*, ed. Otthein Rammstedt, Alessandro Cavalli and Volkhard Krech (Frankfurt am Main: Suhrkamp, 1993). [GA8]

Simmel, Georg, *Gesamtausgabe Band 16. Der Krieg und die geistigen Entscheidungen. Grundfragen der Soziologie. Vom Wesen des historischen Verstehens. Der Konflikt der modernen Kultur. Lebensanschauung*, ed. Gregor Fitzi und Otthein Rammstedt (Frankfurt am Main: Suhrkamp, 1999). [GA16]

Weber, Max, *Gesammelte Aufsätze zur Religionssoziologie* (Tübingen: Mohr, 1988). [GA]

Zweig, Stefan, *Begegnungen mit Menschen Büchern Städten* (Berlin and Frankfurt am Main: Fischer, 1955). [BMBS]

Zweig, Stefan, *Die Welt von Gestern. Erinnerungen eines Europäers* (Berlin and Frankfurt am Main: Fischer, 1962). [WG]

Zweig, Stefan, *Der Amokläufer. Erzählungen.* (Frankfurt am Main: Fischer, 1984). [A]

II. SECONDARY AND OTHER SOURCES

Adorno, Theodor, 'Aufzeichnungen zu Kafka', *Gesammelte Schriften*, 10.1 (Frankfurt am Main: Suhrkamp, 1977).

Ahern, Daniel R., *Nietzsche as Cultural Physician* (University Park: Pennsylvania State University Press, 1995).

Aldrich, Robert, *The Seduction of the Mediterranean: Writing, Art and Homosexual Fantasy* (London: Routledge, 1993).

Alewyn, Richard, *Über Hugo von Hofmannsthal.* Zweite, verbesserte Auflage (Göttingen: Vandenhoeck & Ruprecht, 1960).

Anderson, Mark, 'Kafka and New York: Notes on a Traveling Narrative', in *Modernity and the Text: Revisions of German Modernism*, ed. Andreas Huyssen and David Bathrick (New York: Columbia University Press, 1989a).

Anderson, Mark, *Reading Kafka: Prague, Politics, and the Fin de Siècle* (New York: Schocken, 1989b).

Anderson, Mark, *Kafka's Clothes: Ornament and Aestheticism in the Habsburg Fin de Siècle* (Oxford: Clarendon Press, 1992).

Anderson, Mark, 'Kafka, Homosexuality, and the Aesthetics of "Male Culture"', *Austrian Studies*, 7 (1996), 79–99.

Anderson, Mark, 'Mann's Early Novellas', in *The Cambridge Companion to Thomas Mann*, ed. Ritchie Robertson (Cambridge: Cambridge University Press, 2002).

Arndal, Steffen, 'Ohne alle Kenntnis von Perspektive'? Zur Raumperzeption in Rainer Maria Rilkes *Aufzeichnungen des Malte Laurids Brigge*', *Deutsche Vierteljahrsschrift für Literaturwissenschaft und Geistesgeschichte* (2002), 105–137.

Bachelard, Gaston, *La Poétique de l'espace* (Paris: Presses Universitaires de France, 1957).

Bakhtin, Mikhail, *The Dialogic Imagination: Four Essays*, ed. Michael Holquist, trans. Caryl Emerson and Michael Holquist (Austin and London: University of Texas Press, 1981).

Bauschinger, Sigrid, Denkler, Horst, and Malsch, Wilfried (eds.), *Amerika in der deutschen Literatur. Neue Welt—NordAmerika—USA* (Stuttgart: Philipp Reclam, 1975).

Berman, Nina, 'K.u.K. Colonialism: Hofmannsthal in North Africa', *New German Critique*, 75 (Fall 1998), 3–27.

Berman, Russell A., *Enlightenment or Empire: Colonial Discourse in German Culture* (Lincoln and London: University of Nebraska Press, 1998).

Bertram, Ernst, *Nietzsche: Versuch einer Mythologie*. 8. um einen Anhang erweiterte Auflage (Bonn: Bouvier, 1965).

Best, Otto F., 'Einleitung', in *Expressionismus und Dadaismus*, ed. Otto F. Best (Stuttgart: Reclam, 1974).

Block, Ed, Jr., 'Journey as Self-Revelation: Hugo von Hofmannsthal's *Reiseprosa*, 1893–1917', *Modern Austrian Literature*, 20: 1 (1987), 23–35.

Boa, Elizabeth, 'Global Intimations: Cultural Geography in *Buddenbrooks*, *Tonio Kröger*, and *Der Tod in Venedig*', *Oxford German Studies*, 35 (2006), 21–33.

Boa, Elizabeth, and Palfreyman, Rachel, *Heimat: A German Dream. Regional Loyalties and National Identity in German Culture, 1890–1990* (Oxford: Oxford University Press, 2000).

Börner, Klaus, 'Was die Paradisvögel erzählen—Max Dauthendeys "javanische" Märchen', in *Literatur und Regionalität*, ed. Anselm Maler (Frankfurt am Main: Peter Lang, 1997).

Breidbach, Olaf, *Die Materialisierung des Ichs. Zur Geschichte der Hirnforschung im 19. und 20. Jahrhundert* (Frankfurt am Main: Suhrkamp, 1997).

Brenner, Peter J., 'Die Erfahrung der Fremde. Zur Entwicklung einer Wahrnehmungsform in der Geschichte des Reiseberichts', in *Der Reisebericht. Die Entwicklung einer Gattung in der deutschen Literatur*, ed. Peter J. Brenner (Frankfurt am Main: Suhrkamp, 1989).

Brinkley, Edward S., 'Fear of Form: Thomas Mann's *Der Tod in Venedig*', *Monatshefte*, 91 (1999), 2–27.

Büssgen, Antje, 'Dissoziationserfahrung und Totalitätssehnsucht. "Farbe" als Vokabel im "Diskurs des Eigentlichen" der klassischen Moderne. Zu Hugo Hofmannsthals "Briefe des Zurückgekehrten" und Gottfried Benns "Der Garten von Arles"', *Zeitschrift für deutsche Philologie*, 124 (2005), 520–555.

Clifford, James, 'On Collecting Art and Culture', in *Out There: Marginalization and Contemporary Cultures*, ed. Russell Ferguson, Martha Gever, Trinh T. Minh-Ha, and Cornel West (New York: New Museum of Contemporary Art and Cambridge Mass: MIT Press, 1990).

Corino, Karl, *Robert Musil. Eine Biographie* (Reinbek bei Hamburg: Rowohlt, 2003).

Corne, Johah, 'Asphalt Jungles: Urbanism and Primitivism in Georg Simmel and Wilhelm Worringer', in *Georg Simmel in Translation: Interdisciplinary Border-Crossings in Culture and Modernity*, ed. David D. Kim (Cambridge: Cambridge Scholars Press, 2006).

Corngold, Stanley, *Lambent Traces: Franz Kafka* (Princeton, N.J.: Princeton University Press, 2004).

Cowan, Michael, *Cult of the Will: Nervousness and German Modernity* (University Park: Pennsylvania State University Press, 2008).

Dahme, Hans-Jürgen, and Rammstedt, Otthein, *Georg Simmel und die Moderne. Neue Interpretationen und Materialien* (Frankfurt am Main: Suhrkamp, 1984).

Defoe, Daniel, *A Journal of the Plague Year (1721)*, ed. Paula Backscheider (New York: Norton, 1992).

Dierick, Augustinus P., 'Nihilism and "tierische Transzendenz"' in Gottfried Benn's *Gehirne*', *Orbis Litterarum*, 36 (1981), 211–221.

Dierick, Augustinus P., *German Expressionist Prose: Theory and Practice* (Toronto: Toronto University Press, 1987).

Dierick, Augustinus P., *Gottfried Benn and His Critics: Major Interpretations, 1912–1992* (Columbia, S.C.: Camden House, 1992).

Dodd, W. J., 'Dostoyevskian Elements in Kafka's Penal Colony', *German Life and Letters*, 37: 1 (October 1983), 11–23.

Dunker, Axel (ed.), *(Post-)Kolonialismus und deutsche Literatur: Impulse der angloamerikanischen Literatur- und Kulturtheorie* (Bielefeld: Aisthesis, 2005).

Dürr, Volker, '"Die Mythe Log": Gottfried Benns perspektivistische Poetic des Raums aus dem Geist des Ahistorischen', *Michigan Germanic Studies*, 15: 1 (1989), 51–70.

Edscmid, Kasimir, 'Über den dichterischen Expressionismus', in *Kasimir Edschmid., Frühe Manifeste. Epochen des Expressionismus* (Hamburg: Wegner, 1957).

Eibl, Karl, *Robert Musil: 'Drei Frauen.' Text, Materialien, Kommentar* (Munich and Vienna: Carl Hanser Verlag, 1978).

Eilittå, Leena, 'Art as Religious Commitment: Kafka's Debt to Kierkegaardian Ideas and Their Impact on His Late Stories', *German Life and Letters*, 53 (2000), 499–510.

Elger, Dietmar, *Expressionism* (Cologne: Taschen, 2002).

Eliot, T. S., *The Use of Poetry and the Use of Criticism* (London: Faber and Faber, 1932).

Elsaghe, Yahya A., 'Zur Sexualisierung des Fremden im *Tod in Venedig*', *Archiv für das Studium der neueren Sprachen und Literaturen*, 234 (1997), 19–32.

Elsaghe, Yahya A., *Die imaginäre Nation. Thomas Mann und das 'Deutsche'* (Munich: Fink, 2000).

Emerson, Ralph Waldo, *The Heart of Emerson's Journals*, ed. Bliss Perry (New York: Dover, 1958).

Engel, Manfred, 'Außenwelt und Innenwelt. Subjektivitätsentwurf und moderne Romanpoetik in Robert Walsers *Jakob von Gunten* und Franz Kafkas *Der Verschollene*', *Jahrbuch der deutschen Schillergesellschaft*, 30 (1996), 533–570.

Engel, Manfred, '"Weder Seiende, noch Schauspieler": Zum Subjektivitätsentwurf in Rilkes "Malte Laurids Brigge"', in *Rilke Heute, Bd. 3*, ed. Ingeborg H. Solbrig and Joachim W. Storck (Frankfurt am Main: Suhrkamp, 1997).

Engel, Manfred, 'Rilke als Autor der literarischen Moderne', in *Rilke-Handbuch. Leben-Werk-Wirkung*, ed. Manfred Engel with Dorothea Lauterbach (Stuttgart and Weimar: Metzler, 2004).

Engelberg, Edward, 'Ambiguous Solitude: Hans Castorp's Sturm und Drang nach Osten', in *A Companion to Thomas Mann's* The Magic Mountain, ed. Stephen D. Dowden (Columbia, S.C.: Camden House, 1999).

Engelhardt, Dietrich von, 'Tuberkulose und Kultur um 1900. Arzt, Patient, und Sanatorium in Thomas Manns *Zauberberg* aus medizinhistorischer Sicht', in *Auf dem Weg zum 'Zauberberg'*, ed. Thomas Sprecher, *Thomas-Mann Studien*, 16 (Frankfurt am Main: Klostermann, 1996).

Enjuto-Rangel, Cecilia, 'Broken Presents: The Modern City in Ruins in Baudelaire, Cernudo, and Paz', *Comparative Literature*, 59 (2007), 140–157.

Faath, U., 'Rainer Maria Rilke und Georg Simmel: Wechselwirkung zwischen Philosophie und Literatur', *Blätter der Rilke-Gesellschaft*, 23 (2000), 53–64.

Fieguth, Rolf, 'Zur literarischen Bedeutung des Bedeutungslosen. Das Polnische in Thomas Manns Novelle "Der Tod in Venedig"', in *Studien zur Kulturgeschichte des deutschen Polenbildes*, ed. Hendrik Feindt (Wiesbaden: Harrassowitz, 1995).

Foster, Cheryl, 'Ideas and Imagination: Schopenhauer on the Proper Foundation of Art', in *The Cambridge Companion to Schopenhauer*, ed. Christopher Janaway (Cambridge: Cambridge University Press, 1999).

Foucault, Michel, *The Birth of the Clinic: An Archaeology of Medical Perception*, trans. A. M. Sheridan (London: Routledge, 1989).

Freund, W., Lachinger, J., Ruthner, C. (eds.), *Der Demiurg ist ein Zwitter: Alfred Kubin und die deutschsprachige Phantastik* (Munich: Fink, 1999).

Friedrichsmeyer, Sara, Lennox, Sara, and Zantop, Suzanne (eds.), *The Imperialist Imagination: German Colonialism and Its Legacy* (Ann Arbor: University of Michigan Press, 1998).

Frisby, David, 'Introduction to the Translation', in Georg Simmel, *The Philosophy of Money*, trans. Tom Bottomore and David Frisby (London: Routledge & Kegan, 1978).

Frisby, David, *Sociological Impressionism* (London: Routledge, 1991).

Frisby, David, 'Preface to the Third Edition', George Simmel, *The Philosophy of Money*, 3rd enlarged edn (London: Routledge, 2004), xv–xlvi.

Fuchs, Anne, and Harden, Theo (eds.), *Reisen im Diskurs. Modelle der literarischen Fremderfahrung von den Pilgerberichten bis zur Postmoderne* (Heidelberg: Winter, 1995).

Fuchs-Sumiyoshi, Andrea, *Orientalismus in der deutschen Literatur. Untersuchungen zu Werken des 19. und 20. Jahrhunderts von Goethes 'West-östlichen Divan' bis Thomas Manns 'Joseph' Tetralogie* (Hildesheim: Georg Olms, 1984).

Furness, R. S., *Expressionism* (London: Methuen, 1973).

Ganeshan, Vidhagiri, *Das Indienbild deutscher Dichter um 1900* (Bonn: Bouvier, 1975).

Gerhards, Claudia, *Apokalypse und Moderne. Alfred Kubins 'Die andere Seite' und Ernst Jüngers Frühwerk* (Würzburg: Königshausen & Neumann, 1999).

Geyer, Andreas, *Träumer auf Lebenszeit: Alfred Kubin als Literat* (Vienna, Cologne, and Weimar: Böhlau Verlag, 1995).

Gikandi, Simon, 'Picasso, Africa, and the Schemata of Difference', *Modernism/ Modernity*, 10 (2003), 455–480.

Giobbi, Giuliana, 'Gabriele d'Annunzio and Thomas Mann: Venice, Art, and Death', *Journal of European Studies*, 19 (1989), 55–68.

Girard, René, *Violence and the Sacred* (New York: Continuum, 2005).

Gluck, Mary, 'Interpreting Primitivism, Mass Culture and Modernism: The Making of Wilhelm Worringer's Abstraction and Empathy', *New German Critique*, 80 (Spring–Summer 2000), 149–169.

Goebel, Rolf J., *Constructing China: Kafka's Orientalist Discourse* (Columbia, S.C.: Camden House, 1997).

Goebel, Rolf J., 'Kafka and Postcolonial Critique: *Der Verschollene*, "In der Strafkolonie", "Beim Bau der Chinesischen Mauer"', in *A Companion to the Works of Franz Kafka*, ed. James Rolleston (Columbia, S.C.: Camden House, 2002).

Goetschel, Willi, '"Land of Truth—Enchanting Name!" Kant's Journey at Home', in *The Imperialist Imagination: German Colonialism and Its Legacy*, ed. Sara Friedrichsmeyer, Sara Lennox, and Susanne Zantop (Ann Arbor: Univeristy of Michigan Press, 1998).

Gökberk, Ülker, 'War as Mentor: Thomas Mann and Germanness', in *A Companion to Thomas Mann's* The Magic Mountain, ed. Stephen D. Dowden (Columbia, S.C.: Camden House, 1999).

Goltschnigg, Dietmar, *Mystische Tradition im Roman Robert Musils: Martin Bubers 'Ekstatische Konfessionen' im 'Mann ohne Eigenschaften'* (Heidelberg: Stiehm, 1974).

Görner, Rüdiger, 'Hofmannsthals Orientalismus', in *'Wenn die Rosenhimmel tanzen': Orientalische Motivik in der deutschsprachigen Literatur des 19. und 20. Jahrhunderts*. Publications of the Institute of Germanic Studies, School of Advanced Study, University of London, Bd. 87, ed. Rüdiger Görner and Nima Mina (Munich: Iudicium, 2006).

Görner, Rüdiger, and Mina, Nima (eds.), *'Wenn die Rosenhimmel tanzen': orientalische Motivik in der deutschsprachigen Literatur des 19. und 20. Jahrhunderts*. Publications of the Institute of Germanic Studies, School of Advanced Study, University of London, Bd. 87 (Munich: Iudicium, 2006).

Grill, Genese, 'The "Other" Musil: Robert Musil and Mysticism', in *A Companion to the Works of Robert Musil*, ed. Philip Payne, Graham Bartram, and Galin Tihanov (Rochester, N.Y.: Camden House, 2007).

Gründer, Horst (ed.), *'. . . da und dort ein junges Deutschland gründen.' Rassismus, Kolonien, und kolonialer Gedanke vom 16. bis zum 20. Jahrhundert* (Munich: Deutscher Taschenbuch, 1999).

Gründer, Horst, *Geschichte der deutschen Kolonien. 5 Auflage.* (Stuttgart: Uni-Taschenbuch, 2004).

Habermas, Jürgen, *The Philosophical Discourse of Modernity: Twelve Lectures*, trans. Frederick Lawrence (Cambridge, Mass.: MIT Press, 1990).

Hamburger, Käte, 'Die phänomenologische Struktur der Dichtung Rilkes', in *Rilke in neuer Sicht*, ed. Käte Hamburger (Stuttgart: W. Kohlhammer, 1971).

Hamburger, Käte, *Rilke. Eine Einführung* (Stuttgart: Ernst Klett, 1976).

Hamburger, Käte, 'Die Kategorie des Raums in Rilkes Lyrik', *Blätter der Rilke-Gesellschaft*, 15 (1988), 35–42.

Hamburger, Michael, 'Hofmannsthals Bibliothek: Ein Bericht', *Euphorion*, 55 (1961), 15–76.

Hamlyn, D. W., *Schopenhauer* (London: Routledge and Kegan Paul, 1980).

Harding, Desmond, *Writing the City: Urban Visions and Literary Modernism* (New York and London: Routledge, 2003).

Harvey, David, *Paris, Capital of Modernity* (New York: Routledge, 2003).

Haxthausen, Charles W., ' "A New Beauty": Ernst Ludwig Kirchner's Images of Berlin', in *Berlin: Culture and Metropolis*, ed. Charles W. Haxthausen and Heidrun Suhr (Minneapolis: University of Minnesota Press, 1991).

Hedwig, Anneliese, *Phantastische Wirklichkeit. Kubins 'Die andere Seite'* (Munich: Fink, 1967).

Hegel, G. W. F., *Vorlesungen über die Ästhetik*, in *Ästhetik*, ed. Friedrich Bassenge (Frankfurt am Main: Europäische Verlagsanstalt, 1955).

Heimböckel, Dieter, ' "Amerika im Kopf": Franz Kafkas Roman *Der Verschollene* und der Amerika-Diskurs seiner Zeit', *Deutsche Vierteljahrsschrift für Literaturwissenschaft und Geistesgeschichte*, 77 (2003), 130–147.

Heizer, Donna K., *Jewish-German Identity in the Orientalist Literature of Else Lasker-Schüler, Friedrich Wolf, and Franz Werfel* (Rochester, N.Y.: Camden House, 1996).

Heller, Erich, *The Artist's Journey into the Interior and Other Essays* (London: Secker & Warburg, 1959).

Henninger, Peter, 'Robert Musil's Novellas in the Collection *Drei Frauen*', in *A Companion to the Works of Robert Musil*, ed. Philip Payne, Graham Bartram, and Galin Tihanov (Rochester, N.Y.: Camden House, 2007).

Hoeber, Fritz, 'Georg Simmel', *Neue Jahrbücher für das klassische Altertum, Geschichte, und deutsche Literatur*, 21 (1918), 475–477.

Hoffmann, Martina, *Thomas Manns 'Der Tod in Venedig.' Eine Entwicklungsgeschichte im Spiegel philosophischer Konzeptionen* (Frankfurt am Main: Peter Lang, 1995).

Holitscher, Arthur, *Amerika: heute und morgen. Reiseerlebnisse* (Berlin: Fischer, 1912).

Holub, Robert C., 'Nietzsche's Colonialist Imagination', in *The Imperialist Imagination: German Colonialism and Its Legacy*, ed. Sara Friedrichsmeyer, Sara Lennox, and Susanne Zantop (Ann Arbor: Univeristy of Michigan Press, 1998).

Honold, Alexander, 'Flüsse, Berge, Eisenbahnen: Szenarien geographischer Bemächtigung', in *Das Fremde. Reiseerfahrungen, Schreibformen und kulturelles Wissen*, ed. Alexander Honold and Klaus R. Scherpe (Bern: Peter Lang, 1999).

Honold, Alexander, 'Kafkas vergleichende Völkerkunde: *Beim Bau der chinesischen Mauer*', in *(Post-)Kolonialismus und deutsche Literatur: Impulse der angloamerikanischen Literatur- und Kulturtheorie*, ed. Axel Dunker (Bielefeld: Aisthesis, 2005).

Honold, Alexander, and Simons, Oliver (eds.), *Kolonialismus als Kultur. Literatur, Medien, Wissenschaft in der deutschen Gründerzeit des Fremden* (Tübingen and Basel: Francke, 2002).

Houe, Poul, 'Vanishing Points, Turning Points, and Points of No Return: Geographies of Somewhere, Elsewhere, and Nowhere', *Orbis Litterarum*, 59 (2004), 1–22.

Huyssen, Andreas, 'Paris/Childhood: The Fragmented Body in Rilke's *Notebooks of Malte Laurids Brigge*', in *Modernity and the Text: Revisions of German Modernism*, ed. Andreas Huyssen and David Bathrick (New York: Columbia University Press, 1989).

Huyssen, Andreas, and Bathrick, David (eds.), *Modernity and the Text: Revisions of German Modernism* (New York: Columbia University Press, 1989).

Ihering, Herbert, *Von Reinhardt bis Brecht. Vier Jahrzehnte Theater und Film. Bd. II 1924–1929* (Berlin: Aufbau-Verlag, 1959).

Irwin, Robert, *Dangerous Knowledge: Orientalism and Its Discontents* (Woodstock and New York: Overlook Press, 2006).

Jacobs, Margaret, 'Introduction', *Hugo von Hofmannsthal: Four Stories* (Oxford: Oxford University Press, 1968).

James, William, *Essays in Pragmatism* (New York: Hafner, 1948).

Janaway, Christopher, *Self and World in Schopenhauer's Philosophy* (Oxford: Oxford University Press, 1989).

Janaway, Christopher, 'Nietzsche, the Self, and Schopenhauer', in *Nietzsche and Modern German Thought*, ed. Keith Ansell-Pearson (London: Routledge, 1991).

Janaway, Christopher, *Schopenhauer* (Oxford: Oxford University Press, 1994).

Jayne, Richard, *The Symbolism of Space and Motion in the Works of Rainer Maria Rilke* (Frankfurt am Main: Athenäum, 1972).

Jonas, Klaus W., 'Stefan Zweig und Thomas Mann: Versuch einer Dokumentation', *Modern Austrian Literature*, 14: 3–4 (1981), 99–135.

Kalberg, Stephen, 'Max Weber's Types of Rationality', *American Journal of Sociology*, 85 (1980), 1145–1179.

Kane, Michael, 'Entgrenzung, Grenzüberschreitung und Ausgrenzung um 1900 oder "Gender, Geography, and Orientation"', in *Reisen im Diskurs. Modelle der literarischen Fremderfahrung von den Pilgerberichten bis zur Postmoderne*, ed. Anne Fuchs and Theo Harden (Heidelberg: Winter, 1995).

Kant, Immanuel, *Kritik der Urteilskraft*, ed. Karl Vorländer (Hamburg: Meiner, 1993).

Keith, Thomas, '"Die Welt als ästhetisches Phänomen." Gottfried Benns Nietzsche-Rezeption', *Zeitschrift für Germanistik, N.F.* 10 (2000), 116–126.

Kleinbard, David, *The Beginning of Terror: A Psychological Study of Rainer Maria Rilke's Life and Work* (New York: New York University Press, 1993).

Kontje, Todd, *German Orientalisms* (Ann Arbor: University of Michigan Press, 2004).

Koppen, Erwin, 'Nationalität und Internationalität im *Zauberberg*', in *Thomas Mann. Aufsätze zum Zauberberg*, ed. Rudolf Wolff (Bonn: Bouvier, 1988).

Kozielek, Gerard (ed.), *Das Polenbild der Deutschen 1772–1848* (Heidelberg: Winter, 1989).

Krotkoff, Herta, 'Zur Symbolik in Thomas Manns *Tod in Venedig*', *Modern Language Notes*, 82 (1967), 445–453.

Krysztofiak, Maria, 'Das Spannungsfeld von Großstadt und Provinz in Rilkes *Die ufzeichnungen des Malte Laurids Brigge*', in *Metropole und Provinz in der österreichischen iteratur des 19. und 20. Jahrhunderts. Beiträge des 10. Österreichisch-Polnischen ermanistentreffens* (Vienna: Zirkular, 1992).

Kühne, Monika, '"es geht in einen über, sei man wie man sei." Kafka als Leser Flauberts', *Archiv für das Studium der neueren Sprachen und Literaturen*, 149 (1997), 293–313.

Kundrus, Birthe, *Moderne Imperialisten. Das Kaiserreich im Spiegel seiner Kolonien* (Cologne, Weimar, and Vienna: Böhlau, 2003).

Kundrus, Birthe (ed.), *Phantasiereiche. Zur Kulturgeschichte des deutschen Kolonialismus* (Frankfurt am Main and New York: Campus, 2003).

Land, Nick, 'Art as Insurrection: The Question of Aesthetics in Kant, Schopenhauer, and Nietzsche', in *Nietzsche and Modern German Thought*, ed. Keith Ansell-Pearson (London: Routledge, 1991).

Lefebvre, Henri, *Introduction to Modernity*, trans. John Moore (London and New York: Verso, 1995).

Leighton, Patricia, 'The White Peril and *l'art nègre*: Picasso, Primitivism and Anti-colonialism', *Art Bulletin*, 72 (1990), 609–630.

Leppmann, Wolfgang, 'Time and Place in *Death in Venice*', *German Quarterly*, 48 (1975), 66–75.

Lévy-Bruhl, Lucien, *Primitive Mentality*, trans. Lilian A. Clare (Boston: Beacon, 1966). First published 1923.

Lévy-Bruhl, Lucien, *How Natives Think*, trans. Lilian A. Clare (London: Allen & Unwin: New York, 1926).

Lippuner, Heinz, *Alfred Kubins Roman 'Die andere Seite'* (Bern and Munich: Francke Verlag, 1977).

Lloyd, Jill, *German Expressionism: Primitivism and Modernity* (New Haven: Yale University Press, 1991).

Lloyd, Jill, and Moeller, Magdalena M. (eds.), *Ernst Ludwig Kirchner: The Dresden and Berlin Years* (London: Royal Academy of Arts, 2003).

Luft, David, *Robert Musil and the Crisis of European Culture 1880–1942* (Berkeley and Los Angeles: University of California Press, 1980).

Luft, David, *Eros and Inwardness in Vienna: Weininger, Musil, Doderer* (Chicago: University of Chicago Press, 2003).

Lund, Roger D., 'Infectious Wit: Metaphor, Atheism, and the Plague in Eighteenth-Century London', *Literature and Medicine*, 22 (2003), 45–64.

McBratney, John, *Imperial Subjects, Imperial Space: Rudyard Kipling's Fiction of the Native-Born* (Columbus: Ohio State University Press, 2002).

McBride, Patrizia C., *The Void of Ethics: Robert Musil and the Experience of Modernity* (Evanston, Ill.: Northwestern University Press, 2006).

McLaughlin, Joseph, *Writing the Urban Jungle: Reading Empire in London from Doyle to Eliot* (Charlottesville: University of Virginia Press, 2000).

Martens, Gunter, 'Nietzsches Wirkung im Expressionismus,' in *Forschungsergebnisse: Nietzsche und die deutsche Literatur*, Deutsche Texte 51, ed. Bruno Hillebrand (Tübingen: Niemeyer/DTV, 1978).

Mattenklott, Gert, 'Der Begriff der kulturellen Räume bei Hofmannsthal', in *Hugo von Hofmannsthal. Freundschaften und Begegnungen mit deutschen Zeitgenossen*, ed. Ursula Renner and G. Bärbel Schmid (Würzburg: Königshausen & Neumann, 1991).

May, Keith M., *Nietzsche and Modern Literature: Themes in Yeats, Rilke, Mann, and Lawrence* (New York: St. Martin's Press, 1988).

Meekseper, Cord, and Schraut, Elisabeth (eds.), *Die Stadt in der Literatur* (Göttingen: Vandenboeck & Ruprecht, 1983).

Meredith, Stephen C., 'Mortal Illness on the Magic Mountain', in *A Companion to Thomas Mann's* The Magic Mountain, ed. Stephen D. Dowden (Columbia, S.C.: Camden House, 1999).

Michel, Andreas, 'Formalism to Psychoanalysis: On the Politics of Primitivism in Carl Einstein', in *The Imperialist Imagination: German Colonialism and Its Legacy*, ed. Sara Friedrichsmeyer, Sara Lennox, and Susanne Zantop (Ann Arbor: University of Michigan Press, 1998).

Midelfort, H. C. Erik, *A History of Madness in Sixteenth Century Germany* (Stanford, Calif.: Stanford University Press, 1999).

Mileck, Joseph, *Hermann Hesse: Between the Perils of Politics and the Allure of the Orient* (New York: Peter Lang, 2003).

Miles, David, *Hofmannthal's Novel 'Andreas': Memory and Self* (Princeton, N.J.: Princeton University Press, 1972).

Mistry, Freny, *Nietzsche and Buddhism* (Berlin and New York: de Gruyter, 1981).

Moore, Gregory, *Nietzsche, Biology, and Metaphor* (Cambridge: Cambridge University Press, 2002).

Murath, Clemens, 'Intertextualität und Selbstbezug—Literarische Fremderfahrung im Lichte der konstruktivistischen Systemtheorie', in *Reisen im Diskurs. Modelle der literarischen Fremderfahrung von den Pilgerberichten bis zur Postmoderne*, ed. Anne Fuchs and Theo Harden (Heidelberg: Winter, 1995).

Murti, Kamakshi P., *India: The Seductive and Seduced 'Other' of German Orientalism* (Westport, Conn. and London: Greenwood Press, 2001).

Muschg, Walter, *Von Trakl zu Brecht. Dichter des Expressionismus* (Munich: R. Piper, 1963).

Nenno, Nancy P., 'Projections on Blank Space: Landscape, Nationality, and Identity in Thomas Mann's *Der Zauberberg*', *German Quarterly*, 69 (1996), 305–321.

Nethersole, Reingard, 'Landscape Imagery in Hofmannsthal and Klimt', *Modern Austrian Literature*, 22: 3–4 (1989), 109–126.

Neuhäuser, Renate, *Aspekte des Politischen bei Kubin und Kafka* (Würzburg: Königshausen und Neumann, 1998).

Nienhaus, Stefan, 'Ein Irrgarten der Verschwörungen. Das Venedig-Sujet und die Tradition des Bundesromanes', *Germanisch-Romanische Monatsschrift*, 42 (1992), 87–105.

Noyes, John K., 'Landschaftsschilderung, Kultur und Geographie. Von den Aporien der poetischen Sprache im Zeitalter der politischen Geographie', in *Kolonialismus als Kultur. Literatur, Medien, Wissenschaft in der deutschen Gründerzeit des Fremden*, ed. Alexander Honold and Oliver Simons (Tübingen and Basel: Francke, 2002).

Nussbaum, Martha, 'Nietzsche, Schopenhauer, and Dionysus', in *The Cambridge Companion to Schopenhauer*, ed. Christopher Janaway (Cambridge: Cambridge University Press, 1999).

Nyman, Jopi, 'Re-reading Rudyard Kipling's "English" Heroism: Narrating Nation in *The Jungle Book*', *Orbis Litterarum*, 56 (2008), 205–220.

O'Brien-Twohig, Sarah, 'Beckmann and the City', in *Max Beckmann: Retrospective* (St. Louis: St. Louis Art Museum, 1984).

Oeser, Erhard, *Geschichte der Hirnforschung. Von der Antike bis zur Gegenwart* (Darmstadt: Wissenschaftliche Buchgesellschaft, 2002).

Oesmann, Astrid, 'From Chaos to Transformation: Brechtian Histories Im Dickicht der tädte', *Brecht Yearbook/Das Brecht-Jahrbuch*, 26 (2001), 256–275.

Otis, Laura, *Membranes: Metaphors of Invasion in Nineteenth Century Literature, Science, and Politics* (Baltimore and London: Johns Hopkins University Press, 1999).

Overath, Angelika, *Das andere Blau: Zur Poetik einer Farbe im modernen Gedicht* (Stuttgart: Metzler, 1987).

Pabst, Walter, 'Satan und die alten Götter in Venedig. Entwicklung einer literarischen Konstante', *Euphorion*, 49 (1955), 335–359.

Parkes, Graham (ed.), *Nietzsche and Asian Thought* (Chicago: University of Chicago Press, 1991).

Parkes, Graham, *Composing the Soul: Reaches of Nietzsche's Psychology* (Chicago: University of Chicago Press, 1996).

Parmalee, Patty Lee, *Brecht's America* (Columbus: Ohio State University Press, 1981).

Pasley, Malcolm, 'Nietzsche's Use of Medical Terms', in *Nietzsche: Imagery and Thought*, ed. Malcolm Pasley (London: Methuen, 1978).

Perels, Christoph, 'Vom Rand der Stadt ins Dickicht der Städte. Wege zur deutschen Großstadtliteratur zwischen Liliencron und Brecht', in *Die Stadt in der Literatur*, ed. Cord Meckseper and Elizabeth Schraut (Göttingen: Vandenhoeck & Ruprecht, 1985).

Pernick, Martin S., 'Contagion and Culture', *American Literary History*, 14 (2002), 858–865.

Peters, Paul, 'Witness to the Execution: Kafka and Colonialism', *Monatshefte*, 93 (2001), 401–419.

Petriconi, Hellmuth, *Das Reich des Untergangs. Bemerkungen über ein mythologisches Thema* (Hamburg: Hoffmann und Campe, 1958).

Pieper, Hans-Joachim, *Musils Philosophie. Essayismus und Dichtung im Spannungsfeld der Theorien Nietzsches und Machs* (Würzburg: Königshausen & Neumann, 2002).

Piper, Karen, 'The Language of the Machine: A Post-Colonial Reading of Kafka', *Journal of the Kafka Society of America*, 20 (1996), 42–54.

Plato, *Phaedrus*, trans. Alexander Nehamas and Paul Woodruff (Indianapolis and Cambridge: Hackett, 1995).

Pleister, Michael, *Das Bild der Großstadt in den Dichtungen Robert Walsers, Rainer Maria Rilkes, Stefan Georges und Hugo von Hofmannsthals* (Hamburg: Helmut Buske, 1982).

Porter, Dennis, 'Modernism and the Dream of Travel', in *Literature and Travel*, ed. Michael Hanne (Amsterdam and Atlanta: Rodopi, 1993).

Pratt, Mary Louise, *Imperial Eyes: Travel Writing and Transculturation* (London: Routledge, 1992).

Prusok, Rudi, 'Science in Mann's *Zauberberg*: The Concept of Space', *Proceedings of the Modern Language Association*, 88 (1973), 52–61.

Radkau, Joachim, *Das Zeitalter der Nervosität: Deutschland zwischen Bismarck und Hilter* (Munich: Carl Hanser, 1998).

Rau, Peter, '"Sujet mixte", Zu Durchführung, Funktion und Bedeutung des "Ausländischen"' bei Thomas Mann', *Der Deutschunterricht*, 46: 3 (1994), 88–97.

Reed, T. J., *Thomas Mann: The Uses of Tradition* (Oxford: Oxford University Press, 1974).

Reed, T. J., 'Nietzsche's Animals: Idea, Image, and Influence', in *Nietzsche: Imagery and Thought*, ed. Malcolm Pasley (London: Methuen, 1978).

Reed, T. J. (ed.), *Thomas Mann, Der Tod in Venedig: Text, Materialien, Kommentar* (Munich: Hanser, 1983).

Reed, T. J., *Death in Venice: Making and Unmaking a Master* (New York: Twayne, 1994).

Reichert, Herbert W., *Friedrich Nietzsche's Impact on Modern German Literature: Five Essays* (Chapel Hill: University of North Carolina Press, 1975).

Reif, Wolfgang, *Zivilisationsflucht und literarische Wunschräume. Der exotische Roman im ersten Viertel des 20. Jahrhunderts* (Stuttgart: Metzler, 1975).

Requadt, Paul, *Die Bildersprache der deutschen Italiendichtung von Goethe bis Benn* (Bern and Munich: Francke, 1962a).

Requadt, Paul, 'Gottfried Benn und das 'südliche' Wort', *Neophilologus*, 46 (1962b), 50–66.

Rhein, Phillip H., *The Verbal and Visual Art of Alfred Kubin* (Riverside, Calif,: Ariadne Press, 1989).

Ritchie, J. M., *Gottfried Benn: The Unreconstructed Expressionist* (London: Wolff, 1972).

Robertson, Ritchie, *Kafka: Judaism, Politics, and Literature* (Oxford: Clarendon Press, 1985).

Robertson, Ritchie, 'Musil and the "primitive mentality"', in *Robert Musil and the Literary Landscape of his Time*, ed. Hannah Hickman (Salford: University of Salford, 1991).

Robertson, Ritchie, *The Jewish Question in German Literature 1849–1939: Emancipation and its Discontents* (Oxford: Oxford University Press, 1999).

Robertson, Ritchie, 'Zum deutschen Slawenbild von Herder bis Musil', in *Das Eigene und das Fremde: Festschrift für Urs Bitterli*, ed. Urs Faes and Béatrice Ziegler (Zürich: NZZ-Verlag, 2000).

Robertson, Ritchie, 'Schopenhauer, Heine, Freud: Dreams and Dream-Theories in Nineteenth-Century Germany', in *Psychoanalysis and History*, 3 (2001), 28–38.

Robertson, Ritchie, 'Classicism and its Pitfalls: *Death in Venice*', in *The Cambridge Companion to Thomas Mann*, ed. Ritchie Robertson (Cambridge: Cambridge University Press, 2002a).

Robertson, Ritchie, 'Kafka als religiöser Denker', in *Franz Kafka: Zur ethischen und ästhetischen Rechtfertigung*, ed. Jakob Lothe and Beatrice Sandberg (Freiburg: Rombach, 2002b).

Robertson, Ritchie, 'Kafka as Anti-Christian: "Das Urteil", "Die Verwandlung", and the Aphorisms', in *A Companion to the Works of Franz Kafka*, ed. James Rolleston (Columbia, S.C.: Camden House, 2002c).

Robertson, Ritchie, 'Modernism and the Self, 1890–1924', in *German Philosophy and Literature 1700–1900*, ed. Nicholas Saul (Cambridge: Cambridge University Press, 2002d).

Robertson, Ritchie, 'Kafka's Encounter with the Yiddish Theatre', in *The Yiddish Presence in European Literature: Inspiration and Interaction*, ed. Joseph Sherman and Ritchie Robertson (Oxford: Legenda, 2005).

Robertson, Ritchie, 'Sacrifice and Sacrament in *Der Zauberberg*', *Oxford German Studies*, 35 (2006), 55–65.

Robertson, Ritchie, 'Hofmannsthal as Sociologist: "Die Briefe des Zurückgekehrten"', in *Moderne begreifen: Zur Paradoxie eines sozio-ästhetischen Deutungsmusters*, ed. Christine Magerski, Robert Savage, and Christiane Weller (Wiesbaden: Deutsche Universitäts-Verlag, 2007).

Roche, Mark William, *Gottfried Benn's Static Poetry* (Chapel Hill: University of North Carolina Press, 1991).

Ross, Kristin, *The Emergence of Social Space: Rimbaud and the Paris Commune* (Minneapolis: University of Minnesota Press, 1988).

Rovagnati, Gabriella, 'Sehnsucht und Wirklichkeit: Die Mythisierung des Fernen Ostens bei Hugo von Hofmannsthal', *Zeitschrift für Germanistik*, N.F. 4 (1994), 310–318.

Rüsing, Hans-Peter, 'Quellenforschung als Interpretation: Holitschers und Soukups Reiseberichte über Amerika und Kafkas Roman "Der Verschollene"', *Modern Austrian Literature*, 20: 2 (1997), 1–38.

Said, Edward W., *Orientalism* [25th anniversary edition with a 2003 preface and 1994 afterword] (New York: Vintage Books, 1979/2003).

Sandford, John, *Landscape and Landscape Imagery in R. M. Rilke* (London: Institute of Germanic Studies, 1980).

Scaff, Lawrence A., 'Weber on the Cultural Situation of the Modern Age', in *The Cambridge Companion to Weber*, ed. Stephen Turner (Cambridge: Cambridge University Press, 2000).

Scherer, Frank F., 'Freuds Morgenland: Orientalis-Tick und die Entstehung der Psychoanalyse', in *'Wenn die Rosenhimmel tanzen': Orientalische Motivik in der deutschsprachigen Literatur des 19. und 20. Jahrhunderts*. Publications of the Institute of Germanic Studies, School of Advanced Study, University of London, Bd. 87, ed. Rüdiger Görner and Nima Mina (Munich: Iudicium, 2006).

Schings, H.-J., 'Die Fragen des Malte Laurids Brigge und Georg Simmel', *Deutsche Vierteljahrsschrift für Literaturwissenschaft und Geistesgeschichte*, 4 (2002), 643–671.

Schonlau, Anja, 'Das (Groß)hirn in der Krise. Zu Hofmannsthals "Chandos-Brief" und Benns früher Prosa *Unter der Großhirnrinde*', *KulturPoetik*, 5 (2005), 51–64.

Seliger, Helfried W., *Das Amerikabild Bertolt Brechts* (Bonn: Bouvier, 1974).

Sheppard, Richard, '*Tonio Kröger* and *Der Tod in Venedig*: From Bourgeois Realism to Visionary Modernism', *Oxford German Studies*, 18/19 (1990), 92–108.

Sheppard, Richard, 'Insanity, Violence, and Cultural Criticism: Some Further Thoughts on Four Expressionist Short Stories', *Forum for Modern Language Studies*, 30 (1994), 152–161.

Shiff, Richard, *The End of Impressionism: A Study of the Theory, Technique, and Critical Evaluatioin of Modern Art* (Chicago: University of Chicago Press, 1984).

Shklovsky, Victor, 'Art as Technique', in *Russian Formalist Criticism: Four Essays*, trans. Lee T. Lemon and Marion J. Reis (Lincoln: University of Nebraska Press, 1965).

Simons, Ronald C., and Hughes, Charles C., *The Culture-Bound Syndromes: Folk Illnesses of Psychiatric and Anthropological Interest* (Dordrecht: Reidel, 1985).

Smith, David, 'Nietzsche's Hinduism, Nietzsche's India: Another Look', *Journal of Nietzsche Studies*, 28 (2004), 37–56.

Sokel, Walter H., 'Zwischen Drohung und Errettung. Zur Funktion Amerikas in Kafkas Roman "Der Verschollene"', in *Amerika in der deutschen Literatur. Neue Welt—NordAmerika—USA*, ed. Sigrid Bauschinger, Horst Denkler, and Wilfried Malsch (Stuttgart: Philipp Reclam, 1975).

Sokel, Walter H. *The Myth of Power and the Self: Essays on Franz Kafka* (Detroit: Wayne State University Press, 2002).

Sontag, Susan, *Illness as Metaphor and AIDS and its Metaphors* (New York: Doubleday, 1989).

Spilka, Mark, *Dickens and Kafka: A Mutual Interpretation* (Bloomington: Indiana University Press, 1963).

Spires, John C., *Running Amok: An Historical Inquiry* (Athens: Ohio University Press/Swallow Press, 1988).

Stein, Leon, *The Triangle Fire* (New York: A. Carroll and Graf/Quicksilver, 1962).

Struck, Wolfgang, '"Ein renegatisches Machtabenteuer unter den Negern". Der phantasierte Kolonialismus der literarischen Moderne in Deutschland', in *(Post-) Kolonialismus und deutsche Literatur: Impulse der angloamerikanischen Literatur- und Kulturtheorie*, ed. Axel Dunker (Bielefeld: Aisthesis, 2005).

Tanner, Tony, *Venice Desired* (Oxford and Cambridge, Mass.: Blackwell, 1992).

Taylor, Charles, *Sources of the Self* (Cambridge, Mass.: Harvard University Press, 1989).

Taylor, Charles, 'Two Theories of Modernity', in *Alternative Modernities*, ed. Dilip Parameshwar Gaonkar (Durham, S.C.: Duke University Press, 2001).

Torgovnick, Marianna, *Gone Primitive: Savage Intellects, Modern Lives* (Chicago: University of Chicago Press, 1990).

Turner, David, 'The Function of the Narrative Frame in the "Novellen" of Stefan Zweig', *Modern Language Review*, 76 (1981), 116–128.

Uerlings, Herbert, 'Kolonialer Diskurs und deutsche Literatur. Perspektiven und Probleme', in *(Post-) Kolonialismus und deutsche Literatur: Impulse der angloamerikanischen Literatur- und Kulturtheorie*, ed. Axel Dunker (Bielefeld: Aisthesis, 2005).

Varisco, Daniel Martin, *Reading Orientalism: Said and the Unsaid* (Seattle and London: University of Washington Press, 2007).

Vaßen, Florian, 'A New Poetry for the Big City: Brecht's Behavioural Experiments in *Aus dem Lesebuch für Städtebewohner*', trans. Katharina Hall, *German Monitor* 41, *Bertolt Brecht: Centenary Essays*, ed. Steve Giles and Rodney Livingstone (Amsterdam and Atlanta: Rodopi, 1998).

Vines, Elisabeth L., 'Rilke and Seeing in Time and Space', *Unreading Rilke*, ed. Hartmut Heep (New York: Peter Lang, 2001).

Vogl, Joseph, 'Area Panic: Politische Einbildungskraft und die Frühgeschichte des Amok', in *Die Macht und das Imaginäre. Eine kulturelle Verwandschaft in der Literatur zwischen früher Neuzeit und Moderne*, ed. Rudolf Behrens and Jörn Steigenwald (Würzburg: Königshausen & Neumann, 2005).

Walker, John, 'City Jungles and Expressionist Reifications from Brecht to Hammett', *Twentieth Century Literature*, 44 (1998), 119–133.

Warraq, Ibn, *Defending the West: A Critique of Edward Said's Orientalism* (Amherst, N.Y.: Prometheus Books, 2007).

Weber, Carl, 'The Prodigal Son and the Family In the Jungle: Notes on Brecht's Early Chicago Play and its Contemporary American Staging', *Brecht Yearbook/Das Brecht-Jahrbuch*, 21 (1996), 125–139.

Weinstein, Arnold, 'Afterword: Infection as Metaphor', *Literature and Medicine*, 22 (2003), 45–64.

Willet, John, *Brecht in Context: Comparative Approaches* (London and New York: Methuen, 1984).

Williams, Rhys W., 'Primitivism in the Works of Carl Einstein, Carl Sternheim, and Gottfried Benn', *Journal of European Studies*, 13 (1983), 247–267.

Williams, Rhys W., 'Prosaic Intensities: The Short Prose of German Expressionism', in *A Companion to the Literature of German Expressionism*, ed. Neil H. Donahue (Columbia, S.C.: Camden House, 2005).

Winnacker, Susanne, 'Provisiorien über Brechts Dickicht', *Brecht Yearbook/Das Brecht-Jahrbuch* 18 (1993), 59–71.

Wirkner, Alfred, *Kafka und Die Außenwelt: Quellenstudien Zum "Amerika"-Fragment* (Stuttgart: Klett, 1976).

Wolf, Norbert, *Expressionism*, ed. Uta Grosenick (Cologne: Tashen, 2004).

Worringer, Wilhelm, *Abstraktion und Einfühlung. Ein Beitrag zur Stilpsychologie* (Munich: R. Piper, 1959). (First published 1908).

Wyler-Zimmerli, Cornelia D., *Zeit und Raum: zu Rilke's* Die Aufzeichnungen des Malte Laurids Brigge (Zurich: W. Schneider, 1976).

Wysling, Hans (ed.), *Dichter über ihre Dichtungen: Thomas Mann* (Munich/Frankfurt am Main: Hemaran/S. Fischer, 1975).

Young, Julian, *Nietzsche's Philosophy of Art* (Cambridge: Cambridge University Press, 1992).

Zantop, Susanne, *Colonial Fantasies: Conquest, Family, and Nation in Precolonial Germany, 1770–1870* (Durham, N.C.: Duke University Press, 1997).

Zilcosky, John, *Kafka's Travels: Exoticism, Colonialism, and the Traffic of Writing* (New York: Palgrave/Macmillan, 2003).

Index

colonialism
  city as analogy for 240
  Dauthendey, Max 68–9
  Der Amokläufer 98, 100, 101–2
  exploitation of art 232
  German 8–9, 105–6, 127, 146–7
  Hesse, Herman 47, 62–3, 65–6, 69
  Hofmannsthal, Hugo von 40
  Kafka, Franz 123–30
  and Nietzsche, Friedrich 172–3
  and punishment 146–7
  writing as 8–10, 12–13, 16–17
colours
  Andreas 30
  Der Amokläufer 95–6
  Der Zauberberg 112–14
  'Eingeschlossene Tiere' 55
  Gehirne 189, 190
conflict
  in cities 234–6
  in the psyche 236–8
consciousness, creative 194–5, 218
contagion, pathological
  cholera in Venice 87, 88
  Der Amokläufer 99–100, 103
  Der Tod in Venedig 81–2
  and sexual desire 71–7, 83, 107, 119–20
  transcension of 212–13
Corngold, Stanley 126, 159, 161
cultural identity *see also* European self
  and conflict 234–6
  and desire 75–6
  isolation from 147–9, 151–7, 216
  native perspective in Dauthendey, Max 48
  self-reflection 43–4

Dauthendey, Max
  atmospheric allure 50
  biographical detail 49
  colonialism 68–9
  'Eingeschlossene Tiere' 52, 53–8
  Fernweh 49, 50, 53
  Geschichten aus den vier Winden 58–67
  'Himalajafinsternis' 58–61, 62, 64
  Lingam 46–53, 64, 67–8, 69
  post-colonial criticism of 48
  re-enchantment 17, 47–8, 53
death
  and contagion 76–7, 98, 99, 103, 118
  and creative rebirth 194
  and exotic desire 75–6, 89–90
  and primal unity 175
  submission to 203–4, 209, 210–12
decay, of Venice 81, 84–5
defamiliarization

spatial 73, 77–8, 91, 105, 118
  through travel 19, 103–4
de-individuation of self 80, 176–8, 214
depths of inner self 164–7
Descartes, René 176
'Die Portugiesin' 200–1, 203, 204–6,
  212–14
Dionysus
  Apollonian-Dionysian structure 171,
    175, 217–18, 220, 221
  association with Eastern occult 78, 173
  Dionysian aspects of reality 174–6
  Dionysian forces 166, 225
diseases *see* contagion, pathological
disenchantment
  Andreas 29
  and modern Europeans 18, 24, 26, 51
disillusionment of the exotic 58–67
disorientation
  Andreas 29, 30–1, 33–6
  Der Tod in Venedig 77–8, 79–80, 82–3
  Der Verschollene 136, 138
  'Eingeschlossene Tiere' 54–7
  Fez 39–40
  'Gehrine' 183–5
  magical 60–1
  of personal structure 185
  through travel 20, 64, 91–2
dissolution of self 181, 192–3, 197–8,
  208–9, 220–1
dreams 214, 217, 220–1, 225–6
dream-world (Traumreich) 214–19, 221–3
Drei Frauen
  'Die Portugiesin' 200–1, 203, 204–6,
    212–14
  'Grigia' 175, 185, 193, 200–2, 203–4,
    206–12
  'Tonka' 182, 194, 200, 204
Dutch colonists 62, 65

ecstasis, sexual
  Gehirne 181, 197–8
  'Grigia' 192–3, 208–9
  'Eingeschlossene Tiere' 52, 53–8
  'elsewhere' 130, 132–5, 149, 153, 160–1
enchantment
  with Asian world 53–8
  and disillusion 58–67
epiphany
  Andreas 29, 33, 36
  Aus Indien 64–7
  Die andere Seite 177
  'Grigia' 208–9
  Hofmannsthal, Hugo von 17, 20, 23–4
  Reise im nördlichen Afrika 44

'other,' the (*cont.*)
  Said, Edward 11–13

past, inaccessibility of 44–5
Peters, Paul 127, 128, 146–7, 148n
Piper, Karen 124, 128
Plato
  Phaedrus 86–7
  Platonic love 83, 86–7, 89–90
  Platonic view 113, 114–15
Poland 84–5
post-colonial criticism *see also* Said, Edward
  Dauthendey, Max 48
  Hesse, Herman 47
  identification of 'others' 253
  Kafka, Franz 123–30, 142–3,
    149–50, 161
  power, theory of 11–13
Pratt, Mary Louise 9, 34, 125
primal consciousness
  alternative reality within 174–6, 208–9
  dreams as metaphor for 214
  exotic imagery 182–9
  modern imagination 171–2
  Musil, Robert 200
  narrative structure 179–80
  Nietzsche, Friedrich 169–71
  southern aesthetic 181
primitive worlds
  Benn, Gottfried 186–7
  and dreams 219, 220–1
  Musil, Robert 199–203
primitivism
  depiction of 228–9, 252
  Freud, Sigmund 237
  modernism 231–2
  urban life 229, 234–5, 240–1, 248–9
prostitutes, depictions of 191, 196–7, 230
psyche
  and the city 229
  city as analogy for 235–8
  as part of animal organism 167–9
  repression of 251–2

racist stereotyping 246–7, 255–6
rationality, northern European 182–3,
    188–9, 190, 198–9, 214
reality
  alteration through travel 79–80
  alternative 131–2, 198–9
  effect of exotic on 17
  in primal consciousness 174–6,
    208–9, 219
  rejection modern reality 47, 199–200
  search for new 18–19, 70

sense of 27–8, 68–9
  transformation of 193–4, 195–6
re-enchantment
  Dauthendey, Max 17, 47–8, 53
  Hofmannsthal, Hugo von 18–19, 28
  Reise im nördlichen Afrika 37–46
  Reiseprosa 23, 41 *see also* travel writing
  'Richard and Samuel' 124, 125–6,
    129–30, 133
Rilke, Rainer Maria
  interiority 165
  landscapes 22
  Malte (character) 29, 34–5, 234, 238,
    239, 240
  Paris 126
Rome, as metaphor for the psyche 236–7
Russia 107–8, 130–4, 150–3

Said, Edward
  European opposition to 'other' 10–11
  exotic spaces 2, 5–6, 41, 70, 124
  German Orientalism 8
  language 11–13
  Orientalism 2, 8
  Orientalism 34
  Orientalism 253
  reaffirmation of self 16–17, 253
Saleh 43–4
Schopenhauer, Arthur 166, 168, 173,
    180, 216
'Schweigen der Sirenen, Das' 137
sea, images of 79–80, 82, 83–4, 86, 89, 96
self, the
  Andreas 29, 31–3, 34–5, 36
  autonomy of 167–9
  breakdown of 10–11, 71–7, 167,
    183–7, 193–4, 197–9
  definition 15
  de-individuation of self 80, 176–8, 214
  dissolution 96–7
  dissolution of 181, 192–3, 197–8,
    208–9, 220–1
  European and 'other' 10–11, 75, 253–4
  fragmentation of 29, 31–3, 35–6
  inner depths 104, 164–7
  instability of in exotic setting 202–3
  loss of 46, 84, 87–9, 93–5, 119, 218–19
  transformation of 4–5, 6–7, 23–4, 37
  unification 20, 36, 167–9
sexual desire
  animal nature 54, 56–7, 191, 197,
    204, 244
  contagion, pathological 71–7, 83, 107,
    119–20
  and death 75–6, 89–90